THE INDIGENOUS WORLD 2006

Copenhagen 2006

THE INDIGENOUS WORLD 2006

Compilation and editing: Sille Stidsen
  Regional editors:
  The Circumpolar North & North America: Kathrin Wessendorf
  Central and South America: Alejandro Parellada
  Australia and the Pacific: Sille Stidsen and Jens Dahl
  Asia: Christian Erni and Sille Stidsen
  Middle East: Diana Vinding and Sille Stidsen
  Africa: Marianne Wiben Jensen
  International Processes: Lola García-Alix

Cover, typesetting and maps: Jorge Monrás
English translation and proof reading: Elaine Bolton
Prepress and Print: Eks-Skolens Trykkeri, Copenhagen, Denmark
ISSN 1024-0217 - ISBN 87-91563-18-6

The Indigenous World is published annually in English and Spanish by The International Work Group for Indigenous Affairs.

  Director: Jens Dahl
  Deputy Director: Lola García Alix
  Administrator: Anni Hammerlund

Distribution in North America: Transaction Publishers
390 Campus Drive / Somerset, New Jersey 08873
www.transactionpub.com

This book has been produced with financial support from the Danish Ministry of Foreign Affairs, NORAD, Sida and the Ministry for Foreign Affairs of Finland.

**INTERNATIONAL WORK GROUP
FOR INDIGENOUS AFFAIRS**
Classensgade 11 E, DK 2100 - Copenhagen, Denmark
Tel: (45) 35 27 05 00 - Fax: (45) 35 27 05 07
E-mail: iwgia@iwgia.org - Web: www.iwgia.org

CONTENTS

PART II – INTERNATIONAL PROCESSES

PART III – GENERAL INFORMATION

EDITORIAL
CONTRIBUTORS

EDITORIAL

Although 2005 saw significant progress made in terms of recognising indigenous peoples' rights, this first year in the second UN decade of the World's Indigenous Peoples (2005-2014) also witnessed an endless number of denials or violations of those same rights. The 2005 United Nations World Summit's final document represents an extremely important step forward for indigenous peoples as it consolidates the use of the term indigenous peoples, and reaffirms UN member states' commitment to uphold their human rights. It states a commitment to work at local, national, regional and international levels to advance the human rights of indigenous peoples, and highlights the need to do so in collaboration, or through consultation, with them. As readers of *The Indigenous World 2006* will note, this is a timely and much needed commitment. Many of the country reports included in this volume document what happens when governments and authorities in general do not cooperate with, or at least consult, indigenous peoples when matters influencing their lives and human rights are being decided. In the name of development, free trade or nature conservation, indigenous peoples' rights are denied or violated year after year. This edition of *The Indigenous World* testifies to the fact that this was indeed the case once again in the past year.

The picture is the same the world over. Indigenous peoples remain on the margins of society: they are poorer, less educated, die at a younger age, are much more likely to commit suicide, and are generally in poorer health than the rest of the population. Even in developed countries such as Canada and Australia, statistics show that the life expectancy of the indigenous population is significantly shorter than that of their non-indigenous counterparts. In Australia, the gap is as much as 20 years. And in the United States, one third of indigenous people live below the poverty line, as compared to one in eight of the general population. In developing countries, where improved living standards are high on the agenda, indigenous peoples and their views and considerations are most often ignored when policies and programmes are being designed. The same story repeats itself year after year, in country after country – this year we hear, for example, from Ethiopia how the government has come up with a draft Proclamation on Rural Land Administration and Use that completely overlooks the pastoralists and their need for access to grazing land. The fact that their right to communal ownership of the land has already been sanctioned by other laws is simply ignored. Sadly enough, this is an experience shared by many indigenous peoples around the world. Their rights to land, resources and, more broadly speaking, to practise their distinct livelihoods, need to be claimed and defended again and again, even when they have already been sanctioned by national law or international conventions. In the Philippines, for example, increasing numbers of indigenous communities are getting their land rights officially recognized and are being granted *Certificates of Ancestral Domain Titles*. But the future of some of these ancestral domains is now threatened by an agrarian reform seeking to allocate plots of land to poor landless peasants. Existing laws and policies on land ownership and land use are contradictory, and precedence in this regard has not yet been resolved.

The author of the article on Paraguay puts it quite clearly when he summarizes the situation with the phrase *"the more rights are recognized, the more rights are violated or denied"*. We have indeed witnessed an increasing number of national policies and laws sanctioning indigenous peoples' rights over the past few years but their implementation remains poor, or is undermined by conflicting "national interests". The UN Special Rapporteur on the Human Rights and Fundamental Freedoms of Indigenous Peoples has identified this "implementation gap" between existing legislation and administrative, legal and political practice as one of the main issues to be addressed over the coming years by all who are committed to the indigenous peoples' cause.

As reported in *The Indigenous World* over the past years, the level of organization among indigenous peoples has been increasing steadily, with more and stronger organizations, locally, nationally, regionally and internationally. Their demands continue to be centred around the crucial right to self-determination, and the right to land. And even though ever more instruments are in place to defend these rights, very little has been done to secure their implementation, so there is every reason to believe that the struggle will continue for some years to come. The pressure on indigenous peoples' livelihoods, cultures and even survival is immense. It is impossible to summarize in just a few pages the many different threats to indigenous peoples around the world that are documented in this book. But there is little doubt that the greatest threat in north and south, east and west alike continues to be the ever growing pressure on the world's natural resources. In the name of development or free trade, mining, oil and gas developments, plantations and the like encroach on indigenous peoples' lands and territories and make their life and survival increasingly difficult. The strategies adopted by indigenous organizations around the world to defend their rights vary from all sorts of local organizing and protests – such as the indigenous peoples in Kerala in southern India who have picketed for more than a thousand days in front of a coca-cola factory that is drying up their water sources and polluting their land – to the use of national or international courts - such as in Malaysia where a Court of Appeal confirmed the Temuan Orang Asli's right to their tra-ditional land, or in Paraguay where the state has been enjoined by the Inter-American Court of Human Rights to give the Enxet of Yakye Axa rights over their traditional territory.

It should be stressed that there *are* – important – positive develop-ments for indigenous peoples in some regions, and that the experi-ences from these should be used in a constructive way. Among these is the work of the African Commission on Human and Peoples' Rights, including the adoption of the expert report of the Working Group on Indigenous Populations/Communities which outlines a policy frame-work for protection and promotion of indigenous peoples' human rights. The report was published and widely distributed in 2005. This being said, here too, the challenge of implementing these political achievements in the daily life of indigenous peoples remains to be seen.

As this book goes to print, the much awaited Universal Declaration on the Rights of Indigenous Peoples (commonly known as the "Draft Declaration") has still not been adopted, or even considered, by the UN General Assembly. *The Indigenous World 2006* bears strong testimony to the need for a global standard-setting instrument of this kind, and we sincerely hope that the next edition of the book will bring news of its adoption.

It is our hope that *The Indigenous World 2006* will be used by policy and development planners at all levels, by indigenous activists seeking specific information about experiences in other parts of the world, by scholars and, in general, by all who are interested in hearing indigenous peoples' voices and concerns at this point in time. ❏

Sille Stidsen, Coordinating Editor & Jens Dahl, Director
April 2006

From IWGIA's own world, Board member and Chair of the Board for many years, Georg Henriksen, stood down from his post in November. Georg was instrumental in the founding of IWGIA in 1968 at the Congress of Americanists in Stuttgart, Germany. Years later he became a member of the Board and became Chair of the Board in the early 1990s. No-one has done more for IWGIA over the years than Georg. Thanks to his long and intimate relationship with the Innu of Labrador and his commitment to the rights of indigenous peoples in general, to the support he enjoys from his firm roots in the academic world, Georg has played a prime role in ensuring that IWGIA's work is always based on solidarity without ever losing the organisation's emphasis on a rights-based approach. Although we expect Georg to continue as an active member of IWGIA, we shall miss him as an ever-present member of the Board.

ABOUT OUR CONTRIBUTORS

IWGIA would like to extend warm thanks to the following people and organizations for having contributed to *The Indigenous World 2006*. We would also like to thank those contributors who wish to remain anonymous and are therefore not mentioned below. Without the help of these people, this publication would not have been possible.

PART I – REGION AND COUNTRY REPORTS

The Circumpolar North & North America

This section has been compiled and edited by *Kathrin Wessendorf*, Programme Coordinator for the Circumpolar North Program.

> **Gunn-Britt Retter** is Head of the Arctic and Environmental Unit in the Saami Council and is a member of the Saami Parliament in Norway. Over the past four years, she has worked at the Arctic Council Indigenous Peoples' Secretariat in Copenhagen. (*Arctic Council*)
>
> **Jens Dahl** is a Danish anthropologist and Executive Director of IWGIA. (*Greenland*)
>
> **Laila Susanne Vars** is a Saami from Norway. She has a degree in law and has worked as legal adviser for the Saami Parliament. She is chairperson of the Nordic Saami Lawyers Association and a doctoral candidate at the Faculty of Law, University of Tromso, Norway. (*Sápmi - Norway*)
>
> **Kati Eriksen** is an indigenous Saami from Deatnu valley on the borders of Finland and Norway. She is a mother of two boys. She works as executive officer to the Saami Parliamentary

Council, which is a cooperation organisation between three Saami Parliaments in Finland, Norway and Sweden. She is also vice-chair of the Saami Council. *Mattias Åhrén* is an indigenous Saami from the south Saami area of Sweden. He works part-time as Head of the Human Rights Unit in the Saami Council. He is currently working on his dissertation at the University of Tromso. *(Sápmi - Finland)*

Olga Murashko is an anthropologist and co-founder of the IWGIA local group in Russia. She works in close collaboration with RAIPON on indigenous peoples' and legal rights in the Russian Federation *(National level and Far Eastern region)*. *Gail Fondahl* is chair of the Geography Program at the University of Northern British Columbia. Her research focuses on legal geographies of aboriginal land rights, mainly in the Russian North *(Lake Baikal Region)*. *Anna Sirina* is a senior researcher at the Institute of Ethnology and Anthropology, Russian Academy of Sciences (Department of Siberian Studies). She has carried out fieldwork throughout Siberia and the Far East, and is interested in social anthropology, cultural geography and the history of Siberian ethnology *(Lake Baikal Region)*. *(Russia)*

Gordon L. Pullar (Tani'cak), a Kodiak Island Sugpiaq (Alutiiq), is the Director of the Department of Alaska Native and Rural Development (DANRD) at the University of Alaska Fairbanks (UAF) and the President of the Leisnoi Village Tribal Council. *Dixie Dayo (Masak)*, an Inupiaq, is an Assistant Professor in DANRD at UAF. She is the secretary-treasurer of Bean Ridge Corporation, the ANCSA corporation for her home village of Manley Hot Springs. *Miranda Wright (Tletenesyah)*, a Koyukon Athabascan from the village of Nulato, is an Assistant Professor and the Academic Program Head for DANRD at UAF. She also serves on the Board of Directors of Doyon, Ltd., the ANCSA regional corporation for interior Alaska. *(Alaska (USA))*

Jack Hicks is a social research consultant based in Iqaluit, Nunavut. He served as Director of Research for the Nunavut Implementation Commission and later as the Government of Nunavut's Director of Evaluation and Statistics *(Inuit territories)*. *Mark*

Nuttall is Henry Marshall Tory Professor of Anthropology at the University of Alberta (Canada). He was a Lead Author for the Arctic Council's Arctic Climate Impact Assessment (ACIA) and is currently working on a project examining the social impacts of oil and gas development in northern Canada *(The Northwest Territories). (Arctic Canada)*

Sarah Quick is currently a Ph.D. candidate in Socio-cultural Anthropology at Indiana University. Her research focuses on Métis heritage and performance practice in Canada where she has done fieldwork primarily in Edmonton, Alberta as well as at festivals and performances in Saskatchewan. *(Canada)*

Sebastian Braun is a Swiss anthropologist (sebastian.braun@und. edu). He is assistant professor in the Department of Indian Studies at the University of North Dakota. *(USA)*

Mexico and Central America

This section has been compiled and edited by *Alejandro Parellada*, Programme Coordinator for Central and South America and Editor of *Asuntos Indígenas.*

Maria Elena Martinez Torres, is a researcher/lecturer with the Centre for Research and Higher Studies in Social Anthropology (CIESAS), South-east Unit. She is the author of the book *Organic Coffee: Sustainable Development by Mayan Farmers* (Ohio University Press, 2006). *Mariana Mora,* a doctoral candidate in anthropology at the University of Texas at Austin, is a visiting student at CIESAS-South-east, conducting field work into the political culture of Zapatista autonomy. *Aldo González Rojas,* president of the Commission for Communal Property of Guelatao de Juárez *(Comisariado de Bienes Comunales de Guelatao de Juárez)* in Oaxaca, is also Indigenous Rights Coordinator for the Union of Organisations of Sierra Juárez *(Unión de Organizaciones de la Sierra Juárez)*, Oaxaca. He has been municipal president and used to be director of the indigenist broadcasting company XEGLO

"The Voice of the Mountain". *Séverine Durin* holds a PhD in anthropology. She is a researcher on CIESAS' North-east Programme. She coordinates the project "Urban Indigenous Migration in the North-east of Mexico: the case of Monterrey". *(Mexico)*

Silvel Elías is an agronomist and lecturer at the San Carlos University in Guatemala. He is currently conducting research in Social Geography at the University of Toulouse-Le Mirail. He works as a researcher in the Latin American Faculty of Social Sciences (FLACSO) in Guatemala. *(Guatemala)*

Dennis Williamson Cuthbert (williamson@ns.uca.edu.ni) is an economist and director of the Atlantic Coast Research and Documentation Centre (*Centro de Investigaciones y Documentación de la Costa Atlántica*), attached to the Central American University (CIDCA-UCA). *Gizaneta Fonseca Duarte* is a lawyer and researcher working with CIDCA-UCA. *(Nicaragua)*

Alexis Oriel Alvardo Avila, is a Kuna lawyer. Since 1996, he has been involved in indigenous rights, through the Dobbo Yala Foundation, an indigenous organisation in Panama. He is currently lawyer to the Emberá and Wounaan Congress of Collective Lands, the Wargandi Congress, the Naso People's Congress and forms part of the legal team of the Kuna General Congress. *(Panama)*

South America

This section has been compiled and edited by *Alejandro Parellada*, Programme Coordinator for Central and South America and Editor of *Asuntos Indígenas*.

Efrain Jaramillo is an anthropologist working with the Jenzera Group in Colombia's Pacific region. *(Colombia)*

María Teresa Quispe is a sociologist, member of IWGIA's board and general coordinator of the "Wataniba" Organisation for the Multi-ethnic Human Development of the Amazon (*Organización para el Desarrollo Humano Multiétnico de la Amazonía "Wataniba"*).

Oskar Pablo Pérez, a political scientist, coordinates Wataniba's education work. *Luis Jesús Bello*, lawyer, Ombudsman for Amazonas State, Venezuela, is an expert on indigenous rights with more than 20 years' experience of the issue. *(Venezuela)*

Daniel Peplow is an affiliate professor at the University of Washington, where he teaches environmental justice, and co-director of the Suriname Indigenous Health Fund (www.SIHFund.org). The SIHF provides technology and expertise to indigenous and tribal communities who are self-diagnosing the effects of logging and mining on public and environmental health. *(Suriname)*

Paulina Palacios Herrera is an Ecuadorian lawyer, and the coordinator of Walir Ecuador (Water Laws and Indigenous Rights); she works on women's issues, the environment and human rights in Ecuador. *(Ecuador)*

Jorge Agurto is a social communicator who supports indigenous communities and peoples in Peru to raise awareness of their problems and fundamental rights. He is a promoter with the Indigenous Information Service, SERVINDI. *(Peru)*

Carlos Romero is a lawyer, a social analyst and the author of various works related to indigenous problems and social issues. He runs the Centre for Legal Studies and Social Research (*Centro de Estudios Jurídicos e Investigación Social* – CEJIS), an organisation that advises indigenous peoples in the West and Amazonian areas of Bolivia, particularly with regard to demands for access to lands and natural resources. *(Bolivia)*

Maria de Lourdes Alcantara de Beldi is an anthropologist, scientific coordinator of the "Imaginary and Memory Group" and editor of the Revista Imaginário of Sao Paulo University. For the last five years, she has been working with indigenous youth from the Dourados Reserve in Mato Grosso do Sul. *(Brazil)*

Rodrigo Villagra, is a lawyer and anthropologist, director of the NGO Tierraviva. *Ricardo Morínigo*, is a journalist and sociology student, working in Tierraviva's communications department. Tierraviva is a human rights organisation that supports the territorial demands of the Enxet and Toba Qom peoples of the Paraguayan Chaco. (*Paraguay*)

Morita Carrasco is an anthropologist, lecturer and researcher at Buenos Aires University. She works in the Centre for Legal and Social Studies (CELS), forming part of a team of technical/legal advisors supporting the Lhaka Honhat organisation. (*Argentina*)

José Aylwin is a lawyer and director of the Indigenous Peoples' Rights Observatory (*Observatorio de Derechos de los Pueblos Indígenas*) in Chile, an institution founded in 2004 to document, promote and defend indigenous rights. (*Chile*)

Australia & the Pacific

This section has been compiled and edited by *Jens Dahl*, Director, and *Sille Stidsen*, IWGIA.

Elizabeth Strakosch is a postgraduate researcher in the areas of political rhetoric and indigenous policy at the University of Queensland. (*Australia*)

Rex Rumakiek, originally from West Papua, is Assistant Director of the Decolonisation Campaign Desk at the Pacific Concerns Resource Centre (PCRC); *Peter Emberson* works at the PCRC as editor of its monthly newsletter "Pacific News Bulletin" and is Assistant Director of the Information Section; *Tupou Vere* is Director of the PCRC. (*The Islands of the Pacific*)

Christian Erni is Coordinator of IWGIA's Asia Programme. (*West Papua*)

Asia

This section has been compiled and edited by *Christian Erni*, Programme Coordinator for Asia, and *Sille Stidsen*, IWGIA.

East and South East Asia

Kanako Uzawa is a graduate student of the University of Tromso's
Program in Indigenous Studies in Norway. As a member of the
Rera Association, she is active in cultural preservation and further-
ing the indigenous rights of her people, the Ainu. *Kelly Dietz* is a
doctoral candidate in development sociology at Cornell University
and a board member of the Shimin Gaikou Center. Her research
and activism is focused on militarization, especially within minority and indigenous territories. She was a visiting researcher at
Okinawa's University of the Ryukyus until June 2005. *(Japan)*
Charlotte Mathiassen is a social anthropologist and development
advisor. She has worked with Tibetan communities in the Hima-
layas and on Tibetan issues generally for many years. She has
been an active member of the Danish Tibet Support Group since
1989 and is currently its chairwoman and Nordic representative
in the International Tibet Support Network. *(Tibet)*
*Anthony Carlisle, Shi-chang Chen, Shun-ling Chen, Mag Chin, Re-
becca C. Fan, Pasang Hsiao, Shu-ya Lin, Yong-chin Luo, Jason
Pan Adawai, Pei-shan Ruan and Kimman Tan* are members of
the AIPP-Taiwan mailing list (aipp_taiwan@yahoogroups.com.
hk), via which the report was developed and discussed. The
section on Ping Pu is authored by *Jason Pan Adawai. (Taiwan)*
Maria Teresa Guia Padilla is an anthropologist working for An-
throWatch, a non-governmental organization supporting indigenous communities in ancestral domain titling and in policy
advocacy work (miksgp@anthrowatch.org). *(Philippines)*
Christopher Duncan is an assistant professor in the Department of
Religious Studies and the School for Global Studies at Arizona
State University. *(Indonesia)*
Jannie Lasimbang, is a Kadazan from Sabah, Malaysia. She is Vice-
Chairperson of PACOS Trust, Sabah, a community-based organi-
zation working with indigenous peoples since 1987. She has also
been involved in the Indigenous Peoples Network of Malaysia
(JOAS-IPNM) since its inception in 1992, and is currently the Sec-

retary General of the Asia Indigenous Peoples Pact Foundation based in Chiang Mai, Thailand. *(Malaysia)*

Sakda Sainmi is a Lisu and the Director of Inter Mountain Peoples Education and Culture in Thailand (IMPECT), an indigenous organisation based in Chiang Mai in Northern Thailand. **Helen Leake** has worked for many years with IMPECT and the International Alliance of the Indigenous and Tribal Peoples of the Tropical Forest. She is now working for the Regional Indigenous Peoples' Programme at the UNDP Regional Centre in Bangkok. *(Thailand)*

Graeme Brown is the Ratanakiri Coordinator of Community Forestry International, which works in partnership with the Ratanakiri Natural Resource Management Network, a network of indigenous community people (graemeb@camintel.com). He has worked in Ratanakiri for the past 6 years. *(Cambodia)*

Ian G. Baird, originally from Canada, has been working on natural resource management and ethnicity issues in mainland Southeast Asia for 19 years. He is Executive Director of the Global Association for People and the Environment, a Canadian NGO active in Laos. *(Laos)*

Andrea Martini Rossi is a human rights researcher from Italy. He has worked in Europe, Latin America and Asia and is currently Research Officer at ALTSEAN-Burma in Bangkok. *(Burma)*

Nepuni Piku is from the Memei (Mao) Naga community and is a human rights activist working with the Naga Peoples Movement for Human Rights (NPMHR) in Nagalim. *(Nagalim)*

South Asia

Ina Hume is a consultant on indigenous issues and a cultural recording artist. She established Vanishing Rites in 2004 to develop collaborative media and advocacy projects in the UK and internationally (www.vanishingrites.com). She has written in cooperation with the *Jumma Peoples Network UK*, a human rights organisation aiming to promote the rights of Jummas living in the Chittagong Hill Tracts and abroad. **Sanjeeb Drong** is a

Garo from northern Bangladesh (sdrong@bangla.net). He is a columnist and freelance journalist and currently editor of the indigenous magazine Solidarity. He has published more than 400 articles and four books on indigenous issues. *(Bangladesh)*

Om Gurung is the General Secretary of NEFIN, the Nepal Federation of Indigenous Nationalities. *(Nepal)*

Samar Bosu Mullick is a political activist, teacher and researcher who has worked with and for the indigenous peoples in Jharkhand for over a quarter of a century *(Jharkhand);* **Nandini Sundar** is a professor at the Sociology Department of Delhi School of Economics, Delhi University *(Chhattisgarh);* **Debaranjan Sarangi** is an activist in the people's organisation Prakritik Sambad Suraksha Parishad, which is leading the struggle against mining in Kashipur, Orissa *(Orissa);* **C.R. Bijoy** is a human rights activist based in Tamil Nadu, South India. For decades he has been working closely with Adivasis and their organizations in South India *(Kerala);* **Dolly Kikon** is Lotha Naga, has a Master's Degree from Hong Kong University of Science and Technology and is currently based as an independent researcher and activist in Guwahati, Assam *(Northeast India). (India)*

The Middle East

This section has been compiled and edited by *Diana Vinding,* former Coordinator, and *Sille Stidsen,* IWGIA.

Anna Sophia Bachmann is based in Amman, Jordan and has worked on Iraqi environmental issues since 2004 (bachmanna@gmail.com). She is currently with Nature Iraq (www.natureiraq.org), an Iraqi environmental non-governmental organization focused on the restoration of the Iraqi Marshlands and the sustainable development of Iraq's natural resources. *(The Marsh Dwellers of Iraq)*

Faisal Sawalha and **Ariel Dloomy** provided inputs to the article on the Bedouins in Israel. **Faisal Sawalha** is a high school English teacher in Rahat, one of the seven townships in the Negev. He works with the Regional Council for the Unrecognized Villages in the Negev as their Resource Development and PR person. *Ariel Dloomy* (faisal.rcuv@gmail.com) is the coordinator of the Negev Co-existence Forum for Civil Equality (www.dukium. org) and the editor of their newsletter. *(The Bedouins of Israel)*

Africa

This section has been compiled and edited by *Marianne Wiben Jensen*, Africa Programme Coordinator.

Hassan Idbalkassm is an Amazigh (Berber) from Morocco. He is a lawyer and former president of IPACC and of the Amazigh Association "Tamaynut". He is currently a council member of the *Institut Royal de la Culture Amazigh*. In 2004, he was appointed a member of the Permanent Forum for the Africa region by the president of ECOSOC. *(The Amazigh people of Morocco)*

Jeremy Keenan is Senior Fellow and Director of the Sahara Studies Programme at the University of East Anglia (UK) and Visiting Professor at the Institute of Arab and Islamic Studies at the University of Exeter. *(The Tuareg People)*

Naomi Kipuri is a Maasai from the Kajiado district and an anthropologist by training. She works as a development consultant, conducts research and is especially interested in issues relating to human rights and the rights of indigenous peoples. *(Kenya)*

Benedict Ole Nangoro is a Maasai from Kiteto District in Tanzania. He is currently working with CORDS, a local NGO that works with the indigenous Maasai peoples in collective land demarcation, mapping, registration and titling. *(Tanzania)*

John Nelson is a Policy Advisor to the Forest Peoples' Programme, coordinating a participatory project on Indigenous Peoples and Protected Areas in Central Africa, a support programme for Bagyeli people in the Cameroon oil pipeline zone and Batwa in southwest Uganda, case studies of Baka land use in the Dja Reserve in Cameroon and FSC certification in the Republic of Congo, along with advocacy on the impacts of international financial institutions. *(Uganda and Cameroon)*

Lucy Mulvagh (lucy@forestpeoples.org) is the Forest Peoples' Programme's Project Officer for the Great Lakes region. www.forestpeoples.org. *(Rwanda, Burundi, Democratic Republic of Congo)*

Dr. Albert K. Barume is a lawyer by training, with a Ph.D in human rights. For the last 15 years he has worked as a researcher and activist on issues of indigenous peoples, vulnerable communities and natural resources in the Congo Basin. He has worked in different capacities for a number of international agencies, including the African Commission on Human and Peoples' Rights. *(Republic of Congo (Congo Brazzaville))*

Judith Knight is a Consultant Anthropologist and qualified Museum Curator working in Gabon. She is based at Oxford University where she is completing her PhD on the Babongo Forest People of Central Gabon. *(Gabon)*

Christina Longden has been working with socially excluded societies and individuals since 1995 and has advised governments, NGOs, CBOs and private businesses in matters relating to policy, training and community development (clongden@yahoo.com). She has carried out work for various San NGOs in southern Africa since 2003, and cooperated with some of these in writing for *The Indigenous World* . *(Angola and Namibia)*

Robert K. Hitchcock is an anthropologist and African Studies coordinator in the Department of Anthropology and Geography of the University of Nebraska-Lincoln (USA), and a newly elected member of IWGIA's board. **Diana Vinding** is the new Vice-Chair of IWGIA's board, and a former coordinator in our secretariat in Copenhagen. She has been the Coordinating Editor of *The Indigenous World* in past years and retired from her job recently. *(Botswana)*

Nigel Crawhall has a PhD in Linguistics and is working with the Indigenous Peoples of Africa Coordinating Committee (IPACC). *(South Africa)*

PART II – INTERNATIONAL PROCESSES

This section has been compiled and edited by *Lola García-Alix*, Coordinator of Human Rights Activities.

> *Lola García-Alix* is Coordinator of IWGIA's Human Rights Activities. *(UN World Summit – Reform of the Human Rights Bodies, The UN Commission on Human Rights - 61ˢᵗ session, The Permanent Forum on Indigenous Issues – 4ᵗʰ Session, The UN Working Group on Indigenous Populations)*
>
> *Pablo Espiniella* works in the Office of the High Commissioner for Human Rights as Legal Assistant to the mandate of the Special Rapporteur on the Human Rights and Fundamental Freedoms of Indigenous Peoples (pespiniella@ohchr.org). *(The Special Rapporteur – overview 2005)*
>
> *Kent Lebsock* is Executive Director of the American Indian Law Alliance. *(The UN Draft Declaration on the Rights of Indigenous Peoples)*
>
> *Dina Berenstein* is Project Coordinator of IWGIA's African Commission Programme. *(The African Commission on Human and Peoples' Rights)*
>
> *Patricia Borraz* is a consultant working for Almáciga. This work involves supporting the participation of indigenous organizations and representatives in multilateral negotiations, particularly around issues of environment and sustainable development, through capacity building, communications and information exchange and funding support for their attendance at meetings. *(Indigenous peoples and the Convention on Biological Diversity in 2005)*

PART I

REGION AND
COUNTRY REPORTS

THE CIRCUMPOLAR NORTH

THE ARCTIC COUNCIL

2005 marks the mid-point of the Russian Federation's Chairmanship of the Arctic Council. The Russian Federation has emphasised the importance of indigenous peoples' cultures in the program for its chairmanship. This has been followed up particularly through cultural events and excursions, in which the artistic side of the cultures has been displayed.

The Arctic Council (AC) is an intergovernmental organisation comprising 8 member states with territories in the Arctic realm, six indigenous organisations with the status of Permanent Participants and a number of observers. The more technical and scientific work is carried out by different working groups that meet regularly. The Senior Arctic Officials meet twice a year for broader policy matters and guidance, and reports are brought to a biannual ministerial meeting.

The challenge for the indigenous peoples' organisations, as Permanent Participants (PP), is no longer that of gaining acceptance or recognition of their roles but all too often their shortage of both human and economic resources, which restricts their capacity to participate and contribute in a satisfactory way to all aspects of the Council's work.

Two Senior Arctic Officials meetings were held in Siberia in 2005 and the working groups are in the process of preparing their assessments and reports to be presented to the ministerial meeting in the fall of 2006.

Oil and gas assessment

The Arctic Monitoring Assessment Program (AMAP) working group is preparing an oil and gas assessment and held an oil and gas symposium in St. Petersburg, Russia in September. The symposium benefited

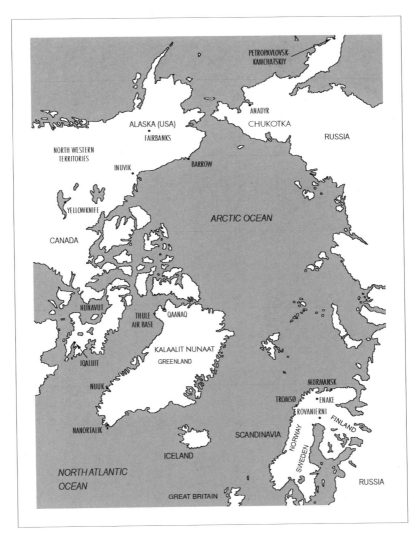

from the broad participation of experts from all over the Arctic region and offered a wide range of presentations discussing issues such as the history of oil and gas development in the Arctic, its socio-economic and environmental effects and the role of impact assessments and development management. Many indigenous peoples' representatives were active in the symposium, both presenting papers and giving speeches. The indigenous peoples focused on land rights and their right to free, prior and informed consent in the processes around access to and use of natural resources. The outcomes of the symposium will feed into the different chapters of the oil and gas assessment.

Protection of Arctic Marine Environment

The Protection of Arctic Marine Environment (PAME) working group is preparing an Arctic Marine Shipping Assessment. The aim is to assemble the best possible information on current shipping activities in the Arctic region. Based on this information, Arctic Council member states will address the environmental, social and economic issues that are of current and possible future significance to the Arctic environment.

For some of the indigenous peoples residing in the Arctic, the marine environment is of the utmost importance and they thus welcome this initiative from the Arctic Council. There is also increasing pressure on resources in the Arctic, largely because of easier access and more advanced extraction technology. This is of great concern to the indigenous peoples, who still rely on fisheries, sea mammals and the ice to hunt from.

Circumpolar Biodiversity Monitoring Program

The Conservation of Arctic Flora and Fauna (CAFF) working group is undertaking a big initiative into monitoring circumpolar biodiversity. For comparative and effective monitoring, similar indicators and methods have to be used and a long process has taken place to include the various monitoring traditions and data management from the different Arctic countries. In 2005, Canada assembled national biodiversity and monitoring experts in a workshop to get the program off the ground. The Permanent Participants were not invited to this workshop, with the explanation that it was meant to be an expert level meeting. This can only be interpreted as meaning that the indigenous peoples are not trusted to be able to select their own experts to work in such a group, or in other words: it is easier to reach an agreement when experts with similar backgrounds and thus similar perspectives on the matters play together and decide the way forward. Once this path is defined, indigenous peoples' perspectives can then be added where they seem to fit in, just to spice the work up.

Community-based monitoring, an initiative raised by the indigenous peoples in the working group, however, adds value to the Circumpolar Biodiversity Monitoring Program (CBMP), as local peoples' observations can either support or reject the findings of scientific research. This is important because, all too often, researchers visit the Arctic to conduct their fieldwork in the summer season, while local people live in the region all year round and make their observations on a regular basis. Many community-based monitoring initiatives are already underway and others are being planned. The indigenous peoples' organisations in the Arctic will create a network of community-based monitoring stations or projects, firstly to protect data management and ownership, but also in order to discuss common indicators for using the data from their various observations in a circumpolar biodiversity monitoring program.

The outcome of the CBMP will be a major contribution to the CAFF Biodiversity Assessment planned for 2010.

Sustainable Development Working Group

The Sustainable Development Working Group (SDWG) is still grappling with how best to achieve sustainable development in the Arctic. The activities of the SDWG are project-oriented, with many projects having been concluded and having delivered recommendations for what needs to be done to improve sustainable development in the Arctic. Many of these are stored on shelves alongside the Arctic Human Development Report (AHDR), delivered to Ministers in 2004. The indigenous peoples' organisations are expecting to see the AHDR, which revealed many gaps in knowledge of the Arctic's socio-economic conditions, followed up. The AHDR could keep the working group busy for many years to come.

The SDWG, however, is in a process of assembling the recommendations from various finished projects, including the AHDR and findings from other Arctic Council working groups, into a Sustainable Development Action Plan, which should become an overall plan for promoting all aspects of sustainable development within the Arctic region. The intention is a good one, but it has been a long process so far. ❏

Source

www.arctic-council.org

GREENLAND

Greenland is a self-governing region within the Danish realm. The first Danish colonial settlement was established in 1721 close to the current capital, Nuuk, on the west coast. In 1953, Greenland became an integrated part of Denmark by law and, in 1979, Home Rule was established following negotiations between Greenland and Denmark. Since then, Greenland has had its own parliament and government responsible for most internal matters. Since 2004, the Danish and Greenland governments have negotiated further self-government for Greenland. The population inhabiting the vast east and west coast of the island numbers 57,000, 88 per cent of whom are ethnic Greenlanders (Inuit).

Elections

The inhabitants of Greenland went to the polls three times in 2005. First they had to appoint two members to the Danish Parliament; then there were the regular elections (every four years) to the 18 municipal councils in Greenland; and then, when the incumbent Greenland Government coalition broke down, elections to the Greenland Parliament were called for November.

Since Home Rule was established, three political parties, the liberal Atassut, the social democratic Siumut and the socialist Inuit Ataqatigiit have dominated the political arena in Greenland. The Greenland Cabinet has always been headed by Siumut, usually in coalition with Inuit Ataqatigiit, and this was also the case following the elections in 2002. However, the coalition broke down in late summer 2005 following disagreements and internal arguments within the Siumut party, as well as a number of scandals.

In recent years, the political picture in Greenland has become more complex and can no longer be described as a traditional dichotomy between liberalism and socialism, these party labels to a large extent no longer being valid. Much depends upon the person in charge of the political party or fraction thereof. This can be seen in the success of a new party, the Democrats, which has profiled itself on a conservative/ status quo policy that is more often characterized as being populist. Although the Democrats emerged from the Greenland Parliament elections in November as the victorious party, a new coalition government (called the "Northern Lights Coalition") was established between Siumut, Inuit Ataqatigiit and Atassut – united at least by a wish to keep out the Democrats.

Self-Government Commission

In the media, much attention was given to Greenland's future constitutional status. A Danish-Greenlandic Self-Government Commission, established in 2004 (see *The Indigenous World 2005*), continued its work in 2005. The work of the Commission revealed a number of divergent viewpoints between Greenlandic politicians not only from different parties but also within the ruling Siumut party. These disagreements relate to the future relationship between Greenland and Denmark and to the strategy to be adopted. There is no doubt that the quest for further Greenlandic control of Greenlandic affairs is supported by a vast majority of the population. However, the Greenland Parliament electoral campaign in the autumn also revealed that the vigorous campaign for independence as advanced by some politicians from Siumut and Inuit Ataqatigiit (and challenged by the Democrats), and reflected in the written media, did not match the immediate concerns of the general public. The future destiny of small and remote settlements, the decision by the Greenland Parliament to try to force people to use airplanes instead of ships and boats, and not least social issues such as a concern for the social and physical security of children, are the main issues for ordinary people.

Annual block grants from Denmark

No less confusing were the positions of the two ruling parties, Siumut
and Inuit Ataqatigiit, in relation to the annual block grants transferred

from Denmark to Greenland every year. There is a widespread feeling in Greenland that the block grant creates a dependency syndrome and passivity. While some politicians claim that independence will open up a new dynamic and responsibility for own affairs, others are of the opinion that economic self-sufficiency is a condition for real political, social and cultural independence. And all politicians seem to agree that more self-rule or independence should be achieved without a decrease in the standard of living.

Three-party coalition government

Considering all the scandals and all the personal fights within the Siumut party, it came as a surprise that they, together with the Democrats, came out the victors in the November Greenland Parliament elections. On the other hand, it also reveals the political stability that has reigned in Greenland for 25 years. The parliamentary system that was introduced following the establishment of Home Rule in 1979 has survived all crises, and Greenland has been able to – *de facto* – become gradually ever more self-governing. In spite of the dependence on the annual block grants from Denmark, the fishing industry – on which the Greenland economy relies to an overwhelming degree – has successfully developed into an important player on the international market. This is, among other factors, attributed to new visions that were introduced with Home Rule and also to those who have been in power. Unfortunately this is often overlooked by the media, who concentrate on scandals and the custom of politicians to intervene in the dispositions taken by Home Rule-owned companies.

The new three-party coalition government established after the elections in November will base its policy on the following general aims:

All initiatives from the coalition partners shall be based on the process towards a self-governing Greenland. From this follows four main aims, which are: to create the fundament for increased equality in the society; to establish a politically and economically self-relying society; to increase people's influence on all levels of society; to ensure environmental sustainability.

The political discussion on self-government versus independence is often led by men, whereas social issues are promoted by women. In the light of what seem to be the main concerns of the general public, this might in part explain the success of women in the elections. While 25 per cent of the candidates were women, they now make up 42 per cent of parliamentary members (31 in total), a number that has been continuously increasing since the first Home Rule Parliament elections in 1979. The new Home Rule Government of eight includes three women.

Foreign relations

Two events that took place in 2005 emphasized that Greenland was *de facto* becoming increasingly independent with regard to matters of foreign affairs.

The first was a partnership agreement between Greenland and Denmark by which Greenland gains more opportunities to negotiate on its own in external affairs, not the least with the European Union.

One key issue in Greenland's position towards the US military presence in the country (radar system) has been its renewal of an agreement from the early 1950s – but with Greenland as an equal partner to Denmark and the USA. The result of the Igaliku agreement of 2004 (see *The Indigenous World 2005*) between Greenland, Denmark and the USA was the establishment of a Joint Committee. This agreement came about when Greenland accepted the upgrading of the Thule radar for use in the US missile defence system. Its scope, however, reaches wider than just military issues. In May 2005, the first meeting of the Joint Committee emphasized the value of the tripartite relationship. The outcome of the meeting was an expectation of concrete cooperation measures in relation to education, environmental protection, research, trade, tourism, etc.

A peculiar incident took place in July on an uninhabited island, Hans Island, in the far north. The island, which is located between Greenland and the Canadian High Arctic, is claimed by both Canada and Denmark. Without notifying the Danish or Greenland authorities, the Canadian Minister of Defence visited the island during the summer. By doing this, he hoped to unilaterally claim Canadian sovereignty to the island, and this resulted in a virtual verbal war between Denmark and Canada. Hans Island, with the Inughuit (Inuit of the Thule area) name of Tartupaluk, is infrequently visited by the Inughuit who since early colonial days have been divided between Canada (Nunavut) and Denmark (Greenland). To the Inughuit, Tartupaluk is part of their traditional homeland, whereas the Canadian government is concerned about authority over shipping routes in case of further global warming, which would allow shipping in Arctic waters. And to both Denmark and Canada, sovereignty over Hans Island will determine the border between the two countries and thus, potentially, control over subsurface resources.

❏

SÁPMI - NORWAY

After innumerable years of in-depth studies and endless political battles between the Sámi people and the Norwegian authorities, resulting in *inter alia* several thousand pages of recommendations and considerations of the Sámi Rights Committee in the early 1980s and late 1990s, the implementation of the Sámi Language Act in 1987 and the establishment of the Sámediggi (the Sámi Parliament) in Norway in 1989, 2005 turned out to be an *annus mirabilis* for the Sámi people in Norway.

New procedures for consultations

Drafted by a working group with representatives from the ministries and the Sámi Parliament, and strongly influenced by the provisions of ILO Convention no. 169, the *Procedures for Consultations Between Central Government Authorities and the Sámi Parliament* came out in 2005. The document was signed by the now former president of the Sámi Parliament, Mr. Sven-Roald Nystø and the now former Minister of Regional Development and Local Government, Mrs. Erna Solberg, in Oslo on May 11, 2005.

The purpose of the procedures is among other things to:

- facilitate implementation of the Government's obligations under international law to consult indigenous peoples
- seek to reach agreement between central government authorities and the Sámi Parliament whenever consideration is being given to implementation of legislation or measures that may directly affect Sámi interests

- facilitate the development of a partnership perspective between
  governmental authorities and the Sámi Parliament that will
  have a strengthening effect on Sámi culture and society.

The consultation procedures apply in matters that may affect Sámi interests directly, such as passing legislative measures or regulations in
areas of culture, religion, intellectual property rights and traditional
knowledge, health and social welfare, sustainable development, etc.

Regular half-yearly policy meetings are to be held between the
minister responsible for Sámi matters and the president of the Sámi
Parliament. The aim of each consultation will be to reach agreement on
proposed measures.

The ministry will follow up this agreement with a public information campaign in 2006.

The Finnmark Act

Probably the biggest event in 2005 was when the Finnmark Act was
finalized and passed through the two chambers of the Storting, the
Norwegian Parliament, in June 2005, after thorough consultations with
the Sámi Parliament resulting in what some might call an historical
agreement. The Sámi Parliament took its decision to give its condi-
tioned consent to the amended Finnmark Act on May 13, 2005. The
conditions included: a strong request for measures regarding coastal
Sámi livelihoods and specifically their rights to the marine resources,
which were not included in the Finnmark Act.

The final Finnmark Act differed substantially from the original
proposition submitted by the Government. Article 3 of the Act, which
regulates the relationship between non-incorporated international law
and the Act itself, was perhaps one of the most challenging, ending
with a so-called partial incorporation of ILO Convention no. 169 into
Norwegian national law. A whole chapter is dedicated to the establishment of a Land Rights Court and a Land Rights Commission that are
supposed to handle land claims from both Sámi and non-Sámi in
Finnmark county.

Despite positive attitudes from many members of the Norwegian parliament, there were however some MPs from both the left and right wing parties who believed that the Finnmark Act was in fact discriminatory to the majority people of Finnmark, as it gives the Sámi minority in this county 3 of the 6 seats in the Land Management Board (Finnmark Estate Board).

The Finnmark Estate

The Finnmark Estate Board will be appointed in January 2006 by the Sami Parliament and Finnmark County and will start the process of establishing the new Land Management regime in Finnmark. It is anticipated that the first Chairman will be a Sámi representative, elected by the Sámi Parliament on behalf of the Sámi in Finnmark. When the Finnmark Act enters into force, around twenty employees will be transferred from the Norwegian State Forest and Land Corporation (Statskog) Finnmark to the new Finnmark Estate. Forty-five thousand square kilometres of land will be transferred to the Estate on the same date. This new Finnmark Estate owns as private landowner and manages 96% of the county, an area that was previously state land.

The Finnmark Estate will hopefully have a bigger say in the use of the land at its disposal, and the Estate Board will be authorised to make decisions that were previously made elsewhere. It will also retain any profits resulting from its activities. While public authorities will still decide such issues as what can be hunted and when, the Estate will decide who is allowed to hunt, on what conditions and what price they will have to pay. The Estate will also have greater freedom to engage in economic development on its own land in Finnmark. However, it is important to note that the Finnmark Estate alone will not decide everything in connection with land in Finnmark. As a private landowner, the Finnmark Estate will have to comply with a number of laws and regulations that govern the management of natural resources.

Change in ministries

In October 2005, due to the Labour party winning the elections, the Ministry of Labour and Social Inclusion replaced the Ministry of Local Government and Regional Development as the ministry with main responsibility for Sámi affairs in Norway. This change was criticised by the newly-elected Sámi Parliament and its first woman president, Mrs. Aili Keskitalo, from Guovdageaidnu/Kautokeino municipality. The Sámi Parliament stressed that the changing of ministry could in fact change the whole scope of Sámi policies, leading to the Sámi people being "clients" rather than an equal people. However, the new minister for Sámi affairs, Mr. Bjarne Håkon Hansen, emphasized in the Norwegian and Sámi media that this would not be the case, and that the change should not have any negative implications on the special status of the Sámi people in Norway, nor should it influence Norwegian Sámi policies in general in a negative way.

Sámi Parliament elections

The elections for the Sámi Parliament were historical in two senses. Firstly, they resulted in the closest race ever between the Labour Party. (a national Norwegian party) and the Norwegian Sámi Association (NSR), resulting in a dead heat and leaving it for a group of just four MPs representing the smallest parties in the Parliament to negotiate with both the Labour and the NSR. The group of four finally reached an agreement with the NSR, making it possible for them to continue uninterrupted in government as they had done since the first elections in the late 1980s. Secondly, the number of women MPs increased from 17. 95% (7 out of 39 MPs) to a sensational 51% (22 of 39 MPs), a result which was strongly influenced by an active campaign in all parties to get more women to run for election.

The Nordic Sámi Convention

Another encouraging development in the work on Sámi rights issues in Norway in 2005 was the progress in the work on a Nordic Sámi Convention. The proposal from the expert group of representatives appointed by the governments of Sweden, Finland and Norway and the Sámi parliaments of the respective countries was presented in Helsinki on November 18. The proposal for a Sámi Convention, which *inter alia* includes an overarching provision recognizing the Sámi people's right to self-determination, will undergo hearings and a political procedure that requires signatories from the three state parliaments involved and also signatories from the respective Sámi parliaments. The Convention cannot be enforced without the Sámi parliaments' consent.

With the fundamental bill of rights set forth in the Nordic Sámi Convention and the recognition of Sámi land rights in Finnmark as a framework for all future Sámi politics, the Sámi people's lengthy quest for equality and justice has finally been rewarded with some appreciable and noticeable progress.   ❑

SÁPMI - FINLAND

Finland still treats its approximately 7,000 Saami as a national linguistic minority rather than an indigenous people. Two major Saami issues dominated the discussions in 2005. These were the Enare logging dispute and the production and screening of Saami children's programs on a national television channel.

The Enare logging dispute[1]

In the 1990s, the Finnish Forestry Service (*Metsähallitus*),[2] the company through which Finland today manages the lands in the Saami areas that Finland claims belong to the state, heavily increased the logging of old forests in Enare municipality. Continued access to winter grazing in old forests, rich in lichen, is fundamental to reindeer herding. Finland claimed that it wanted to negotiate with the reindeer herders but, in these so-called negotiations, the reindeer herders were heard but their position never seriously taken into account.

In 2005, the logging of old forests in the Enare area had reached such proportions that, if nothing was done immediately, traditional reindeer herding in the area would disappear. As a consequence, in 2005 the WWF and Greenpeace joined the Saami's struggle, demanding that Finland (the Finnish Forestry Service) stop all logging activities in old forests in the Enare area. The local reindeer herders and Greenpeace established a camp called a "Forest Rescue Station" in the Enare old forests, to protest against further logging.

SAK (*Suomen ammattiliittojen keskusjärjestö*), the Central Organisation of Finnish Trade Unions, which is Finland's biggest trade union with more than one million members and with a strong indirect connection to the ruling Finnish Social Democratic Party, responded to

these protests by calling for a boycott of reindeer meat. Enare municipality (a public body and thus directly bound by international law,
with a duty to remain neutral in case of conflict between different
members of the municipality, be they Saami or Finnish) responded by
collecting signatures, demanding that Greenpeace abandon the camp
and leave the area. Enare municipality further demanded that the reindeer herders supporting the protests against further logging should
identify themselves, so that the boycott of reindeer meat could be directed against them personally.[3]

The workers of the state-owned Finnish Forestry Service - encouraged by the company, and thus indirectly by the Finnish government
- protested at Greenpeace's presence in the area. They did so dressed
up in the Saami people's traditional clothes. Non-Saami people mas-
querading as Saami constitute an enormous offence to the Saami people.

The state-employed Finnish Forestry Service workers further established a so-called "Anti-Terror Info Center" next to the Forest Rescue Station, with the approval of the Finnish Forestry Service. From the
"Anti-Terror Info Center", the state workers subjected the reindeer
herders and their supporters to intimidation and violence. Reindeer
herders received threatening phone calls in the middle of the night,
single reindeer herders were bullied in local bars etc. The Finnish Forestry Service's workers also blew horns and used sirens night after
night to prevent the reindeer herders and their supporters in the Forest
Rescue Station camp from sleeping. They burned crosses outside the
camp in a "Ku Klux Klan" fashion, and drove highly dangerous heavy
forest harvesting machines into the heart of the camp. The police arrived - but suggested that the behavior of the masked men was "normal" for the area and that they would not take action *unless a crime had
been committed.*

The UN Human Rights Committee criticizes Finland

The United Nations has on several occasions criticized Finland (and
other countries with a Saami population) for violating Saami land

rights - thus endangering Saami culture. For example, in October 2004, the Human Rights Committee reiterated its concern over Finland's failure to settle Saami ownership rights to land.[4] The Human Rights Committee found the situation of the Saami people so alarming that it called on Finland to report back to the Committee within one year with regard to what action it had taken to resolve their land rights. This report was due in November 2005.

Domestic bodies also underlined Finland's obligation not to violate the Saami people's rights. The Finnish Ombudsman against Discrimination recently stated that failure to protect the Saami reindeer herding rights constituted discrimination in working life.[5] The Finnish government's own Committee on Equality in Working Life[6] has stressed the need to recognize the Saami people's rights as an indigenous people, particularly highlighting the importance of securing the continued existence of reindeer husbandry. It calls on authorities to systematically promote the possibility for the reindeer herders to continue their traditional livelihood. Finland has essentially ignored the findings of these bodies.

Finland also ignored the Human Rights Committee's request last year to refrain from any action that might adversely prejudice a settlement on the issue of Saami land rights. Finland has not changed one single policy, directive etc. in order to accommodate the Committee's request and halt the draining and destruction of the Saami areas. The logging and mining industries continue to expand into Saami territory in a manner that severely diminishes or even prevents the Saami people from continuing to pursue their traditional livelihoods in a sustainable manner. The government continues to authorize all logging operations on Saami territory, resulting in disappearing pasture areas, without the consent of or even consultation with the Saami.

Further, the privatization of land in Saami areas continues without any notice being given to the Human Rights Committee's request that Finland stop such activities. For example, the Forestry Service continues to sell land on the private market at the same pace. Obviously, the Saami people will have lost these lands even if it is later concluded that the land was indeed not for Finland to sell. Finland has ignored the

Saami parliament's plea to halt such transfers until a solution to the Saami right to land has been found.

The Nellim case

The UN Committee has already been made aware of one instance in which Finland has engaged in an activity that the Committee explicitly requested it to refrain from. In an interim decision issued in November 2005 (HRC communication no 1433/2005), the Committee requested that Finland halt logging activities in the Nellim area of northern Finland which, if pursued, would have meant the end of traditional Saami reindeer husbandry in the area. As the logging in Nellim is subject to a pending case under the Optional Protocol to the International Covenant on Civil and Political Rights, we shall only repeat here that, in this case, the Finnish Forestry Service logged forests of fundamental importance to Saami reindeer husbandry, disregarding the Committee's explicit request that Finland refrain from such activities. Not even when a Finnish District Court ordered the forestry measures to stop did Finland halt the logging. Rather, Finland used technicalities to get around the decision of its own court.

On Monday 14 November, 2005, the Committee notified Finland of its decision that the logging must stop. On Friday 11 November, the Finnish Forestry Service had around 10 people logging in the relevant area. From Monday November 14 to Wednesday November 16, at 3 pm, the Forestry Service had all its logging staff, around 40 people, logging in the area. At 3 pm, Helsinki finally made a phone call to Nellim and told its Forestry Service to stop the logging. During the almost three days when the Finnish Forestry Service knew about the Committee's decision but before Finland had actually called a halt to the logging, large areas of important grazing land were destroyed for the foreseeable future, perhaps forever.

Furthermore, following the halting of forestry measures in the Nellim area, the Finnish Forestry Service simply moved its logging activities to other parts of Saami areas, some of them equally sensitive for reindeer husbandry. For example, the Forestry Service is currently logging in the reindeer herding-sensitive Pitkajarvenvaara grazing areas, as in Nellim, without consulting the reindeer herders.

And yet another of many examples, the Ministry of Trade and Commerce has granted the mining company Inco Limited a licence to start prospecting in five places on important reindeer herding land in the Enare area. The permission was granted without consulting the relevant Saami bodies, who have on several occasions expressed their negative view of Inco's activities in the area.

Media rights

In October 2005, the Finnish National Broadcasting Company *Yleisradio OY* (YLE) decided that Finland would not join Nordic cooperation in producing Saami children's programs. Norway and Sweden have screened Saami children's programs for the past ten years and have tried repeatedly to contract YLE into the cooperation also. Following YLE's decision, Saami parents decided to take action. A delegation comprising Saami children, their parents and the president of the Saami parliament visited Helsinki for two days on 12-13 December 2005. The delegation met a number of parliamentarians, members of YLE's board and YLE executives. After the visit, YLE's board decided that a new study on funding and screening of Saami children's programs would be carried out together with the delegation. The study is to be ready in March-April 2006 and YLE will make its final decision accordingly. Members of the delegation were very happy following YLE's decision but are still closely monitoring the situation to ensure that YLE does not bury Saami children's media rights under alleged budget constraints. ❑

Notes

1   The description of the Enare logging dispute is a shortened version of documents by the Saami Council, written by Mr. Mattias Åhrén.
2   The Finnish Forestry Service or *Metsähallitus* is both a state commercial enterprise and governmental body.

2   The Finnish Forestry Service or *Metsähallitus* is both a state commercial enterprise and governmental body.
3   This is not the first time Enare municipality has tried to put such pressure on the reindeer herders. In the 1990s, when the Saami initiated a court case asking for an injunction against envisaged logging by the *Finnish Forestry Service*, through its municipal board and mayor, Enare municipality threatened the Saami with blocking of an ongoing renovation of a slaughtering house. A complaint was filed with the Ombudsman against Discrimination who reprimanded the municipality, holding that it had exerted inappropriate pressure on the authors by formally asking them to withdraw from their legal proceedings.
4   See CCPR/CO/82/FIN/Rev.1
5   See *Arbetslivs- och Jämställdhetsutskottets betänkande 7/2003* rd.
6   *Arbetslivs- och Jämställdhetsutskottets betänkande*

Other sources

Saami Council: *Briefing Note on the Logging Dispute in Enare.*
Saami Council: *Observations by the Saami Council on Finland's responses to the Human Rights Committee's Concluding Observations with regard to Finland's Fifth Periodic Report*
Both available at: www.saamicouncil.net

RUSSIA

The numerically small indigenous peoples of the Russian North, Siberia and the Far East are unique peoples with separate cultures and traditions and living a traditional way of life. The term "numerically small" is used by the Russian Federation for indigenous groups that number less than 50,000 individuals in order to distinguish them from larger ethnic groups. The small numbered peoples have specific legal rights and are protected by the constitution of the Russian Federation. There are 41 numerically small indigenous peoples in the Russian North, Siberia and Far East, constituting a total number of about 250,000 individuals.

The 5th Congress of indigenous peoples

In April 2005, 333 indigenous delegates, representing 41 indigenous peoples, took part in the 5th Congress of the indigenous peoples of the Russian North, Siberia and Far East in Moscow. Many guests were invited and the Congress was opened by a number of high-ranking government officials, such as the Minister for Regional Development and the Minister for Foreign Affairs. The Congress re-elected the president of the Russian Association of the Indigenous Peoples of the North (RAIPON), the national umbrella organization, Sergey Nikolaevich Haruchi, for his third term. This was only possible, however, after changing RAIPON's charter, which led to heightened discussions during the meeting and, finally, to a vote by secret ballot on the part of all indigenous representatives.

Furthermore, candidates were put forward for a Public Chamber that was established in fall 2005, consisting of NGOs and other civil society actors and which acts as an advisory body to the Russian president Putin. In December 2005, Pavel Sulyandziga, first vice-president of RAIPON, became a member of this Chamber.

Federal legislation

The three most discussed federal laws in 2005 that directly affect indigenous peoples were the new Forest Code, the new Water Code and the Law on Subsoil. None of these laws have been passed through the Duma however. While drafts of the Forest and Water Codes were adopted by the Duma at the first reading, the second readings were postponed repeatedly and, so far, the laws have not been reintroduced. Both laws aim to privatize resources in an extensive manner, lending the future owners almost unlimited rights of exploitation without regard to the protection of nature and biodiversity. In the case of the new Water Code, the owner of the waters would be allowed to exploit all resources commercially and, similarly, the new Forest Code would allow the new private owners to extensively hunt in the forests and carry out logging activities.

At the end of July 2005, the Duma's Committee on Nationalities submitted a draft Federal law "On Protection of Primordial Habitat and Traditional Lifestyle of indigenous numerically small peoples of the Russian Federation". The law was prepared in cooperation with RAIPON experts. It incorporates the legal basis of notions related to the primordial habitat and traditional lifestyle of indigenous peoples and recommends a procedure to assess the impact of any and all projects that affect the indigenous peoples' habitats and lifestyles.

Law on Subsoil

A new government variation on the Federal law "On Subsoil" was passed to the State Duma and draft-related work started in mid-October 2005. The draft law submitted by the government totally ignores indigenous peoples' rights. At present, efforts are being made by RAIPON's experts to prepare proposals for a draft law with an empha-

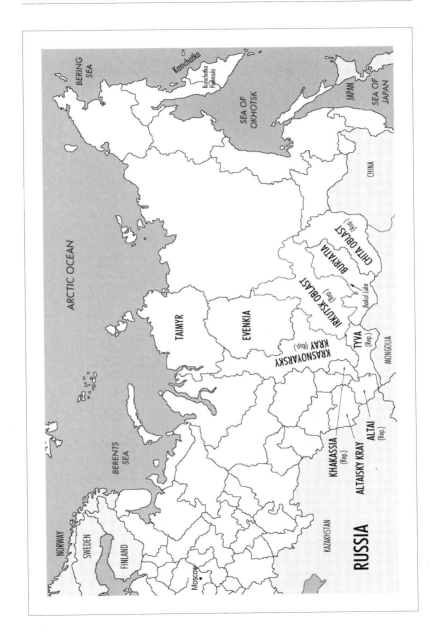

sis on protecting indigenous peoples' rights in the development of natural resources.

When the law on subsoil was presented in March 2005, a government official openly stated that the main aim of the law was to introduce procedures by which industry could apply for licenses. The network of pipelines in Siberia, described below, is also regulated by this law.

The Far Eastern region

The Russian Far East is a hot spot in terms of enforcement of indigenous peoples' rights. Large-scale projects in the field of oil and gas extraction are being implemented and the construction of giant pipelines to transport oil and gas from Sakhalin, Kamchatka, and Central Siberia to countries in the Pacific region has started.

A round table meeting on "Indigenous Peoples and Industrial Companies: Experience and Prospects" was held on August 24-25 2005 in Vladivostok. Representatives of Russian and transnational companies, the Plenipotentiary representation of the Russian Federation President in the Far Eastern Federal Okrug, leaders of the Far East regions, State Duma deputies and other representatives of authorities and of the business community, as well as World Bank and ILO experts, took part in the round table meeting.

Following reports by the World Bank, IFC and ILO, representatives of the Sakhalin Energy, Exxon, Rosneft and BP companies made presentations of their "charitable activities", as they called them, focusing on Sakhalin indigenous peoples. However, the tenor of the companies' presentations changed after listening to reports from indigenous peoples' representatives from the regions and after hearing the claims made with regard to the lack of impact assessment of the projects on the habitat and traditional lifestyle of indigenous peoples. The indigenous peoples' representatives demanded that companies carry out such assessments and, jointly with representatives of indigenous peoples, outline action plans aimed at mitigating the negative consequences and allocating compensation proportional to the estimated impact to the indigenous peoples. Representatives of the companies, including the state-owned oil company Rosneft, offered to set up joint working groups with RAIPON to produce a strategy for assessing the damage to indigenous peoples and their development plans, inviting representatives of indigenous peoples from corresponding regions to participate in these groups.

Sakhalin Island

Two pipelines that are pumping oil and gas from the Okhotsk Sea shelf will cross the length and breadth of Sakhalin Island. These pipelines will cross 1,103 rivers and brooks comprising salmon spawning areas and will split the migration routes of wild animals and domestic reindeer. The full length of the land pipelines will lie on seismic zones of potential earthquake magnitude 8-9 and will cross 44 tectonic faults of different types no less than 55 times. The danger to the population is clear and the projects will undoubtedly have an impact on Sakhalin Island's eco-system and close-lying areas of water.

In January and July 2005, the Sakhalin Association of Indigenous peoples of the North and environmental organizations carried out protest actions by blocking the roads in the north of the island. Those roads are used by companies for transporting materials to the pipeline construction sites. Indigenous peoples demanded assessments of the pipeline projects' impact on indigenous lands and way of life. As a result of the protest action, the oil company agreed to create a working group to discuss the project. However, at the end of 2005 it became clear that the working group was acting without indigenous representatives. This means that Sakhalin Energy Investment Company (SEIC) and Exxon Mobil are refusing to carry out a social impact assessment / "ethnological expert report". Based on regional appeals, RAIPON has made an appeal to the Ministry of Natural Resources and the General Prosecutor. RAIPON has taken an active part in the protest of the Sakhalin indigenous peoples by participating in the protest action in the north of Sakhalin in January and by picketing Exxon Mobil oil company's office in Moscow in July 2005.

Kamchatka

According to the information from Kamchatka's Association of indigenous peoples and an article from the newspaper "Aborigen of Kamchatka", oil and gas development in the Kamchatka shelf of the Okhotsk Sea has already started and it is crucial that proper conditions are provided for indigenous peoples. However, no impact assessments have been conducted and few steps are being taken to protect indigenous peoples' rights.

The indigenous peoples are formulating their demands for implementation of the federal law "On fishing", which was signed by Mr. Putin. It contains standards fostering the priority access of indigenous peoples to water resources. However, executive authorities are reluctant to fulfil the standards of this law, pointing to the lack of implementation mechanisms.

A process of reorganizing the administrative-territorial structure in the Far East has started, in its first stage focusing on the unification of the two administrative regions of the Kamchatka Peninsular: the Kamchatka Region and the Koryak Autonomous Okrug. A referendum on unification was held on October 23, 2005. The unification aims to simplify the mechanism for solving big economic tasks in the region and it is important that indigenous peoples prepare their demands in the process of this unification. The indigenous peoples make up 35 percent of the total population of Koryak Autonomous Okrug, and their position is quite strong, e.g. they have four deputies in the regional Duma. In Kamchatka, the indigenous population constitutes about 2% of the population; their position is weak and the region's administration has a negative attitude toward the demands of the indigenous peoples, e.g. indigenous peoples have far fewer fishing rights in Kamchatka region than in Koryak Autonomous Okrug.

Lake Baikal region

In the 1970s, the indigenous Evenki people living north of Lake Baikal in Eastern Siberia experienced the effects of a mega-project when the Baikal-Amur Mainline Railroad (BAM), dubbed "the project of the century", was built through their homelands.[1] Their traditional hunting, reindeer herding and fishing had already been reshaped by 50 years of Soviet institutions and the railroad further affected their way of life, bringing in thousands of construction workers, providing electricity and paved roads, cutting their access to pastures and haylands, polluting the lands and waters adjacent to the tracks. Now the Evenki face a new "project of the century" — the "Eastern Siberia-Pacific Ocean Pipeline", the world's longest pipeline (4188 km), crossing six major political-administrative regions of the Russian Federation. Transneft, a Russian oil transport company, hopes to move oil from Siberia to the Pacific coast where it can be shipped to markets throughout Asia. On December 31, 2004, the Russian prime minister signed an order for the construction of such a pipeline.

Since the collapse of the Soviet Union, the Evenki and other indigenous peoples of the Russian Federation have experienced a paradox of increased (if unrealizable) legal rights to their traditional land and resources along with a decreased *de facto* ability to benefit from these lands. Many Evenki in the area to the north of Lake Baikal have been reduced to dependence upon subsistence fishing and hunting. Their reindeer herds were appropriated by the state in the 1930s, then annihilated by it in the 1980s. Their ability to reach traditional hunting grounds has been compromised by the withdrawal of state transport and skyrocketing fuel costs. Under the Soviet system everyone had a waged job; now unemployment officially stands at 40-60% in the villages and more accurately reaches 70-80%.

Threats from the proposed pipeline

The initial proposed pipeline route failed an environmental impact assessment in 2003, largely due to its proximity to Lake Baikal (12 km at its closest). Transneft then chose a second route, significantly farther north (80-100 km from the lake). Although given approval to proceed with surveying work on that route in 2004, Transneft decided that costs were too high, and in 2005 chose to pursue a third route, similar to the first but now running less than 1 km from the lake, along the BAM railway line.[2]

The area is highly seismic, with earthquakes ranging well past 9 on the Richter scale. Its montane rivers feed into the north end of Baikal, an elongated and exceedingly deep lake that holds approximately 20% of the world's fresh water. With the collapse of local economic activities, the Evenki are highly dependent on the fish of Lake Baikal and its rivers. While Transneft touts a safety record on a par with Western companies, it has not built pipelines through such terrain. Many Evenki thus consider this project "a bomb, it will at some point explode."[3]

Local consultations

Russian law requires that citizens be provided with a chance to participate, and make their views known, in environmental impact assessments. Transneft was slow to provide information and host public hearings: the Evenki only discovered plans for the pipeline with the first influx of workers:

> They've already been living here two times, those who want to build a pipeline. Last year and now. The surveyors, the construction workers. No, we heard mostly from them. We don't know the details. I haven't talked with them, I just heard that they are living here.[4]

Then, during this past summer (July-August 2005), Transneft finally organized a series of public hearings along the route. Environmental assessment documents were made accessible for review in certain centres, and villagers invited to visit these, or the head office in the region's capital, Severobaikalsk, to further express their views. Yet many Evenki found this approach problematic, given their stark poverty:

> Recently this Muscovite came to ask these guys [about their opinions of the pipeline]. He said, "Come to see me in Severobaikalsk." They said to him, "How are we to get there?" To get to Severobaikalsk you need 90 rubles. There and back. And for 90 rubles, how many loaves of bread can you buy? 10 loaves. You either buy the bread or go there. [5]

Local aspirations and apprehensions

Neither the Evenki nor other locals are entirely opposed to the pipeline. Surveying in three villages (July 2005) indicated that 48% of the local population oppose construction of the pipeline while 35% support it "given adherence to ecological requirements" and 7% support it outright.[6] Their main concerns are threefold. Given that the local population depends so heavily on the fish and other biological resources, but also that their lands and waters retain a spiritual as well as an economic significance, they want assurances that the potential for environmental degradation will be minimal. Indeed, Lake Baikal was designated a UNESCO World Natural Heritage site in 1996. The UNESCO World Heritage Centre has indicated its grave concern at the project, and the need for an environmental impact assessment that meets international standards. Second, given the rampant unemployment, local Evenki would like to benefit directly from the construction, through jobs. Third, they demand that the compensation and rents to be collected from the pipeline transecting their homelands be shared with them.

Transneft's promise of jobs for locals is obviously alluring, especially to many parents who see their adult children with few and declining options for local work. Yet it appears a red herring: Transneft assures that 40 persons from the Severobaikalsk Region (akin to a county) will be hired and trained. The population of the region (including the city of Severobaikalsk) is approximately 41,000 (with 1.7% of this being Evenki): thus 40 positions amount to 0.1% of the population. There is no guarantee that any of these will be villagers or Evenki; most are likely to come from the region's capital and only city, Severobaikalsk (with a population of 25,400).

Locals also hope that, whatever the route of the pipeline, its rental payments may invigorate the local economy. The size, and more importantly the "focus" of compensation and rental payments will depend on legal interpretations and political manipulation. How will these payments be shared between republic, region and local municipal (village) governments? A few Evenki families have petitioned for, and received, extensive land holdings on which to rebuild and pursue reindeer herding; they do not own these lands, but have permanent use rights. Would these families have a right to compensation where the pipeline transects their lands? Some argue that clan collectives should receive payments, suggesting the resurrection of traditional governance structures.

Until late 2005, though President Putin had criticized environmental concerns for slowing economic development, Russia's Ministry of Natural Resources had supported the need to protect Lake Baikal in this instance. However, in mid-November the Ministry reversed its position, and agreed to approve the project on technical and economic grounds. Transneft plans to begin construction in 2006. The Evenkis' concerns remain unanswered, the benefits they could receive poorly defined and not at all guaranteed, and compensation very much open to legal interpretations, which in turn are subject to political manipulations. They look bleakly at a new "project of the century" that threatens to provide few if any benefits, and may impose huge costs on their way of life, health and cultural survival. If legal developments to protect indigenous rights to land have progressed in theory over the last decade in the Russian Federation, in practice they remain largely unattainable for these peoples. ❑

Notes

1 About 35,000 Evenki live throughout Siberia – they are the most dispersed living and second largest "indigenous numerically small people". Their numbers along the BAM track (depending on what width zone one draws) are around 5,000. There are around 700 Evenki living in the Severobaykalsk region where research for this article was conducted.
2 Environmental NGOs are using the fact that the route has changed to demand a new environmental impact assessment - so far without much success.
3 Comment made by an Evenki community member at a public hearing on the pipeline hosted by Transneft, Kholodnaya village, Severobaykalsk Region, Buryat Republic, 13 July 2005.
4 Comment made by an Evenki female, in her 40s, Kholodnaya village, July 2005. (Exact age and date of interview withheld to maintain anonymity.)
5 Comment made by an Evenki male, in his 40s, Kholodnaya village, July 2005.
6 Based on surveys conducted among 127 persons (24% of the adult population) in the villages of Kholodnaya, Dushkachan and Uoyan, July-August 2005. This included mostly Evenki, but other nationalities as well.

ALASKA
(USA)

As of the last federal census, conducted in 2000, there were 119,242 Alaska Natives in Alaska representing about 19% of the total Alaska population. The four largest groups are the Yup'ik (Eskimo) of western Alaska, the Inupiat (Eskimo) of Northwest and Northern Alaska, the Athabascan Indians of interior Alaska, and the Tlingit and Haida Indians of Southeast Alaska. Smaller groups are the Aleut and Tsimshian. Alaska Natives, as the indigenous people of Alaska are usually known, occupy over 200 villages across Alaska as well as living in the urban centers. The Alaska Native Claims Settlement Act of 1971 (ANCSA) settled aboriginal land claims in Alaska by using business corporations as the vehicle through which to receive the settlement. Legal title to 44 million acres of land and a cash settlement were transferred to 12 regional corporations and over 200 village corporations. The cash settlement of US$962.5 was for lands lost and amounted to about three dollars per acre. There are also 229 federally recognized tribal governments in Alaska that retain a special government-to-government relationship with the US government.

Alaska Natives and mining

The mining industry in Alaska continues to grow, and increasingly influences the Alaska economy. Alaska Natives must balance employment opportunities and cash generation with traditional values and protecting the environment for subsistence uses.

During 2005 the mining industry contributed US$2 billion to the Alaska economy, of which US$96 million was for exploration. As most

mining activities are on or near lands owned by Alaska Native corporations, the corporations can potentially make significant financial gains
from the mining. This creates a dilemma for many Alaska Natives, however, as they fear that the mining activities may threaten the environment and thus their traditional food supply. To Alaska Natives living on
the land, hunting and gathering continues to be the preferred lifestyle
and contributes not only food but enhances one's indigenous spirit.

Sharing and natural resource development

In an attempt to provide equity among the regional corporations established under ANCSA, the US Congress inserted a provision (Section 7(i)) that required 70% of all profits generated from the development of natural resources to be shared among all of the other corporations. This provision was enacted so that a corporation with resource
rich lands would need to share its wealth with corporations that did not
have extensive natural resources and thus all Alaska Natives would experience a financial benefit. Individual corporations also share their
wealth with their Alaska Native shareholders when the corporations
make a profit and declare cash dividends, just as other business corporations do. Some corporations are able to share far more of their wealth
than others. For example, the NANA regional corporation in Northwest
Alaska distributed 65% of its profits to its Inupiat shareholders in 2005.
This was made possible by the financial success of the NANA-owned
Red Dog mine, the world's largest zinc mine. This mine has been so successful that NANA distributed US$9.9 million under ANCSA's Section
7(i) to other Alaska Native corporations in December 2005.

The Pebble Mine

Alaska's mining industry must follow strict environmental regulations and is required to actively involve local communities in its
planning process. It must also consider the possible impact on other
resource development when making decisions, such as the possible

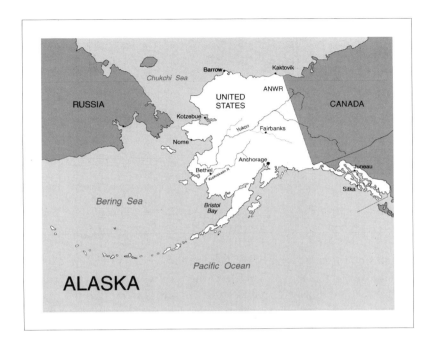

damage to the large commercial fishing industry in the Bristol Bay region. A large mine, called the Pebble Mine, is being proposed on the Alaska Peninsula in that region. If developed, opponents say it may threaten the largest commercial and sport fishing industry in the world. Fish is also a subsistence food that not only provides nutritional value but also a cultural way of life. Alaska Natives harvest this abundant resource for personal use or to share with family and friends and throughout Alaska. Active community associations have been formed opposing the opening of this gold and copper mine, as it could be one of the largest open pit mines in the world if developed.

The Arctic National Wildlife Refuge

The year 2005 was expected by many to be the year that would see the opening up of the vast Arctic National Wildlife Refuge (ANWR) to oil development. With the Republican Party in control of the US Senate and the House of Representatives as well as the White House, many assumed the ANWR would be opened up in 2005. Despite a strong push in the US Congress, led by Alaska's powerful Senator Ted Stevens, this was not to be.

In the days just prior to Congress' Christmas break, Senator Stevens attempted to gain Senate approval to open up the ANWR to drilling by attaching the approval language to a bill appropriating funding for the war in Iraq, relief for Hurricane Katrina victims and money to combat the avian flu threat. This controversial political move drew heavy criticism, some from his Republican colleagues. The Senate voted 48-45 to strip the ANWR language from the bill and then unanimously passed the bill without the drilling language. Twenty-five moderate Republicans asked that it be taken out because they felt it would jeopardize passage of the US$54 billion bill.

The Inupiat village of Kaktovik, the only indigenous community within the boundaries of the ANWR, continues to be divided on the idea of drilling in the refuge. Once considered to be strongly in favor of drilling for economic reasons, a 2005 petition not to open the refuge attracted the signatures of 57 of the village's 188 adults. The Gwich'in Steering Committee, representing the Gwich'in Athabascan Indians of Alaska and Canada, has continued to actively oppose refuge drilling. The Gwich'in consider the Porcupine Caribou herd, which has its calving grounds within the ANWR, as crucial to preserving their way of life.

If the ANWR is opened up to oil drilling, some Alaska Native corporations will be involved because they long ago negotiated drilling rights with the US government. Because these agreements were not part of the Alaska Native Claims Settlement Act, revenues generated from oil development would not be required to be shared with other regions. This situation became an issue at the 2005 Alaska Federation of Natives (AFN) annual convention held in Fairbanks in October. Ahtna, Inc., the regional corporation representing the Copper River Athabascan Indians, proposed a resolution to the convention calling for support for the oil drilling corporations to share revenue generated from ANWR lands. After some contentious debate, the resolution was withdrawn in the name of Native unity. In 1983, the Arctic Slope Regional Corporation, representing the Inupiat of the Arctic Slope, traded 101,000 acres of land it owned within the Gates of the Arctic National Park for drilling rights to 92,160 subsurface acres within the ANWR. New efforts to secure US Congressional approval for drilling in the refuge are expected in 2006.

Alaska Native government contracting controversy

Under the US Small Business Administration's 8(a) program, most small minority and disadvantaged contractors are eligible for federal contracts up to a specific amount without participating in competitive bidding. The system is called "sole-source" contracting. Unlike other eligible small businesses, however, Alaska Native and Native Hawaiian organizations have no limit for federal contracts and are automatically included in the government program. Some Alaska Native corporations have found government contracting very profitable but when a few of the large dollar value contracts went to Alaska Native corporations, several small businesses and the media called for an investigation claiming abuse of the program. The US Government Accounting Office (GAO) is now conducting a study into how well the no-threshold, sole-source program for Alaska Native, tribal and Native Hawaiian businesses is reaching the goals set for the program to promote tribal self-sufficiency and job creation.

Health and Education

There are slightly more than 30 Alaska Natives holding Ph.D. degrees out of the nearly 120,000 Alaska Natives. Recognizing the shortage of Alaska Natives with Ph.D.s, the University of Alaska has begun efforts to increase the number. With more Alaska Natives attending the university, there is a need for more doctoral-level Native faculty members to teach and serve as role models. Dr. Graham Hingangaroa Smith, a Maori from New Zealand, and Pro Vice-Chancellor (Maori) of the Uni-

versity of Auckland, is assisting the university in developing a comprehensive plan to increase the number of Alaska Native Ph.D.s. He
was instrumental in implementing a successful plan in New Zealand
with the goal of producing 500 Maori Ph.D.s in five years   ❏

Sources

Anchorage Daily News
The Washington Post

ARCTIC CANADA

Inuit territories

The Inuit live in four different regions of the Canadian Arctic. Nunavut is the largest region, with an area of 2.1 million square kilometers – roughly the size of continental Europe. As of the last national census in 2001, 22,500 Inuit lived in Nunavut, comprising 85% of its population. The Labrador Inuit Association has 5,300 members, 8,800 Inuit live in Nunavik (in northern Quebec), and 3,000 Inuvialuit live in the far north-west of the Northwest Territories. These figures will be updated by the 2006 census.

Nunatsiavut

Thirty years in the making, Nunatsiavut ("Our beautiful land") and the Nunatsiavut Kavamanga (Nunatsiavut government) became a legal and constitutional reality on December 1, 2005. This happened because Labrador's 5,300 Inuit voted for the Labrador Inuit Land Claims Agreement (LILCA) in May 2004, and it was then approved by the Newfoundland and Labrador legislature and the Canadian Parliament. The LILCA gave the Inuit of Labrador ownership of 15,800 square kilometres of land, and resource and management rights to another 56,700 square kilometres of land known as the Settlement Area, plus a range of financial and other benefits. Nunatsiavut is not a "territory" at the federal/territorial level of the Canadian political system (as Nunavut is) but rather a sub-jurisdiction within the province of Newfoundland and Labrador.

The LILCA is unique in that it provides for Inuit self-government rather than "self-government through public government" such as exists in Greenland and Nunavut. In the latter case indigenous people exercise effective control because they are the majority in the jurisdiction (and this could change if they were ever to become a minority of the population), whereas in Inuit self-government the legislation sets out decision-making structures which only Inuit can be elected to govern. However, though there are few non-Inuit living in the area, each of the five community governments will be required to have at least one non-Inuit as a council member.

Labrador's Inuit leaders are now creating the governmental structures they need to operate their new jurisdiction, and are preparing for the election of the first Nunatsiavut Assembly. The Executive members of the Labrador Inuit Association have been sworn in as the transitional heads of the Nunatsiavut Kavamanga until the first elections are held, no later than December 1, 2007.

Nunavik

Nunavik continues to edge closer to the establishment of Nunavimmiut Aquvvinga – the People of Nunavik's Steering Body, or Nunavik government. The first phase of the implementation plan would see the amalgamation of the existing stand-alone public bodies created by the 1975 James Bay and Northern Québec Agreement (JBNQA), which are the Kativik Regional Government, Kativik School Board and the Nunavik Regional Board of Health and Social Services. The drive to combine their powers, responsibilities, roles, functions, authorities, assets, jurisdictions, obligations, resources and privileges into one unified entity came not from within those organizations but from the Makivik Corporation, the regional Inuit representative organization.

2005 also saw the Makivik Corporation, the Government of Canada and the Government of Nunavut edging closer to signing the Nunavik Inuit Land Claims Agreement, which will resolve the outstanding aboriginal claims of Nunavik Inuit to the area offshore of Québec (the Nunavik Marine Region) and to Northern Labrador and an area offshore of Labrador. Inuit claims to the offshore areas were excluded from the negotiations that resulted in the JBNQA back in the 1970s.

If the draft agreement is ratified by all parties, the Nunavik Inuit will own 80% of all the islands in the Nunavik Marine Region, receive Can$86 million as capital transfers and funds to assist them in imple-

menting the treaty, and will see the creation of co-management (joint Inuit/government decision-making) regimes to address wildlife, land management and environmental issues. With such an agreement, all the outstanding Inuit land claims in Canada will have been concluded.

Nunavut

The urgent shortage of public housing continued to be a pressing issue in Nunavut in 2005. Asked what could be done to reduce the territories' high rate of tuberculosis and other disturbing health indicators, the Chief of Staff of Nunavut's only hospital told the national media, "Housing, housing, housing and housing".

Hopes of getting the federal government to finally commit to funding the construction and maintenance of the estimated 3,300 units that are needed to address the immediate housing shortage (and 250 per year after that) were raised by the vague agreements reached at a First Minister's Meeting held in Kelowna, B.C. in November (see also the article on Canada in this book). The meeting was called by the Liberal Prime Minister, and consisted of representatives of the federal government, the 13 provincial governments and the national aboriginal organizations. One of the many commitments that the Prime Minister made was to build 1,200 housing units in "the Far North". No one knew quite what that meant. The three northern territories, plus Nunatsiavut and Nunavik? Plus the northern provinces? This became a mute question when the Liberals were defeated in a federal election before they could implement any of the promises they had made at Kelowna. The Liberals failed to seriously address the northern housing crisis during their more than a decade in office, and the incoming Conservatives have made no promises to do so either.

The election of a national Conservative government could have a big impact on Nunavut's capital city, Iqaluit. One of the Conservatives' major campaign promises was to boost Canadian sovereignty over the Arctic, and among their specific proposals was the building of a deep-sea military-civilian port in Iqaluit. Three new armed naval heavy ice-breakers and 500 armed forces personnel would be based there. It remains to be seen whether the new federal government will prioritize money for armed icebreakers over money for desperately needed public housing.

Inuvialuit Region

The Joint Review Panel for the Mackenzie Gas Project, an independent seven-member body established to evaluate the potential environmental and social impacts of a Can$ 7-billion natural gas megaproject that would stretch from the Beaufort Sea to Alberta, has begun holding community hearings. This panel and a second group examining the project's engineering and economics will hold hearings throughout 2006 from Sachs Harbour on Banks Island in the north to Calgary, Alberta in the south (see also the section below on the North West Territories).

"I can't complain," said Thomas Berger, who as the one-man commissioner of the Mackenzie Valley Pipeline Inquiry stopped an earlier version of the proposal in 1977. Berger no longer seems worried that the oil companies will trample unopposed over fragile northern environments or over the rights of people seeking to protect traditional livelihoods and lifestyles. "The recommendations I made have been carried out," he told the national media.

> *I recommended to the government they should settle land claims first. They have done that... I recommended environmental values should be protected. That, to a great extent, has been achieved.*

> *Thirty years ago, the idea of reviewing these projects and considering land claims, taking into account environmental issues -- all that was in its infancy. Industry now realizes these are matters they have to take into account. I think that's progress.*

The public hearings will allow community residents to express their views on this.

The Northwest Territories

The Canadian North is on the verge of major developments in the oil and gas industries. In the Northwest Territories (NWT), 2005 was dominated by discussion over the regulatory process and procedures for the environmental assessment for the Mackenzie Gas Project. Public hearings begin in Inuvik in January 2006. The Can$7 billion Mackenzie Gas Project is a joint proposal by Shell Canada Limited, Conoco Phillips Canada (North) Limited, Exxon Mobil, Imperial Oil Resources Ventures Limited and the Aboriginal Pipeline Group (collectively referred to as the Proponents). This represents a megaproject for northern Canada, one that would develop natural gas from three fields in the Mackenzie Delta area for delivery to markets in Canada and the United States, as well as power further development in Alberta's oil-sands industry. The total length of the pipeline would be about 1,300 kilometers from its beginning in Inuvik, down to Alberta.

Technical hearings by the National Energy Board and hearings on environmental, social and economic issues conducted by a Joint Review Panel, will be carried out in 26 communities in the Northwest Territories, along with communities in Alberta (including the major cities of Edmonton and Calgary), and are expected to last for one year. A decision on approval of the Mackenzie Gas project will also be based on these testimonies and information

With most Aboriginal groups having had land claims settled, and with optimism over high natural gas prices kickstarting talks in 2000 to get the pipeline built, the Inuvialuit, the Gwich'in and the Sahtu Dene will be one-third owners of the pipeline and currently form the Aboriginal Pipeline Group (APG). On the surface, at least, Aboriginal leaders are key supporters of the project, arguing that oil and gas development is the only way Aboriginal communities – and the economy of the Northwest Territories as a whole – can achieve jobs and prosperity. Yet 2005 was characterized by dispute, with each player (Aboriginal, federal and territorial governments, industry) pushing its own interests and struggling to reach agreement on the most appropriate way forward for the project. While Aboriginal leaders demonstrated their support for the project, they also argued that it was the responsibility of both industry and the Canadian government to meet the costs of social and economic impacts, and to settle housing and education concerns. Access and benefits agreements also dominated the agenda of talks between Aboriginal groups such as the Sahtu and Imperial and other proponents. Such concerns appear to have been resolved and the Canadian Liberal government announced that it would be giving Can$500 million to Aboriginal communities to help deal with social and economic impacts. However, one of the major stumbling blocks for the proponents remains the unresolved land claim of the Deh Cho in the central Mackenzie Valley. The proposed pipeline route is approximately 40% in Deh Cho traditional territory. Although not opposed to the project, nor to membership of the Aboriginal Pipeline Group, for the Deh Cho a land claim settlement is a precondition before discussions can begin. The Deh Cho argue that they are entitled to revenue from the Mackenzie gas pipeline paid to them directly as a separate level of government. They are also asking for greater clarity around royalty sharing, better environmental assessment, greater understanding of the social impacts, and a guaranteed voice on the Joint Review Panel. There are signs that the Mackenzie Gas Project proponents, including the Aboriginal Pipeline Group are becoming impatient with the Deh Cho position – the chairman of the APG has given the Deh Cho until 30 June 2006 to join the group or lose out on the opportunity.

A number of NGOs, northern and southern, have also established a wide array of positions on the pipeline, and are likely to argue that the project has to be in Canada's interest as a whole. Beyond the rhetoric of leadership about economic opportunities and the future of the NWT, at the community level there remain widespread concerns over the social and environmental impacts of the pipeline. The support of Aboriginal political and business leaders has given industry, government and the media the impression of unequivocal support for the Mackenzie Gas Project, yet the majority of Aboriginal voices have been muted. The extent of opposition to the pipeline remains unknown and the hearings process will give Aboriginal peoples living in Mackenzie Delta and Valley communities an opportunity to express their feelings, anxieties and concerns. For Aboriginal peoples – and all residents of the NWT -- the hearings offer the opportunity and space for open conversation and debate, for the exchange of information and ideas and for a greater understanding of the scope of the project before a final decision is made and before the specific conditions are set out. ❏

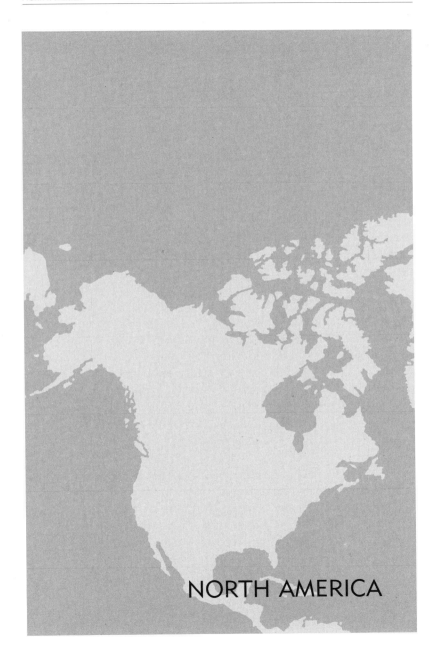

NORTH AMERICA

CANADA

Canada's *Constitutional Act* (1982) specifies three Aboriginal groups: First Nations (often known as "Indians"), Métis and Inuit. First Nations form the largest percentage of the total Aboriginal population (62%), followed by Métis (roughly 30%). This total population is divided roughly equally between those who live in urban environments and those who live in rural areas. According to Canada's 2001 census, the highest concentrations of Aboriginal peoples are found in the Prairie Provinces.

First Nations hold historical claims to territories (reserves) in the provinces through the land surrenders and treaties negotiated with either British colonial administrators or the Canadian government. The *Constitutional Act* protects these treaty rights. There are discrepancies between provinces and territories as to specific treaty rights and whether treaties and reserves were ultimately established. For example, most First Nations in British Columbia do not have treaties with the Canadian government since the province did not historically recognize their land or resource claims. This situation is currently changing, with many British Columbia First Nations in negotiations to establish treaties.

First Nations are culturally, linguistically and regionally diverse groups of peoples and their current national organization, the Assembly of First Nations, often reminds the public of this. Many First Nation peoples live off-reserve in order to access urban centers.

Métis are historically associated with the mixed-heritage populations that arose out of European interests in the fur trade. Their consciousness as a separate nation is most often attributed to early19[th] century events in Manitoba. The only place where Métis have been able to secure land is in Alberta, through a provincial agreement in 1938. With constitutional recognition in 1982, "Métis" has expanded to

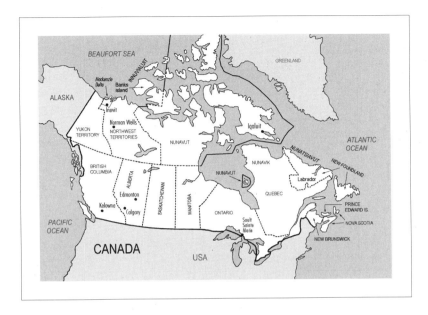

include people who may not identify with the historical Métis populations of western Canada. Currently the Métis National Council represents Métis in some regions of Ontario as well as Manitoba, Saskatchewan, Alberta and parts of British Columbia, while the Congress of
Aboriginal Peoples represents other Métis organizations as well as
"Non-status Indians" and off-reserve peoples.

"Non-Status Indians" either never obtained treaty and/or status
rights or lost these rights because of *Indian Act*[1] policies. In 1985, Bill
C-31 was passed in order to address the discriminatory problems of
the *Indian Act* and to provide the legal impetus for some "Non-status
Indians" to regain their status, primarily those women (and their children) who had lost their status through marriage to any "non-status"
individual, including Métis and "non-Status Indians." In many areas
of the provinces, the boundaries between First Nations, Métis, "Non-
Status Indians" and individuals who have recently regained their status are complicated and blurred since there is a history of intermar-
riage and alliances, as well as changing provincial and federal policies,
with which to contend.

The Kashechewan water treatment scandal

In October 2005, national attention was captured by a water treatment scandal on the road-inaccessible Kashechewan reserve in northern Ontario. In early October, officials tested E. coli in the water supply and began chlorine treatment, which then exacerbated children's skin conditions. Media coverage of the skin sores as well as the overall poverty and crowded living conditions on the reserve spurred government moves to airlift many from the reserve to cities in Ontario. By the end of the year, most of the 1,000 evacuees had returned home, and the government had promised a financial package to overhaul the water treatment facility as well as provide adequate housing over the next few years. Kashechewan thus became a rallying point for long-standing problems in reserves' water supply and sub-standard housing conditions. The Canadian government had announced funding to overhaul water treatment facilities in 2003 and four facilities were completed in 2005 (two in Ontario and two in Alberta). However, likely due to the publicity of Kashechewan, two further new water treatment projects were announced and the media broadcast the appalling living conditions on several other reserves.

The Kelowna Commitments

The media attention on Kashechewan thus bolstered the fervency of meetings that had begun in 2004 between Prime Minister Paul Martin's Liberal government and Aboriginal organizations. These meetings culminated in the First Ministers Conference on Aboriginal issues held on November 24 and 25, 2005 in Kelowna, British Columbia. This conference was the first occasion since the various constitutional talks in the 1980s for Aboriginal leaders, First Ministers, territorial and provincial Premiers and the Prime Minister to come together to discuss Aboriginal issues. Representatives from the Assembly of First Nations, the Inuit Tapiriit Kanatami (the national Inuit organization), the Métis National Council, the Congress of Aboriginal Peoples and the Native

Women's Association of Canada attended and were active in the pre-conference planning. Many indigenous activists were also at Kelowna, albeit outside the meetings as protesters. Among them were the Grass-roots Peoples Coalition, which saw the meetings as bypassing the long outstanding reparations from the Canadian government over Aborigi-nal and Treaty rights, and representatives from the National Associa-tion of Friendship Centres, who were seeking to draw attention to ur-ban Aboriginal issues.

The overall goal of the conference was to address the gap between quality of life for Aboriginal peoples and other Canadians. The Cana-dian government offered a ten-year set of initiatives, with a five-year financial commitment. In his conference speech, Paul Martin under-scored the moral imperative of this commitment through the dismal statistics of Aboriginal rates of suicide, diabetes, infant mortality, low high school graduation and unemployment. He also acknowledged the need to understand the diversity within and between Aboriginal communities, the differences between Inuit, Métis and First Nations as well as the differences between northern, urban and reserve settings and, finally, the unique needs of Aboriginal women.

Health, housing and education were key areas of discussion, and the federal government committed Can$1.8 billion towards education, Can$1.6 billion towards housing and infrastructure and just over Can$1.3 billion towards health care for the next five years. The educa-tion plan includes implementing First Nations jurisdiction and control over education on-reserve or for self-governing First Nations, ensur-ing that the curriculum in all primary and secondary classrooms in-cludes local Aboriginal perspectives and learning approaches. It also looks into developing national centres for Inuit and Métis learning. Besides immediate needs in housing and clean water supply, the hous-ing plan includes more jurisdictional control for First Nations as well as support programs to build skills in construction, management and operations. The Health care package continues the "Aboriginal Health Blueprint" set out in September 2004: doubling the number of Abo-riginal health professionals while halving the rates of infant mortality, diabetes, youth obesity and youth suicide in ten years. In addition, Can$200 million was set aside mainly to address future initiatives in economic opportunities, and Can$ 170 million for policy capacity, accountability and treaty negotiations—these areas all under the umbrella of strengthening relationships between Aboriginal peoples, Aboriginal organizations and the Canadian government.

Residential school claims

2005 also saw an Agreement in Principle between the Assembly of First Nations, the Canadian Government and church organizations to resolve claims of physical and sexual abuse of former students of residential schools. Every province and territory, with the exception of Newfoundland, New Brunswick and Prince Edward Island, had church-run residential schools, instituted through these churches' missionary activities with indigenous peoples. After Canada's 1867 Confederation, these schools were jointly operated by the churches and the Canadian government. They continued until the 1970s when most schools shut down, although the last federally-run school did not close until 1996. An estimated 80,000 people still alive attended such schools, and this agreement hopes to resolve the more than 12,000 claims by former students against the churches and the Canadian government that have not yet been brought to trial. The Canadian government will make Can$1.9 billion available for compensation to students, as well as funding for the next five years for the Aboriginal Healing Foundation.

Election prognosis for 2006

What may possibly call a halt to some of the above mentioned agreements is the upcoming election on January 23, 2006. In an historical move, the Conservative Party called for and later won a no-confidence vote with the support of the other opposition parties on November 28, 2005 and forced the upcoming elections. What these elections mean for Aboriginal peoples has been the subject of concern, considering the many agreements recently made, and Aboriginal organizations have been tracking party campaigns closely. The Conservative Party has indicated that it would replace the Kelowna agreement with a new set of initiatives. Aboriginal organizations have been urging their members to vote and have even pointed to several ridings where their votes could sway election outcomes. Further, the newly-formed First Peoples National Party is also on the docket, with five candidates in Alberta, Ontario and British Columbia ridings.

Land claims and settlements

After many years of negotiation, two land settlements have been resolved in Ontario. In February, the Wahta Mohawk community and the governments of Canada and the province of Ontario announced the resolution of a claim dating back to 1918 when 40% of the Wahta Mohawk reserve was taken by the government and handed over to Ontario without the consent of the First Nation. The negotiation process began in 1993 and, after several years of consultations with the affected communities, the settlement will give back a major portion of the area taken (3,300 of 4,000 hectares) as well as compensate the Wahta Mohawk with Can$9.7 million for the value of the lands not returned and the loss of not having use of these lands since 1918.

To the west, in May, the Rainy River First Nations agreed to a settlement of a 90-year-old grievance. In 1914-1915, Canada wrongfully surrendered six of their reserves and caused much hardship in relocating their people. The "Rainy River Land Claim" began in 1982 but it was not until 1997 that the governments of Canada and Ontario agreed to address the claim. The final negotiated settlement consists of Can$71 million in compensation for the market value of approximately 6,048 hectares of provincial land as well as the opportunity to purchase up to 12, 677 hectares of replacement land.

In June, the Thames First Nation in Ontario was granted Can$15 million in a purely financial settlement to redress the past misappropriation of monies earned from selling the First Nation's land by a Superintendent of Indian Affairs between 1830 and 1854.

In November, in British Columbia, the Songhees First Nation settled an agreement over 1.13 acres of land that Canada had taken for a rail spur in 1920. The agreement requires the land to be returned and the Songhees First Nation to be compensated with Can$1,240,000.

Finally in April, the Innu of Betsiamites and the government of Canada agreed to begin negotiations to resolve the Innu claims that Highway 138 and the bridge over the Betsiamites River in Quebecwere constructed on or near their reserve without proper authority and consultation.

Treaty rights on trial

Recent court cases have both reaffirmed and limited treaty rights. In November, the Supreme Court of Canada ruled unanimously for the Mikisew Cree First Nation's appeal that a 118-kilometre road proposed through (and later along the boundary of) their reserve at Peace Point, Alberta was impermissible. The proposed road would have crossed trap lines of Mikisew families as well as others; it would have also interfered with their moose hunting grounds. Since the federal government only released information about this road as it would to the general public, the Supreme Court argued that they did not follow the proper procedures for consultation over the road's possible interference with the Mikisew's treaty rights – hunting, trapping, and fishing rights – as outlined in Treaty 8.

In July the Supreme Court, however, did not rule in favor of Mi'kmaq logging rights in Nova Scotia and New Brunswick. In the court's interpretation, since the Mi'kmaq could not prove that they traded logs before their treaty rights were established in the1760-61 Peace and Friendship Treaty then they could not log without legal permits today. The court also argued that the Mi'kmaq could not establish territorial claims to the areas in which they had illegally cut logs. The consequences of this ruling may put considerable burden of proof on First Nations in future claims: they must show a connection between past and contemporary uses of resources, and they must provide evidence of occupation, which some analysts say would require extensive archaeological research.

Self-Government

Self-government agreements are under negotiation with several groups to refashion existing government relationships or to establish anew their Aboriginal rights to control the interests of their own communities. These are multi-stage negotiations over land, resource and jurisdiction issues before the final agreement is instituted (see *The Indigenous World 2002-2003, 2004, 2005*).

The Miawpukek First Nation, a Mi'kmaq community on the South Central Coast of Newfoundland, signed a Self-Government Framework Agreement and a Land Transfer Agreement with the Government of Canada and the Government of Newfoundland and Labrador in April 2005. The Miawpukek First Nation has thus officially begun the process of establishing its future legislative powers and has government approval to expand the Samiajij Miawpukek Reserve by approximately 2,331 hectares.

However, based on a July 2005 vote across four Ontario First Nations, the Grand Council of the United Anishnaabeg Councils' proposed self-government agreement was not ratified since the number of supporting votes needed from the First Nations' members was not achieved. Although disappointed by the results, the United Anishnaabeg Councils leaders were proud of the voter turn-out and respected the outcome.

Treaty negotiations in British Columbia

In August 2005, the Yekooche First Nation, along with provincial and federal representatives, signed an Agreement in Principle and thus joined five other British Columbia groups in the last stage before the final treaty agreement in the negotiation process. The Yekooche First Nation consists of around 200 members in a community northwest of

Fort St. James in north-central British Columbia, and this agreement outlines proposed treaty lands that would add land to join up three of their four reserves, along with a Can$6.5 million cash settlement. The agreement also works towards delineating harvesting and hunting rights for migratory birds and plant life in areas near their reserve lands, although their fishing rights are still to be negotiated.

Métis harvesting rights

Stemming from the Supreme Court's 2003 *R. v Powley* decision that allowed Métis harvesting rights initially in Sault Ste. Marie in Ontario, Métis members within the Métis National Council (MNC) have been able assert these rights to limited degrees (see *The Indigenous World 2005*). One example of the many still to be worked out across the MNC-affiliated provinces is in Alberta. Here the Métis provincial representative bodies were successful in mapping out an interim Métis harvesting agreement with the province in 2004 but, in 2005, the Assembly of Chiefs of Treaties 6, 7, and 8 called for a termination of these rights because the province had not properly consulted them. In addition, to deal with the repercussions of the *Powley* decision, Canada gave the MNC resource funding and, with this, the MNC assembled a team of expert researchers to study historic and territorial Métis boundaries. In 2005, they met in order to formulate a "MNC Historic Database" with web accessibility for further genealogical research.   ❑

Notes and sources

1   The Indian Act, passed in 1876, is the legislation that provides the federal government with the legal framework of authority over Indians and the lands reserved for Indians. At one time it governed all aspects of status Indian lives, affecting their livelihood, lifestyle and social choices, on and off reserve.

Assembly of First Nations: www.afn.ca
British Columbia Treaty Commission: www.bctreaty.net

Department of Indian and Northern Affairs Canada: www.ainc-inac.gc.ca
First Peoples National Party of Canada: www.fpnpoc.ca
Métis National Council: www.metisnation.ca
Métis Nation of Alberta: www.metisablerta.ca
Statistics Canada:
http://www12.statcan.ca/english/census01/home/index.cfm
United Anishnaabeg Councils: www.uac.org

UNITED STATES OF AMERICA

The year's events were marked by the background of the continuing wars in Afghanistan and Iraq. These efforts still involve many
Native American soldiers. They also amount to a huge expenditure for
the federal government which, in response to record national deficits,
has tried to cut services it deems unessential. For some tribes, this
means that Bureau of Indian Affairs (BIA) contracts are lost. BIA contracts provide resources to tribes to run social, economic, ecological,
educational and other programs; cutting these resources will not only
mean a loss of tribally controlled programs but also a loss of tribal
employment opportunities. The Northern Cheyenne Tribe in Montana,
for example, will probably lose 35 jobs because of this. Any loss of employment opportunities on small, underdeveloped reservations is a
disaster. On the other hand, those tribes who are involved in manufacturing contracts for the Department of Defense are gaining employment and revenues. Sioux Manufacturing, of the Spirit Lake Nation,
North Dakota, for example, which manufactures personal and vehicle
armor, runs three shifts and made about US$20 million in profits this
year.

The economy

The evaluation of the 2000 census data continues and, in January 2005,
a Harvard University based study showed that socio-economic conditions for Native Americans had greatly improved between 1990 and
2000. Income had risen by around 20%, with tribes who operate gaming facilities seeing a higher average rise than tribes who do not. The
authors emphasized that the most important reason for improvements,
however, was self-determination; the abolition of colonial and bureau-

cratic processes allows tribes to act and react more quickly and efficiently, as well as culturally appropriately, to socio-economic needs. They also took note of the fact that, despite these improvements, the average income in Native America is still less than half the average for the United States overall.[1]

A growing number of Native-owned businesses are contributing to a better economy on the reservations. Corporate tribal casinos have increased their revenues significantly over the past years, to US$19 billion in 2004, and it is thus not surprising that several tribes are continuing to expand gaming operations. For example, the Little Traverse Bay Bands of Odawa Indians in Michigan is planning to open a US$197.4 million casino complex, and the Northern Arapaho Tribe in Wyoming is expanding its current casino while building a new one.

Again, as impressive and encouraging as these figures might seem, it must be emphasized that almost a third of all Native Americans live below the poverty line, as compared to about one eighth of all Americans. In comparison to all other racial or ethnic groups, Native children are the most likely to live in conditions of poverty.

Tragedy

The sometimes extreme conditions Native children live in were highlighted on March 21, 2005, on the Red Lake Reservation, an Ojibwe reservation in northern Minnesota. A sixteen-year-old student killed nine
people in Red Lake High School that day, before taking his own life.
Between then and July, three more young students committed suicide,
continuing an extremely alarming nationwide trend that sees increasing
numbers of Native youths taking their own lives. The school shooting
brought the conditions of poverty and hopelessness to brief national
media attention. The Federal Bureau of Investigation (FBI) brought
charges against a friend of the shooter, who is the son of the tribal chairman, as co-conspirator, and detained him under very unclear circumstances. In December, this student pleaded guilty to "threatening inter-
state communications" – he had been in regular e-mail contact with the
shooter prior to the tragedy – after the FBI tried to charge him as if he
were an adult with conspiracy to commit murder. While the media attention has all but disappeared from Red Lake, the community is still
trying to heal the wounds and to put measures in place that will allow a
similar tragedy to be prevented in the future. For a short while, the tragedy put conditions on some reservations in the spotlight. But many reservations are dealing with youth suicides and ways to prevent them on
a daily basis, and without adequate resources.

Sports mascots

One of the greatest controversies in Native American issues this year
came from a decision made by the National Collegiate Athletic Association (NCAA), the governing body of collegiate athletics.
   Ever since the 1950s, Native American and other civil rights activists have opposed the use of Indian mascots, logos and nicknames for
school, university and professional sports teams. They see these practices as a continuation of colonial rule, and as an inaccurate portrayal
of Native cultures, therefore perpetuating – mostly negative – stereotypes.

Hundreds of schools and universities have changed their nicknames and logos but some have decided not to do so. Following years of calls from civil rights activists, the National Congress of the American Indians, many tribal government resolutions and professional organizations, the NCAA ruled on August 5, 2005 that Native American related nicknames, mascots or logos that are deemed "hostile and abusive in terms of race, ethnicity or national origin" would no longer be tolerated at any NCAA-sponsored tournaments. Schools who continued these practices would no longer be allowed to host such tournaments. The organization published a list of eighteen schools that would fall under the new guidelines. The Florida State University "Seminoles", the Central Michigan University "Chippewa" and the University of Utah "Utes" were subsequently exempted because they could show that tribal governments supported their use of their tribal names. However, the responses to the NCAA often showed a shocking residual racism that is normally hidden, and a widespread ignorance of Native American culture, history and contemporary situations, coupled with indifference about these issues. The debate made clear how much Native American culture has been appropriated by the dominant society, which largely assumes that it has the right to dictate the terms by which Native America can be defined.

Sovereignty

Federal courts heard a host of sovereignty-related cases in 2005. As expected in the extremely complex and sometimes contradictory legal arena that is federal Indian law in the United States, the results were mixed. Sovereignty for tribes still rests on a case-by-case basis.

The Supreme Court handed a victory to the U.S. Forest Service in a sacred site case. The Forest Service has tried to protect the area around a Medicine Wheel in the Bighorn Mountains, Wyoming. The site is on National Forest land but is used for ceremonies by several tribes. The Forest Service tried to accommodate the sacred use of the site by restricting, but not barring, the economic development of 23,000 acres surrounding the site. Wyoming Sawmills sued against such restriction of economic development on federal lands on the grounds of religion but its case was dismissed by a Court of Appeals, which ruled that the timber company lacked legal standing. The company appealed to the Supreme Court, which declined to hear the case. While this implies that the Forest Service policy stands, it is not an indication as to whether or not the Supreme Court has reversed its opinion on sacred sites on federal lands. In earlier years, it had favored economic development over tribal religious needs.

The 9th Circuit Court of Appeals ruled for the sovereignty of federally recognized tribes in determining membership. In the case, *Lewis v. Norton*, siblings sued the government in order to force the tribe to accept them as members. The tribe, the Table Mountain Rancheria of California, operates a successful casino and distributes about US$350,000 yearly to each of its fewer than 100 members. The Lewis siblings' father had been admitted as a member, and their grandparents had been on the original enrollment list. While the court showed sympathy to the siblings' pledge, it emphasized the tribe's sovereign immunity and its right to resolve "purely intramural matters such as conditions of tribal membership" according to its own rules. This decision re-emphasizes the fact that tribes alone determine the criteria for membership, and that membership is not always based upon biological descent, nor does it have to follow federal standards for equal rights.

In October, in another development connected to tribal sovereignty, the National Labor Relations Board (NLRB) held that tribes are subject to federal labor laws. Specifically, this decision means that tribes have to allow labor unions to organize in their enterprises. This decision overturned thirty years of precedent that had exempted tribal enterprises from labor laws. State governments are already exempt from federal labor laws, and if tribes are sovereign entities, they argue, they should receive the same exemption. Tribes had used the exemption from labor laws in casinos, but it also allowed them to be more competitive in the manufacturing and service industries. The decision is expected to be challenged through the courts.

Land cases

In March, the Supreme Court decided on the case *City of Sherill v. Oneida Indian Nation of New York* (see *The Indigenous World 2005*), and handed an astonishing defeat not only to the Oneida Nation but to Indian tribes overall. The Oneida Nation had repurchased some of the 250,000 acres that had been illegally appropriated by New York in the 19th century. The Oneida had then declared that the properties, within the city limits of Sherill, were tax exempt because they lay within the lands delineated as Indian country by the 1794 Treaty of Canandaigua, and automatically reverted into tax-exempt trust land status, owned and controlled by the reservation government, now that the injustice had been resolved. A lower court sided with the Oneida in 2003, and the U.S. Solicitor General filed a court brief in favor of the Oneida Nation.

In a surprise decision, the Supreme Court decided that while the Oneida Nation held a valid claim for the stolen lands, once these lands were purchased, even if within reservation boundaries, they were not tax exempt until expressly returned to trust status by the Secretary of the Interior. The government has been more than cautious in granting trust status to tribal lands, mostly because of fears that Indian tribes would use these plots to build casinos. More surprising than this technical decision, however, was the court's argument.

The majority decision held that because the lands had been governed by state, county and city authorities, and because the Oneida Nation had waited for so long to seek justice, "we hold that the Tribe cannot unilaterally revive its ancient sovereignty, in whole or in part, over the parcels at issue". While the court made clear that the land claim was valid, it closed one avenue of remedy; in doing so, it showed an amazing lack of understanding of the historical forces that had prevented the Oneida from seeking justice earlier. The court also established a new criterion for land cases by basing its decision on the finding that a reversion of the parcels to trust status, or in other words to tribal authority, would have "disruptive practical consequences" for the city and its citizens. It was not long before lower courts latched on to this formulation in other Indian land claim cases. In the meantime, local governments presented the Oneida Nation with a multi-million dollar bill for overdue property taxes.

In June, judges of the 2nd Circuit Court of Appeals used the *Sherill* decision to deny a Cayuga land claim, *Cayuga Nation v. New York*. Even though the judges acknowledged that the 64,000 acres in question had been illegally acquired, they cited the *Sherill* case to argue that the Cayuga had waited too long to bring the case to court. The claim for remedy was dismissed because it was seen as too "disruptive" for non-Indian communities. New York governor Pataki (Republican) was quick to declare the decision a "tremendous victory for property owners and tax payers". The plaintiffs, the Cayuga Nation of New York and the Seneca-Cayuga Tribe of Oklahoma, plan to appeal against the ruling. If it stands throughout the courts, then the *Sherill* decision has fundamentally changed the legal landscape and would allow for any land claims to be denied on the basis of "disruption" of the established status quo.

Trust fund case

The *Cobell v. Norton* class action lawsuit (see *The Indigenous World 2005*) entered its ninth year this year. This lawsuit revolves around the mishandling of more than US$100 billion of Indian trust fund money by the Department of the Interior since 1887. The government, acting as a warden of Indian landowners, collected lease money for grazing and mineral exploitation but never paid the individual Indian account holders. Judge Lamberth declared in July that the case "serves as an appalling reminder of the evils that result when large numbers of the politically powerless are placed at the mercy of institutions engendered and controlled by a politically powerful few". The case has been riddled with overt attempts by the government to destroy records and deceive the court. This year, the Bush administration asked for the replacement of the judge for alleged bias. Representing some 500,000 Native Americans, the leading plaintiff, Eloise Cobell, offered a US$27.5 billion settlement but the case seems to be deadlocked for the moment.

Corruption scandal

This year also saw the slow but steady investigation of a corruption scandal of historic proportions that started with several casino-operating tribes and has reached the highest government levels. The Saginaw

Chippewa Tribe of Michigan, the Agua Caliente Band of Cahuilla Indians of California, the Mississippi Band of Choctaw and the Coushatta Tribe of Louisiana hired lobbyist Jack Abramoff, who then convinced them to hire public relations specialist Michael Scanlon, both of whom had very close ties to House Majority Leader Tom DeLay (Republican). In 2004, the story broke that the tribes had paid the two men over US$45 million dollars. Senator John McCain (Republican) started an investigation into these fees before the Senate Committee on Indian Affairs. The Coushatta Tribe of Louisiana alone, it turned out, had paid Abramoff US$32 million dollars over three years; leaders of the tribe had transferred funds earmarked for housing, health care, and education programs to the lobbyist. Some of these funds had then been redirected to former Christian Coalition director Ralph Reed to lobby against other tribes' casino plans. Abramoff, Scanlon and Reed worked to shut down the Tigua Tribe of Texas' casino, and then offered the tribe their million-dollar services to reopen it. Abramoff and Scanlon also ran election campaigns for members of the Agua Caliente and Saginaw Chippewa tribes.

The corruption scandal came to engulf Tom DeLay and other high-ranking national politicians in 2005. Abramoff got tribes to contribute money to the National Center for Policy Research, a non-profit organization allied with conservative causes, which subsequently used part of the money to pay for overseas trips for the politicians, including a golfing excursion to Scotland. Abramoff also used tribal money to rent a skybox in a football stadium, which was then used by mostly Republican politicians, and funneled some money to an anti-Palestinian settler in Israel. After Abramoff was indicted for fraud charges on his own purchase of a casino operation, in October 2005, President Bush's nominee for the second highest post at the Department of Justice withdrew his nomination over ties to Abramoff. Michael Scanlon entered a plea agreement on charges of conspiracy to defraud tribes and bribe a public official, and started to cooperate with the authorities. In November, Representatives Tom DeLay and Bob Ney (Republican) became a focus of the corruption investigation, as did former Department of Interior deputy secretary Griles, former White House official Safavian, and a host of other political figures. In December 2005, Abramoff was negotiating a plea agreement on the bank fraud charges. By this time, the sum of tribal money involved was estimated to be nearly US$80 million. The complex web that Abramoff spun is too complicated to easily summarize but some analysts think it might become the largest political scandal in Washington since Watergate.

What the investigation clearly shows is that competition between casino-operating tribes has led some of them to campaign against others, and to use the same methods of influencing national politics as other interest groups, namely money. The investigation has also led to calls for even stricter rules within the Indian Gaming Regulatory Act (IGRA) of 1988. Tribes and the National Indian Gaming Association (NIGA) are opposed to any amendments to the IGRA because they fear that this would result in a diminution of sovereignty. Paradoxically, state governments are also opposed to such a reform, because it would take away the means of pressuring tribes to provide higher percentages of gaming revenues to the states.

Kennewick Man and the notion of Indigenousness

Finally, it might be of interest to note that scientists have started to study the over 9,000-year-old human remains known as Kennewick Man, found in 1996 in the state of Washington. The remains, taken by some scientists to represent an early Polynesian or European presence in North America, led to a long court battle under the Native American Graves Protection and Repatriation Act (NAGPRA), which decided in favor of a study of the remains in 2004. Tribes had wanted to rebury the remains without study, claiming the Kennewick Man to be an ancestor of theirs. This decision has led to efforts to change NAGPRA's definition of "Native American". While currently the definition is "of, or relating to, a tribe, people, or culture that is indigenous to the United States," the new definition would read "is or was" indigenous. The court ruling in 2004, based on the old definition, determined that the remains were not Native American since no link could be established between them and contemporary Indian nations. Therefore the remains can be studied.

Senator McCain (Republican), the chairman of the Senate Indian Affairs Committee, introduced a bill to include the new definition in the law. This happened in response to the court ruling, and would support the claim of the tribes to rebury the remains without study. The bill had the support of the whole committee but, in July, the Bush administration opposed the proposed amendment and the Department of the Interior announced that it agreed with the outcome of the Kennewick Man case. This represents a change in policy. Until 2004, the government had fought in favor of the tribes, and against the scientific study, in order to uphold NAGPRA as the law of the land.

On a wider level, it remains extremely unclear how people who lived in North America 9,000 years ago cannot be indigenous to the continent, but a lawyer representing a group of scientists opposing the amendment said that they "weren't American Indians as we know those people today". She argued that some of the first Americans were not related to present-day Native Americans: "They're different. Kennewick Man is different. This man walked our country and he wasn't an American Indian as we know it today." If one defines cultural change as representing a fundamental disruption, one would of course be hard pressed to find any indigenous peoples anywhere. But perhaps that – the denial of indigenousness to contemporary peoples – is exactly what is intended.   ❑

Note

1   **Jonathan B. Taylor and Joseph B. Kalt:** *American Indian on Reservations: A Databook of Socioeconomic Change Between the 1990 and 2000 Censuses.* Available online at: http://www.ksg.harvard.edu/hpaied/pubs/documents/AmericanIndian-sonReservationsADatabookofSocioeconomicChange.pdf

MEXICO AND
CENTRAL AMERICA

MEXICO

2005 was noteworthy for its increased coordination between indigenous struggles and those of other sectors of Mexican society, through the battle to defend their natural resources and, more broadly, the launch of the Sixth Declaration of the Lacandona Forest. Renewed interest on the part of transnational capital in the country's natural resources put increased pressure on indigenous territories. A series of controversial laws promoting natural resource privatization has been approved in recent years and many communities have been, and continue to be, pressured into becoming companies to sell assets that belong to all humanity such as water, air and biodiversity. Organised resistance had its triumphs and also its defeats, in the form of much repression. Political violence increased, particularly in Oaxaca and Guerrero.

Onslaught against indigenous territories and institutions

The so-called *Oportunidades* and *Procampo* government programmes deliver individualized economic resources that neither resolve the health, food and education problems (*Oportunidades*) nor encourage the agricultural production (*Procampo*) of those targeted by them. On the contrary, they create dependency and erode indigenous community institutions such as the General Assembly because this latter is not consulted when deciding who receives support or whether this is the kind of support that is really needed in the communities. In actual fact, this "support" for agricultural production ends up lining the pockets of the large agroindustrialists who collude with government technicians to encourage indigenous and peasant farmers to purchase agricultural inputs and machinery which, in the end, they do not use de-

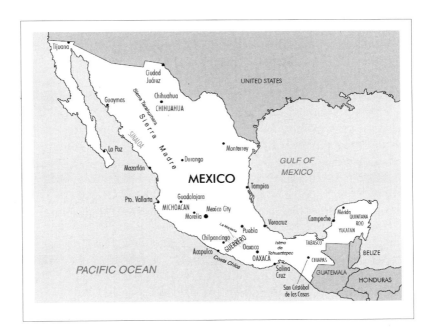

spite having bought. Moreover, the food aid programmes that are distributed in Mexico contain foods not produced in the country and these have become big business for the ruling classes and political parties. And yet they pay no compensation for the damage caused to impoverished rural populations when they deprive them of the possibility of producing their own food, or encourage them to eat foods alien to their dietary culture, which in the past was a form of resistance.

Offering payment for environmental services or establishing protected natural areas is another way of stripping indigenous peoples of their land because, when communities sign contracts or agreements containing conservation commitments, they lose their decision-making capacity over the land. In addition to the legal framework and government programmes that are eroding the foundations of Mexican indigenous communities, megaprojects are being promoted on their lands such as: the construction of highways that make possible the rapid transit of goods between the Gulf of Mexico and the Pacific Ocean, benefiting US global trade with the Far East; the construction of

maritime ports for deep sea vessels, which will form the hub of multi-
modal transport; the construction of dams to generate the electricity
needed by foreign companies wishing to invest in industrial corridors
(primarily in the Pacific) and in which the communities' approach to
and care of the environment count little given that all legal means and
coercive actions are used to evict them (the case of La Parota in Guerrero is the most visible at international level but there are other similar
evictions taking place, primarily in Nayarit, Jalisco, Oaxaca and Chiapas, towards the Pacific Ocean). In 2005, a strong boost was given to
mineral prospecting in Oaxaca, under the pretext that this industry
could become a source of employment. And yet the studies are being
conducted without the knowledge of the indigenous communities.

The struggle against La Parota dam

In 2005, the conflict around the planned construction of La Parota dam
in Guerrero[1] intensified, resulting in three murders, dozens of injuries
and clashes between peasant farmers and the police force. According
to government figures, the dam will produce around 1,332 million
KWh a year, equivalent to the annual consumption of Guerrero state.

The indigenous and peasant farmers who have organised against
the dam are warning that it would flood 17,000 hectares of high biodiversity forest, and would directly displace more than 25,000 people. In
all, 72,000 inhabitants would be affected, turning this dam into a veri-
table "eco- and ethnocide".

With the plans for La Parota dam, the government is violating
agrarian legislation, the state and federal constitutions and international agreements relating to the environment and the rights of indigenous peoples, such as ILO Convention 169. It is even ignoring the
recommendations of the World Commission on Dams (WCD). Community members opposing construction of La Parota have organised
into the Council of Cooperatives and Communities against La Parota
(*Consejo de Ejidos y Comunidades en contra La Parota* - CECOP).

In July 2005, more than 70 organisations throughout the country,
along with others from abroad, organised a "National Meeting against

La Parota Dam" in the Aguas Calientes community, Acapulco municipality. The organisations attending the meeting agreed that not one centimetre more of land would be handed over to those promoting their dispossession and that they would defend the environment. In addition, they agreed to form a united front to defend their land and water and the peoples' economic, social, cultural and environmental rights, as part of their human rights.[2]

Indigenous Peoples' Forum parallel to the World Water Forum

The World Water Forum was held in Mexico in March 2006, organised by business people with the consent of governments. Many parallel fora were held, organised by Mexican and international civil society. The *Law on National Waters* was discussed, which pronounces the state's ownership of all the country's water and gives federal government the powers to allocate it to private individuals (thus commencing its privatisation) without having to ask the consent of the indigenous and peasant peoples and communities who have safeguarded it since time immemorial.

The "Tlatokan Atlahuak" Declaration of the Parallel Forum of Indigenous Peoples reaffirmed the sacred nature of water and the importance of preventing its privatisation. The neoliberal model, which views water as a commodity, and the fact that the World Trade Organisation is promoting the privatisation of this public utility throughout the world, were both rejected.

Mining

The Mining Law empowers the federal government to issue mining concessions even to transnational companies, without the need to seek the consent of the indigenous communities and peoples who have lived on these lands since time immemorial. In the Nahua communities of the Sierra de Manantlan in Jalisco, 16 concessions covering virtually the whole biosphere reserve of the same name have been allocated. In 2005, the indigenous resistance in Ayotitlán to attempts by the Minera Peña Colorada company to surface mine ferrous deposits in the area led to lawsuits and appeals, and they requested a suspension of the company's activities in their settlements.

Against bioprospecting

The indigenous political agenda of strengthening traditional knowledge and recovering and encouraging sustainable practices in the face of the interests of capital assumes greater significance in Chiapas. The region is known as one of the planet's "bio- hot spots" as the state contains 40% of the country's biodiversity as a whole plus a high percentage of the whole continent's biodiversity. In addition, this state contains a large proportion of the creole seeds that gave rise to many of the foods consumed in the world today, a significant number of plants with curative properties that form the basis of many medicines, and forms the main route of Central America's biological corridors.

This exceptional biological wealth has been identified as one of the state's main comparative advantages in relation to its national and international economic market integration, as reflected in the priority Governor Pablo Salazar has given to the tourism and eco-tourism sectors, including ambitious infrastructure programmes and initiatives to attract private investment.[3] In the legal sphere, federal and state initiatives and reforms are aimed at facilitating the private exploitation of these biological resources and the privatisation of their gene banks. Laws governing access to and protection of genetic resources, protection of traditional knowledge and industrial property (approved by the Senate and currently being discussed in the Chamber of Deputies) require indigenous communities to register their ancestral knowledge of how to use local plants and encourage its patenting and consequent privatisation.

In 2005, the federal state approved the law on biosecurity and genetically modified organisms, known popularly as the Monsanto Law, which promotes the development of transgenics in Mexico and implements the privatisation of the country's genetic resources, granting patents over indigenous knowledge. Far from protecting the health and biological diversity of crops that have their origins in Mexico, such as maize, beans, squash, tomatoes, cotton, avocados, etc., this law enables the importation and sowing of transgenic seeds on national territory.

In the same year, the law on biodiversity conservation and environmental protection in Chiapas state was discussed. In the words of the Environment and Natural Resources Minister this would mean that "opportunities for legal markets for genetic resources and biodiversity are opened up in Chiapas".[4] In March 2005, in an act that violated the country's national sovereignty, the Mexican Constitution and ILO Convention 169, Governor Pablo Salazar opened up the draft bill to international consultation, eliminating indigenous and peasant farmers - the people whose knowledge and territories would precisely be the most affected - from the participation process. In the face of this action, successful protest on the part of different organisations from Chiapas, such as the 19 that make up the Council of Doctors and Traditional Birth Attendants of Chiapas (*Consejo de Médicos y Parteras Tradicionales de Chiapas* - Compitch) and the environmental organisation *Maderas del Pueblo del Sureste* (Wood for the People of the South-East) managed to get approval of this initiative halted.

As an alternative to this vision, members of these organisations countered with a concept of collective and cross-generational ownership. In an action aimed at reflecting this alternative vision, the doctors and traditional birth attendants of Compitch freely disseminated their traditional knowledge, knowledge that has historically been guarded and protected jealously amongst very few people, so that it would remain in the public domain and thus could not be patented. In a conversation with the researcher Neil Harvey, a Tzeltal doctor from Compitch explained, "We must teach each other what we know about medicinal plants. If [this knowledge] only belongs to one person, it is as if it were not ours, but it is everyone's. If someone else wants it, we will give it to him, if someone needs it; this must be between equals and in support of those who need it."[5]

Radicalising the struggle

Sixth Declaration of the Lacandona Forest

After 12 years of struggle to obtain recognition of the rights of indigenous peoples, in June 2005 the Zapatista National Liberation Front
(*Ejército Zapatista de Liberación Nacional* - EZLN) launched a new national political initiative with the Sixth Declaration of the Lacandona
Forest. This calls upon different sectors of Mexican society, including
workers, peasant farmers, indigenous peoples, young people and ho-
mosexuals, to build a long-term political force defined as "anti-capitalist, left-wing and grass-roots up" and which is positioned outside the
party political system. For this, it proposes conducting the "Other
Campaign", in order to differentiate it from the presidential campaigns
of 2006, describing this as "a national campaign to forge a new way of
conducting politics, for a left-wing programme and for a new constitution". The aim of the Other Campaign is to coordinate the demands of
the Indian peoples with those of other sectors in the country, establishing closer relations by listening to the voices of all those who go un-
heard. The Other Campaign commenced on 1 January 2006 with a six-
month trip by Delegate Zero[6] around all the states in the Republic with
the aim of listening to the views of different players on the country's
current situation. In this regard, the initiative itself holds the challenge
of constructing a diverse political force both in terms of its content and
the participation of its players, without sidelining the demands of Indian peoples, as has been the case throughout Mexico's political history. The people, groups, families, organisations and communities that
signed up to the Sixth Declaration have met to discuss the content and
organise the logistics of the Other Campaign when it passes through
their states. Supporters will come together in a national conference in
June 2006 when the joint programme of struggle will be produced on
the basis of information gathered during the course of the Other Campaign.

   As part of the preparatory events, a meeting was held in August
2005 with representatives of indigenous communities and organisations in the Zapatista community of Javier Hernández. Here, delegates

explained the main political agendas of the national indigenous movement in the context of the Other Campaign. Noteworthy points discussed and proposals emanating from this meeting included the struggle to preserve the biodiversity and for the right to land, and against land privatisation. In addition, emphasis was placed on building indigenous autonomy as the basis for constructing sustainable practices and processes alternative to neoliberalism. In the words of the *Consejo Indígena Popular de Oaxaca* (CIPO) representative, "In order to contribute to global transformation, we say no to taking power but yes to building a counterforce, with the territory as our basis, the social movement as our instrument and autonomy as our platform".

Autonomy

The Good Government Committees

August 2005 marked two years since the establishment of regional autonomous government in the Zapatista areas. The previous multi-service centres, known as *Aguascalientes*, became *Caracoles* and the seats of the Good Government Committees, after a long consultation from the Zapatista National Liberation Army in August 2003. Given that the 2001 constitutional reforms on indigenous rights and culture failed to establish the legal framework for exercising indigenous autonomy, the Zapatistas established autonomous regional governments alongside the official municipal authorities. In these two years, the Good Government Committees have consolidated their way of working by means of a system of collective and rotating representation to resolve problems at regional level, coordinate between municipalities, establish project priorities, decide how resources are to be distributed in the region etc. Two representatives from each autonomous municipality belonging to a *Caracol* form a Good Government Committee. These representatives live in the *Caracol* and exercise their collective authority for a short period of time (one week to two months) before being replaced by another two representatives from each municipality. This rotation avoids any concentration of power or the formation of *cacicazgos* (chiefdoms), as has been the case in a large number of local authorities in the recent past in Chiapas. In June 2005, through the Sixth Declaration of the Forest, the EZLN delegated complete responsibility for supporting and monitoring the way in which the Good Government Committees operate to the Zapatista grassroots, also on a rotating basis.

This expression of autonomous indigenous government continues the self-learning process and practice of Zapatista political culture known as "leading by obeying". In the words of one Zapatista grass-roots supporter, "Previously, the government took decisions on our lives. It was the oppressor. Now we are the government, it is a government of the people, we govern amongst ourselves. It is no longer a government with authority over life but one that is at the service of the people."

Indigenous National Congress

The peoples organised since 1996 in the National Indigenous Congress (*Congreso Nacional Indígena* - CNI) held their 16th meeting in the Erupción de Rebeldía Caracol in Lago Azul de Zirahuen, in the Purepecha community of the same name, in Michoacán, on 18 and 19 June 2005. The final declaration of this meeting overwhelmingly rejected the laws and proposals recently amended and created by the Mexican government to privatise everything that is born of Mother Earth and their traditional knowledge. They asserted their rejection of, and decision not to comply with, all programmes aimed at dividing and privatising territories and destroying communal organisations, such as the Programme for Certification of Cooperative and Communal Rights (PROCEDE and PROCECOM), the Programme of Payment for Environmental Services and the territorial re-organisations of their peoples. The Indian peoples that make up the National Indigenous Congress (CNI) recognise the San Andrés Accords as the supreme constitution of Indian peoples.

In March 2006, the EZLN and the CNI urgently organised the 6th Indigenous National Congress, to be held in the Ñañu village of San Pedro Atlapulco in May 2006. It made clear the decision of the native peoples not to request legal recognition of their rights through dialogue but to exercise such rights and autonomy in practice. The call to attend responded to the EZLN's invitation to build "a great anti-capitalist and left-wing force that can work to build a new national programme of struggle and a new constitution with the aim of putting an end to the war of capitalist devastation".[7] Now we realise that the war of conquest is not yet over, and that foreigners can still seize our lands through government ploys. We are no longer seeking dialogue with those in power; what we are seeking is that they should fall, disappear and, with them, the wealthy, who have left us suffering in the dark for more than 500 years. The time has come to rise up in a great civilian and peaceful movement to occupy by force the place that is rightfully ours in our Mexican nation. We can no longer wait for the powerful to listen to us. They are not interested in us. They despise us."[8]

The Congress discussions will focus on an evaluation of the indigenous struggle since the 2001 constitutional reforms, which were in breach of the San Andrés Accords, and on conducting an assessment and evaluation of the impacts of neoliberal capitalism on indigenous peoples and the nation as a whole.

Repression and resistance

Guerrero
In Guerrero, the Amuzgo, Tlapaneco, Mixteco and Nahua peoples make up 13.75% of the total population. Since the time of the so-called "dirty war" of the 1960s and 70s, around 500 people have been murdered or "disappeared" for political reasons. The indigenous population has suffered this state terror disproportionately. In recent years, according to reports from different human rights NGOs, there has been an increase in the number of complaints made against the Mexican army for human rights violations, detentions and forced disappearances, torture, illegal deprivation of personal freedom, injury, house raids, robbery, rape and murder.[9]

Ten years on from the Aguas Blancas massacre

28 June 2005 marked the 10-year anniversary of the massacre in Aguas
Blancas, Guerrero, when 17 indigenous and peasant farmers were
murdered by the Motorized Police. Five hundred students, teachers,
peasants and indigenous marched from the outskirts of the settlement
to the entrance to Aguas Blancas and to the monument to those who
died. During this action, they demanded the reopening of the case and
punishment of those responsible, including former governor Rubén
Figueroa Alcocer and General Mario Arturo Acosta Chaparro who has
also been accused by various social and human rights organisations of
being involved in state repression during the dirty war.

Social organisations organised the Aguas Blancas Ten Years of Impunity forum in Coyuca de Benítez, where it was emphasised that full
justice had not been carried out, and that the recommendations of the
Supreme Court of Justice and of the Inter-American and National Human Rights Commissions had not been enforced. The Voice of the
Voiceless (*Voz de los sin Voz*) Human Rights Centre said that the massacre was "a case that continues to enjoy impunity. We concur that
there are continuing violations of human, economic and social rights;
conditions of poverty have not improved for the community, as stipulated by the National Human Rights Commission".[10]

Tenth Anniversary of the Community Police

Ten years ago, in the face of state impunity and violence in the area, the
inhabitants of Costa-Montaña de Guerrero created their own community police and justice system. Over the years, the community police
has shown how collective rights can be exercised "in practice", without asking the government's permission. The Costa-Montaña community justice system has shown what civilian security means, prioritising the protection of men and women and not that of the official apparatus. One of its greatest values has been that it is free and reciprocal.
In all, crime has been reduced by 95% in relation to the period prior to
its establishment. The Costa-Montaña community justice system in
Guerrero is defined as a multicultural, inter-municipal and multilingual justice system. The Regional Coordinating Body of Community

Authorities (CRAC) groups together a total of 62 Mixteco, Tlapaneco, Nahua and *mestizo* settlements in Malinaltepec, San Luis Acatlán, Marquelia, Copanatoyac and Metlatónoc. According to Superintendent Zósimo Avilés Mendoza, in these ten years the CRAC has handled 1,484 cases, of which 1,203 were resolved through reconciliation; 247 are pending resolution and 34 suspects are on the run. In this process, five community police officers have died in gunfire.[11]

Oaxaca and Chiapas

Political violence in Oaxaca and Guerrero has intensified over the last four decades. Alongside this political violence can be seen the systematic repression suffered by organisations or movements that oppose the establishment of megaprojects or policies emanating from the capital. In Oaxaca state, during 2005 some 130 social activists were imprisoned while more than 150 arrest warrants were also outstanding, all with the aim of demobilising the social organisations and promoting the presidential candidacy of Governor Ulises Ruiz Ortiz (from the PRI). At the end of 2005, a resurgence of paramilitary groups could be observed in Chiapas, attempting to put a stop to the Other Campaign and its sympathizers and supporters.

Migration

In a scenario marked by neoliberal policies, an important sector of the population has opted to migrate in search of work abroad or in other regions of the country.

New players in Monterrey

In recent decades, Nahua, Tenek, Otomíe, Mixteco, Zapoteco and Mazahua people, among others, have arrived in the Metropolitan Area of Monterrey (AMM). Most of them were born in the states of San Luis Potosí, Veracruz, Hidalgo and, to a lesser extent, Querétaro and Oaxaca. In the AMM, they are employed in ethnic niches such as domestic service, gardening, building and itinerant sales. Depending on the estimate, the indigenous population varies between 20,000 and 30,000 people.

With the opening of an office of the National Commission for Indigenous Development (*Comisión Nacional para el Desarrollo de los Pueblos Indígenas* - CDI) in Nuevo León in 2005, the growing number of indigenous people in Monterrey was recognised at federal level. At state level, the Ministry of Education has, since 1998, been working to raise awareness of the need to respect cultural and linguistic diversity among non-indigenous teachers and pupils in more than 65 primary schools with indigenous children.

This growing visibility is also accompanied by brutal discrimination on the part of some government departments, beginning with the municipal trade inspectors who hound and bribe the itinerant Nahua, Otomíe, Mazahua and Mixteco sellers. In addition, state agencies such as Integral Family Development (*Desarrollo Integral de la Familia* - DIF), justify the rounding up of indigenous children (even babies) found on the street into centres under the pretext of eliminating child labour. In reality, they are quite simply denying indigenous women workers the right to look after their children themselves and take them with them while they sell.

As a result of an investigation requested by the CDI into the situation of indigenous women in the Metropolitan Area of Monterrey, the Centre for Higher Research and Studies in Social Anthropology, Northeast Unit, recommended prioritising issues of health in Nuevo León, with particular focus on reproductive health, network strengthening via communication and legal advice.   ❑

Notes

1   Three years ago, the state announced the megaproject consisting of the construction of a hydroelectric dam in La Parota, which the Federal Electricity Commission hopes to build to the north of Acapulco.
2   See www.mapder.org, www.hic-al.org
3   **Rosa Elvira Vargas y Angeles Mariscal** , *La Jornada*, 25 March 2006.

4 **Angélica Enciso**, *La Jornada*, 8 March 2005.
5 **Neil Harvey**, *La Jornada*, 11 June 2005.
6 Delegate Zero is the name the Zapatist leader Sub-Comandante Marcos is currently using.
7 Invitation to the 4th National Indigenous Congress.
8 Words spoken by Delegate Zero at a meeting with members in Nurio, Michoacan on 3 April 2006.
9 See report from the **Centro de Derechos Humanos de la Montaña**, Tlachinollan
10 **Misael Habana de Los Santos**, *La Jornada*, 29 June 2005.
11 **Rosa Rojas**, *La Jornada*, 15 October 2005.

GUATEMALA

For the indigenous peoples of Guatemala (60% of the country's total population), 2005 offered little progress in terms of human development but, at the same time, was a very active year in terms of indigenous struggles. These took place in three broad areas: firstly, the struggle against neoliberal policies such as the mining projects, free trade agreements, the law on public service concessions and the water law, in the face of which the indigenous organisations managed to organise various forms of collective action to pressure the state into reviewing these measures. Secondly, the progress made - still in its early stages but significant - in the battle for fundamental rights, including land and the struggle to combat racist and discriminatory practices, principally those caused or tolerated by state structures. Thirdly, the circumstances caused by the passage of tropical storm Stan, which affected primarily indigenous areas and highlighted their great social, economic and political vulnerability, a historical product of the long process of social exclusion characteristic of the Guatemalan nation.

Mining projects encouraged with government support

Despite widespread popular protest, mining company Montana Exploradora, which is running the Marlin Project, commenced activities on the Sipacapa indigenous territory, San Marcos department, in the west of the country, with the support of the government and the World Bank. The government refused to suspend the company's contract or provide a period in which to hear the indigenous organisations' proposals to renegotiate the terms of the concession. The formation of a High-level Mining Commission, comprising government and civil society representatives, was however agreed and, in a document entitled

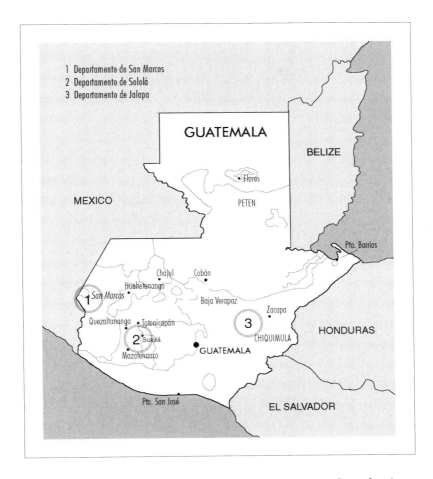

1 Departamento de San Marcos
2 Departamento de Sololá
3 Departamento de Jalapa

"Mining Policy Guidelines", this commission proposed mechanisms for achieving a consensus that would ensure community participation, environmental and health protection, and guarantee that the benefits obtained would be shared between the transnational companies and the Guatemalan population. However, as expected, these proposals were not taken into consideration by the government in the amendments to the Mining Law proposed by the Ministry of Energy and Mines, as these introduced only changes to government royalties and ignored the issue of community participation.

Alongside this, the indigenous communities in question invoked their constitutional right to hold a "Popular Consultation" on 18 June, with the support of the Supreme Electoral Court, in which an overwhelming majority of the inhabitants of Sipacapa municipality rejected the mining project. As was to be expected, however, official sectors and economic interests linked to mining rejected the validity of this consultation. It should be noted, in this regard, that there were two sides to the anti-mining protests, and that these did not always coincide in their rhetoric: the first was that of the environmental and popular organisations, for whom the main problem consisted of the environmental and health threats that might be caused by mining. The second was that of the indigenous organisations themselves, for whom approval of the mining contracts signified above all a violation of their fundamental rights as contained both in the Constitution of the Republic and other international agreements, principally ILO Convention 169. Despite this latter having been ratified by the country, the government refuses to elaborate the necessary instruments to put it into practice.

The Water Law

Discussions in the Congress of the Republic on draft bill of law 3,118, entitled the "General Water Law", caused collective indigenous protest unprecedented in recent history. For a week, communities blocked highways and paralysed a large part of the country and, given the magnitude of the protests and afraid that the situation would become ungovernable (perhaps also with an eye to the Bolivian and Ecuadorian situations), Congress hastened to postpone discussions on this law. But why is water, more than any other issue, such a sensitive one for indigenous communities, and why did Congress give way so easily to this pressure?

The aim of the draft bill was, among other things, to centralise water administration by creating the Vice-ministry of Water Resources, to prohibit practices that cause a decline in water sources, encourage sustainable use by encouraging equity, solidarity and social participation but, in addition, authorise special licences for water use. This last point clearly created much uncertainty amongst indigenous communities, for whom water is one of the most important of life's resources. It is powerfully clear that the government was justifying the strategic value of this law in the context of free trade agreements,[1] in which guaranteed water access will be a clear need for new transnational investment. However, for indigenous populations, who have developed processes by which to socially manage their water using local institutions that protect and regulate its access and use, any state interference in issues of water is viewed with mistrust, particularly given the historical experience of dispossession and misappropriation that has encouraged the illegal use of water, to the benefit of outside interests.

It is clear that the government saw the indigenous protests as a good excuse to suspend approval of the Water Law, knowing full well that this initiative would come up against even greater opposition from the private sector, primarily the large agricultural, industrial and commercial companies who make indiscriminate use of the water through improper possession and uncontrolled contamination, without having to make any payments for the decline in environmental services provided by the water. Without any struggle whatsoever, these greater interests found themselves the main winners in this suspension of the water law. And yet the authenticity and legitimacy of the indigenous movement cannot be denied, for it cannot be reduced – as some political analysts have hastily and disparagingly sought to do - to mere political manipulation.

Indigenous uncertainty in the face of free trade agreements

The struggle against the free trade agreements between Central American countries and the United States (CAFTA–RD)[2] has served to rearticulate the social movement in the Central American region and, perhaps as never before, this issue has acted as a catalyst for indigenous and peasant interests. During 2005, strong social protest was mounted, including indigenous and peasant marches, road blocks, occupations of public buildings, press releases, fora and other actions to expose the unsuitability of these agreements and the threats they imply, particularly for the most marginalised sectors of society, concretely indigenous and peasant farmers. On 10 March, as a matter of "national urgency", Congress approved the FTA in order to put a stop to this social movement. Even so, the protests culminated in a national strike on 14 March, organised by the main representative civil society organisations. This was put down violently by the police force. And yet protests continued throughout the year at various points around the country, achieving little however in terms of changing the government's decision to implement the agreement.

From these protests against the CAFTA–RD, it is clear that there is great uncertainty as to the implications these agreements will have on the situation of indigenous peoples. Despite the fact that the government has conducted a widespread media campaign to publicise the advantages of the agreements, the population is unaware of their real content and believes the national and local economy will be seriously affected by the arrival of large transnationals linked primarily to the food and agriculture sector.

The struggle for land and the Land Registry Law

The indigenous and peasant organisations continued their struggle for access to land and for rights over their ancestral territories throughout the year. The most interesting case in which progress was made was that of the Santa María Xalapán indigenous community, in Jalapa department, which after many years of negotiations managed to recover a portion of its land (140 has) that had been taken by private owners. The problem was resolved by the government purchasing these lands from the private owner and returning them to the community. But, in general, demands and proposals around agrarian issues were ignored or repressed by the government, such as the cases of the violent evictions of peasants and indigenous who were occupying various large estates around the country.

The 1996 Peace Accords, which brought 36 years of armed conflict to an end, committed the state to undertaking concrete actions to seek a solution to the agrarian problems affecting the country. In this regard, consideration was given to creating mechanisms to modernise the way in which land ownership is recorded. On 15 June, after many years of negotiations, and largely due to lobbying on the part of the peasant organisations, Decree 41-2005 the "Law on Land Registry Information" was approved. The final content of this law left out many of the original proposals discussed at the negotiating table, however, such as regulating the excess lands of the large estates and returning seized lands to the indigenous.

The indigenous communities have great expectations and also uncertainties as to the way in which the land registry will deal with indigenous lands and territories. In its articles 65 and 66, the law stipulates recognition of communal lands in order to undertake the measuring and registration of the whole area and allows for the measuring of individual areas only if all of the joint owners request it. It also guarantees the existence and use of indigenous ceremonial places. However, the indigenous organisations have warned of the possibility that the law may be used as a legal means by which to seize lands. For this reason, in a press release published on 1 September 2005,[3] the National Coordinating Body of Peasant Organisations (*Coordinadora Nacional de Organizaciones Campesinas* - CNOC) warned that the organisations had to continue their struggle for recovery of their communal lands, and avoid the privatisation of lands on which are to be found water sources, forests and archaeological sites.

A light at the end of the tunnel in the war on racism and discrimination

After a long drawn out case, the courts finally issued their first conviction (albeit with minimum sentences) in a case of racism and discrimination. This sets a precedent for what is a very common social practice in the country, and which is manifested primarily in the social exclusion of the country's indigenous population. In this case, the courts convicted individuals who had racially insulted the indigenous Nobel prize winner Rigoberta Menchú. However, thousands of cases occur every day in the country and go unpunished, precisely because the court processes are so long, costly and complicated.

Tropical storm Stan highlights the social exclusion of indigenous peoples

In its trajectory across Guatemala during the first week of October 2005, tropical storm Stan caused great destruction, primarily in the indigenous areas of the country's western highlands (*Altiplano Occidental*). More than 90% of the 700 people who died were indigenous, buried in the mudslides that destroyed their villages. It is estimated that in Panabaj, a hamlet of the Tz'utujil indigenous people, of Santiago Atitlán, in Sololá department, there were 100 deaths and 600 disappearances. Five thousand more people were affected and virtually all infrastructure and public services were destroyed. The impact of material damage and loss of human life was similarly considerable in hundreds of other small indigenous settlements.

In general, the western part of the country, which is the most densely populated and home to the greatest concentration of indigenous people, was severely affected by destruction of roads, schools, housing, loss of crops and different economic activities, to such a point that many places were paralysed and cut off for several weeks. The government's reconstruction efforts prioritised rebuilding those areas that suffered the greatest damage but, in general, reconstruction was extremely slow and politicised, such that by the end of the year most of the damage remained unrepaired, primarily small-scale infrastructure such as drinking water systems, access roads, irrigation systems, rural schools and other services in the most remote communities in the interior of the country. Rural women, particularly indigenous, were seriously affected, although very little was done to ascertain the magnitude of the impact, nor was an opportunity created for them to play a more central role in designing reconstruction agendas.

Stan's passage emphasised the deep social, economic and political vulnerability that most of the Guatemalan population suffer from, particularly in the indigenous areas, which have historically been overlooked in the country's development processes. This is why they live in high risk areas and their production activities are constantly affected by natural phenomena. Stan also highlighted the political manipulation that takes place in reconstruction processes, an aspect that was strongly questioned by the indigenous organisations. It was noted that the government's concern was limited to repairing immediate large-scale damage, generally under the same conditions of vulnerability as before. The need to implement fundamental in-depth changes that could help overcome future insecurity, and which would at the same time highlight risk management as a national priority involving all social sectors, was overlooked.

Stan's passage highlighted the great solidarity of the Guatemalan people and of international cooperation in such emergencies but, above all, showed how social networks and social capital can be activated at local community level, making it possible to mobilise collective mutual support efforts in order to overcome the crisis.   ❏

Notes

1   *Prensa Libre*, 19 September 2005.
2   CAFTA-RD stands for Central America/Dominican Republic Free Trade Agreement. This is the Free Trade Agreement that has been agreed between the governments of Costa Rica, El Salvador, Guatemala, Honduras, Nicaragua and the Dominican Republic, and the United States.
3   *Prensa Libre*, 1 September 2005. *La CNOC ante la aprobación e implementación de la Ley del Registro de Información Catastral –RIC.*

NICARAGUA

2005 was marked by the political instability of the national state. Conflicts between the main political parties impacted on the stability of the different state powers and public service institutions. The Office of the Ombudsman for the Defence of Human Rights (*Procuraduría para la Defensa de los Derechos Humanos* - PDDH) proved to be one of the most noteworthy in this regard. The lack of institutional stability became clear when three Special Ombudsmen resigned, including the Reverend Norman Bent, Special Ombudsman for Indigenous Peoples.

A subsequent rethink of the scope of the PDDH led to an open selection process to hire two special ombudsmen for indigenous peoples in the Caribbean Coast, with their administrative headquarters in the two regional capitals of Bilwi and Bluefields. An operating budget to cover the costs of the posts has not yet been established, however. The only actual appointment by the end of 2005 was that of the Special Ombudsman for the North Atlantic Autonomous Region (RANN), although some local sectors were questioning this choice because the person appointed spoke only Spanish, in a town with a majority English-speaking Miskito population, in addition to his political affiliation to the Constitutional Liberal Party (*Partido Liberal Constitucionalista*).

In the midst of this instability and uncertainty, one positive piece of news was the appointment of Javier Williams Slate as Vice-chancellor of the Republic in July 2005. This young lawyer is the first public official of Miskito-Creole origin to occupy this post in Nicaragua. Although the Vice-chancellor had previously acted as ambassador in Belize and Jamaica, this event was a real surprise within the Bolaños government, which has often been marked as class-based and exclusive.

Garífuna summit of Central America and the Caribbean

In November 2005, the Garífuna Summit[1] was held in the municipality of Corn Island, South Atlantic Autonomous Region (RAAS). Four heads of state attended: Enrique Bolaños Geyer, President of the Republic of Nicaragua, and three prime ministers from English-speaking countries: Said Musa (Belize), Roosevelt Skerritt (Dominica) and Ralph E. Gonsalves (Saint Vincent and Grenada). Representatives from Guatemala, Belize, Honduras, Costa Rica, Saint Vincent and Grenada, Dominica and Nicaragua signed the Summit Declaration declaring, above all, a commitment to preserve the Garífuna culture. In this respect, the States party agreed to support the decision of the Nicaraguan government, in its position as President pro tempore of the Central American Integration System (SICA), to include in the 27th ordinary meeting of SICA heads of state a Joint Action Plan to safeguard the cultural heritage of the Garífuna. In addition, a representation from the Caribbean Common Market (CARICOM) expressed an interest in signing a Free Trade Agreement to encourage cultural and commercial links between Central America and the Caribbean.

A new General Law on Education

In July 2005, the National Assembly approved in principle a new General Law on Education. It should be noted that the current law in this regard is 105 years old and represents a great limitation on the country's educational development. The new legislation establishes a higher budget for education, better conditions for teachers and recognises only bilingual intercultural education in the Autonomous Regions of the Caribbean Coast of Nicaragua. And yet this new law also has many deficiencies. The existing Regional Autonomous Education System, for example, is not envisaged in the new legislation, nor is the organisational set-up for bilingual and intercultural education, as established in the National Education System.

Regional elections

The most important political events in the Caribbean Coast focused on preparing for the forthcoming regional elections on 5 March 2006. The Caribbean Coast elections, coming as they do prior to the national elections in November 2006, are viewed by national political parties as a yardstick by which to measure their popularity. The Supreme Electoral Council (CSE) is banking on a high turnout, even though it only managed to respond to a small fraction of the requests for identity documents during 2005. This institution forms a stumbling block to this aspect of civic participation if one recalls that, of all the Caribbean

Coast population able to vote, almost 35% have no identity documents.

Seven political alliances and parties will participate in the March 2006 elections. The indigenous political organisation Yapti Tasba Masraka Nanih Asla Takanka (YATAMA) and the Party Movement for Coastal Unity (*Partido Movimiento de Unidad Costeña* - PAMUC) are the regional parties with the highest membership. A third regional organisation, the Multi-ethnic Indigenous Party (*Partido Indígena Multiétnico* - PIM) has joined an alliance with the Constitutional Liberal Party (*Partido Liberal Constitucionalista*). The national parties will also have a presence via the Sandinista National Liberation Front (*Frente Sandinista de Liberación Nacional* - FSLN), the Nicaraguan Liberal/Conservative Party Alliance (*Alianza Liberal Nicaragüense con el Partido Conservador* - PLN-PC), the Alliance for the Republic (*Alianza por la República* - APRE) and the Herty 2006 Alliance (*Alianza Herty 2006*), in the contest for the 90 posts of councillor available in the North and South Atlantic Regional Councils.

Social panorama

The vulnerability of indigenous communities to natural disasters and institutional abandonment became all the more evident in July when an uncontrollable plague of rats ruined the crops in a very poor area of 14 Miskito communities along the banks of the Wangki and Coco rivers, Waspán municipality, in the RAAN, and in the municipality of San José del Bocay, Jinotega department. By October, the plague had spread to 76 neighbouring communities. In response to the emergency, indigenous leaders and the municipal mayors of San José del Bocay and Wiwilí, Jinotega department, and the mayor of Waspán municipality obtained food aid from national and international bodies. For its part, central government, through the Ministry of Agriculture, Livestock and Forests (MAGFOR), distributed rat poison to exterminate the plague and, at the start of 2006, will provide maize, bean and rice seed to encourage new crop production. Despite these actions, hunger was prevalent in this part of the country by the end of 2005, and the crisis worsened when 21 cases of the illness "Grisis Siknis" appeared, a type of collective hysteria that had already affected this area of the RAAN two years ago.

Another social problem that occurred in the Autonomous Regions, and the origins of which lie in the global oil crisis, was the almost one-month-long protest on the part of one sector of coastal society in the air terminals of Bilwi and Waspam towns in the RAAN, in protest at the spiralling cost of air fares. User dissatisfaction did not manage to freeze prices however. By the end of the year, a return air fare from Managua to Bilwi cost more than US$140 , a consequence of the 40% increase in prices throughout 2005.

On another note, after almost one year of research, the 2005 Human Development Report for Nicaragua was officially published in July 2005 by the UN Development Programme (UNDP). The most outstanding feature of this publication was the fact that it was exclusively devoted to the Autonomous Regions of the Caribbean Coast. The document, entitled "Informe de Desarrollo Humano 2005" Las Regiones Autónomas de la Costa Caribe ¿Nicaragua asume su diversidad? (Human Development Report 2005. The Autonomous Regions of the Caribbean Coast. Does Nicaragua accept its diversity?), begins by proposing an analysis that goes beyond measuring human development indices in the RAAN and the RAAS. Instead it confronts the reality of the coast's ethnic diversity within a mono-ethnically conceived state and the necessary challenge of constructing an ethnically inclusive state. The basic documents prepared for the report cover different thematic issues such as autonomy, human development, socio-cultural capital, production systems and markets, the state of indigenous and ethnic languages, citizenship and identity, use and ownership of lands, etc. It is the largest and most complete investigative effort ever undertaken into the social aspects and socio-political problems of Nicaragua's Caribbean Coast.

Natural disasters

The hurricane season that battered the Caribbean islands also affected Nicaragua's Caribbean Coast. The natural phenomenon of greatest impact was category 3 hurricane Beta, which hit the national territory in the coastal area of the Miskito community of Sandy Bay Sirpi, in the municipality of Desembocadura de Río Grande, in the South Atlantic Autonomous Region (RAAS), in October 2005. Four people of indigenous origin died as a result of this disaster and, in the communities of Sandy Bay Sirpi, Karawala, Walpa and Kara, 200 houses were reported destroyed and another 173 damaged, in addition to the loss of crops and forested areas.

Demands for the human rights of indigenous peoples

On 23 June 2005, the Inter-American Court of Human Rights (IACHR) again issued an historic ruling in favour of the human rights of indigenous peoples in Nicaragua. The Court had already previously ruled in favour of the indigenous community of Awas Tingni's communal property rights and, this time, the Court ruled in favour of the political rights of the indigenous political organisation, YATAMA.

YATAMA's lawsuit arose after it was prevented from participating in the municipal elections of 2000 when the Supreme Electoral Council – by means of a reform to the Electoral Law – prevented popular membership organisations from participating in these elections. In response to the new requirements, YATAMA had to turn from an organisation with its support base in the Miskito indigenous territories into the Western model of a political party to be able to participate in the elections. However, despite the organisation's efforts, its involvement in the elections was finally refused by the Electoral Council.

The IACHR convicted the Nicaraguan state of discrimination and denial of indigenous communities' participation, with their own forms of political organisation, in the 2000 electoral process. In its ruling, it ordered the Nicaraguan state to reform the Electoral Law, to include in it provisions guaranteeing indigenous political participation in accordance with their own forms of organisation and to pay US$80,000 to YATAMA for material damage caused in 2000. The Nicaraguan government stated its desire to comply with the Court's ruling but, by the end of 2005, six months after the ruling and only three months before the next regional elections, there was still no sign that a reform of the

Electoral Law would form part of the legislative agenda of the National Assembly in 2006.

Indigenous communities of the Pacific and centre of Nicaragua

In the last three months of the year, indigenous community leaders from the towns of Matagalpa and Muy Muy in Matagalpa department, in association with the Chorotega Coordinating Body (*Coordinadora Chorotega*) and the Indigenous Movement of Nicaragua (*Movimiento Indígena de Nicaragua* - MIN) organised the first popular consultation workshops on the draft "General Law on Indigenous Peoples". The communities of the Pacific and centre of the country hope to hold consultation workshops throughout the first six months of 2006. The most important activity for the coming year could be the presentation of this draft law, in a ceremony which for the first time will bring together community leaders from the Pacific and centre with the Council of Elders of Nicaragua's Caribbean Coast (*Consejo de Ancianos de la Costa Caribe de Nicaragua*).

The most important demand arising from this draft law is that of the right to property. Although these communities have titles granted by the Spanish Crown, most of their territories were leased to the municipalities many years ago, and land rights over these areas are currently a cause of complex dispute between the state and the communities in question.

Progress in the legalisation of indigenous territories through Law 445

2005 was a positive year in terms of legalising the indigenous and ethnic territories of the Caribbean Coast. For the first time, the National Commission for Demarcation and Titling (*Comisión Nacional de Demarcación y Titulación* - CONADETI), which is the body responsible for issuing communal property titles within the context of Law 445, this year obtained funding of 11.3 million córdobas (approximately US$678,000) out of the General Budget of the Republic to implement its work and fulfil its tasks and attributions. A summary of this year's work of the Intersectoral Commissions for Demarcation and Titling (*Comisiones Intersectoriales de Demarcación y Titulación* - CIDT), the technical bodies in the process, reveals that the CIDT-RAAN received and processed a total of 25 requests to title communities and territories while the CIDT-RAAS received a total of 7 requests. For its part, the CIDT-Jinotega, which is a special case in the process, dealt with the five requests for titling of all the indigenous territories in the BOSA-WAS biosphere reserve.

The first titles issued through Law 445 were presented by Enrique Bolaños Geyer, President of Nicaragua, in the town of Waspam, on 5 May 2005. The titled territories comprise areas in the municipalities of Siuna, Bonanza and Waspán, in the RAAN, and the municipalities of Wiwilí and San José del Bocay in Jinotega department. In total, it is calculated that 35,000 people have benefited, living in 85 communities on two Mayangna territories: Mayangna Sauni As and Mayangna Sauni Bu; and three Miskito: Kipla Sait Tasbaika, Li Lamni Tasbaika Kum, and Miskito Indian Tasbaika Kum.[2]

These titles must be directly registered by CONADETI on the corresponding Property Registers, which are held in Bilwi, the administrative centre of the RAAN, and in the town of Jinotega. The process was put on hold throughout 2005 because serious technical problems arose, given that a part of the territories was already registered under national agrarian reform titles that had to be cancelled. In addition, the final stage of regularisation of the titled territories, which consists of leasing agreements or the expulsion and/or relocation of settlers, represents a difficult task. In 2006, an interinstitutional committee will be organised comprising territorial commissions, state bodies, and regional and municipal representatives, and this will have the task of completing the legalisation of these territories.

Final considerations

The vulnerability of the autonomous regions to poverty, serious social problems, natural disasters and institutional abandonment became clear once more in 2005. This reality was faithfully reproduced in the UNDP's Human Development Report 2005, which documented very low human development indices in Nicaragua's Caribbean Coast, weak autonomous institutions and the great challenges facing the development of both coastal society and Nicaraguan society in general. The challenge of achieving an authentic democratic, participatory and representative state is as relevant in Nicaragua as the need to come to terms with its national ethnic diversity.

In addition, and despite the fact that the indigenous and ethnic communities of the Caribbean Coast were affected by the country's political, economic and social tensions, they also made significant progress in claiming their rights, with the first delivery of communal property titles, issued in the context of Law 445, to five indigenous territories. Although progress in the process of legalising territories is slow and there is insufficient technical and financial resources to meet the demands of the communities, this first titling is of great symbolic value and constitutes a significant reference point for future actions.   ❑

Notes and references

1   The Garífuna are an ethnic group of African origin whose communities were originally spread along the Atlantic coast of Central America and various islands of the Caribbean, but are now also found in the United States, where there are around 100,000 immigrants.
2   Presidency of the Republic. "Entrega de Títulos Comunitarios a Cinco Territorios Indígenas Ubicados en la Reserva de la Biosfera de BOSAWAS". *Páginas Azules*. No. 42. 23-29 of May 2005. Pg. 3.

El Nuevo Diario, 11 July, 17 July, 26 July, 12 October, 25 October, 12 November, 15 November and 5 December 2005.
La Prensa, 12 March, 10 June, 29 June, 1 July, 30 October, 26 November, 29 November and 7 December 2005.
Williamson Cuthbert, Dennis y Fonseca Duarte, Gizaneta, 2005: "Avances en la Legalización de los Territorios Indígenas en la Costa Caribe". *Indigenous Affairs* 4/05:44-50. IWGIA-Wani.

Interviews

Aminadad Rodríguez, Coordinator of the Indigenous Movement of Nicaragua.
Simos Hernández Pérez, President of the National Coordinating Body of the Indigenous Community of Matagalpa.
Matilde Ramos Rivas, Secretary of the Diriangén Regional Coordinating Body.

PANAMA

There are seven indigenous peoples in Panama: the Ngöbe, Bugle, Bribri and Naso in the western region and the Kuna, Emberá and Wounaan in the eastern region. They account for almost 200,000 individuals, representing 8.4% of the national population.

Poverty among the indigenous population is alarmingly high, a fact that is shameful in a country known for its high per capita income. Panama is, in fact, considered to have the second worst distribution of wealth on the American continent.

The indigenous have 5 representatives in the National Assembly, out of a total of 78. There are three from the Ngöbe-Bugle and two from the Kuna Yala comarcas. Nonetheless, these indigenous representatives are nominated by the political parties and not by the communities themselves, which means they lack independence of opinion. With the constitutional changes that took place in 2004, it is now possible for indigenous representatives to be nominated for the National Assembly without going through the political parties but we shall have to wait until the Electoral Code has been amended to see how this will be regulated.

Panama has five territories legally known as Indigenous Comarcas. These are special political divisions for indigenous peoples.[1] Despite the fact that there are five legally recognised territories, there are other indigenous peoples that still do not enjoy this status. Such is the case of the Naso, the Bribri and part of the Emberá and Wounaan population, along with two Kuna populations.

Proposed laws

The Naso people have produced a draft bill for the creation of the Tjër Di Naso Comarca. This bill of law was presented to the National As-

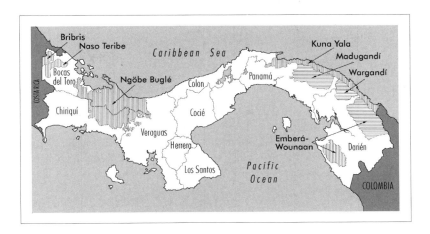

sembly for consideration at the start of 2005. This is the second time it has been presented because, on the first occasion in early 2004, it was rejected by deputies from the 1999-2004 assembly. With the election of new representatives, the first debate on the bill could now begin in the Indigenous Affairs Committee of the Assembly of Deputies. Following its debate, the proposal was approved by the seven-member committee, six of whom are indigenous. Approved at its first reading, it was thus submitted to the assembly for a second debate before 78 deputies. By order of the President of the Assembly of Deputies, Mr. Elías Castillo, its discussion was however postponed and, to date, we still do not know what its fate will be, although it is still on the agenda for discussion.

In the case of the Emberá and Wounaan, their lands were not protected by Law 22 of 1983 so they decided to organise under the name of the Congress of Collective Lands (*Congreso de Tierras Colectivas*). Like the Naso, they presented a draft bill to the National Assembly for recognition of their territorial rights. This proposal is still being discussed by the Indigenous Affairs Committee and will hopefully soon be approved.

For their part, the Bribri people still have no draft bill but they have conducted a socio-economic and land tenure study of the lands they occupy in order to produce one. This study was conducted by the Na-

tional Land Administration Programme and will serve as the basis for
a future law recognising this people's territorial rights.

Territorial conflicts

There are many conflicts over indigenous territories, primarily due to
invasion by settlers. These people do not respect the comarcas or legalised territories. Such is the case, for example, of the Kuna de Madun-
gandi and Kuna de Wargandi comarcas which, in spite of being legalised, are often prey to settler invasions.

For this reason, the traditional indigenous authorities have presented complaints to the government authorities, particularly to the Ministry of Government and Justice and the National Department for Indigenist Policy regarding these invasions. Claims for environmental
damage have also been made to the National Environmental Authority. These complaints have not been successful, however, and the invasions continue.

To address this issue, the Ministry of Government and Justice and
the National Department for Indigenist Policy have set up an inter-institutional commission and, within the Department for Indigenist Policy, a technical committee to deal with these complaints.

The inter-institutional commission has visited the areas of conflict
but has not yet presented its reports. In the Wargandi case, the technical committee made a number of short, medium and long-term recommendations but no decisions have yet been taken in this regard.

The committee's recommendations included the following:

Short-term:

- To compile and analyse the data from the land tenure study undertaken by the National Department for Agrarian Reform.
- To request that the Chepigana local authority appoint the head
  of the Wargandi police.

- To send a radio communication two weeks in advance providing information on the actions and activities of national government.

Medium-term:

- To request that, in accordance with the stipulations of the law, the Agrarian Reform should define peasant land ownership with land title rights.
- Alternative 1: with the support of the police and the Ministry of Government and Justice, to empower the traditional indigenous authorities to be able to implement evictions through their own competent decision-making and expressive bodies (General Congress), given that the law requires that the indigenous preserve, conserve and safeguard the jurisdiction of their comarca.
- Alternative 2: to ask the comarca authorities to make demands through the competent administrative bodies.

A similar situation is occurring on the lands of the Emberá and Wounaan communities. Their ancestral lands are being invaded by settlers. However, this is now with the consent of the Darién Sustainable Development Programme (*Programa de Desarrollo Sostenible de Darién -* PDSP), through the mass land titling that is taking place in Darién Province with funding from the Inter-American Development Bank. The PDSP has hired in the services of a Spanish company to conduct registration and measurement of lands for private titling. This has come up against the opposition of the indigenous communities because private lands are often measured within the indigenous communal territories without the communities being notified. They only realise what is happening when the company is actually taking the measurements and, on some occasions, measurements are taken within their ancestral lands without their realising, private land titles even being granted.

For this reason, the Congress of Collective Lands and the communities, through their lawyers, have presented 51 appeals against land allocation requests with the aim of getting the Panamanian state to recognise the communities' territorial rights by means of judicial and administrative lawsuits. For the moment, these cases have not been resolved.

Intellectual property rights

During 2005, the Dobbo Yala Foundation, the Congress of Kuna Culture and the Emberá and Wounaan Congress of Collective Lands held workshops, meetings and activities within the context of a project entitled "Protecting collective rights in accordance with the traditional practices and knowledge of the Kuna and Emberá of Panama on traditional medicine". The key issue for the project is to conserve and protect traditional knowledge of medicinal plants in accordance with the customary norms and practices of the Kuna, Emberá and Wounaan communities. Work is being undertaken to create legal protection mechanisms and visit protocols for these communities, with the active participation of their traditional authorities and the users and holders of traditional knowledge themselves. For this reason, the objectives are three-fold:

- to define the ownership and transmission of traditional knowledge by studying the patterns and concepts of ownership of medicinal plant knowledge;
- to identify the customary norms governing the use of traditional knowledge that guide the formulation of protocols for its transmission, use and protection;
- to identify, evaluate and facilitate collaborative decision-making and the role of traditional authorities in traditional medicinal plant knowledge.

During this period, organisational and planning activities were undertaken in a participatory manner jointly with the traditional authorities and technical staff of the General Congress of Kuna Culture and the Emberá and Wounaan Congress of Collective Lands. Discussion groups and interviews with key informants were conducted among

Kuna and Emberá-Wounaan users and holders of traditional knowledge in the indigenous communities with the participation of traditional authorities, facilitated by indigenous lawyers speaking their native language. During this phase, the project's objectives were widely disseminated at national level, along with its methodology and expected outcomes. The preliminary results consist of systematizing the information obtained in the discussion groups and interviews, and this activity will be complemented in the next stage of work, which consists of producing a proposed Draft Bill to protect indigenous peoples' traditional medicinal knowledge.

Kuna General Congress

A Kuna General Congress was held on 24, 25, 26 and 27 June 2005, its second meeting of the year. This is the highest-level political and administrative decision-making body in Kuna Yala Comarca. Three days of debates within the Congress, in which reports from the Executive Committee, the commissions, (boundary, statute and tourism), the projects (bilingual intercultural education, environmental education, handicrafts) and the Congress on Culture were discussed and debated, along with the merger of the Institute for Koskun Kalu Research (*Instituto de Investigación Koskun Kalu* - IIKK) and the Institute for the Integral Development of the Kuna Yala (*Instituto para el Desarrollo Integral de Kuna Yala* - IDIKY), plus approval of the 2006 budget and reports from public officials.

It should be noted that this Congress was attended by other Panamanian indigenous authorities, such as the head of the Emberá and Wounaan Congress of Collective Lands and a delegation of Emberá and Wounaan representing these peoples. Their aim was to find out about and exchange experiences on indigenous traditional organisation and to forge links of solidarity. At the end of the meeting, the Kuna General Congress issued a resolution of support and solidarity with these people, who are demanding recognition of their ancestral rights from the state.

A key point in the Congress was the election of a new traditional
authority by the indigenous delegates. It should be recalled that there
are three traditional authorities in Kuna Yala.   ❑

Note

1   The comarcas are: the *Kuna Yala Comarca*, created by means of Law No. 2 dated
    16 September 1938 and organized by Law 16 dated 19 February 1953. This
    comarca is largely inhabited by Kuna people. The *Emberá de Darién Comarca*,
    created by means of Law No. 22 dated 8 November 1983 and regulated by Ex-
    ecutive Decree No. 84 dated 9 April 1999, the decree by which the Organic Ad-
    ministrative Charter of the Emberá-Wounaan de Darién was adopted. The *Kuna
    de Madungandi Comarca*, created by means of Law No. 24 dated 12 January 1996
    and regulated by means of Executive Decree No. 228 dated 3 December 1998,
    the decree by which the Organic Administrative Charter of the Kuna de Madun-
    gandi comarca was adopted. This is a second Kuna comarca. The *Ngöbe-Bugle
    Comarca*, created by means of Law No. 10 dated 7 March 1997 and regulated by
    means of Executive Decree No. 194 dated 25 August 1999, the decree by which
    the Organic Administrative Charter of Ngöbe-Bugle Comarca was adopted. The
    Kuna de Wargandi Comarca, created by means of Law No. 34 dated 25 July 2000
    and for which regulations still have to be established. This is the third Kuna
    comarca.

SOUTH AMERICA

COLOMBIA

In early 2005, the US National Intelligence Council published a report on global trends over the next 15 years that would have an impact on the security of the American continent.[1] With reference to Latin America, the report highlighted that "militant indigenism", together with new and old "armed actors" would contribute to destabilising the region's peace. The report referred directly to Evo Morales' Movement to Socialism (*Movimiento al Socialismo* - MAS) in Bolivia, the Confederation of Indigenous Nationalities of Ecuador (*Confederación de Nacionalidades Indígenas del Ecuador* - CONAIE) and the Peruvian Nationalist Movement (*Movimiento Etnocacerista* - ME). It also linked Hugo Chavez' Bolivarian Movement (*Movimiento Bolivariano*)[2] in Venezuela with these trends which, it considers, is riding on the back of this anti-North Americanism, seeking to incorporate it into its plans for a continental rebellion against the US. Although it makes no direct reference to the indigenous movements of Colombia or other of the sub-continent's countries, it does indicate the disastrous consequences for the global economy if ethnic groups were to block access to the energy resources (oil, gas, coal) on their territories (in Colombia, the indigenous own 30% of the national territory). Faced with this scenario, the Colombian President, Álvaro Uribe Vélez, is viewed by the US State Department as the representative of US interests in the Andean region.

This vision is not a new one. Nor is it new that some analysts who defend globalisation seek painstakingly to establish links between terrorism, organised crime and social movements that are struggling for land, the environment, territorial autonomy, development alternatives, human rights and justice, and against racial discrimination and socio-political exclusion.

What is new in Colombia is that this interpretation of reality has injected life into a socio-economic project and state model born of the

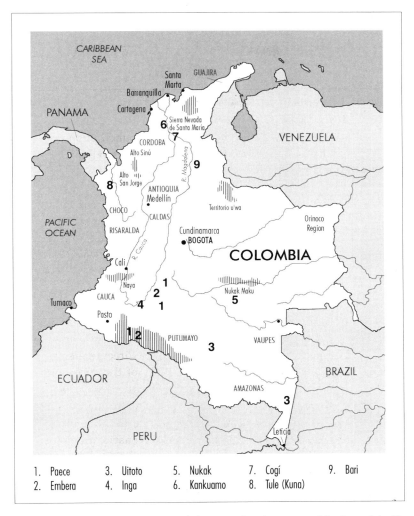

1. Paece   3. Uitoto   5. Nukak   7. Cogí   9. Bari
2. Embera   4. Inga   6. Kankuamo   8. Tule (Kuna)

deaths and violent evictions of thousands of peasant, black and indigenous families from their land by means of terror and human rights
violations. And in 2005, this model of society, which bases its *raison
d'être* on force, became yet more entrenched.

Colombians will remember 2005 as the year in which a legal framework was constructed that would guarantee impunity for those

who committed or supported the massacres of the previous decade and in which the spoils of war, taken by blood and force - land, belongings and political space - were legalised.

Uribe's re-election, the Plan Colombia and the Free Trade Agreement

The re-election of President Bush and the increased Republican majority in both the US Senate and Chamber of Representatives breathed new life into President Álvaro Uribe's aspirations to remain in power.[3] Clearly, Uribe's rhetoric of "God and Fatherland" was ideologically and linguistically in tune with that of President Bush. Moreover, and this is important for Uribe's "Democratic Security" policy, there would be a greater chance that military assistance would now be maintained (between 700 and 800 million US dollars a year) for a further four years. But what undoubtedly revitalises his possibility of re-election, and something for which the Uribe government has been working untiringly in terms of overcoming all obstacles (constitutional reform and consent of the Constitutional Court to this reform), is the possibility of signing a Free Trade Agreement as soon as possible. Presidents Bush and Uribe were eager to finalise negotiations in 2005 because the law empowering the Bush government to sign this type of agreement was due to expire that year. Pressure from the Bush government for Uribe to sign the treaty was not as successful as had been hoped, however, and this has now been postponed until 2006.

Indigenous peoples: an extra spoke in the wheel

The indigenous have sought to involve themselves in the Colombian political system with acceptable levels of autonomy. The real problem is that democratic involvement in political life is just not possible in an exclusive and authoritarian political system such as Colombia's.

This is not necessarily an ethnic stance on the part of the indigenous organisations. For them it is more important to actively participate in building a new system that will make tolerance, solidarity and respect for cultural differences possible. While they are seeking to strengthen and adapt their own institutions to this challenge, they are also testing out democratic principles in order to join with other black and peasant organisations, and other social sectors excluded from the Colombian political system.

With the risk of having a wide desert to cross with the 2006 re-election of Uribe and his authoritarian style, in 2005 some indigenous organisations began to demonstrate their opposition to neoliberalism and globalisation. It is this resistance that has become the extra spoke in the wheel of Uribe's steamroller. We shall now look at the most noteworthy features of this resistance and the events leading up to it.

The General Environmental Law

The General Environmental Law was debated throughout 2005. Indigenous, black, peasant, NGO, environmentalist and academic sectors focused their activities on raising public awareness of the disadvantages and possible implications for Colombia of approving a law that would enable the logging companies to tear down the country's natural forest heritage. But at all costs, and despite wide opposition to the law, the government pushed forward with the proposal and the law was passed in December.

Two weeks after having approved the General Environmental Law, however, it was for Uribe himself to accept that the law was going to damage the country's natural forests and that necessary changes would have to be made to ensure that logging interests could not affect them.

Failure of anti-drugs policy

The *Plan Colombia* was approved by the US Congress in October 1999 in the context of that country's anti-drugs policy. As drugs trafficking has become the main source of the economic and military empowerment of the armed groups (guerrillas and paramilitaries alike) and as these groups (since September 11, 2001) have been added to the US Defense Department's list of terrorist organisations, the anti-drugs war has gradually come to be defined as a *war on terrorism*.

By establishing a causal relationship between terrorism and drugs, the social problems of the coca growing regions have become a phenomenon to be dealt with in military terms. Prior to implementation of the economic development proposals designed for these regions, they must first undergo a "military solution".

With the spread of illegal crop production, many areas of the country became part of the so-called *Grey Zone*, classified as easily accessible to the armed players. The inhabitants of the Grey Zone thus came to be considered a part of the funding strategy, when they were not seen as potential auxiliaries in terrorist actions.

Now, 6 years on, despite the millions of litres of glyphosate that have been poured onto the Putumayo and Nariño forests and which, between 1999 and 2004, destroyed around 260,000 hectares of coca crops, the satellite photographs ordered by Colombia and the United Nations show that the cultivation area has actually increased by more than 90,000 hectares, clearly demonstrating the failure of the anti-drugs policy. And yet the glyphosate, with the addition of powerful surfactants, has had devastating effects on the crops of peasant and indigenous farmers, on their domestic animals and on the biodiversity. And this is without considering the approximately 200,000 peasant and indigenous farmers who have fled to neighbouring Ecuador to avoid a war precipitated by paramilitaries, guerrillas and the army for control over the region.

Despite this failure, the possible fumigation of coca and poppy crops in natural parks is now being discussed and, as if this were not a sufficient affront to the environment, they are considering the use of fungi which, whilst destroying the coca and poppy crops, would also devastate all the plant and animal species of the region. Environmentalists and biologists have warned of the effects of using these organisms which, in addition to affecting "all types of living being", have an enormous capacity for mutation, with the potential to turn entire regions of the Amazon and Pacific into a disaster zone.

The Free Trade Agreement

Another issue on which Uribe will have to pay a political price for his decision is the signing of the Free Trade Agreement. Various of the country's social and economic sectors have also taken this up. The indigenous population of Cauca has played a worthy role in this opposition. They held a popular consultation on the FTA in five municipalities in order to enforce their right to be consulted and to participate in decision-making on a treaty that was going to affect their lives. Out of a possible electorate of 68,000 (the total indigenous population of Cauca is 173,000), 51,330 voted. Of these 50,000 voted NO to the Free Trade Agreement, i.e. 98%. This civic exercise is being repeated by other social sectors and we believe that it is one method of resistance and a way of showing one's disagreement with authoritarian policies that *de facto* impose a decision that favours the few and powerful but compromises the future of all Colombians.

Indigenous and popular mandate for life

The real opposition to affect Uribe has come from the Cauca indigenous. They have highlighted the social poverty of the president's socio-economic policies and his authoritarian plans.

This opposition began at the end of 2004 with indigenous protests, first in Cauca and then among the Embera peoples of Caldas, Antioquia, Valle, Risaralda and Córdoba. This cultural and political mobilisation has taken the shape of marches, mobile congresses and permanent assemblies and has the aim of

"expressing our commitment to uniting and working to weave a reciprocal solidarity with all peoples. A solidarity that is urgent in order to defend life in all its forms of biological and cultural existence. We know we cannot do this alone and that we need each other if we are to understand, resist and create a country and world that is both possible and necessary".

The central themes of these protests have focused around denouncing the government's democratic security policy and the consequences of neoliberal adjustment, which in socio-economic terms has led to land concentration and ruin for the peasantry, and in political terms to a proliferation of conflict and social instability. Hence their demand that the Uribe government should respect the autonomy of their peoples, their right to life and international human rights instruments.

But perhaps the most important thing about these protests is that they have again put social and political conflict at the top of the agenda, conflict that is being caused by an absence of any agrarian policy in tune with the needs of the rural population.

Rebirth of the struggle for land

Through these protests, the indigenous – now joined by black, peasant and other popular sectors – have highlighted the exclusive policies in the Colombian agricultural sector. In one decade these policies have concentrated landholding and displaced two million peasant, black and indigenous men and women, giving rise to an agrarian counter-reform that has placed 4 million hectares of land in idle hands, expanding livestock ranches that create neither employment nor development. This dispossession is now in the process of being legalised by Uribe's Justice and Peace Law. And, given this vision and mandate, the indigenous are beginning to occupy unproductive ranches in a number of zones in Cauca. After several weeks of clashes, including violent evictions and injuries along with further occupations, on 13 September 2005 Uribe was finally forced to address land demands in Cauca and publicly recognise the country's serious land distribution problems. But the Cauca indigenous have not stopped there. Thinking on a countrywide level, they are suggesting that the Colombian people now hold a *public hearing* on land tenure in Colombia.

Privatization of natural resources on indigenous territories

At the end of 2005, a new grouping of economic agents began to take shape, its efforts and actions aimed at seeking to control natural resources, particularly the increasingly important strategic resources required for capital development. This is presumably what is worrying the US National Intelligence Council, as referred to above, although it does not mean that the geopolitical and geostrategic interests of legal and illegal economic groups, armed or not, now take second place. But pressure on (or the "seduction" of) various indigenous peoples to become partners in exploitation of their resources can already be seen.

The organisations that are now mobilising for the right to life have sensed that this is the greatest challenge facing them in the future because, as they have stated in their press releases, *"The social conflict over land in our country is affecting all of us because the Colombian state is not guaranteeing the social function of the land and is acting continually in favour of the landowners"*. This is why, *"The aim of this process is to create unity, integration and a struggle for land and for the defence of natural resources, for the indigenous, black and peasant communities of Cauca"*. ❏

Notes

1   *Mapping the Global Future: Report of the National Intelligence Council's 2020 Project.*
2   Supporters of Chavez often state that a central component of the Bolivarian movement is the liberation of Indians, blacks, *mestizos* (mixed white and Indian ancestry) and *mulattos* (mixed white and black ancestry) from the oligarchy. This has led some analysts to characterize "Chavismo" as being "national ethnic populism".
3   Colombian elections will be held in 2006.

VENEZUELA

2005 was characterized by greater political stability in Venezuela. With the local elections at the start of 2005, and the sound defeat of the opposition parties, these latter decided to withdraw from the legislative (National Assembly) elections arguing that the necessary electoral guarantees were not in place. Despite this situation, and the disappearance of the opposition from the National Assembly, once the elections were over all international observers were agreed that the process had been a transparent one. Although turn-out was low, a traditional phenomenon in Venezuelan parliamentary elections, the process had taken place without further mishap.

Four indigenous deputies were elected as a result of these elections, three permanent and one substitute. The National Assembly continued its work, two of the results of which are the Organic Law on Indigenous Peoples and Communities (LOPCI) and the Organic Law on Local Authorities, both highly important pieces of legislation for indigenous peoples.

And yet beyond this apparent internal stability, the international scene was characterized by a war of words between the Venezuelan and US governments. The CIA now considers Venezuela as "the most worrying country in Latin America" and the threat of direct US intervention was present throughout the year, in both political discourse and public opinion. A senior US army officer was expelled from the country, accused of espionage. Similarly, a religious group of US origin the "New Tribes", was also expelled. This group has had a significant presence within the Amazonian indigenous territories since the 1970s, providing health services, schools and airports. The "New Tribes" were accused by President Chávez and his government of extracting from the country both considerable strategic information and valuable mineral and biological resources.

1 Wayyú   3 Warao   5 Yagarana   7 Yekuana
2 Pumé   4 Pemón   6 Yanomami

The debate around the Free Trade Area of the Americas (FTAA) also held a significant place in the national political debate. The old dispute between pan-Americanism, this time represented by the FTAA,
and the Latin Americanism of the Bolivarian Alternative for Latin
America and the Caribbean (*Alternativa Bolivariana para las Américas -
ALBA*), supported by Chávez, became clear. Venezuela, or more specifically the indigenous territories in the south of the country, is proving to be a strategic area for American ambitions (water, biological diversity, etc.). The Venezuelan government is warning that the FTAA

poses a serious threat to their inhabitants while the ALBA offers them an alternative that will ensure their survival.[1]

Finally, continuing violations of indigenous peoples' fundamental social rights were observed throughout 2005. The so-called "Bolivarian revolution" initiated by President Chávez is making great efforts to achieve a social balance and social justice, implementing immediate public policies in this respect that will have a significant and direct impact on the excluded population. These policies, which generally run parallel to the government ministerial system and are directly financed out of the profits of oil exploitation, have been called "Missions". And yet the failure to adapt these "Missions" to indigenous cultural norms and the indigenous environment has created side effects and led to the persistence of human rights violations.

Expulsion of the religious "New Tribes" mission

On 12 October 2005, day of "indigenous resistance", in a programme broadcast live throughout Venezuela, President Hugo Chávez ordered the expulsion from Venezuela of the whole delegation of the evangelical "New Tribes" mission.

New Tribes has had a significant and often controversial presence among the indigenous peoples in the south of Venezuela. At times with more than 200 missions in the Venezuelan Amazon, their presence in the area has made them a great source of knowledge on the Piaroa, Panare and Yanomami peoples, as well as on the biological and mineral resources of the Amazon. Their sites are equipped with small airports, light aircraft, motor launches and modern satellite equipment.

Since their arrival in Venezuela, the different indigenous peoples with whom they have worked have suffered the fervour of their evangelizing activities. Indigenous deities have been rejected, along with their myths and beliefs. Their dances and rituals have been prohibited, their whole world vision altered, given that those who refuse to renounce their culture are branded heretics.

Nevertheless, after the announcement of the expulsion of the "New Tribes", the indigenous supported them. Wherever they set up base and where state services were lacking, the "New Tribes" formed a kind of parallel state, offering high quality health and education services. These were geographically, culturally and linguistically remote areas. So expelling the New Tribes missionaries has required the design of an interdisciplinary work plan to avoid any negative effects. It is worrying that the government's response implies the continuing presence of a large number of soldiers in the area, given that this presence currently represents a threat to indigenous rights. These are personnel untrained in the rights of indigenous peoples. Numerous complaints have been made about violations related to authoritarian attitudes, the illegal removal of food products that the indigenous use for small-scale trade or for their own consumption. We are certain that these attitudes are not part of the state's policy, but the government must recognise the deficiencies in military training, at least with regard to their work with indigenous peoples.

The Missions as social policy

Social justice in Venezuela is one of the five central pillars or fundamental "equilibria" in the transition towards the Bolivarian revolution. Along with social equilibrium, there is economic, political, territorial and international equilibrium, all forming the broad outlines of the country's social and economic development plan for the 2001-2007 period.

And yet the situation that was current in 2005 among Venezuela's indigenous communities and peoples clearly shows that there is still much to do if the much longed for social justice is to be achieved.

With a view to achieving this equilibrium, the Venezuelan state chose to implement a model by which to strengthen public policy on the basis of programmes parallel to the traditional ministerial system, known as "Missions". One sector that has undoubtedly suffered most severely from exclusion is that of the indigenous peoples. However, the failure to adapt these "Missions" to the different indigenous cultures has meant that objectives are not being achieved and basic social rights are being violated. We shall now take a look at the situation of indigenous peoples in Venezuela during 2005 from a rights-based perspective:

Right to education

The education system in indigenous communities still suffers from many failings. It is true that new and modern study centres have been created in indigenous areas, with good infrastructure and significant technical advances. And yet these "Bolivarian Schools" sit alongside small community schools lacking in the most basic of educational resources.

The incorporation of the School Feeding Programme into these Bolivarian schools, alien to indigenous eating patterns, has created disturbing distortions in their socio-economic balance. The level continues to be of extremely low quality in the main, and the lack of appropriate materials is only one of the reasons contributing to this problem.

Nevertheless, the Ministry – at regional and national level – has shown itself open to a complete transformation of the formal education system for indigenous peoples. The state recognises the right and need to adapt the proposal for "Bolivarian education" in the case of indigenous communities. For this reason, they are creating, from within the Ministry itself and with the involvement of various players, proposals for curricula that are adapted to each indigenous community or people. It should be noted that the great difficulty in implementing this right relates to the lack of staff trained for such a task throughout the country. The state's efforts, however, are many and it has entered into various alliances with different institutions, including national and international universities.

Right to health

This area remains one of the greatest violations of rights suffered by indigenous Venezuelans.

The high mortality and morbidity indicators are the result of failings in the health system in these zones. The implementation of the "Barrio Adentro" Mission, by which Cuban doctors provide health in poor areas and slums, has not been able to make up for the lack of dispensaries, medicines and health professionals. And, in addition, these services are not reaching the indigenous communities, remaining as they do largely in the provincial towns.

During 2005, work recommenced on implementing the Yanomami Health Plan, with the aim of providing basic health services to the Yanomami population, traditionally excluded from basic services. Violations of the Venezuelan Yanomami population's right to health have been particularly worrying, with infant mortality rates among the under threes reaching more than 50%. The Ombudsman for Amazonas State, Luis Bello, denounced this situation caused, in his opinion, by "the presence of numerous endemic and epidemic illnesses on their territories and by the Ministry of Health and Social Development's failure to establish effective public policies that would enable the problem to be tackled".[2] The health situation of Warao communities in the Orinoco Delta is also of particular concern.

Right to food

By means of the "Mercal" Mission, different basic food items are sold at a low price in poor areas and slums, including in the indigenous communities. During 2005, meals cooked in communal "soup kitchens" were also distributed by a number of food programmes in indigenous communities. However, these projects, aimed at populations with nutritional deficiencies, are causing undesirable side effects in traditionally self-sufficient indigenous communities. In fact, they represent a serious threat to the communities' endogenous development, causing a weakening of traditional farming, hunting and fishing practices.

In addition, this clashes with the government's credit policies and different subsidies and grants intended to encourage endogenous development projects in these communities.

Legislative developments

The law of greatest importance for the rights of indigenous peoples, entitled the Organic Law on Indigenous Peoples and Communities (*Ley Orgánica sobre Pueblos y Comunidades Indígenas* - LOPCI), was approved during the first quarter of 2006.

However, it has to be said that some fundamental points were not adequately addressed. Among other things, we believe that the use of natural resources for traditional activities has not been protected, nor the relevant sanctions removed. The Attorney-General's Office demonstrated a conservative position in this regard, tending towards limiting those rights already recognised in the Constitution.

In addition, the Organic Law on Local Authorities was also approved. Three indigenous National Assembly representatives participated actively in discussions on the drafting of this law. Through their participation, it was possible to get the concept of "Indigenous Municipalities" included.

Political participation

The national indigenous movement and, with special effort, the movement in Amazonas State, is continuing to make progress in terms of occupying political spaces within different state institutions.

2005 was an electoral year on different levels. Mayors were elected throughout the country, along with representatives to the National Assembly.

In Amazonas State, the indigenous political movement, known as PUAMA, again won seven mayoral posts.

At national legislative level, indigenous representatives were also elected. Three of them are permanent representatives of the indigenous peoples in the National Assembly. In addition, one Amazonian leader was elected as substitute representative for Amazonas State.

In terms of the representatives' participation within the National Assembly, their work has been more fruitful. Leaders with more train-

SOUTH AMERICA   153

ing and experience in the socio-political *"criollo"* world normally occupy these spaces. And these processes, while not being simple, often
require political clarity rather than technical specialisation. The case of
the mayoral posts is different, where public management requires certain professional strengths and technicalities that elected grassroots
leaders do not necessarily possess. The "Western" nature of public bureaucracy creates tension with traditional forms of "leadership" and
great efforts are required to ensure a "clean" encounter between two
radically differing worlds. The National Indian Council of Venezuela
(*Consejo Nacional Indio de Venezuela* - CONIVE) has made significant
efforts to close this cultural gap by running a school for indigenous
leaders. Nevertheless, it is clear that the process will take a few years
yet and will only be successful insofar as it is accompanied by a process of social awareness raising – within schools, for example – which,
whilst guaranteeing respect for multi-ethnic identities will also ensure
the acquisition of certain Western tools that are essential for a relationship between equals.   ❑

Notes and reference

1   With Venezuela's entry into Mercosur during 2005, and the declarations made
    at the IV Summit of the Americas (held in November of the same year in Buenos
    Aires) regarding certain changes in geostrategic power relations in South Amer-
    ica in favour of Latin Americanist strategies and opposed to US neoliberal dic-
    tums, the Venezuelan proposal for building a Bolivarian Alternative for Latin
    America and the Caribbean (ALBA), in opposition to the FTAA, has taken on a
    new spirit.
2   **Bello, Luis Jesús, 2005**: *Derechos de los pueblos indígenas en el nuevo ordenamiento
    jurídico venezolano.* IWGIA, Venezuela, 2005. p 28.

SURINAME

The year 2005 marked the 30th anniversary of Suriname's independence from the Netherlands and was also the fifth time general elections had been held. While elections have been generally free and fair since independence in 1975, Suriname has had to cope with land rights issues and periodic eruptions of violence. For this reason, the simultaneous occurrence of the anniversary and the elections attracted international attention.

The ruling "New Front" coalition lost its overall majority in the parliamentary elections of May 2005. Its presence in the 51-seat National Assembly fell from 33 to 23 seats. President Runaldo Venetiaan initially failed to secure the necessary two-thirds majority in the National Assembly. By contrast, the National Democratic Party, under former military coup leader Désiré Bouterse, doubled its tally from seven to 15 seats. The United States threatened to break off diplomatic relations and the Netherlands threatened to withhold development aid if Bouterse was elected president. The international community has viewed Bouterse with suspicion since his brutal governance during the 1980s. Venetiaan was finally re-elected, after a three-month stalemate, to a third five-year term as president in a special election among legislators in August 2005.

Approximately 50,000 indigenous and tribal residents (10% of the total population) live in over 50 villages in Suriname's interior region. Five culturally distinct groups of Maroons (Ndyuka or Aukaner, Saramaka, Paramaka, Aluku or Boni, Matawai, and Kwinti) and four Amerindian groups (Wayana, Carib, Arowaks and Trio) live along the rivers in eastern Suriname, where gold mining occurs.

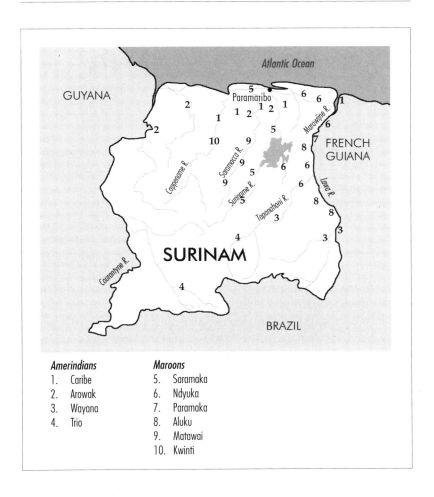

Amerindians
1. Caribe
2. Arowak
3. Wayana
4. Trio

Maroons
5. Saramaka
6. Ndyuka
7. Paramaka
8. Aluku
9. Matawai
10. Kwinti

Human rights

Racially discriminatory Mining Act

Together, the Association of Indigenous Village Leaders in Suriname, Stichting Sanomaro Esa, the Association of Saramaka Authorities and the Forest Peoples Programme have submitted four reports to the United Nations Committee on the Elimination of Racial Discrimination (the CERD Committee). The most recent submission, in January

2005, focused on the imminent adoption of the racially discriminatory Mining Act by the National Assembly. The draft Mining Act was tabled in January 2005 pending the national elections. Now that the elections are over, however, and the same coalition of parties that previously formed the government has maintained its overall majority in the National Assembly and will again form the government, the draft Act is once again on the agenda for imminent enactment.

According to Natalie Prouvez, secretary of the CERD Committee, Suriname's draft Mining Act is racially discriminatory against the Maroons and the Amerindians for three reasons. First, it fails to recognize, guarantee and secure their rights to their lands, territories and resources; second, the act fails to protect the indigenous communities from the negative social, cultural, environmental and health consequences of natural resource exploitation; and third, the draft Mining Act does not provide indigenous and tribal communities with adequate access to the courts in Suriname to seek protection under the law. This conclusion is supported by the 2005 Inter-American Development Bank's Country Environment Assessment for Suriname (IDB 2005), which states that, by national law Amerindians and Maroons have no formal rights to land in the interior. As a result, large-scale mining and logging concessions are granted on tribal lands without prior consultation or informing the tribal people. Consequently, the new mining law was drafted without consultation of Maroon and Amerindian representatives.

In west Suriname, concessions have been granted to BHP/Billiton and Suralco/Alcoa, who plan to construct a hydroelectric dam that will force Amotopo, a Trio indigenous community, from its lands and flood the lands of at least four other communities (Wanapan, Section, Washabo and Apura). In the east, the state has granted gold mining concessions to Suralco/Alcoa and Newmont Mining on the traditional lands of the Paramake Maroon people. The indigenous people are being excluded from, and may no longer conduct subsistence activities in, these areas. According to Carlo Lewis, village chief of Apura, we are not against development, but our way of life has to be taken into account. We are already no longer allowed to hunt and we cannot go to the supermarket like the people in the city, because we live from the forest.

Court case

In August 2005, the Inter American Court of Human Rights (IACHR) gave its judgement on the Moiwana case, which was championed by human rights activist Stanley Rensch, former president of the IACHR. In 1986, during Bouterse's rule, 40 people were murdered during an attack on the N'djuka Maroon village. The massacre took place during Suriname's civil war and was one of many assaults on tribal peoples perpetrated by the military government while they sought rebel leaders throughout the country. In August 2005, the IACHR ordered Suriname to pay US$3 million in compensation to survivors of the massacre. The Inter-American Court also ordered the government to create a development fund to support the education, health and housing of the Moiwana survivors.

New Association for Small-Scale Gold Miners

In support of the expanding gold mining industry, a gold mining association is being established to organize small-scale gold miners. The World Wide Fund for Nature (WWF) and the Inter-American Development Bank donated US$150,000 to finance the association. Through the organization, miners will be given information on how to improve their gold mining activities, production and price. The task of the association is to coordinate gold mining activities and make proposals regarding codes and regulations related to mining. The WWF was recently criticized, however, for excluding indigenous and tribal peoples living in the concerned territories from full involvement in meetings, discussions and decisions that shape development and environmental policy (Chapin 2004, Dowie 2005). Josin Aluma Tokoe from COICA (*Coordinadora de las Organizaciones Indígenas de la Cuenca Amazónica* – the Coordinating Body of Indigenous Organizations in the Amazon Basin) has criticized the WWF for leaving out indigenous and tribal peoples altogether from its vision of development and conservation in the Guiana Ecoregion Complex.

Mercury pollution – monitoring risk and reducing exposure

An estimated 30 to 60 tons of mercury are released into the environment in the interior rain forest region along the Tapanahony River (Drietabbetje, Sella Creek and Godo Olo) each year by miners who use it to extract the gold from soil and river sediments (Pollack et al. 1998, Gray et al. 2002). Rachael van der Kooye, a Suriname national, is currently implementing an environmental awareness project in the region. Miners and people living in the surrounding villages are exposed to mercury poisoning, and it is feared that the incidence of birth defects in children and toxicity in adults is increasing as a result of mercury pollution.

In a similar initiative, tribal villagers along the lower Saramacca River asked the Suriname Indigenous Health Fund (SIHF) for help in finding a solution to the mercury problem. Villagers performed tests and showed that some people living in the area had high mercury levels in their bodies. They were worried about their children, who are most vulnerable. They want to have the option to test themselves routinely so they can monitor mercury levels over time. They would also like help in finding ways to reduce the mercury in their bodies. To accomplish this, villagers want to test different types of fish from different locations so they know which fish to select for their diet in order to reduce their risk of exposure. Finally, they are requesting health assessments to determine the effects of mercury on their community's health.

The recent development and commercialization of automated portable mercury analyzers now makes it possible to perform real-time on-site measurements of mercury bioavailability in fish and people. Proposals are now being developed to make this technology available to villages interested in the self-diagnosis of public and environmental health problems. The proposals under development are based on a three-point plan developed by villagers that calls for a cooperative approach to monitoring risk, measuring impact and reducing mercury exposure from gold mines.

Villagers along the Saramacca River also expressed concern at the deteriorating quality of the water near their villages. The river provides fish (the main source of protein), a bathing place and water for household use. They have been observing signs of pollution in fish for some time. The fish they catch often spoils rapidly. Fish flesh is often mushy and smells bad. Fish from the Saramacca River often have strange black spots and, after cooking, dirty black foam is left on the bottom of the pan. Villagers find that the fish they have traditionally consumed is tasting worse over time. It is worth mentioning that the exact same observations were made by the Captain of Gran Santi (Lawa River) a couple of years ago. The Lawa River suffers severely from pollution due to small-scale gold mining.

Villagers lament the absence of clean drinking water. In the rainy season, they rely on rain water, which is collected in buckets or, for the better off, larger storage tanks. Until recently, water from the Saramacca River was used for consumption in the dry season. Now this is no longer an option. Water consumed during the dry season reportedly causes diarrhoea, stomach cramps and fever. In the absence of boreholes or water pumps, there is currently no other local source of drinking water. Villagers suspect that the large-scale gold mines in the area are responsible for the pollution of the Saramacca River. Another possibility is that water pollution is being caused by small-scale miners working further upstream, on tributaries of the Saramacca River.

Concluding remarks

Without immediate and urgent attention, indigenous and tribal peoples - who remain without guaranteed rights and effective remedies - will suffer irreparable harm to their physical and cultural integrity and their individual and collective dignity and well-being. Indigenous and tribal communities must be consulted before the Mining Law is enacted. They must be consulted on all conservation, resource extraction and management initiatives that directly impact on their lands. Furthermore, villagers should lead efforts to set up long-term mercury programs to monitor and mitigate the effects of mercury from gold mines on their community's and their environment's health.   ❑

References

Chapin, M., 2004: A challenge to conservationists. *World Watch.* Nov/Dec:17-31.

Dowie, M., 2005: Conservation refugees: when protecting nature means kicking people out. *Orion.* Nov/Dec:16-27.

Gray, J.E., V.F. Labson, J.N. Weaver, and D.P. Krabbenhoft, 2002: Mercury and methylmercury contamination related to artisanal gold mining, Suriname. *Geophysical Research Letters,* 29(23):201-204.

IDB, 2005: Inter-American Development Bank, *Country Environment Assessment (CEA) Suriname,* draft Report, February 2005.

Pollack, H, J. de Kom, J Quik, L Zuilen, 1998: *Introducing Retorts for Abatement of Mercury Pollution In Suriname.* Organization of American States. Paramaribo, Suriname.

ECUADOR

2005 was a year of political transition for the Ecuadorian indigenous movement. A period in which political participation - via an electoral alliance – had formed a real threat to their organisational fabric and strength was followed by the ousting of President Lucio Gutiérrez by an urban population organised as "outlaws",[1] and this gradually led to a rebuilding of the indigenous grassroots movement.

Ecuador comprises fourteen indigenous nationalities: Kichwa, Siona, Secoya, Cofán, Huaorani, Shiwiar, Shuar, Achuar, Chachi, Epera, Tsa'chila, Huancavilca, Awa and Afro-Ecuadorian. They live in the country's three natural regions: coast, inter-Andes or mountain and Amazon.

The indigenous movement is organised into three regional organisations: the Confederation of Indigenous Nationalities of the Ecuadorian Amazon (*Confederación de Nacionalidades Indígenas de la Amazonía Ecuatoriana* - CONFENIAE), the Confederation of Peoples of the Kichwa Nationality of Ecuador (*Confederación de Pueblos de la Nacionalidad Kichwa del Ecuador - Ecuador Runacunapac Riccharimui* - ECUARUNARI) and the Confederation of Indigenous Nationalities of the Ecuadorian Coast (*Confederación de Nacionalidades Indígenas de la Costa Ecuatoriana* - CONAICE). In turn, each of these is made up of provincial federations or organisations of nationalities and peoples.

Ecuador has signed ILO Convention 169, and recognises the collective rights of "indigenous peoples who identify themselves as nationalities". In addition, it has ratified most of the international human rights instruments.

Ecuador's indigenous nationalities are organised into the Confederation of Indigenous Nationalities of Ecuador (*Confederación de Nacionalidades Indígenas del Ecuador* – CONAIE).

Participation in the political system

The indigenous movement has participated in Ecuadorian electoral democracy since 1996, holding seats in parliament, the Constituent Assembly and on local councils. In 2003, the indigenous movement participated in the government of ex-Col. Lucio Gutiérrez but withdrew after eight months, weakened by a clear strategy to undermine their organisational structures. The Gutiérrez government was following a policy of involving itself in all areas of the indigenous movement with a paternalistic rhetoric that stripped "the Indian" of his dignity and his political position.

During 2005, the urban population began rebuilding its strength around a new social energy: the *outlaw identity* that emerged as a strong criticism of the political system and, particularly, of Lucio Gutiérrez. Resorting to despotism, he remoulded the Supreme Court of Justice to suit his needs and those of economic and political interests. On 20 April, after a week of fierce popular demonstrations, the Armed Forces and the National Police withdrew their support of the President, and he was thus ousted by the "outlaws". Indigenous participation in these events was scarcely even symbolic, however, being represented only by leaders or small groups. The reason lies in the divide and rule policy that had been promoted by Gutiérrez in his efforts to weaken the powerful organisational strength that CONAIE had previously enjoyed.

Following the change in President, and coinciding with a new leadership within CONAIE, a process of relative calm took place in the anti-indigenous strategy.

Territorial issues

Organisational work during 2005 revolved around a process of reflection amongst the indigenous nationalities and peoples in relation to their territories, territorial management and the significant threats challenging them.

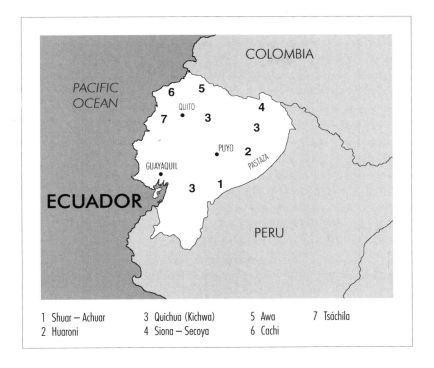

| 1 Shuar – Achuar | 3 Quichua (Kichwa) | 5 Awa | 7 Tsáchila |
| 2 Huaroni | 4 Siona – Secoya | 6 Cachi | |

Cases are occurring in different regions of the country whereby various environmental organisations are advising local governments on regulations, local agreements, conservation projects and proposals on territories that were originally indigenous. Payment for environmental services is presented as part of the multilateral organisations' formula to alleviate poverty and generate income from a sector other than agriculture. Despite this rhetoric, in reality, this is turning into big business, a private market for environmental services relating to CO_2 emissions. In addition, the water sources and upland plateaux, largely community territories, are at the centre of multiple "private conservation" interests. The need to preserve them has become a kind of craze among the municipalities and local authorities, to the detriment of a population assumed to be predatory and which is accused of being the main cause of environmental degradation. These mechanisms are seriously threatening the indigenous territory of the Kichwa peoples of the inter-Andean region for example. Indigenous rights have been brushed aside, turning the indigenous into poor people who represent a threat to the ecosystem.

On the Ecuadorian coast, too, indigenous nationalities are facing serious threats to their territories. The ancestral inhabitants of extensive areas of primary forest have been rapidly pushed inland. The region has been parcelled up into different private ecological reserves. By purchasing land, attempts are being made to divest the indigenous nationalities of their common heritage, rich in biological diversity and now the sphere of interest of a conservationism that offers no place for indigenous management. This is particularly the case of the Chachi and Awa nationalities, besieged by conservation projects on all sides, by logging companies and by those selling environmental service certificates. In the case of the Huancavilca, they are resisting oil exploitation, the passage of an oil pipeline and direct alienation of their lands, at the mercy of businessmen and invaders. The Tsa'chila nationality find themselves ambushed, their territory surrounded by monocropping and land invaders, with a total absence of public policies.

Contractual rationale behind the indigenous territories

The mega-diversity that characterises Ecuador revolves fundamentally around the indigenous territories. A number of the nationalities have managed to get some areas of their ancestral territory recognised them by the Ecuadorian state. They are opposed by those interested in getting their hands on the natural resources they contain, and this involves various different actors. People are beginning to realise the goldmine that "environmental business" can represent in regions of primary forest, the Amazon and the fragile ecosystems of the inter-Andean region. The way in which rights are acquired over these territories is now governed by a legality that is replete with legal defects and violence but apparently in line with private law, which enables any agreement to be signed between free parties.

A number of legal concepts are becoming established, legal within Ecuador's property law and land market, by means of which the ancestral territories can be appropriated. On 19 September 2005, the Organisation of the Huaorani Nationality of the Ecuadorian Amazon (*Organización de la Nacionalidad Huaorani de la Amazonía del Ecuador* – ONHAE) and EcoGenesis Development LLC signed a Usufruct Agreement covering two areas: the first an allotted area of 613,750 has. and the second a plot of 29,019 has. The usufruct relates to the use, enjoyment and partial disposal of both "properties" *with the aim of attracting investment for projects to develop the resources existing in the lands.* Usufruct is granted for a period of 30 years, additionally committing the Huaorani nationality to renouncing any claim or action against those to whom the usufruct is awarded.

A document in legal format has appeared,[2] in which the indigenous representative grants general power of attorney, wide and sufficient enough to *undertake all necessary contracts and negotiations, both inside and outside of the country, with the aim of securing the sale of and/or placing of environmental services on OISE's lands (Organización Indígena Secoya del Ecuador - Secoya Indigenous Organization of Ecuador).* According to the person who provided this electronic document, an identical document was signed in the middle of 2005 and registered in Quito.

Over the past 11 years or so,[3] different communities, particularly in the inter-Andean region, have signed forestry contracts with the FACE Forestation Programme in Ecuador – the PROFAFOR company. They are in a similar format in all cases. The company recognises its origins in the Forest Absorbing Carbon Dioxide Emission (FACE) Foundation founded in 1990 at the initiative of N.V. Samenwerkende Elektriciteitsproduktiebedrijven (Sep), the Dutch Electricity Generating Board.[4] The aim of the company is forestation and reforestation to offset carbon dioxide emissions. This company signed an agreement with the Ecuadorian Institute for Forest and Natural Areas and Wildlife (*Instituto Ecuatoriano Forestal y de Áreas Naturales y Vida Silvestre* - INEFAN) - an obsolete institution following the structural reforms implemented in Ecuador in order to modernise the state under the neoliberal model - with the aim of financing activities of forestation and reforestation on private land.[5] The aim of the contract is to obtain exclusive rights to capture and offset CO_2 by means of forestation and reforestation on a particular plot of land where the company is working. The one referred to for this report related to a community plot of 350 hectares. The contract requires exoneration of the company supplying the species planted from all liability and payment in cash for forestation activities, while the community will lose all rights over these lands for 20 years.

On 30 August 2004, before a Public Notary in the town of Puyo, a Contract for Environmental Services was authenticated between the Organisation of Shiwar Nationalities of Pastaza in the Ecuadorian Amazon (*Organización de Nacionalidades Shiwiar de Pastaza de la Amazonía Ecuatoriana* – ONSHIPAE) and Mr Marco Alejandro Vélez Palacios. This contract relates to lands totalling 89,377 has. belonging to the Shiwiar and Bufeo communities. The aim of the contract is to authorise Vélez Palacios to

   a) *act and intervene directly in promoting, managing, marketing and any other legal, judicial, extrajudicial, contractual etc. proceedings that may be required with public and/or private bodies, with the aim of organising, under the best terms and conditions, programmes for the conservation of forests and environmental services in general;*
   b) *sign agreements and contracts with third parties, either individuals or corporate bodies, nationals and/or foreigners with the aim of managing funds, receiving donations, implementing investment programmes, and offering guarantees to those interested in preserving, conserving, protecting etc. these lands;*
   c) *coordinate the raising of funds, management, control, signing and intervention in the planning, execution and supervision of development plans and projects, conservation projects, environmentally sustainable projects or projects of a social, cultural, educational or humanitarian nature under terms that may be agreed with the bodies with whom the negotiations are being conducted.*

It is a one-year renewable contract, and the Shiwiar will pay him 15% of the profits generated by his actions, although they will be responsible for all the conservation tasks. In case of termination of the contract, ONSHIPAE must pay a fine of US$200,000 within five days to Vélez Palacios.

Finally, there is an agreement between the Federation of Kichwa Organisations of Napo (*Federación de Organizaciones Kichwas del Napo* – FONAKIN) and the Probenefit Project. The Probenefit Project is a project financed by the Ministry of Education and Science of the Federal Republic of Germany to promote implementation of the Convention on Biological Diversity. This project *comprises an interdisciplinary team made up of a non-profit making NGO (the Institute for Biodiversity), the Institute for Public International Law and the Department of Ecology of Gottingen University plus the Future Technologies Consultancy of the Association of German Engineers....it also includes a medium-sized pharmaceuticals firm (Dr. Wilmar Schwabe S.L.) that is interested in conducting investigations in the Ecuadorian Amazon with the aim of producing plant extracts.* The area of work is the Sumaco Biosphere Reserve.[6] The aim of the agreement is related to designing a model for and assessing the feasibility of accessing the biological resources and traditional knowledge of the Reserve, subsequently being able to "discover" plant extracts that may help in developing marketable remedies. The agreement sets out the steps to be followed. It includes FONAKIN's obligations to undertake the work with the communities, to help in defining research areas and to keep the regional indigenous federations CONFENIAE and CONAIE informed, along with the whole Kichwa population of the Amazon.

These contracts, signed within the context of Ecuadorian civil law, suffer from many procedural defects and are in complete violation of the rights recognised and guaranteed to indigenous nationalities and peoples by the Ecuadorian state. The different parties' interest in the territories can be seen in all of them, the readiness to imposing extremely harsh conditions on those signing them, the need to "legitimise" these legal acts by signing them with the representative organisations of the nationalities. CONAIE is seeking mechanisms by which to cancel these documents, which are so harmful to the life, future and territorial rights of the nationalities. And yet these probably represent only a few of the contracts that must have been signed or are currently being negotiated. It is important is to put a stop to the use and abuse of legal forms of Ecuadorian contractual law to the detriment of the indigenous, as such actions hark back to the days of the 1492 conquest: exchanging gold for trinkets.

Another ongoing problem: oil and indigenous peoples

The Kichwa community of Sarayaku is standing firm in the face of the Argentine oil company CGC's actions. During 2005, national awareness of the community grew with the clear discovery of 1,250 kilograms of *pentolita* (explosive) buried on their territories for seismic exploration. In addition, the community has been actively supported by many other organisations who are commencing or maintaining resistance in the face of extraction activities, environmental services[7] and, particularly, oil exploration.

The Achuar and Shuar nationalities decided to organise themselves into an Inter-federational Committee based around resistance to oil exploitation on the part of the nationalities living in the central southern Amazon. In the case of the Achuar, resistance has been ongoing for more than a decade in the face of different attempts to explore in their territory, including international campaigns on a number of occasions. However, faced with the head on resistance of these nationalities, a strategy of divide and rule has been deployed in relation to this committee. An Achuar leader was co-opted by the Burlington company to sign a Tripartite Agreement between indigenous leaders, state representatives and the company. At the end of 2005, the indigenous organisations made known a document signed years previously between the Ecuadorian Army and various representatives of the oil companies working the oil and gas fields of the Ecuadorian Amazon, by means of which the armed forces undertook unreservedly to protect the companies' installations and interests. The Achuar leaders have demanded that National Congress force the Army to cancel the agreement as it is in violation of Ecuadorian sovereignty and the army's dignity.

Regeneration of peoples and nationalities

The regeneration of the Pasto people, who live either side of the Co-
lombian/Ecuadorian border and who celebrated their first assembly -
reaffirming their existence as a people - in 2005, is an extremely positive sign. In addition, in the context of the change in government noted
above, they have strengthened their community authorities as the basis
on which to structure the Ecuadorian indigenous movement. There has
been an organisational revival within all its bodies in general.

The protest for Life, Water and against the Free Trade Agreement between Ecuador and the United States of America, which took place in November 2005, can in part be explained by this process of strengthening of
the organisational fabric of the indigenous movement, particularly the inter-Andean Kichwa. There was also a symbolic presence in the protest of
representatives from various Amazonian and coastal peoples.

Another process, in the middle of the year, that highlighted the increased strength of the indigenous movement was the collective criticism that emerged in the internal debate on the Development Project
for Indigenous and Black Peoples of Ecuador - PRODEPINE, financed
by the World Bank, IFAD (International Fund for Agricultural Development) and the Ecuadorian state. This project commenced within the
context of the UN Indigenous Decade, and the indigenous organisations' assessment was that it had been damaging to their organisational fabric and their own historical development. Implementation of this
project had meant a tripling of the "letterhead organisations", a strong
tendency towards dividing the grassroots organisations, hundreds of
projects commenced that had led to unsatisfied expectations in terms
of the aim of "poverty alleviation", a strong "clientilist" tendency created among small NGOs, specialist professionals emphasising the formula of "development with identity" whilst implementing projects of
the most basic developmentalism. After a long debate within CONAIE,
this organisation asked the Ecuadorian state not to sign up to a second
phase of the project, requesting at the same that state policies should
address the needs of the indigenous peoples and nationalities of Ecuador.   ❑

Notes

1   This term was coined by the ousted Col Gutiérrez himself in the midst of popu-
    lar protests against a government characterized by corruption, speculation and
    despotic action.
2   Although its authentication before a Public Notary was not verified. This is the
    act that tends to make these contractual forms "sacred", very specific to private
    law governing sales or purchases and to the constitution of real rights over pri-
    vate property.
3   Of the various documents we have been able to find, the oldest date back to
    logging contracts signed between communities and this company in 1994.
4   Recorded in this way in the whereas clause of these contracts.
5   It is surprising to note that, in a regime that protects private property, there is an
    agreement between a public institution devoted to protecting public forested
    land and a private company devoted to activities on private lands.
6   Not recognised as such in Ecuadorian legislation for any purpose.
7   In 2003, the Sarayaku community was also tempted with a proposal to hand
    over its territory for the environmental service business but this proposal was
    not approved by the Assembly.

PERU

A ccording to a recent World Bank publication, 48% of Peru's population can be considered indigenous, if you include all households in which the head of household or his wife have parents or
grandparents whose mother tongue is/was an indigenous language. If
you restrict the criterion to only those households where the head of
household or his partner uses an indigenous language then the percentage drops to 25%. In numbers, this means that out of the 26+ million Peruvians, between 6.5 and 12.5 million of them can be considered
to be indigenous, depending on whether you use the first or second
criterion.[1]

The same source corroborates the link between indigenousness and
poverty, indicating that 43% of all poor households are indigenous If
we consider only those households living in extreme poverty, this figure increases to 52%.

General issues

The historic and structural exclusion that characterises the situation of
indigenous peoples was one of the reasons why the Commission for
Truth and Reconciliation[2] recommended creating a public decentral-
ised body to establish public policies in favour of these peoples. This
request was supported by the organisations themselves, who were
struggling to replace the bankrupt National Commission for Andean,
Amazonian and Afro-Peruvian Peoples (*Comisión Nacional de Pueblos
Andinos, Amazónicos y Afroperuanos* - Conapa) with a higher-level institution of greater power and status.

In this context, the process to elect the nine peoples' representatives
that would form part of the Governing Council of the National Insti-

tute for the Development of the Andean, Amazonian and Afro-Peru-vian Peoples (*Consejo Directivo del Instituto Nacional de Desarrollo de los Pueblos Andinos, Amazónicos y Afroperuanos* – INDEPA) began in August. After an unprecedented, complex and, in some cases, controversial electoral process, the four Andean, three Amazonian and two Afro-Peruvian elected representatives were announced on 16 December.

Expectations of INDEPA are limited given that the government has thus far shown a lack of suitable politicians, professionals and technicians to promote indigenous issues. INDEPA could, in the future, benefit from the institutional powers it enjoys to revitalise indigenous issues if the new government, to be inaugurated in July 2006, can appoint suitable people to run this body and if there exists a firm political will to support its initiatives. Nonetheless, the outlook is dismal, for any references to indigenous demands are few and far between in the proposals being made by the presidential candidates.

The Camisea gas project

One of the most controversial issues between indigenous peoples/communities, the business sector and the state is the impact of the Camisea gas project, which continues to make the news after causing four spillages in one 15-month period. A study conducted by the Supervisory Body for Energy Investment (Osinerg) identified more than 40 critical points along the 174-kilometre length of the Camisea gas pipeline, most of them located within the forest section. Despite the fact that *Transportadora de Gas del Perú* (TGP) – the company responsible for carrying gas from Camisea to Lima - has been fined three times for ruptures in the gas pipeline and other environmental damage, it has had to pay no penalties, having lodged appeals each time.

Gas damage has affected both Andean and Amazonian peoples located along the gas pipeline route. A forum held on 27 April in the town of Ayacucho reported the impacts of the project in the Andean

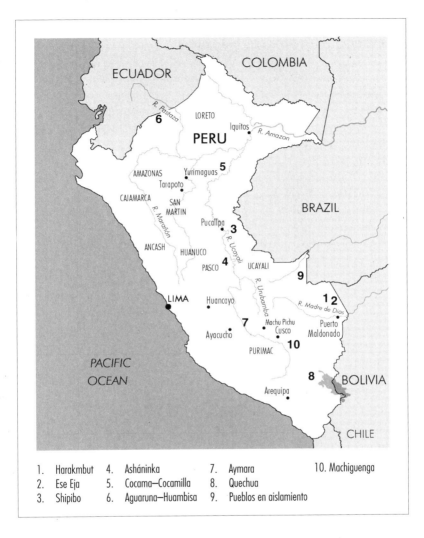

1. Harakmbut	4. Asháninka	7. Aymara	10. Machiguenga
2. Ese Eja	5. Cocama–Cocamilla	8. Quechua	
3. Shipibo	6. Aguaruna–Huambisa	9. Pueblos en aislamiento	

area as being: damage to vegetation, depopulation of wildlife, limited financial compensation to owners of agricultural lands and unfulfilled employment expectations.

New General Environmental Law

Public pressure in favour of environmental legislation that is capable of addressing the scale of environmental problems and conflicts facing the country led to a significant achievement when, after 20 years, Peru approved a marginally modern and viable legal framework for the environment. This relates to the General Law on the Environment, No. 28611, approved on 16 October 2005. Work began on the Environmental and Natural Resources Code in the mid-1980s and this was promulgated in 1990, but it caused such a strong reaction among the business sector that amendments were made that cancelled out all its practical effectiveness.

This legislation contains specific mention of the rights of indigenous peoples. Article 70 of the law in question establishes that, "in the design and application of environmental policy and, in particular, in the process of environmental territorial organisation, the rights of indigenous peoples, peasant and native communities recognised in the Political Constitution and in international treaties ratified by the state must be safeguarded. The public authorities shall promote their participation and integration in environmental management".

Law on Peoples and Communities in Congress

Contrary to the communities' interests, Congress used Law 28159 to set up a Special Commission to Review Legislation on Peasant and Native Communities. In November, this finally approved a report that was unanimously rejected by the indigenous organisations because it did not recognise the pre-existence of indigenous peoples, nor guarantee the communities either their territorial integrity or their ownership of natural resources. Among other things it did not guarantee their participation in the use, management and preservation of the resources existing on their territories and it retained the possibility of granting mining, logging and gas/oil concessions on communal lands against the wishes of the population.

The Free Trade Agreement

Unlike the above case, which embroiled the organisations in fruitless discussions, one issue of the utmost importance has still not received sufficient attention from the indigenous organisations. This relates to the negotiations around the Free Trade Agreement (FTA) with the United States. These have been accompanied by a powerful government-promoted media campaign in favour of signing the FTA, which has led to confusion among wide sectors of the population. It has fallen to the National Convention of Peruvian Agriculture (*Convención Nacional del Agro Peruano* - CONVEAGRO) to lead the opposition to the FTA and organise protests, given the consequences this treaty will have for the country's agricultural and livestock producers, who are mostly indigenous.

CONVEAGRO's main technical queries relate to the removal of price bands, which will leave some Peruvian agricultural products temporarily unprotected while US subsidies will, however, remain in place. According to CONVEAGRO, this situation will affect more than 90% of the country's producers. The organisation states that the negotiations have handed over sensitive products market to the world's number one superpower and that this represents a latent threat to Peru's food security and sovereignty.

By the end of the year, a proposal that the FTA should not be debated by the current parliament, which is now largely discredited, but by the new parliament that will sit from 28 July 2006, was beginning to gain greater acceptance among different social and political sectors.

Andean issues

Majaz mining project

Peasant communities in the north shook that part of the country for several weeks by organising one of the largest protests in opposition to the Río Blanco mining project being run by Majaz, a subsidiary of the British company Monterrico Metals. The action began with a march by

3,000 community members and seizure of the camp on the Piurana mountain, 3,000 metres above sea level. Police and army repression led to the death of one community member, with 18 more seriously injured. Wide protests subsequently took place in rural and urban areas around Piura and Cajamarca, along with an overwhelming strike under the slogan: "Piura's water rises in Ayavaca".

The driving force behind these actions came from the environmental fronts of the provinces of Ayavaca and Huancabamba in Piura, and San Ignacio and Pacaipampa, in Jaén province, Cajamarca region. They decided to defend their water, lives and land, convinced that metal mining in the area would destroy the plateau on which the Río Blanco project was located, in addition to contaminating the sources of the Quiroz, Shinshipe and Marañon rivers, waters that in turn feed the Piura and Cajamarca valleys. The villagers denounced the fact that the mining concession had been awarded without the authorisation of the land owners, the communities of Segunda and Cajas (Huancabamba) and Yanta (Ayavaca) and those inhabiting its area of influence.

Mining and political persecution

One issue of great concern is the political persecution of national, regional and local leaders of communities affected by mining, and who belong to the National Confederation of Communities Affected by Mining (*Confederación Nacional de Comunidades Afectadas por la Minería* - CONACAMI) and other similar social organisations. This relates to approximately 600 leaders denounced by the state authorities in 18 regions of Peru. The persecution takes place by means of judicial complaints, police surveillance and the orchestration of smear campaigns accusing the community leaders of advocating violence.

One clear example of this persecution was the accusation made by the Public Prosecutor of Huancabamba against the president of CONACAMI, Miguel Palacín Quispe, accusing him of being the intellectual author of the protests undertaken by Huancabamba and Ayavaca villages, despite the fact that he was called upon by the Ministry of Energy and Mines to form part of a commission that travelled to the

area to intercede in favour of peace and dialogue, along with Monsig-
nor Daniel Turley and Javier Aroca of Oxfam America.

In September, the state – through the Peruvian Agency for International Cooperation (*Agencia Peruana de Cooperación Internacional* - APCI)
- rescinded the NGO CONACAMI's legal status because its activities
did not correspond to that of an NGO proper. This administrative decision, of a clearly political nature, was taken in the face of pressure from
the mining companies to get the state to quieten down those communities that were acting against mining activities.

The serious issue here is that not-for-profit associations, such as
NGOs, are governed by the Civil Code and protected by the Political
Constitution of Peru, which specifies that they cannot be dissolved by
administrative acts. The only legal route by which to dissolve an association is that of article 96 of the Civil Code, which empowers the
Public Prosecutor's Office to request dissolution when the objectives
of the association or its activities run counter to public order or good
practice.

Another of the blackmailing mechanisms to which the business
and mining sector has been resorting is to request the intervention of
the National Supervisory Body for Tax Administration (*Superintenden-
cia Nacional de Administración Tributaria* - SUNAT) to determine who
finances the NGOs representing and defending the communities in
mining/environmental conflicts and how. In this context, in October
Oxfam International was the victim of tendentious reports claiming,
falsely, that it was linked to acts of violence, despite being an organisation that condemns violence and works to promote human rights.
Oxfam described the reporting, broadcast by a Sunday TV programme
on 23 October and seeking to discredit its work on behalf of the community's rights and in favour of dialogue between them and the mining companies, as a "slanderous campaign".

It is precisely the failure to promote any institutionalised channels
of dialogue between state and civil society that is one of the most serious deficiencies of Alejandro Toledo's government, whose mandate
will come to an end in July 2006 without having fulfilled his commitment to establish a high-level commission for dialogue between the
state, companies and communities.

The extent of disagreement became clear in September when two parallel events were organised in the same southern town of Arequipa. One brought together the pro-business sector and the other the communities affected by mining, who denounced the "exclusive and million-dollar 27th Mining Convention" aimed at reaching exclusive agreements and lobbying the government and the few people invited from civil society.

Amazonian issues

The Camisea case

The Machiguenga Council of the Urubamba River (*Consejo Machiguenga del Río Urubamba* - COMARU), the Body of Machiguenga Native Communities (*Central de Comunidades Nativas Machiguengas* - CECONAMA) and the Federation of Yine Yami Native Communities (*Comunidades Nativas Yine Yami* - FECONAYY) organised a river stoppage in protest at the government's lack of attention to its demands. Its main requests are that there should be a halt in the allocation of oil and gas concessions until safety can be ensured, and that an independent social and environmental audit should be undertaken by an international body of known repute, with its results made public and its recommendations binding. They are asking that, as the Inter-American Development Bank (IDB) financed the gas pipeline, it should also finance the audit and support the demands of the affected populations, in strict compliance with its own Operational Policy. They are also asking that the IDB review the 20 conditions imposed on the state and the company for granting of the loan for the transport phase.

The fourth spillage, which took place on 24 November, was of considerable size and affected territories of high biodiversity such as the Machiguenga Communal Reserve. Walter Kategari, head of COMARU, denounced the fact that the pipeline rupture occurred within this Natural Protected Area, compromising the source and basin of the Parotori River, the Picha River and part of the Lower Urubamba, "seriously affecting the communities of Camana, Mayapo, Puerto Huallana and Carpintero and those downstream of the Lower Urubamba River".

The indigenous organisations battled virtually all year to get the public hearings for allocation of Plot 56, adjacent to Camisea – known as Camisea 2 – suspended until the causes of the spillage had been clarified and measures adopted that would guarantee that something like this could not occur again but the Ministry ignored these requests.

The indigenous organisations have serious concerns because they have always demanded that all damage should be investigated, punished and compensated for and because they have had no response to their request to exclude the area of Plot 88 that is superimposed on the Territorial Reserve of the Kugapakori, Nahua, Nanti and others, given the vulnerability of these peoples in isolation to oil and gas activities.

Other protest actions
The Amazonian organisations have been active in various protests with the aim of drawing attention to their demands. Atalaya made the news on 30 September by organising a river stoppage which, by means of teams located at various points along the Urubamba River, stopped dozens of barges belonging to the Pluspetrol company. The actions went as far as seizing the small airport in Atalaya and blockading the new Atalaya-Satipo highway with the aim of cutting off food and personnel supplies to the main Camisea camp. This action was organised primarily by indigenous communities, with the support of the local and regional authorities of Atalaya and Ucayali respectively. Their main demand was that resources should be allocated to compensate for the damage and indirect injury caused by the project, given that the Ucayali region does not benefit from the project's royalties despite being an area of permanent river transit, which has led to the contamination of the Urubamba River and a decline in hydrobiological resources.

Another action that merited public attention was that of 300 indigenous from the Canaan de Cachiyacu community, of the Shipibo people, Ucayali region, who, on 8 July, and bearing traditional arms such as arrows, machetes and spears, peacefully but firmly took control of nine of the 26 oil wells belonging to the Canadian company Maple Gas

Corporation and closed the valves. The indigenous denounced the fact that they were receiving no benefits from the royalties paid by this company to the state despite the fact that the extraction was taking place on part of their titled territories. Their requests for dialogue were never answered by the authorities. Maple Gas indicated that this action had reduced extraction from 270 to 80 barrels of oil a day and that it was paying royalties of more than a million dollars a year to the state. The President of Ucayali Region acknowledged that his authority was planning various development projects in the region but that the slow pace of state bureaucracy had delayed their implementation.

One of the clearest triumphs of the Amazonian movement was the successful territorial defence of Chorinashi community in the face of the logging concession granted to the *Consorcio Forestal Amazónico* (CFA) run by Spanish citizen, Carlos Salcedo Noya. The situation had the region on tenterhooks, given the threat of immediate eviction and police mobilisation in the area, which is in Atalaya province. In response, a great March for Peace was organised by the Defence Front for the Interests of Atalaya (*Frente de Defensa de los Intereses de Atalaya*) in support of the community. A woman from the Yine people, Daysi Zapata, head of the Indigenous Organisation of the Atalaya Region (*Organización Indígena de la Región Atalaya* - OIRA) stated, "We are peaceful people. That is why we fought against the violence of Sendero Luminoso in the past and why we are now fighting against the violence of abusive businessmen and the arrogance of the justice system". The symbolic struggle of the Chorinashi received the backing of the committees of the Ashâninka Army of Gran Pajonal (*Ejército Ashâninka del Gran Pajonal*).

The Chorinashi Native Community, located in Tahuanía district, Atalaya province, Ucayali region, is legally recognised by the Peruvian state by means of a resolution dated 13 August 1991. They did not manage to obtain their title, however, having ceded part of their territory to the Diobamba community, which had been superimposed on them. As part of the agreement, the Chorinashi community was to move to the Cohenga stream with the support of Diobamba and the authorities. Problems arose when, in 2002, the National Institute for Natural Resources (*Instituto Nacional de Recursos Naturales* - Inrena) awarded logging concession units that were superimposed on those of the Asháninka ancestral territory and which included not only the territory in the possession of Chorinashi but also part of the proposed Inuya Tahuanía Communal Reserve, drawn up by AIDESEP in 1996. This formed the origin of a conflict between the CFA, which groups together various concession-holding companies, and the Chorinashi community, the OIRA federation and the national organisation, AIDESEP.

This conflict created controversy at various levels, particularly when some institutions such as the Coordinating Body of Indigenous and Peasant Agroforestry of Peru (*Coordinadora Agroforestal Indígena y Campesina del Perú* - COICAP) endorsed the process for the logging concession and accused those supporting Chorinashi of harbouring ulterior motives. On the other side, AIDESEP, headed by Haroldo Salazar, firmly defended Chorinashi's position and denounced the illegality of the concession.

The conflict had a happy ending for Chorinashi on 2 December 2005 when agreements for the physical and legal regularisation of 34,790.21 has. of the community were reached, along with return of its ownership. The CFA agreed to back down as civil party in the various criminal cases against indigenous leaders.   ❑

Notes and reference

1   **World Bank, 2005:** *Indigenous peoples, poverty and human development in Latin America: 1994-2004.*
2   The transitional government presided over by Valentín Paniagua created the Commission for Truth on 4 June 2001, and this was ratified and complemented by President Alejandro Toledo on 4 September of the same year, finally being called the Commission for Truth and Reconciliation. The commission was created as a body responsible for clarifying the events that took place during the violence that Peru suffered between 1980 and 2000 and apportioning responsibility for them. Its aim was also to propose initiatives affirming peace and reconciliation between all Peruvians.

BOLIVIA

National elections were held on 18 December 2005 following the resignation of President Carlos Mesa in June and the formation of a transitional government under the President of the Supreme Court of Justice, Eduardo Rodríguez, who organised the electoral process. The deep contradictions evident throughout the country were thus neutralised, avoiding a civil conflict between Bolivians.

The result of the elections meant that the Movement to Socialism (*Movimiento al Socialismo* - MAS), headed by the indigenous leader Evo Morales and the intellectual Alvaro García Linera, obtained 1,535,000 votes (53.7%) as opposed to 819,000 for the liberal Jorge Quiroga (28.6%). These were historic results, not only given the high concentration of votes among the two leading parties, in a country whose electorate is traditionally fragmented, but also because the vote favoured a Bolivian symbol of struggle against the empirical North, against the neoliberal model and against the colonial and racist oligarchy.[1]

The Bolivian population is largely indigenous. According to the 2001 census of people aged 15 or over, 62% of individuals identified themselves with one of the 50 indigenous peoples or native populations. Nonetheless, the Bolivian state has racialized its social relations and, despite having had their collective rights formally declared, indigenous peoples have still not had their territories returned or their autonomy or development with identity made effective.

Bolivia, a state in crisis

Since 1985, and in application of the "Washington Consensus", a series of neoliberal reforms designed by the multilateral agencies have been applied in the country. The pillars of the "first generation" of reforms

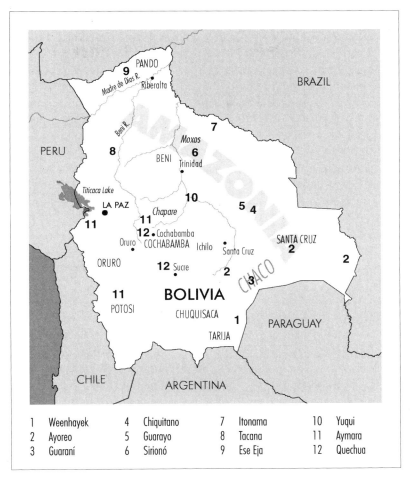

1	Weenhayek	4	Chiquitano	7	Itonama	10	Yuqui
2	Ayoreo	5	Guarayo	8	Tacana	11	Aymara
3	Guaraní	6	Sirionó	9	Ese Eja	12	Quechua

comprised monetary adjustment, fiscal reform, closure of the state
mines, the mass lay-off of workers, market opening and trade liberalization, and the free hiring/firing of labour.

The "second generation" of reforms were based on the "capitalization"[2] ("privatization") of the six largest public companies: the *Empresa
Nacional de Electricidad* (ENDE), the *Empresa Nacional de Telecomunica-
ciones* (ENTEL), *Lloyd Aéreo Boliviano* (LAB), the *Empresa Nacional de*

Ferrocarriles (ENFE), *Yacimientos Petrolíferos Fiscales Bolivianos* (YPFB) and the *Empresa Metalúrgica de Vinto* (Romero Bonifaz, 2005 : 39-40).

The dismantling of the state companies, the bankruptcy of a number of producers reliant on them and the mass lay-off of workers all skewed the economy. Out of the economically active population as a whole, 83% are involved in the informal sector, whilst only 24% of the population have direct links with the modern capitalist economy.

Among the "third generation" of reforms were the constitutional reforms of 1994 that formally acknowledged the country's ethnic diversity, recognised indigenous peoples' economic, social and cultural rights, established uninominal constituencies for the election of half of the representatives to the Chamber of Deputies, and established the Constitutional Court, the Council of the Judiciary (*Consejo de la Judicatura*) and the Ombudsman as part of legal reforms by which to monitor constitutionality, the discipline of judicial bodies and the defence of society respectively.

Living conditions in the country

Average annual income in Bolivia varies between US$800 and US$1,000, the lowest on the continent. According to the last national census, 60% of the population were living in conditions of poverty.

Of this percentage, 34% live on less than two dollars a day whilst 14% survive on less than one dollar a day. The situation in rural areas is even more dramatic: 90% survive under conditions of poverty whilst 60% live in a situation of extreme poverty.

In addition, the statistics for mother and child mortality indicate that 60 of every 1,000 live born babies will die before their first birthday, whilst 390 women in every 100,000 die in childbirth.

The flight of economic surpluses abroad

The organic incorporation of strategic sectors of the national economy into transnational capital has changed the financial structure of the state. State revenue now comes from the following sources: credits and donations 40%; direct and indirect taxation 34%; non-tax revenue 15%; company taxes 11% (Romero Bonifaz, op. cit.: 648).

Business contributions to state revenue represent only 11% of the total, despite the fact that they have taken over the running of strategic sectors of the national economy, the same sectors which – when they were being managed as public companies – were creating 70% of state revenue.

The main source of state revenue is now loans and donations. The former represent on average 34% of the total, whilst the second represent 6%. Credit comes from three multilateral institutions: the World Bank, the International Monetary Fund and the Andean Community of Nations. This explains why, despite the fact that Bolivia has benefited from the writing off of virtually all its bilateral external debt, its public debt over the last four years has grown by 26%, increasing the country's political and economic dependence.

The main leakage of economic surplus takes place through oil profits, which total 1,500 million dollars a year, of which only - on average - 160 million finds its way into the State Treasury. The way in which this surplus is taken out of the country is by the companies declaring and calculating their profits in their country of origin, thus avoiding tax. As of 2004, 11 out of 18 oil companies had declared zero profits for the last four years.

The structural problems of the state

The breakdown between the state and the economic structure is expressed in a lack of control over economic surpluses. In a backward and dependent country, characterized by a diverse economic structure, this is a particularly complex phenomenon. Seventy-six per cent of the population are involved in simple trading or agricultural economic systems, with purely reproductive aims and subjected to increasingly unequal exchange relations within a process in which labour is subjected to capital.

Conflicts with indigenous peoples are the result of a monocultural
state existing alongside a multicultural and multicivilisational society,
a mix that does not permit the articulation of heterogeneous cultures
and different historical periods. The dislocation between the state and
the regions is related to the primary export nature of the economy and
the application of models based on development poles or enclave investments associated with the extraction of particular strategic com-
modities, determining the configuration of core and peripheral regions.

This situation is made worse by the multi-activity and multi-centre
nature of the dominant labour activities, particularly in rural and semi-
rural areas. However, the strengthening of ethnic identity in Bolivia
goes beyond fragmented societal structures, which explains the great
organisational and mobilising capacity of Bolivia's social movements.

The public agenda

As the state structures have become exhausted, there has been a need
to adopt measures to completely reorganise the country. At the initiative of the indigenous peoples, a commitment has been made to hold a
Constituent Assembly, a measure resisted by the economic elites of
Santa Cruz and Tarija who, to counteract this initiative, have proposed
granting autonomy to the departments, including powers over natural
resources, the main strategic interests of which are concentrated in
these two regions of the country.

In addition, gas being the main strategic sector of the national economy and its defence the focal point of agreement of the social movements, the demand for nationalization of the oil and gas industry has
taken on greater strength. 48.7% of the national territory has oil and
gas potential. However, the neoliberal energy policy dismantled
Yacimientos Petrolíferos Fiscales Bolivianos, YPFB, through the sale of oil
fields, pipelines, refineries and marketing networks at knock-down
prices. Gas reserves are under the control of the oil companies: Repsol,
Petrobras, Maxus and Total, who control 80% of the reserves via shared
risk contracts. Meanwhile, the Chaco and Andina companies that

emerged from the capitalization (privatization) process and which are run by British Petroleum and Repsol, control 15% of the reserves.

Before privatization, oil and gas were owned by YPFB, an organisation that could sign operating or partnership contracts in return for 50% of the profits. Marketing and distribution channels were a state monopoly. With the neoliberal measures, the production chain was ruptured, gas and oil ownership was restricted to those fields not declared commercial and reserves were reclassified as either existing or new, reducing state participation in the new ones from 50% to 18%.

Despite the fact that companies operating in Bolivia enjoy many advantages,[3] their contributions to state revenue represent only 5.9% of annual income but 32% of total exports. The scale of the social and political crisis affecting the country can be explained by the population's frustration at state participation in the income generated by gas and oil exploitation.

In June 2004, former president Carlos Mesa called a binding referendum to define a new energy policy, and a popular mandate emerged to return oil and gas to state ownership and re-establish YPFB. Since then, efforts have been made to agree a new oil and gas law, and this finally came into effect in May 2005. It includes the return to state ownership of oil and gas at the wellhead, and the creation of a direct tax on oil and gas which, when added to the 18% royalties, will enable state participation in oil profits to reach the equivalent of 50%.

In addition, it states that YPFB will be re-established on the basis of a return of the Bolivians' shares that were transferred in the privatization process; the promotion of industrialization processes; the recognition of three types of contract with private operators: operating, partnership and shared production; the forced migration of all oil company contracts to the new legal system and it also includes a section on indigenous rights.

Some experts warn of failings in the new law. On the one hand, restitution of oil and gas at the wellhead is not total as the state has to access this domain from the subsoil. On the other, the re-establishment of YPFB has no real capital basis: the Bolivians' shares in the privatised companies were investment securities and not actual cash.

And yet it establishes the indigenous right to prior consultation, to participate in the profits, to obtain compensation for damages and environmental monitoring. The oil companies operate in blocks that are superimposed on indigenous territories (known as *"Tierras Comunitarias de Origen"* – TCOs - or Native Communal Lands) claimed by the indigenous peoples. Repsol has 22 blocks covering an area of 4.9 million hectares, superimposed on top of 17 TCOs in the Amazon and Chaco regions, threatening the life of communities of Chiman, Moseten, Tacana, Mojeña, Yuracaré and Guaraní peoples. The Guaraní communities are also affected by construction of the Bolivia-Brazil gas pipeline, owned by Transredes (ENRON – Shell) and Petrobras, which is 3,150 kms long. In addition, there is the Cuyabá lateral gas pipeline, owned by ENRON-Shell, which is 626 kms in length, affecting 24 Chiquitano and 2 Ayoreo communities. The Yacuiba - Rio Grande gas pipeline, owned by Transierra (Repsol and Petrobras), is 431 kms long.

Another important issue on the national agenda relates to indigenous territorial demands. By virtue of the Agrarian Law, approved in 1996, Native Communal Lands are recognised in favour of the indigenous. The peoples of the lowlands have presented 54 TCO requests covering an area of 23.3 million hectares, of which 28 are in the Amazon, covering an area of 12.7 million hectares, 16 are in the Chaco, covering an area of 5 million hectares, and 10 are in the Eastern region, covering an area of 5.5 million hectares.

In relation to the highlands, it should be noted that, as from 1997, emulating the protest actions over indigenous territory in the lowlands, the *ayllus, marcas* and *suyus* of the Andean and sub-Andean region, organised within the Council of Ayllus and Marcas of Qullasuyu (*Consejo de Ayllus y Marcas del Qullasuyu* - CONAMAQ), began a process to re-establish their ancestral territories via the presentation of 174 demands for TCOs. In Chuquisaca department, three requests for 961,000 hectares have been presented, in Cochabamba four requests for 456,000 hectares, in La Paz 38 for 1.2 million hectares, in Oruro 80 requests for 7.9 million hectares, and in Potosí 49 requests for 4.2 million hectares.

The slow attention being paid to indigenous demands can be seen in the fact that only 5 million hectares have been titled in the lowlands

and 500,000 hectares in the highlands, thus making this one of the aspects that is creating the most inequality and conflict.
The historical challenge facing Bolivia's indigenous peoples is that of reshaping the structure of government on the basis of a reconstitution of their territoriality. This would enable them to achieve structural transformation and consolidate themselves as a socio-political subject of power. To this end, their increased hegemony will need to be based on a strengthening of their organisations, on their capacity for collective action, on their majority control of Parliament and the Executive and on the receptive attitude of the international community, particularly neighbouring countries.
❏

Notes and source

1   Evo Morales emerged as leader of the peasant coca producers, persecuted and stigmatized by the US embassy. He has vehemently fought the neoliberal model, particularly the oil companies. The fact that he is indigenous has meant he has been the victim of many discriminatory attitudes in Bolivia's racist and exclusive society.

2   The capitalization was brought in by means of Law N° 1544 dated 21 March 1994.
   The capitalization consisted of attracting "strategic partners" (private companies), who would be chosen and whose capital contributions would be determined by international public tender, with the Bolivian state transferring the public companies' assets, in shares, to Bolivian residents who were of adult age as of 31 December 1995. These shares, together with worker contributions, were deposited in individually funded pension schemes invested in securities on the capitals market, and managed by *Administradores de Fondos de Pensiones* (AFP), with the state assuming these companies' liability.

3   Repsol and Amoco have the lowest production and exploration costs of 200 companies in the world. Production of a barrel of oil costs a global average of 5.6 dollars, as opposed to only one dollar in the case of Repsol and 0.96 cents in the case of Amoco for operations undertaken in Bolivia, according to the publication Global Upstream Performance Review, quoted by the former presidential delegate for a review of capitalization in his official reports.

Romero Bonifaz, Carlos, 2005: *El Proceso Constituyente Boliviano. El hito de la quarta marcha de tierras bajas.* CEJIS, 2005.

BRAZIL

After three years in power, Luiz Inácio Lula da Silva's government is notable for its great lack of respect for - and complete lack of knowledge of - Brazilian indigenous reality.

2005 ended with the greatest number of Indian murders in Brazil - 38 - in the last 11 years and the least number of indigenous land recognitions. According to information from the Ministry of Justice, only five Indigenous Lands (*Tierras Indígenas* - TIs) were declared in 2005. Lula da Silva's government has declared an average of six lands per year, a total of 18 with 8,749 hectares and authorized 55, totalling 9,843 hectares.[1]

The result of this demarcation process is that Brazil now has an area of 1.1 million km^2 set aside for indigenous peoples in the country. The National Indian Foundation (FUNAI) recognises 604 Indigenous Lands, of which 480 are either demarcated, or authorised and in the process of demarcation, whilst the other 124 are in the process of identification or recognition.

Faced with an increasing indigenous population and the serious problem of land reoccupations, tension between the *fazendeiros* (landowners), loggers and illegal squatters is increasing on a daily basis and the credibility of the institutions that are supposed to be supporting the indigenous population, for example, the National Foundation for Indigenous Health (FUNASA) and FUNAI is declining considerably in the eyes of these people.

According to demographic data[2] from 1991 to 2000, published in October 2005, there has been a 150% increase in the indigenous population since 1991.[3] The number of indigenous now totals 734,127, an annual rate of increase almost six times greater than that of the general population. A large part of this increase is due to people living in urban areas, primarily in the south-west of Brazil.

1. Cinta Larga   3. Macuxi   5. Guaraní   7. Guajajara
2. Yanomami   4. Xavante   6. Ticuna

Faced with this reality, indigenous problems are worsening. A report by Amnesty International denounces the fact that Brazil's indigenous peoples continue to suffer from, among other things, violence, poverty, hunger, discrimination and conflict over land. For this reason, Amnesty recommends, "the Brazilian government give urgent priority to defining clear policies and specific strategies to deal with persistent human rights issues and land problems affecting the Brazilian population."[4]

According to statements by the Forum for Defence of Indigenous Rights (FDDI), *"the Lula government has demonstrated its incapacity to deal with our country's ethnic plurality. One of the clearest examples was the delay in authorizing the Raposa-Serra do Sol Indigenous Land, which led the indigenous to denounce Brazil to the Organisation of American States (OAS). This latter recommended that the Brazilian government implement precautionary measures to protect the lives of this land's inhabitants."*

Land disputes and identification

Despite the fact that FUNAI is, very slowly, recognising and returning the indigenous lands, this represents a drop in the ocean in relation to the problems of hunger, malnutrition and violence being suffered by the Brazilian Indians.

Within this slow process,[5] in 2005 the Ministry of Justice stated that the following indigenous lands were recognised as TIs, together totalling 4,124,448 has.: the TI Trombetas-Mapuera with 3,70,418 has., located in the states of Amazonas, Pará and Roraima, where the Wai Wai, Hixcariana and groups in voluntary isolation live, the TI São Domingos do Jacapari y Estação (Amazonas state), of the Kokama, with 133,630 has., the TI Mirim (Amazonas state) of the Tikunas, with 20,400 ha, the TI Araça`y of the Guarani-Ñadeva, with 2,721 has., and the TI Awá (Maranhão) of the Guajá Indians with 37,980 has.

No-one knows when authorisation of these lands will take place. The slowness of bureaucracy and, in addition, the arbitrary nature of Brazilian justice, are leading the indigenous population to lose faith in the Brazilian state and to decide to take things into their own hands. Such was the resolution taken in February by the General Assembly of the Tupinikin and Guarani people, held in the hamlet of Combois, with approximately 350 Indians, in the sense that there will need to be a struggle to recapture their lands, now occupied by the Celulosa Aracruz company. In 1979, the indigenous population began to fight to recover its lands; in 1997, FUNAI identified 18,071 hectares as lands traditionally occupied by the Tupinikin and Guaraní. To date, around 11,000 has. are still in the hands of the Aracruz company.

The same occurred with the Karajá, who decided in that same month to occupy one of their lands located in the municipality of Aranã, Goiás state. Despite the fact that the 704 has. of Aranã land has already undergone the whole process of authorisation and has been registered since 2001 in the name of the Karajá, the area continues to be illegally occupied by the Arica estate.

Lands authorized

According to the president of FUNAI, Mércio Pereira Gomes, the objective of Lula da Silva's government is to have authorised 100 Indigenous Lands by 2006. According to this same official, the President of the Republic has already authorised 55, with a total of around 160 territories left (100 in the process of demarcation and 60 in the identification phase). It is estimated that, by the end of Lula's government, authorised Indigenous Lands will cover 12.5% of the national territory.

According to the general coordinator of the Coordinating Body of Indigenous Organisations of the Amazon (COAI), Jecildo Cabral Saterê-Mawé,

"The policy of Lula's government towards the indigenous sector is shameful and disappointing. The greatest problem for Brazilian indigenous peoples is the absence of effective public policies. This results in difficulties in guaranteeing the Indians their right to their lands through the justice system. The problem is not one of recognising and demarcating territories. Once they are authorised, these areas suffer all kinds of pressures. The state lacks any kind of organisational set-up to deal with this problem."

The conflicts between Indians and non-Indians do not disappear once the former have had their territories demarcated. The arbitrary nature of Brazilian law, together with a permanent lack of monitoring, leads to constant abuses of human rights and breaches of ILO Convention 169, which has been adopted by Brazil.

"Brazil is being denounced within various bodies at international level for its failure to respect human rights, for example, the complaints to the

OAS made by the Indigenous Council of Roraima and by the Federal Public Prosecutor's Office of Minas Gerais State. The violation of the human rights of indigenous peoples in Brazil emerges in these complaints, informing international public opinion of the Brazilian state's failure and lack of ability to comply with its social and legal responsibilities. Alongside this, and in contrast, all international financial commitments are being enforced to the letter."[6]

Given the above scenario, we will now list some examples of the Indigenous Lands that have been legalised and, in some cases, suspended:

- Ñanderu Marangatu, March, of the Guaraní Kaiowá people, in the municipality of Antonio João, in the extreme southwest of Mato Grosso do Sul state, covering an area of 9,317 has. The Guaraní Kaiowás' demand began in 1995 but it was only in 2001 that FUNAI began the demarcation work, which was concluded in 2004. At the end of 2005, this indigenous population was evicted once more from its authorised land by decision of the President of the Supreme Federal Court, who ruled that the land should be cleared with the intervention of the Federal Police.

- Raposa Serra do Sol, 15 April 2005. Through its authorisation, the Brazilian state recognised the right of the approximately 16,000 Indians who live on an area of 1.7 million hectares in the northwest of Roraima state, thus increasing the conflict between rice farmers, who settled there during the 1990s, and the indigenous population.

- Espírito Santo (Amazonas state), with an area of 33,849 has. for a population of 121 inhabitants, permanently occupied by the Kokama people.

- São Sebastião (Amazonas state), with an area of 61,058 has. for a population of 224 Kaixana and Kokama Indians, in the municipality of Tocantins.

- Maranduba with an area of 375 has. and a population of 31 inhabitants of the Karajá ethnic group, in Santa Maria das Barreiras and Araguacema in the states of Pará and Tocantins.

- Tabalascada with an area of 13,014 has., with 302 inhabitants from the Wapixána and Macuxi ethnic groups, in Roraima state.

Unlike other regions of Brazil, the scope of authorisation of Indigenous Lands in the Brazilian Amazon is the result of an evaluation of intricate relationships between permanently occupied lands, lands used for productive activities and lands essential for the preservation of the environmental resources necessary for physical and cultural reproduction. In this context, the superimposition of areas that characterise the indigenous territory are essential for their survival.

Indigenous movements

2005 was marked by regional conferences[7] of indigenous peoples, the main aim of which was to plan a programme of proposals and demands in preparation for the National Conference that is to be held in April 2006, and for the national indigenous protests: "Indigenous April – Free Land".

According to Vilmar Guarany, [8] "These conferences resulted in proposals from the Indians themselves, in other words, what they want for themselves. They form a framework for an indigenous presence in the proposal for a new Brazilian indigenist policy. In addition to the right guaranteed in the Brazilian Constitution of 1988, the Indian Statute that has been going through National Congress since 1991 and the validity of ILO Convention 169, in Brazil a readjustment of indigenist policy is needed." [9]

The main outlines of the discussions were: issues of land, education and health, the environment, autonomy, and protection and self-determination. These discussions were aimed at increasing the autonomy of the Indians themselves so that they can become key players in the social, political and economic spheres of the country.

Among the proposals approved were: recognition, demarcation, authorisation and registration of Indigenous Lands; resources from the Union to compensate the occupants of authorised Indigenous Lands, the acquisition of cultivable land for urban villages; and the creation of State Indigenous Councils (Consejos Indígenas Estaduales - CIEs).

One of the main results of these regional conferences was the creation of the National Council for Indigenous Policy (CNP) in May, set up by indigenous organisations and NGOs supporting the indigenous cause. This council was responsible for organising the "Indigenous April – Free Land" protests. One of its objectives is to coordinate and harmonise the formulation and implementation of specific and differentiated public policies aimed at indigenous peoples on the part of the Federal Government. Indigenous peoples will be represented through socio-cultural regions and the number of councillors per region will be proportional to the indigenous population in that region.[10]

However, in September, at the Regional Conference of Indigenous Peoples of the states of Goiás, Tocantins and east of Mato Grosso, held in Pirinópolis (Goiás state), the Indians claimed that FUNAI was having difficulty in accepting this body.

The "Free Land" national indigenous protests have provided continuity to "Indigenous April", involving around 700 leaders from 89 indigenous peoples. Organised by the Forum for the Defence of Indigenous Rights (FDI), the main demand is for 14 TIs, in addition to specific public policies in the areas of health and education.

New organisations have also been created, including: the International Alliance for Indigenous Peoples in Isolation, the result of the 1st International Meeting (8 to 10 November, Belém-PA, Pará state) on Indians in voluntary isolation living in the Amazonian countries and the Gran Chaco. The aim is to demand that governments of the countries where these Indians are found should take measures to protect their habitat, their rights and to respect their decision to have no contact with official bodies, if this is what they wish.

General news

A number of conflicts between Indians and non-Indians resulted in cowardly fought struggles. The impunity provided by the Brazilian justice system is referred to in documents published by Amnesty International. The following are worthy of note:

- The summary execution of the leader, Truká Adenilson dos Santos, and his son Jorge Vieira, aged 16. Known as Dena, he played a fundamental role in the struggle for the traditional territory of Isla de Assunção. He was murdered in public by plain clothes police officers.
- In July, Dorival Benitez was killed by gunfire from illegal occupants in the region of Sete Quedas, Mato Grosso do Sul, during the indigenous occupation of the area known as Sombrerito. Another two indigenous individuals were seriously wounded, Ari Benitez and Silvio Iturbe. The Guaraní-Kaiowá indigenous had decided to occupy the Sombrerito *fazenda*, which is in the process of being identified as an Indigenous Land.
- On 2 October, another indigenous murder took place, this time in the Acre region, near the town of Cruzeiro do Sul. Alberto da Silva Katukina had his throat slit. He was a teacher and leader of the Katukina people who lived on the Campinas/Katukina Indigenous Land, near the BR 364 highway.
- Land disputes caused another murder, this time that of the Guaraní Kaiowá leader Dorvalino Rocha, on 24 December, on the part of men hired as security guards by the *Fazenda Fronteira*, situated in the municipality of Antonio João – (Mato Grosso do Sul state).

What measures were taken by the Brazilian justice system in the face of so many deaths? Very few. In the case of Dorvalino Rocha, for example, after confessing to the crime, the guard João Carlos Gimenes was released by federal police officer Penélope Automar.

National shame: discredit and condemnation of the Brazilian government

In addition to the increased murders and violence against Indians, the national and international press characterized Brazil as a country in which hunger is killing its indigenous children.

The hardest hit region was that of Mato Grosso do Sul, which has 29 villages with an indigenous Guaraní population of around 30,000 who today live on little more than 20,000 hectares. And yet there are 100,000 hectares of lands recognised as being of traditional indigenous occupation. Part of these indigenous lands are now subject to legal actions that are challenging the identification reports and return of ownership. The most scandalous case is that of a TI that was authorised in the municipality of Antonio João, the Guaraní Ñanderu Marangatu Indigenous Land, already mentioned earlier.

Suspension of Ñanderu Marangatu's authorisation led to the Indians having to withdraw from three *fazendas* in Antonio Joao following police intervention that caused the death of Dorvalino Rocha.

In a news release entitled *"Brazil: Government and judiciary fail Brazil's indigenous peoples once more"*, Amnesty International stated that the government had failed to protect Indian rights to land. It also added that the Federal Police, supported by the *fazendeiros,* had used violence to remove the Indians from their ancestral land and that the Guaraní Kaiowá camped there were suffering from hunger.

The Brazilian government's agrarian policy is marked, in this state in particular, by an uncertainty created by the threat of legal action against demarcation processes.

Yvy-Katu, Indigenous Land of the Guaraní-Ñadeva, Mato Grosso do Sul, officially recognised by the Ministry of Justice on 4 July, celebrated its victory for only four days. On 8 July, a preliminary injunction issued by the High Court of Justice at the request of the Pedra Branca *fazenda* suspended the effect of this resolution recognising the territory as their permanent possession.

This seems absurd to the indigenous as, *"they seem to be playing with us. Someone recognises the land as ours and then someone else comes along and immediately says it's not. We're not toys and our land is not a business to make money out of. We hope that the authorities take us seriously and respect our rights. The land is ours and we are a part of that land..."*

Indigenous health

Indigenous health during the year went completely downhill. The National Health Foundation, FUNASA, responsible for indigenous health in Brazil, underwent a reform in 2004 at the behest of Lula da Silva's government. The new model centralized the system's management and left a trail of disasters through failure to implement the federal budget resources.

Throughout Brazil, the indigenous protested at a lack of resources that was leading to increased malnutrition (in Mato Gross do Sul) and increased malaria, STIs and tuberculosis (Yanomami indigenous lands).

The children are the ones who suffer the most. As of May 2005, 19 children had died of malnutrition in Mato Grosso do Sul.

The deaths and malnutrition are the result of many factors. These include the loss of land, which leads to the disorganisation of our economy, our way of producing, of feeding ourselves and of organising our families. Failing to respect the provisions of the Federal Constitution and ILO Convention 169, public policies for indigenous peoples still do not take into account our way of being, of living, thinking and organising. The basic food baskets are delivered to our houses without questioning whether the type of food is in line with our customs. [11]

According to morbidity and mortality indicators, average infant mortality among indigenous children (55.8 deaths per thousand live births) is double that recorded among the Brazilian population as a whole. In some Special Indigenous Health Districts (DSEI) such as Medio Purus, in the Amazonian region, it is as high as 185.2.

"Indigenous health is scandalous! Millions are wasted by FUNASA on seminars and meetings while our children die of malnutrition, as in Mato Grosso do Sul. The emergency measures adopted provide relief but no cure. The problem requires coordination of government actions, which is currently non-existent, and special public policies for indigenous peoples." [12]

Complaints regarding the failure to include indigenous representatives in the Brazilian government's discussions, and thus decision-making, on indigenous affairs are constant. The lack of knowledge of or openness towards more equal dialogue results in the few public policies and communication channels aimed at this population being completely inadequate and ineffective, culminating in a total disregard for this population. ❑

Notes and references

1   In comparison we have: José Sarney (1985-1990), declared 39 Indigenous Lands and authorized 67 with an area of 14,370,486 hectares, Fernando Collor (1990/92) declared 58 Indigenous Lands and authorised 112, with an area of 26,405 hectares; Itamar Franco (1992/1994) declared 39 Indigenous Lands with 7,241 hectares and authorised 16, resulting in 5,432 hectares; Fernando H. Cardoso (1995/2002) declared 118 Indigenous Lands and authorised 145 with a total of 41,043 hectares.

2   **Instituto Brasilero de Geografía y Estadística, 13 December 2005:** *Tendencias Demográficas: un análisis de los indígenas con base en los resultados de la muestra de los Censos Demográficos 1991 y 2000.*

3   This research was undertaken with self-declared indigenous. The analyses are broken down by municipality, by rural or urban environment and by specific rural residence (those located in rural areas of municipalities that have Indigenous Lands)

4   Report of *Amnesty International*, December 2005.

5   First, a technical team is sent to recognise the land and, after recognition, a report is produced that can be challenged by the states, municipalities or other interested parties. These reports and protests are sent to the Ministry of State and Justice. The next step is to publish a Declaratory Resolution, which can be suspended later by a preliminary injunction. The land can only be authorized by the President of the Republic and will be later noted in the Registry and in the Secretariat for the Union's Heritage.

6   Manifesto against the Lula government's indigenist policy.

7   Maceió (AL), Dourados (MS), Florianópolis (SC), Pirinópolis (GO), Cuiabá (MT), Porto Velho (RO), São Vicente (SP) and Belém (PA)

8   Vilmar Guarany is a lawyer, an indigenous Guarany M'bya from Rio Grande do Sul, responsible for Defence of Indigenous Rights with FUNAI, and head of the commission that organised 15 regional conferences.

9   CIMI (Indigenous Missionary Centre) document, 28 March 2005.

10 Brazilian Amazon with nine representatives, northeast and east with five, south and southeast with four and centre east two, totalling 20.

11 Document condemning the government. Silvio Paulo (Guarani), Anastácio Peralta (Guarani), Nito Nelson (Guarani), José Bino Martins (Guarani), Ladio Veron (Guarani), Rosalino Ortiz (Guarani).

12 **Manifesto against the Lula government's indigenist policy http://www.amazonia.org.br/noticias/noticia.cfm?id=155248**

PARAGUAY

During 2005, the situation of indigenous peoples in Paraguay, who now total around 20 peoples with a population of some 87,099 individuals,[1] changed in form but not in content.

The government's institutional framework

The Paraguayan Institute for the Indigenous (*Instituto Paraguayo del Indígena* - INDI) is the main body responsible for implementing state indigenist policy, primarily in relation to the administrative processing of community land claims and direct or indirect intervention through aid and development projects in the communities. Of the 412 communities existing in the country, 185 have no legal security over their lands,[2] and it is INDI that has to purchase back the lands claimed, which are now largely in the hands of private owners. And yet to do this it needs to be allocated a sufficient budget, something that has not been forthcoming for at least the last five years. This constitutes an ongoing and "structural denial"[3] of rights and, to date, everything points to the likelihood that there will be no substantive reforms aimed at changing this historic tendency on the part of the Paraguayan state.

Law 904 of 1981 continues to be the organic law governing INDI and the land claims process despite the fact that, as we shall see later, it is in the process of being amended.

In institutional terms, no changes took place in the formal structure of indigenist policy during 2005, although as mentioned above the political and legal process of reforming and amending Law 904/81 was initiated. INDI's president was, however, replaced in August, with Ms. Marta Dávalos taking over from Col. Oscar Centurión. Her background is a technical one and she thus tried to bring about changes in the internal functioning of the institution in order to ensure that more favourable action could be taken in the many cases of indigenous land claims or defences. However, this initial goodwill soon succumbed to INDI's endemic incapacity to resolve problems, caused by structural conditions and problems far removed from her sphere of influence.

A project to strengthen INDI predates Ms. Dávalos' appointment, financed as a non-refundable credit by the Inter-American Development Bank (IBD). In this context, consultations were held with numerous indigenous communities and organisations in relation to reforming this institute. The proposals that resulted from these consultations induced complaints and uprisings against the Dávalos administration, however, on the part of certain indigenous sectors, and this misguidedly resulted in a draft reform of Law 904/81 along with consequences that we shall consider further on.

The domestic and international legal framework

In terms of the positive constitutional reforms that have been taking place in Latin America, Paraguay is a forerunner in its wide recognition of the rights of indigenous peoples, as established in Section V of its Constitution. This recognises, among other principles and rights: indigenous peoples' prior existence to the state, their right to communally own their lands in a size and quality sufficient for their preservation, the internal customary/political autonomy of the communities, and more. This constitutional framework was consolidated with the adoption of ILO Convention 169 by means of National Law No. 234 of 1993. In addition, a large number of human rights treaties and conventions[4] combine to strengthen this legal framework, making Paraguay a country with high legal standards on indigenous rights and a clear will to ratify human rights instruments. Needless to say, the degree of contradiction between these laws and their enforcement is such that the historic and current reality of Paraguay's indigenous peoples shows them to be inversely proportional to each other: the more rights are recognised, the more they are violated or denied.

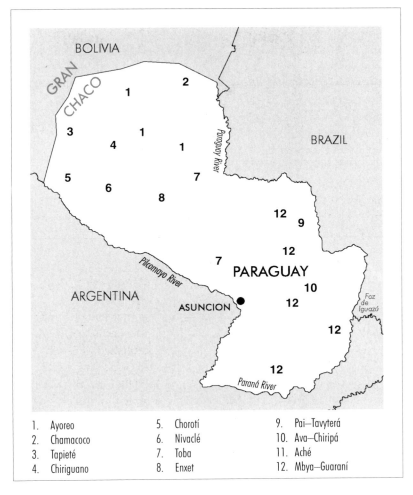

1. Ayoreo	5. Chorotí	9. Pai–Tavyterá
2. Chamacoco	6. Nivaclé	10. Ava–Chiripá
3. Tapieté	7. Toba	11. Aché
4. Chiriguano	8. Enxet	12. Mbya–Guaraní

Judging by other news from Latin America, noted in *The Indigenous World*,[5] this is a growing trend as global market interests increasingly set their sights on the natural resources that still remain under the occupation of indigenous peoples. The rights gained by indigenous peoples over their territory, supposedly protected by constitutions and the ratification and signing of Convention 169 by various countries, are taking a battering not only from actual situations (illegal invasions, evictions, etc.) but also from restrictive statutory laws and judicial and administrative measures challenging these rights. And, this said, we come back to the Paraguayan case: the process of strengthening INDI, the institutional reform sponsored by the IDB and with which indigenous sectors - including former indigenous INDI officials, the urban indigenous and some Eastern and Western region communities - were dissatisfied, has ended up in a draft reform of Law 904/81 that is diametrically opposed to the constitutional framework.

Following an extensive and much publicised indigenous public demonstration in the capital's Plaza Italia, where they camped out for more then a month, the protest came to an end in November 2005 with the approval of Law 2,822 which "basically consists of a re-editing of the text of the current law…, from which the legislators removed some articles and included others, without modifying its legislative formulation (regulatory with regard to indigenous rights and organic with regard to INDI), in a conceptual framework that continues the current assimilationist line that was present from the start."[6] In sum, the amended law is nothing but a bad repetition of a law that was already out of step with Section V of the Constitution and ILO Convention 169. It was for this very reason that consultation of the country's indigenous peoples had been needed for some time, along with the corresponding approval and promulgation of a statutory law addressing this issue, but Law 2,822 in no way fits this bill. Following preliminary approval of the Law, the Commission for Self-determination (*Comisión por la Autodeterminación*), the Federation of Indigenous Organisations of the Eastern Region (*Federación de Organizaciones Indígenas de la Región Oriental*) and the Network of Private Indigenist Bodies (*Red de Entidades Indigenistas Privadas*) mobilised against it.

Rulings of the Inter-American Court

Paradoxically, but perhaps not surprisingly, this reform of Law 904/81 was commenced after the Paraguayan state received an historic and most overwhelming sanction against it with the Inter-American Court of Human Rights' (IACHR) ruling on 17 June in favour of the indigenous Enxet community of Yakye Axa. In this ruling, the Court established that Paraguay had violated the judicial rights and guarantees enshrined in articles 8 and 25, the right of ownership in article 21 and the right to life in article 4.1 of the American Convention on Human Rights (the Convention) to the detriment of the community's members and in relation to articles 1.1 and 2 of this Convention. The Court argued, however, that there was insufficient evidence to convict the Paraguayan state of the deaths of 16 of the community's members. In its ruling, the Court demanded reparation for these violations, requiring the state to adopt various measures, including most importantly the identification of the community's traditional territory and its transfer to them at no cost within a period of three years from notification of the ruling. Other measures included the creation of a fund to purchase these lands within a year, ongoing assistance in terms of basic services until the lands had been returned, and then the subsequent implementation of a development programme plus - and this is of interest to us in this section - an obligation on the part of the state to "adopt in its domestic law, within a reasonable period, the legislative, administrative and any other measures that may be necessary to guarantee indigenous peoples' effective enjoyment of their property rights".

It should be noted that the community and its representatives have presented a request for interpretation to the Court to clarify, among other things, what parameters will be used when identifying the traditional lands for demarcation, as these had been clearly indicated by the community throughout the course of the domestic and even international court case.

The preliminary approval of Law 2,822 continues to fly in the face of the IACHR's demands on the Paraguayan state in terms of adapting its domestic law to include the restitution of indigenous peoples' lands.

Lastly, it should be noted that, as at the time of writing this report, the submissions period within the IACHR is about to come to an end in the case of the Enxet community of Sawhoyamaxa vs. Paraguay, which could mean that there will be a second conviction of the Paraguayan state in early 2006 for violations similar to those in the Yakye Axa case, i.e., violation of territorial rights, judicial guarantees and the right to life of the Sawhoyamaxa members and community. It is to be hoped that such a ruling will be forthcoming because the government has made no changes in response to the circumstances that led to the first ruling and its efforts have also been insufficient and meagre in terms of implementing the compensation measures ordered in favour of the Yakye Axa community. Another two cases are also pending before the Inter-American Commission on Human Rights, the case of the Xakmok Kásek community and that of the Kelyemaga Tegma community, the first of these being on the point of referral to the Court for in-depth analysis.

Indigenist public policies

The lack of budgetary allocation for INDI has been notable, as has been its use as a "fire fighting mechanism" in the numerous conflicts suffered by indigenous communities.

There are specific projects being financed by the World Bank and the IDB within the so-called "megaprojects", such as the Chaco Integration Corridors Project (*Proyecto de Corredores de Integración del Chaco*), the Roads for the Inhabitants of Western Region project (*Ruta de las Residentas de la Región Oriental*) (construction of roads funded largely by the IDB), and the World Bank's Safe Water Project in indigenous communities in the Chaco.

Although part of the problem with these projects is that the assistance provided varies from good to very bad, the crux of the problem is that the issue of territorial guarantees is sidelined and delayed. Many of these projects do envisage purchasing or titling lands.[7] This is done, however, as a project component handled by the counterpart ministries to the multilateral agencies, such as the Ministry for Public Works. The expert advice of these ministries as to whether the lands to be purchased form part of a traditional territory or not is thus subordinated to decision-making bodies that have visions, aims and interests very different to those that INDI, rightly or wrongly, represents. They therefore very often purchase unnecessary lands, push through he purchase of others which, although they are claimed lands, are not next in line in terms of progress of their administrative processes and, of course, they are also open to influence peddling in which the overpricing of land is common currency. In addition, the possibility of gaining control over this purchase process is even less given that the authorities, valuation experts and relevant sectors deal first with private owners, then with communities and almost never with established indigenous organisations or private indigenist organisations, these latter being those most able to at least question and challenge irregularities in the process.

Finally, although there are some local and regional actions and programmes that may be having some success, there is a great lack of health and education policies at national level, and there is also a dearth of positive measures that would enable indigenous participation in state affairs and public policy making.

The activities and demands of indigenous players and their allies

As previously explained, the indigenous demonstration in the Plaza Italia began in protest at the marginalisation they had been suffering since the change in INDI's management team. They were calling for the removal of Ms. Davalos and her entourage, camping out in the square and attracting the attention of press and public alike. The initial demand was that the recommendations made during the consultation on INDI's strengthening process be fulfilled but, once these demands had been passed on to parliamentary representatives sitting on the Human Rights and Indigenous Affairs Committee, they were turned into a draft bill that was approved with surprising haste – rather unusual for an indigenous issue if you consider the delays and denials involved in the transfer of land to indigenous ownership. The indigenous of the Plaza Italia requested the same priority treatment from the Senate, and this was accompanied by an unusually favourable media campaign, which raised the population's awareness, albeit in a rather paternalistic way.

It was at this point that the Commission for the Self-determination of Indigenous Peoples (*Comisión por la Autodeterminación de los Pueblos Indígenas* - CAPI), the Federation of the Eastern Region (*Federación de la*

Región Oriental) and the Indigenist Network (*Red Indigenista*) took action, somewhat belatedly, warning the senators of the nonsense in republishing a bad law that needed to be changed and which was even a serious retrograde move in terms of guaranteeing indigenous rights, for example by authorising public and private sector exploitation of the mineral and water resources on indigenous lands. The Senate finally approved the law, however, in a full session in which representatives known to be unfavourable to indigenous rights voted through the draft law with virtually no amendments.

The indigenous of Plaza Italia took this as a triumph and, as a sign of their acceptance of this approval, they demobilised and moved their makeshift encampment. CAPI, the Federation of the Eastern Region, the Indigenist Network, and even INDI's management took this as a political blow from more powerful sectors and a clear retrogression in indigenous rights, and so they came up with a plan of action aimed at achieving a total veto of approved Law 2,822.

In November, and through unprecedented joint work, some 1,200 indigenous people descended on Asunción to demand that the government veto the approved law. For six days, the indigenous participated in protest actions, primarily outside the parliamentary buildings, where they called for a meeting with the President of the Republic, Nicanor Duarte Frutos, who avoided meeting them on a number of occasions.

Given this lack of response from the head of state, the indigenous decided to march on the presidential palace. Police in Asunción tried to prevent them from doing so and, to this end, a hundred anti-riot police were deployed in the surrounding streets, attempting to attack the demonstrators. Undeterred, and with full media coverage, the indigenous marched on the presidential palace where they forced the President to receive their representatives. After the meeting, the creation of a special commission, made up of indigenous and government representatives, was stipulated to analyse the new law.

This commission has now achieved a partial veto of 13 of Law 28,222's articles, those that most seriously compromised already established rights. CAPI, the Federation and their allies have begun a process of mobilisation and constant monitoring of this process with the strategic aim of achieving the greatest possible participation of the communities and organisations in a consultation process that could end in the approval of an implementing law that will ensure full validity of Section V and ILO Convention 169 and consolidate progress in indigenous rights and their enforcement.

Most typical violations of the rights of indigenous peoples

It was noted above that indigenist policies, either of a public or private nature, good or bad, are limited in the face of certain structural problems and conditions. These include the following: the expansion of an agro-export model based on the intensive use of natural resources; the concentration and reconcentration of land, primarily for intensive soya cropping in the country's Eastern Region and livestock raising in the Chaco and north of the country which, in turn, has accelerated environmental and social erosion (exploitation of forest resources, widespread use of pesticides, invasion of indigenous lands, restricted access to privately owned lands for traditional activities), and led to increased capital gain on lands; rural poverty leading to a rural exodus; widespread violence, cultivation of and trafficking in drugs, and all this with direct consequences for the conditions and quality of life of indigenous communities and their members. The indigenous communities find themselves in the geographic, physical and symbolic eye of this storm of irrational productivism and its many consequences. And if the state does not actually support this as a national development policy, then it turns a blind eye to it or is incapable of controlling it, given that the production model extends beyond the national or regional legal, political or ideological framework to include paralegal or directly illegal systems and organisations such as internal or cross-border mafias which, in Paraguay, have a longstanding and symbiotic relationship with the established authorities.

In this context, the struggle for political power that is currently underway in the inner circles of the government party, so defining in terms of the country's political and economic future, has serious consequences for the struggle of indigenous peoples, their organisations and allies. The aims and challenges are at least clear: to achieve consolidation of a favourable legal framework, overcoming the retrogression caused by Law 2,822, to achieve unified positions within the indigenous movement, to force government institutions to respond and enforce international rulings in favour of the petitioning communities, and to achieve an end to - and reparation for - human rights violations committed against people and communities.

The battle ground will not be an easy one, but smoke can be seen and the war paint is on in the indigenous camp.   ☐

Notes and references

1   **Dirección General de Encuestas, Estadísticas y Censos (DGEEC), 2002:** *National Indigenous Census 2002.*
2   This figure is deceptive in terms of the proportion of legal guarantees for indigenous lands, as the indigenous census intentionally did not record whether the guaranteed lands held were sufficient for the communities, bearing in mind the minimum required by Law 904/81 of 20 hectares per family in the Eastern Region and 100 in the Western Region. Given this legal parameter, the number of communities without sufficient land would increase considerably to around 50% of the country's communities.
3   **Ramírez, Andrés, 2005:** Derechos de los pueblos indígenas: voces discrepantes frente a una crisis terminal en *Derechos Humanos en Paraguay 2005.* CODEHUPY, 2005, Asunción, pp. 469-480.
4   The American Convention on Human Rights itself (National law 1/89), the Optional Protocol of San Salvador on Economic, Social and Cultural Rights (National law 1,040/97), the Convention on Biological Diversity (Law 253/93) and many more.
5   See for example the reports on Brazil, Argentina and Peru in *The Indigenous World 2005.*
6   **Ramírez , Andrés**, op. cit. p. 474.
7   This largely entails support for the measuring and public recording of lands already purchased by the state, however, and does not provide funds for land purchases, which is in fact the main requirement and deficiency in guaranteeing the indigenous their lands.

ARGENTINA

During 2005, Argentina's response to indigenous demands for their rights continued in the form of delays, silences, omissions, denials and violence. Violent evictions, police repression, persecution and legal harassment all took place in response to indigenous demands for respect of their rights. Demands for titling of lands and territories were not endorsed. On the contrary, they were unjustifiably delayed. Freedom of association and political participation were challenged, and the federal administration appeared not to know what direction to take in its indigenist policy. The federal state's inability to formulate an effective policy with the indigenous reached absurd levels in 2005 when a provincial government submitted the constitutional prerogative of recognising a community's possession and ownership of its lands and territories to a referendum. And this issue was only aggravated by the Supreme Court of Justice which, on being presented with the case, decided to wipe its hands of the issue. The attitude of national parliamentarians has not been so very different this year, leaving a draft emergency bill pending that would have put a stop to compulsory evictions of indigenous from their ancestral lands for four years.

Indigenist policy at the federal level: two examples

Indigenous participation in formulating state policy

The National Institute for Indigenous Affairs (*Instituto Nacional de Asuntos Indígenas* – INAI) is responsible for implementing federal policy on indigenous issues. It is supposed to be supported by a group of indigenous representatives from throughout the country but, for various reasons, it has not been possible to set this group up. In 2005, community assemblies were held at village and provincial level but the process came to a halt before the national elections, the time when indigenous voices demanding due respect for their rights most needed to be heard in all their force.

Consultative meeting in the Congress of the Nation

On 12 May 2005, an indigenous delegation attended the Congress of the Nation to debate a draft bill with a group of legislators that sought to prevent "enforcement of evictions" (against indigenous peoples) for four years, whilst at the same time ordering INAI to "define indigenous lands in order to title them in favour of communities". Without entering into a debate on the possible intentions of the policies, the bill was due to be heard by the legislative assembly for its approval during this period, but this was not possible. The organising of a consultative meeting should have been normal practice in Argentina, which has ratified ILO Convention 169, but it takes more than good intentions to respect the opinions and authority of the indigenous themselves in issues of direct interest to them. Despite the efforts made by the president of the Chamber of Deputies' Population and Human Resources Committee, the meeting was not what it should have been. Not because procedures appropriate to the cultural norms of the affected peoples were lacking but because the meeting did not have the due and legitimate participation of genuine leaders and representatives. This was due to an absence of financial resources to ensure this presence. For this reason, only indigenous people living in the state capital were able to attend, or those who happened to be passing through. The failure to set aside specific funds within INAI's national budget for due consultation with the indigenous peoples is indicative of Argentina's lack of respect for international law.

Deficiencies in local governments' indigenist policy

Indigenous culture: political merchandise in Formosa province

In 2005, the Formosa government, through the Ministry of Tourism, organised the 2nd Meeting of Native Peoples of America. A grand event that claimed to be demanding cultural plurality but which was denounced by the province's indigenous people as a scheme on the part of Governor Gildo Insfrán to cover up the numerous violations of

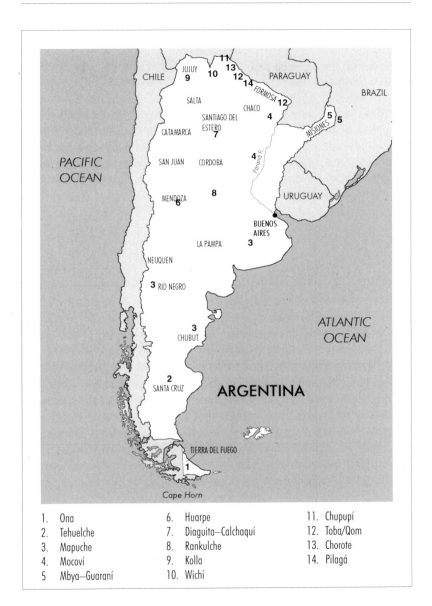

1. Ona
2. Tehuelche
3. Mapuche
4. Mocoví
5 Mbya—Guaraní

6. Huarpe
7. Diaguita—Calchaquí
8. Rankulche
9. Kolla
10. Wichí

11. Chupupí
12. Toba/Qom
13. Chorote
14. Pilagá

their rights, some of which have been of national importance. Such was the case of the investigative journalism conducted by a free-to-air TV channel into the repressive practices of party activists on election day, when indigenous voters had their identity documents confiscated, and were barricaded in their communities, later taken by force to vote for the "right" candidates. In fact, this conference took place in an electoral year, two months after an international complaint had been presented by the Nam Qom community to the Inter-American Commission on Human Rights[1] and one week after the trial of three of its members, accused of murdering a police officer, in a confused event while they were out on traditional hunting activities.

A legal absurdity: law 7352 on a referendum in Salta province

A pathetic event took place in the context of the Lhaka Honhat organisation's land claim, when it found itself in a process of friendly resolution before the Inter-American Commission on Human Rights (IACHR). In April, the Salta government unilaterally decided to break off the friendly negotiation process on the basis of the false argument that Lhaka Honhat had made no comments with regard to the government's proposal for land distribution presented via the IACHR. The government therefore decided to send a proposal for a referendum to the provincial legislature so that the people of Rivadavia could say whether they wanted the indigenous ancestral lands (of state plots 55 and 14) to be handed over to their "current indigenous and non-indigenous occupants"[2] or not. There were not even any second thoughts when various federal state bodies warned of the unconstitutionality of the referendum, on the basis that indigenous rights could not be submitted to a popular decision.

On 11 August 2005, Lhaka Honhat asked the Supreme Court of Justice to rule on the call for a referendum, and presented an appeal known as a "declaratory action" (*acción declarativa de certeza*). On 28 September, the Court issued its ruling stating that it was not competent to hear the issue and that it was for the petitioners to present their demand before the ordinary courts of Salta province. Only one of the seven members of the Court, along with the Attorney-General of the Nation (who had already issued his opinion on 24 August), stated that the issue raised was of the Court's original competence, as the arguments made by Lhaka Honhat directly and immediately called into question clauses of the National Constitution that needed essential clarification when judging the affected right. Although the minister did not venture an opinion on the unconstitutionality of the referendum, he at least recognised the Supreme Court's competence to rule on the issue. There is no doubt that indigenous rights cannot be subject to consultation, and that the procedure employed was in breach of ILO Convention 169. The formula used is illegal in that it offers the alternative option of voting not to provide lands. All that can be added in this regard is that, unfortunately, the majority of Court members did not warn that this failure to enforce the territorial rights of the indigenous, along with the government's actions in this regard, constituted a flagrant threat to their survival as peoples.

On the Pilagá people

On 23 November 2005, the Supreme Court once more ruled that an appeal made by indigenous communities who will be affected by construction works on provincial highway No. 28 (Formosa province), being undertaken with funding from the Inter-American Development Bank (IDB), was not within its competence. The communities of the Pilagá people argued in their appeal that the works would negatively affect their ancestral territory and they therefore requested a change of route. The communities also requested a ruling on the unconstitutionality of provincial law 1439/94, which declares lands legitimately belonging to them as being of public use and thus subject to expropriation. In this case, the Supreme Court decided that as the works were being undertaken by the Formosa Water Resources Department, albeit with IDB funding from a Ministry of National Planning programme, the federal state was not responsible. The judges argued that although the petitioners were trying to claim that this was of the court's original competence, their statement that the works would create a threat of flooding in the communities meant that it clearly was not as the provincial administrative and judicial authorities were responsible for assessing whether works would affect rights specific to the provincial sphere, such as environmental rights.

Security forces and the legal system

The Wichí communities of the Itiyuro river basin, in Salta, better known as the highway 86 communities, have been denouncing the theft of timber from their ancestral lands. In 2005, faced with the apathy of the local authorities, they decided to take things into their own hands and prevent a logging company's lorry from leaving their lands. For more than 60 days they peacefully asked to be heard. And an answer was not long in the coming: on 8 July, with a warrant from the provincial judge, Nelson Aramayo, 50 police officers descended on the community of Pozo Nuevo to recover the lorry. Taking advantage of the fact that community leaders were not in the area as they had travelled to Salta to present a petition to the government, the operation ended in violent repression. The elder, José Galarza, cacique of Tonono community, who had not travelled for health reasons, suffered the impact of forty bullets, both rubber and real, and had to be admitted to Tartagel hospital. His son, José Galarza, who came to the defence of his father, and Salomón Abraham were also wounded. None of the community members were armed or put up any resistance.

Outcome of some old land conflicts

We shall look here at three examples of the many claims outstanding in our country in relation to the titling of traditional lands. Three typical cases in which the battle has been fought against local governments, with the lukewarm participation of the federal state, which is ultimately responsible for protecting indigenous rights.

The Casiano community: dispossession of land by individuals
For more than 16 years, the Mapuche people of Casiano-Epugner community, in Río Negro province, have been denouncing the occupation of their lands by an individual, Mr. Abbi Saad, who argues that he is the owner of these lands. In 2003, the community was ac-

cused of misappropriation. In June 2004, the Casiano-Epugner community submitted the results of an investigation to the state prosecutor that proved Abbi Saad's illegitimate possession in order to obtain his eviction. Provincial law 2287 establishes that in a complaint of dispossession of a Mapuche community or settler, the prosecutor must evict the person or persons in question and return the lands to the community or settler. The prosecutor therefore undertook to resolve the claim within a week. One year later, given his clear failure to do anything, the Casiano-Epugner community decided to take the government to court to obtain final and unconditional recognition of their possession and ownership rights over these lands. Abbi Saad's eviction had been ordered more than 10 years ago for violation of provincial land law 279 but this was never enforced through the negligence and complicity of government officials. In December, the provincial Mapuche organisation the Indigenous Advisory Council (*Consejo Asesor Indígena*) held a *Futa Trawn* (Mapuche assembly) in which it denounced the two organisations jointly responsible for implementing indigenous territorial rights, the state-run Council for the Development of Indigenous Communities (*Consejo de Desarrollo de Comunidades Indígenas* - CODECI) and the National State Land Regularisation Programme (*Programa Nacional de Regularización de Tierras Fiscales*) (created in 1996), for delaying the processes and not fulfilling their objectives.

Cuña Pirú
On 6 December, the Yvy Pita, Ka'Aguy Poty and Kapi'i Poty communities of the Mbyá Guaraní people in Cuña Pirú valley (Misiones province) held a meeting with officials from the federal state, local government and authorities of the La Plata National University. In 1992, the Celulosa Argentina S.A. company gave this university more than 6,000 has, part of the ancestral Mbyá Guaraní territory traditionally used by these communities. In 1999, the university signed an agreement with the Misiones Ministry of the Environment by virtue of which the lands became the university's private natural resource for 20 years. The communities therefore mobilised, asking to form an active part of these agreements and requesting that the definitive title to

the lands be issued to them. The university wants to conserve the environment, rich in biodiversity, and to conduct - as it has done to date - academic training activities. It claims to recognise the communities but does not know much about the specific rights of indigenous peoples and so it does not appear ready to recognise the communities' title to their lands of traditional use and is offering to transfer ownership of 700 hectares to them, with the rest being subject to a joint management plan. This proposal has not been accepted by the communities, who are demanding respect for their rights as established in the national constitution (article 75 paragraph 17) and ILO Convention 169. For the moment, the positions are sharply opposed and INAI has been asked to act as mediator, proposing an alternative which, we hope, will bring justice to the historic demand of these communities.

Lhaka Honhat

This organisation's struggle, which includes more than 40 communities of the Chulupí, Chorote, Tapiete, Toba and Wichí peoples in Salta province, continues unabated. Following the illegal referendum organised by Salta province, and in the face of unjustified delays on the part of the Inter-American Commission on Human Rights in issuing its report, which may well convict the Argentine state for violating the human rights of indigenous peoples, a ten-person delegation travelled to the capital to talk to the president. Nobel Peace Prize winner Adolfo Pérez Esquivel and the Mothers of the Plaza de Mayo supported the initiative, asking President Néstor Kirchner to agree to an audience. To attract public attention, a number of well-known personalities and organisations from around the world endorsed an advertisement in a national daily newspaper in which the communities called on the president to prevent their traditional lands from being divided. Wearing the national football team's colours to show that they too were Argentinians, on 29 November a demonstration took place in the Plaza de Mayo in Buenos Aires, awaiting an audience from the president. On 30 November, they returned to their communities with a promise that this meeting would take place on 13 or 14 December. Two weeks later they travelled to the capital once more where they waited patiently until 15 December, with no luck. After 21 years of claiming title to their traditional lands, and five years of friendly negotiations with the government under the supervision of the IACHR, they returned once more with no more than a promise that the president "would receive them" at some stage. This illustrates yet again the federal state's inability or unwillingness to put together a policy with the indigenous peoples within the framework of international standards governing their specific rights.

The indigenous movement's policy

In 2005, the Argentine Republic played host to the Indigenous Peoples' Summit (s) of the Americas, held on the occasion of the Fourth Summit of the Americas (Mar del Plata, 3 and 4 November).

From 27 to 30 October, delegates from indigenous organisations from a number of American countries met in Buenos Aires. During the meeting, workshop debates and artistic presentations were organised along with plenary sessions at which a document to be presented to the Presidential Summit was discussed and formulated. Indigenous demands focused on recognition of self-determination. The Organisation of Indigenous Nations and Peoples in Argentina (*Organización de Naciones y Pueblos Indígenas en Argentina* - ONPIA) and the Assembly of First Nations of Canada (AFN) were responsible for convening and organising the indigenous summit. In the context of the so-called Peoples' Summit of the Americas, attended by NGOs and representatives of the World Social Forum, another indigenous summit took place in Mar del Plata on 3 and 4 November. This was organised by the Mapuche Confederation of Neuquén (*Confederación Mapuche del Neuquén*) and the Commission of Indigenous Jurists of Argentina (*Comisión de Juristas Indígenas de la República Argentina*). In a lengthy document, those attending demanded recognition of the self-determination of indigenous peoples, the ownership of territories, lands and natural resources, and approval of the American Declaration and Universal Declaration on the Rights of Indigenous Peoples, among other things. ❏

Notes

1   In March 2005, members of the Nam Qom community of the Toba people in
    Formosa denounced before the IACHR the fact that on 16 and 17 August 2002,
    an operation on the part of more than 100 police officers had burst into the com-
    munity in search of the alleged authors of the death of a police officer, with the
    result that mass and indiscriminate arrests had taken place, with indigenous
    individuals forced to make statements under torture in the capital's police sta-
    tion. When they complained of this to the provincial courts, the judge decided
    there was insufficient proof as witnesses had stated that, "the police are our
    friends, we have nothing against them". This contrasted with the testimonies of
    community members.
2   For the referendum to be valid, it needed to have more than 50% of votes cast in
    its favour. Of the 16,762 people on the electoral register, 5,049 voted YES, 131
    voted NO and 34 spoilt their vote. This therefore means that the total votes cast
    represented 31% of the electorate. Other people turned up to vote in the na-
    tional elections but did not vote in relation to the referendum. The government
    had at the last moment passed a new statutory decree amending the law so that
    the referendum could be held alongside the legislative elections. To ensure the
    effectiveness of this manoeuvre, the government concealed the amendment.

CHILE

N ine indigenous peoples (the Aymara, Colla, Diaguita, Kawéskar, Lickanantay, Mapuche, Quechua, Rapa Nui and Yámana) inhabit the current territory of the Chilean state. The indigenous population in Chile totals more than one million people, with the Mapuche being the most numerous, accounting for almost 90% of the country's indigenous population.[1]

As in other parts of the continent, these peoples have formed the object of cultural assimilation and territorial dispossession policies. During the 19th century, the Chilean state occupied territories thus far in the hands of the indigenous, taking their lands from them and imposing its laws and culture on them. In the case of the Mapuche in the south of the country, their population was arbitrarily confined to 3,000 *reducciones* (reserves) of a communal nature on around 5% of their original territory of almost 10 million hectares. During the 20th century, the state promoted the individual ownership of these lands, along with their subsequent transfer into non-indigenous hands. The military regime (1973-1990) concluded by dividing the still remaining Mapuche communities and promoting policies for their assimilation into the rest of the population. The smallholdings that this process of division gave rise to contributed to the impoverishment of the communities and the migration of their inhabitants towards the urban centres, where it is now estimated that 80% of the Mapuche population live.

Legislation

In 1993, following the end of the military regime, Congress approved legislation (law no. 19,253) to create the National Corporation for Indigenous Development (*Corporación Nacional de Desarrollo Indígena* - CONADI) to act as a steering committee for indigenous policy, and recognised indigenous rights over their lands, languages and cultures. This law, however, did not recognise indigenous peoples as such, only recognising them as "ethnic groups", nor did it recognise their traditional organisations. It recognised neither their political rights - such as autonomy and indigenous justice systems – nor their territorial rights – such as those over natural resources. For these reasons, it falls far below the standards established in applicable international instruments, such as ILO Convention 169, which has not been ratified by Chile to date. Nor does the Political Constitution of Chile recognise indigenous peoples and their rights. In 2005, the government of President Lagos (2000-2006) presented a proposal to Congress with this aim.[2] This proposal, which was not put to the indigenous peoples for prior consultation and which did not recognise the collective rights that indigenous peoples are now claiming in the country, did not gain a favourable reception in the National Congress.

During 2005, the government presented two draft legal reforms to Congress in relation to indigenous peoples. The first, of a constitutional nature, was with the aim of creating a territory and special administration status for Easter Island, territory of the Rapa Nui, and the second, of a legal nature, was to establish a maritime coastal area for native peoples. These draft bills, which were far from meeting the Rapa Nuis' demands for autonomy or recognising the Mapuche-Lafkenches' rights over the natural resources of the coastal region, and also far from current trends in international law governing this area, are still being processed through Congress.

Discrimination

Indigenous peoples in Chile are subjected to numerous forms of discrimination. On a political level, they have no representatives in the National Congress. Their representation in national government, as well as in regional and local government, is negligible in proportion to their number. On an economic level, discrimination can be seen in the levels of indig-

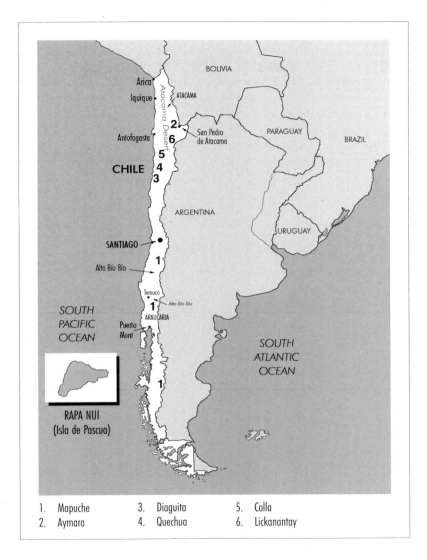

1. Mapuche   3. Diaguita   5. Colla
2. Aymara   4. Quechua   6. Lickanantay

enous poverty, which are much higher than those of the non-indigenous population.[3] To this must be added the discrimination that affects indigenous peoples in environmental terms. This became clear in 2005 with the (state-sponsored) construction of numerous wastewater treatment plants (17 in the Araucanía region) on or near the lands of Mapuche communities (a total of 42 Mapuche communities were affected), and with the efforts of a logging company (Arauco SA) to dump the waste from its cellulose plant on the Pacific Ocean in the territorial waters of the Mapuche-Lafkenche.[4] And finally, discrimination against the indigenous can be seen in the treatment the justice system has meted out to the Mapuche in recent years, in the context of the land conflicts involving their communities. Many of their leaders have been convicted of actions of a "terrorist" nature, which contrasts sharply with the impunity that the non-indigenous enjoy for crimes committed against the Mapuche.

Public policy and indigenous peoples

Sectoral policy

The policies promoted by the state over the last decade in relation to indigenous peoples have not only been insufficient but also contradictory. For example, through the indigenous lands fund created by a 1993 law, CONADI promoted a programme aimed at protecting and extending indigenous lands. According to CONADI's records, a total of 406,000 hectares had been acquired via the market as of 2005, transferred by the state to and/or regularized for indigenous peoples throughout the country. Of these, 200,000 corresponded to Mapuche territory. Less than a quarter of this amount (81,000 hectares) however corresponds to new lands acquired for the indigenous, the three remaining quarters relating to the transfer of state lands, most of them of indigenous ancestral ownership, and to the regularisation of pre-existing titles of indigenous ownership.

The numerous problems with this policy – including inadequate state funding to deal with indigenous demands for misappropriated lands and a lack of mechanisms to address those demands for ancestral lands,[5] the fragmentation of indigenous communities by prioritising individual titling of the lands acquired or transferred over that of community ownership, and the lack of state support to develop production among the recipients,[6] - have been noted by different analysts and denounced by the indigenous organisations.[7]

Economic globalization

Alongside this sectoral policy, the Lagos government's efforts have been focused on expanding the global economy and free trade towards the indigenous peoples' territories, rich in natural resources. Alongside the signing of free trade agreements with the largest world economies (the United States and the European Union, among others), the government therefore supported and/or implemented a series of investment projects on indigenous lands or on those lands claimed by indigenous communities. These projects, which include mining projects on the territories of the Andean peoples in the north, and logging, water, highway and hydro-electric projects on Mapuche territory, have been implemented without adequate consultation of the indigenous peoples and without considering any benefit sharing mechanisms. These same projects have had a serious impact on the culture, environment and economy of indigenous peoples, and this has been denounced by indigenous organisations and documented by the Special Rapporteur, Rodolfo Stavenhagen, in the report of his trip to Chile in 2003.

The Ralco hydro-electric plant

The Ralco hydro-electric project, which was commenced with state support at the start of the 1990s by Endesa Chile – a subsidiary of Endesa España – in the Alto Bío Bío, on the ancestral territory of the Mapuche-Pehuenche, reached completion in 2004. Ralco resulted in the flooding of 3,500 hectares of land inhabited by the Pehuenche and the relocation of around 500 members of their communities. Faced with resistance on the part of the affected Pehuenche communities, who had demonstrated their opposition to its construction from the start, the project was imposed through joint illegal action by the state and the company. As a consequence, five Pehuenche women submitted a complaint to the Inter-American Commission on Human Rights alleging violation of their rights, including the right to life, ownership and legal protection, and a compensation agreement was reached with the Chilean state in 2003. This agreement committed the government to a series of undertakings, including the creation of a new municipality in the area, material compensation of the plaintiffs, the establishment of mechanisms to solve the land problems of the Pehuenche communities, the strengthening of Pehuenche participation in the area's development institutions, and monitoring of the Ralco plant's environmental obligations, along with the promotion of processes for understanding and dialogue with indigenous peoples in order to introduce a constitutional reform for recognition of their rights and ratification of ILO Convention 169. It should be noted that most of the commitments made by the Chilean state - with the exception of the creation of the Alto Bío Bío municipality and some of the material compensation for the plaintiffs – remain unfulfilled to date, as was denounced by the petitioners in this case before the Inter-American Commission on Human Rights in Washington DC, in a hearing held in October 2005.

Mining and the Andean peoples

In recent years, large mining investment projects have been promoted on the territory of the Andean peoples (Aymara, Lickanantay, Quechua, Colla and Diaguita) in the north of the country. These projects are having a significant impact on their ecosystems, in particular their waters, causing the drying up of wetlands, meadows and springs essential to development of the agro-pastoral economy specific to their communities, and threatening the survival of ancestral settlements. The most serious impacts of mining on the indigenous territories in this part of the country in 2005 included the following:

• the destruction of archaeological sites and contamination of the Lickanantay *ayllu* (territory) of Chiu Chiu as a consequence of the expansion of the Talabre tailing reservoir, which belongs to the state company *Corporación del Cobre* (CODELCO Chile);

- the loss of the Lickanantays' water rights in the Loa River basin, as a consequence of its monopolization by a number of mining and also water companies;
- and the monopolization of water rights in the Colla territory by mining companies and the drying up of meadows and wetlands as a consequence of the over-exploitation of water resources, the most serious case being the environmental impacts caused by the Maricunga mining company.

To this must be added projects that were being negotiated during 2005, threatening the rights of Andean communities, such as:

- the request for water extraction in Salar del Huasco by the mining company *Doña Inés de Collahuasi*, which is compromising the Aymara's plateau (*altiplano*) habitat and the Pica and Matilla hydrological system;
- plans by CODELCO-Chile and the National Petroleum Company (*Empresa Nacional de Petroleo* - ENAP) to exploit the Tatio geyser – an ancestral site of the Lickanantay communities of Toconce and Caspana – for geothermal energy production. During 2005, the state granted this territorial area to the communities for tourism purposes;
- and the imminent approval by the 3rd Region's Regional Environmental Commission of the Pascua Lama mining project, by means of which Minera Nevada Ltd. (a subsidiary of Barrick Gold Corporation) intends to exploit a gold deposit located under the glaciers that form the source of the waters making up the hydrological system of the Huasco river and its tributaries, in the upper basin of the river, where the ancestral territory of the Diaguita people is to be found.

The criminalization of Mapuche demands

The previously mentioned inadequacies of and contradictions in public policy, in particular the proliferation of investment projects on their ancestral territories, have in recent years caused indigenous peoples to take action in the face of violations of their rights to land and natural resources. In the case of the Mapuche, these actions have not only been harshly repressed by uniformed police but they have also been pursued through the justice system by the Public Prosecutor's Office and the government. Consequently, many Mapuche leaders and community members have been charged with - and convicted in court of - committing various crimes, including crimes of a terrorist nature, recourse being made to current anti-terrorist legislation.

In this regard, the ruling passed by a criminal court in Temuco, Araucanía region in July 2005, in case RIT No. 080/2004, should be noted. In this case, 8 Mapuche (including two *longko* or traditional Mapuche chiefs - Pascual Pichún and Aniceto Norín – who are currently serving a sentence from another case for the alleged crime of "terrorist threat of fire") were accused of forming an illegal terrorist association, charges made by the Public Prosecutor's Office, the government, the local authorities, one logging company and various large landowners of the area.

It should be noted that use of anti-terrorist law N° 18,314 in Chile to try Mapuche has been questioned by human rights defenders and international human rights bodies.[8] This is because this legislation enables procedural guarantees to be curtailed, to the detriment of those under investigation. The law therefore enables the use of so-called "faceless" witnesses or experts, increased periods of detention, increased periods of investigational confidentiality, and substantially increased penalties for the crimes in question.

This ruling brought a long case against the Arauco Malleco Coordinating Body of Communities in Conflict (*Coordinadora de Comunidades en Conflicto Arauco Malleco*) to an end. And although the ruling made no comment as to whether the Mapuche were terrorists or not, or whether the crimes for which they had been tried were terrorist acts or not, in practice it questioned the government and Public Prosecutor's efforts to use anti-terrorist legislation to bring Mapuche to justice for actions committed in the context of land conflicts in the south of the country.

In March 2005, in another issue related to the legal system, the end of the investigation into the death of Alex Lemún Saavedra was decreed, a 17-year-old boy who was shot dead by police during their investigations on a logging estate being occupied by the Mapuche. The military court that heard the case decided that, on this occasion, there had been no crime because - according to the defence put forward by the police officer - he had shot at the youth in self-defence. This was despite the fact that the meticulous investigation brought to light no evidence of any shots other than those fired by the police, leaving those responsible for his death unpunished.

It must finally be noted that, during 2005, numerous complaints were made regarding the excessive use of violence on the part of the police force against indigenous people, organisations and communities when enforcing legal procedures, these actions causing devastating consequences for their victims.[9] There were many cases in which the police acted in an excessive and disproportionate manner in the context of judicial actions – eviction orders and search warrants - against Mapuche individuals and communities, with the consequence of a great many people being arrested or injured.[10]

Conclusion

In summary, during 2005 – which formed the last year of President Lagos' government - far from moving towards greater recognition of and respect for indigenous rights in the country, the situation of legal defencelessness of those very rights continued. In addition, and as a consequence of the development of a contradictory public policy in relation to these peoples, their territorial rights continued to be violated by investment projects affecting their lands and natural resources, as did the individual rights of their community members, such as the right to liberty and judicial guarantees, criminalizing their demands and protests for land.   ❏

Notes and references

1   The results of the 2002 census, in which 692,000 people (4.6% of the total) stated
    that they belonged to an indigenous people, contrasts with the census of 1998 in
    which 998,000 (1,350,000 including the under 14s) did so.
2   In line with the government's proposal, the final paragraph of article 1 was re-
    placed as follows:
    "... the law shall guarantee the right to conserve, develop and strengthen the spiritual,
    social and cultural identity, languages, institutions and traditions of the indigenous
    peoples that live on the national territory".
3   While poverty affects 35.6% of the indigenous, it affects only 22.7% of the non-
    indigenous. Average indigenous incomes are less than half that of the non-in-
    digenous population (World Bank, 2001, in Stavenhagen's (UN Rapporteur)
    2003 report from his mission to Chile).
4   See www.mapuexpress.net
5   This is aggravated by the rise in value of the lands being acquired by CONADI
    for the Mapuche in the south of the country, which has quadrupled over the last
    decade according to CONADI statistics (2005). To tackle this situation, the Com-
    mission for Historic Truth and New Treatment, in its final report for 2003, pro-
    posed state expropriation as a way of resolving the problem of lands misappro-
    priated from the Mapuche in the past (see www.coordinacionindigena.cl), al-
    though this has not been considered to date.
6   The Origins Programme, funded by the Inter-American Development Bank and
    the Chilean state, has been trying to tackle this problem, often without success,
    since it was established in 2001.
7   See www.observatorioderechosindigenas.cl
8   The international bodies that have questioned the use of this legislation against
    the Mapuche include: the International Human Rights Federation (2003), Am-
    nesty International (2004), Human Rights Watch and the Indigenous Peoples'
    Human Rights Watchdog (2004). To this must be added the concern of and rec-
    ommendation made on this issue by the UN Special Rapporteur for Indigenous
    Rights (2003), and the UN Committee on Economic, Social and Cultural Rights
    (2004).
9   The Health Service of Araucanía Norte, a government organisation, published a
    report in 2004 giving an account of the psychological effects caused by police
    repression, particularly among boys and girls living in the indigenous commu-
    nities in Araucanía.
10 By way of example, we can mention the eviction from the Las Encinas indige-
    nous home ("hogar indígena") in Temuco during September 2005, which resulted
    in 54 students being arrested, a number of them with injuries of varying natures
    and degrees. Also the eviction of Mapuche students from Temuco cathedral
    during October, and the dramatic raids on rural Mapuche communities follow-
    ing the fire at the family home of farmer Jorge Luschsinguer, which took place
    in April 2005.

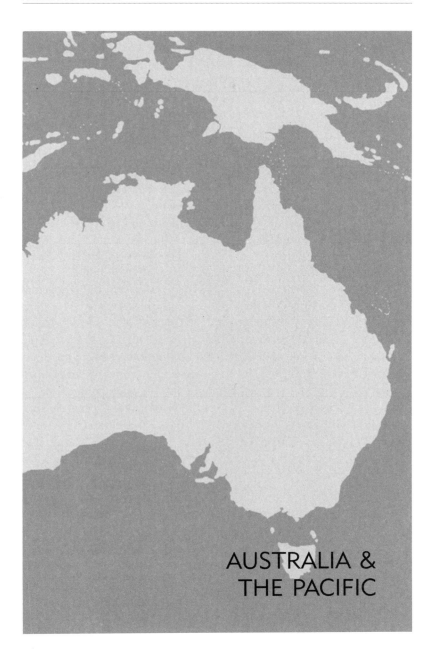

AUSTRALIA &
THE PACIFIC

AUSTRALIA

A round two and a half percent of Australian citizens identify as indigenous, and this proportion continues to grow. Although indigenous peoples belong to hundreds of different cultural communities and language groups, the common experiences of colonization have led to the formation of a national indigenous identity and political movement. A prominent cultural and political distinction, however, exists between the Torres Strait Islander people of Northern Queensland and other groups (often collectively termed "Aboriginal").

Subjected to violent dispossession, marginalization and strict state control since the time of white settlement, the indigenous population carries a heavy socio-economic burden. The gap between indigenous and non-indigenous life expectancies remains stable at about 20 years, less than ten percent of the indigenous population has completed senior schooling, and access to basic services in remote communities is limited. Nor have the many fundamental political demands of indigenous Australians been met. Despite fitful political progress that led to the granting of citizenship in the 1960s, and limited autonomy and land rights during the 70s, 80s and 90s, there has never been any mainstream recognition of indigenous sovereignty. A state apology for the "stolen generations" of removed and institutionalized indigenous children remains unforthcoming.[1]

The Howard paradigm

In the 1990s, public support was growing for formal political "reconciliation" between indigenous and non-indigenous Australians. There was even support for the drafting of a treaty, to establish political relations of equality in the absence of a historical "founding docu-

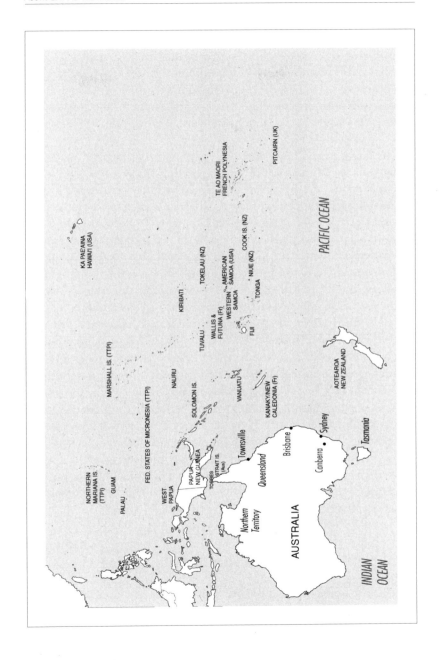

PITCAIRN (UK)

TE AO MAORI
FRENCH POLYNESIA

PACIFIC OCEAN

KA PAE'AINA
HAWAI'I (USA)

COOK IS. (NZ)

TOKELAU (NZ)

WESTERN
SAMOA (USA)
AMERICAN

NIUE (NZ)

KIRIBATI

TONGA

WALLIS &
FUTUNA (Fr)

FIJI

MARSHALL IS. (TTPI)

TUVALU

NAURU

AOTEAROA
NEW ZEALAND

FED. STATES OF MICRONESIA (TTPI)

VANUATU

SOLOMON IS.

KANAKY/NEW
CALEDONIA (Fr)

NORTHERN
MARIANA IS.
(TTPI)

GUAM

PALAU

WEST
PAPUA

PAPUA
NEW GUINEA

TORRES
STRAIT IS.
(Aus)

Townsville

Brisbane

Sydney

Tasmania

Northern
Territory

Queensland

Canberra

AUSTRALIA

INDIAN
OCEAN

ment" recognizing mutual sovereignty. By the time the Reconciliation Commission delivered its recommendations in 2000 after a 12-year process of consultation, however, the political landscape had changed. The progressive Labor federal government was gone, replaced in 1996 by a conservative coalition dedicated to governing for the "forgotten" white mainstream. Its leader, John Howard, has overseen a "revolution in indigenous policy".[2]

His strategy has been to focus attention on "practical" issues of indigenous health and education, separating these from "symbolic" issues of rights and historical injustice. The latter concerns are then dismissed as being self-indulgent, divisive and counterproductive. Federal outrage over indigenous disadvantage is long overdue, but Howard's particular approach has undermined indigenous autonomy and progress towards reconciliation. Firstly, he has focused attention on indigenous responsibility for indigenous problems, highlighting "black-on-black" violence, alcoholism and welfare dependence. By rejecting historical injustice and marginalization as contributing factors, he has eliminated the moral imperative for settler Australia to take responsibility for or make concessions to the indigenous population. Secondly, he has sought to integrate indigenous individuals into the Australian economic and political "mainstream". They can only enjoy the benefits of economic and social equality if they enter the settler community on *its* terms, leaving behind collective indigenous identities and political grievances. Needless to say, the political projects of indigenous self-determination and national reconciliation have disappeared from public debate under the current government.

In 2005 Howard continued his program of reform, building on major changes made in 2004. His government also flagged its intentions of making further legislative changes in the near future.

Sharing responsibility, denying rights

In 2004 Howard made his boldest move in the sphere of indigenous politics - abolishing the Aboriginal and Torres Strait Islander Commission (ATSIC). This was a nation-wide body elected by indigenous peoples, designed to both provide a legitimate elected leadership capable of advocacy and negotiation and to administer funds and provide services to indigenous communities. This dual role caused some problems to ATSIC, which found itself in the difficult position of both taking money from the government and criticizing its policies. It was increasingly plagued by allegations of corruption and disconnection from the indigenous grassroots membership. The surfacing of decades-old rape charges against its elected president gave Howard his opening. On 16 March 2004, ATSIC was abolished by parliament, and replaced with the National Indigenous Council (NIC), an advisory panel of "distinguished indigenous leaders" to be appointed by the government. Service delivery was returned to mainstream government departments.

ATSIC had provided a system of allocating funds and handling specific requests for resources and infrastructure. In its absence, "Shared Responsibility Agreements" allowing indigenous communities to negotiate directly with the government have been introduced. The first and most controversial of these agreements was struck in December 2004 with the Western Australian community of Mulan. This isolated community had been petitioning unsuccessfully for petrol pumps to be installed, and finally decided to cut a deal with the federal government. In return for the A$172,000 needed to install the pumps, the community leadership would undertake several hygiene programs, including ensuring that children's faces would be washed daily. In 2005, 120 more shared responsibility agreements were signed with Aboriginal communities across Australia, making them a major part of funding allocation and a significant new political development. The Woorabinda community in Queensland procured a public pool, go-karts and sports facilities with the promise to increase school attendance by enforcing a "no school, no pool" policy, while Pipalyatjara in Southern Australia gained a mechanic's workshop on the undertaking that no services would be provided free of charge to friends or relatives.

It is not yet clear how the government will enforce the terms of these agreements, with Howard only promising a "commonsense response" in the event of non-compliance. While some indigenous people defend Shared Responsability Agreements, others in the broader indigenous

community see them as patronizing and controlling. Aboriginal leader Mick Dodson emphasizes that public infrastructure and services
are rights, not concessions or handouts. To access basic services and
infrastructure available to all non-indigenous Australians, Aboriginal
communities are forced to "sit up and beg".[3] Aboriginal Senator Aden
Ridgeway believes that the system "has the potential to turn into
blackmail".[4] Perhaps the most fundamental objection is that shared
responsibility agreements focus on individual behaviour and ignore
structural and systemic aspects of indigenous disadvantage.[5]

Still, considering the dire needs of many indigenous communities,
it is likely that they will continue to sign up. In fact, these communities
may be playing the government's game better than it realizes - it has
recently become clear that Mulan had introduced the hygiene measures
and face washing long before striking any deal over petrol pumps.

Privatization of communal land

Movement toward tenure reform on indigenous land has been ac-
celerating over the past year. Currently, land returned to indigenous
peoples under native title and land rights is owned collectively by the
community, and is inalienable. Around twenty percent of Australia is
owned by indigenous groups or is the subject of ongoing native title
claims (most of this land is in the arid interior, where late settlement and
unsuitable farming conditions meant the indigenous population was
not forcibly dispossessed). Debate now centres on whether communal
ownership is socially desirable and economically viable.

Howard made his position clear early on, stating that he is "looking
more towards private recognition of Aboriginal title".[6] His government
argues that, while indigenous people may be rich in communal assets,
they are unable to convert these into steady incomes or enter the mainstream economy. This is summed up in the now-popular saying that
Aborigines are "land-rich but dirt-poor". Greater individual control of
assets would allow indigenous people to borrow against their assets,
and convert them into money through sale and lease.

The Northern Territory has long been a proving ground for federal indigenous policy. In 1976, it became the site of the first (and still the most comprehensive) Aboriginal land rights legislation. On 5 October 2005, Minister for Indigenous Affairs Amanda Vanstone announced that it would become a test case yet again. The Aboriginal Land Rights (Northern Territory) Act 1976 will be reformed to allow the government to lease townships from indigenous collective owners, and then sub-lease this land to others. Under the government's proposal, the terms of these leases would be set at 99 years, and the maximum annual rent payable to indigenous communal owners at 5 percent of the total land value.

Several prominent Aboriginal political figures have expressed support for this position, but many inside and outside the indigenous community fear that it marks a gradual rolling back of land rights and native title. If this proposal is in fact the first move in a political campaign to introduce freehold title on indigenous land, then indigenous communities will be facing a major attack on their rights and communal identity. Freehold systems in places such as Alaska and Papua New Guinea have led to indigenous social and political fragmentation, and in many cases to loss of land altogether. Vanstone, however, assures us that "despite what you may hear, I can confirm that no changes are planned to the inalienable communal nature of Aboriginal land".[7]

Dismantling an indigenous "eyesore"

The collection of tents outside Canberra's old parliament house has long been a site of indigenous organization and protest. This "tent embassy" was established in 1972 to advance indigenous land rights and sovereignty and to represent the Aboriginal nations. Over time, many white politicians have found themselves pulling up a folding chair to discuss issues with indigenous activists at the site, but there have also been repeated attempts to close the embassy down.

The most recent attack began in February 2005 when government Senator Gary Humphries announced a new inquiry into the relevance of the site:

The embassy as it stands is doing more harm than good to the reconciliation process. It has gone beyond the role an embassy serves, becoming an unattractive and intimidating camping ground. This is not appropriate for the parliamentary triangle.[8]

Released in December 2005, the report recommends the removal of permanent campers and the establishment of an "educational and historical centre". Michael Anderson (co-founder of the original embassy) said that this attempt to memorialize the site was inappropriate because the struggle for rights and recognition was not yet over.[9]

Building regional connections

As opportunities for political expression of indigenous aspirations within the Australian political context narrow, indigenous people are increasingly looking to regional and international fora. In 2005, Australian indigenous activists began to work more closely with Pacific indigenous groups and play a more prominent role in regional politics.

From April 26-28, 2005, the Pacific caucus of Australian and Pacific indigenous representatives met in Brisbane to prepare for the UN Permanent Forum on Indigenous Issues meeting in May in New York. At this meeting, Aboriginal barrister and leader Mr Mick Dodson took over the Pacific indigenous seat at the UN from Ms Mililani Trask of Hawaii. The Caucus agreed that there was little to be gained and much to be lost by working within the APEC (Asia Pacific Economic Cooperation) regional structures, which are dominated by great power interests. It also highlighted the fact that the UN Millennium Goals offered little to indigenous peoples. They undertook the substantial challenge of increasing the profile of regional indigenous issues at an international level, and of working together to gain greater respect for indigenous issues within Pacific nations.

The Australian political context is unique, and its Aboriginal people have a set of needs somewhat different from their Torres Strait Islander and Pacific counterparts. Nonetheless, basic issues of dispossession, land rights and political marginalization remain the same, and the benefits of working together to address these issues have not fully been appreciated. Despite differences of emphasis, the Australian and Pacific indigenous representatives have made a commitment to pool knowledge and experiences and to combine in international political action.

Conclusion

The federal government's attempts to "share responsibility", reform land tenure and archive the tent embassy are all part of a broader project: the exclusion of rights-based discourse and *collective* indigenous experiences, identities and demands from the public sphere. In their place, individualized concepts of responsibility and agency have become the staples of mainstream indigenous politics. Instead of viewing indigenous people as an autonomous group that must be integrated into the national political framework, they have been redefined as individuals who must one by one enter the pre-existing "mainstream" society and economy.

As noted above, indigenous commentators are divided on the value of the Howard approach. Some reject it altogether, while others are prepared to engage in dialogue with the government. But even those most enthusiastic about the new schemes give hints that they have not relinquished dreams of political recognition and social justice. In a BBC interview, NIC member Warren Mundine stated that supporting welfare and land reform does not "mean we've given up on a treaty, an apology and any compensation due to us. By having a strong economy and a healthy, educated and safe society, we are better able to fight for our rights and social justice."[10] He and other indigenous leaders display a pragmatic understanding of Australian political realities; after nine years of Howard's agenda dominating and reshaping public life, social justice and rights-based platforms are unlikely to win any political popularity awards. At some point in the future, however, the basic issues of indigenous/settler relations will re-emerge and demand resolution. Paradoxically, if Howard does succeed in addressing "practical" indigenous disadvantage and improving the day-to-day lives of indigenous peoples, they may be in a stronger position to fight for their basic political rights.   ❑

Notes and references

1   The "stolen generations" is a popular name for the thousands of indigenous children who were removed from their families by the government and raised in institutions. Children of mixed parentage were particularly targeted to further the policy of indigenous "assimilation" into white society. Although this government policy was formally discontinued in the 1970s, indigenous children continue to be removed at seven times the rate of non-indigenous children. For further information see *Bringing Them Home: Report of the National Inquiry into the Separation of Aboriginal and Torres Strait Islander Children from their Families*, 1997.
2   **Paul Kelly**, *The Australian*, 8 December 2004
3   **Carol Martin** interviewed on ABC radio, 9 December 2004
4   **Aden Ridgeway**, *Sydney Morning Herald* 11 December 2005
5   **Larissa Behrendt**, 8 December 2004
6   Howard quoted in *The Australian* 19 February 2005
7   Government brochure: *Northern Territory Land Rights Act: Unlocking the potential* www.oipc.gov.au/documents/OIPC_LandRightsActBrochure.pdf
8   Senator Gary Humphries, media release 16 February 2005
9   *The Australian* 26 December 2005
10 4 February 2005

THE ISLANDS OF THE PACIFIC

The Pacific is a vast region covering 32 million square kms and a third of the earth's surface. Possessing over 10,000 islands with a landmass of 130,000 sq. kms, it is home to 11.3 million people. This vast expanse of ocean has 22 island nations, 14 of whom have achieved political independence, while the remaining are still under colonial rule.

Self-determination

The issue of self-determination will continue to be a major concern for the 3 million indigenous peoples of the Pacific islands in the fore-seeable future. Self-determination is applied differently and at different levels to the occupied nations. There are two groups that are now rallying for a resolution to their problems under the UN Second Decade of Decolonization that started in 2001 and will end in 2010. The first group consists of 5 territories that are on the UN List for Decolonization.[1] These include Guahan (Guam), American Samoa, Kanaky (New Caledonia), Tokelau and Pitcairn. These territories are self-governing according to the UN decolonization terminology. They are effectively in the process of decolonization. The second group consists of territories that are not on the UN List and are fighting an uphill battle to get listed in order to be given the due process. These countries include West Papua (Indonesian New Guinea), Te Ao Maohi (French Polynesia), Wallis and Futuna, the Moluccas and Rapanui (Easter Island).

The Pacific Islands Forum and the Pacific Plan

The Pacific Islands Forum is the South Pacific region's inter-govern-
mental organization with 16 full member states and three observers
(French Polynesia, New Caledonia and Timor Lorosa'e). In the October
2005 meeting of Forum Leaders in Papua New Guinea, French Polynesia gained Associate Membership following a review of membership categories. The aim of the Forum is to enhance regional cooperation.

The better part of 2004 and 2005 saw the Pacific Islands Forum Secretariat (PIFS) assembling together an initiative called the Pacific Plan
which will have a direct bearing on the lives of all those who call the
Pacific their home. The goal of the Pacific Plan is to: "Enhance and
stimulate economic growth, sustainable development, good governance and security for Pacific countries through regionalism".

For the region's indigenous peoples, a small breakthrough in the
Plan under sustainable development is the "recognition and protection of cultural values, identities and traditional knowledge". The Plan
supports the development of a strategy to maintain and strengthen
Pacific cultural identity and the creation of an institution to advocate
for and protect traditional knowledge and intellectual property
rights.

In all, PIFS spent one year drawing up this new model, which involved broad consultations with all Forum member states and an array of stakeholders. But much criticism surrounded the development
of the plan. Some of the concerns were directed at several of the defini-
tions the Plan held on its key objectives. Another was the hurried way
in which the consultation process was carried out and, in most cases,
many Pacific peoples felt that adequate opportunity was not afforded
to Pacific Island communities to review the plan and to comment on its
relevance for its peoples. In March 2005, Pacific indigenous peoples
from 16 different countries attending a Pacific Regional Consultation
on the UN Permanent Forum on Indigenous Issues called for a moratorium on the plan because the plan "fails to provide evidence that its

implementation will result in any social, economic, cultural or political benefit to the people of the Pacific Basin".

In September, another call was made by 12 Pacific regional non-governmental organizations for the Pacific Forum Leaders to heed the calls of their peoples and consider extending the consultation period. Despite all this, this controversial Plan was endorsed in October 2005 at the Forum Leaders' meeting in Papua New Guinea.

Instability within traditional structures

In connection with the decolonisation processes, the Pacific island states are still working out the complex integration of old and new systems of governance. In the process of nation building, the island communities are often at odds with traditional political and cultural systems and processes.

In modern systems of governance, individual merit, neutrality, equality before the law, freedom of expression and the rights of the individual form the basis. In traditional governance systems, however, it is obligatory for people to be loyal to kin and community, and adhere to consensual and consultative values. These systems tend to be dominated by male elders, do not encourage collective thinking or the participation of women and youth in decision-making processes, and roles are traditionally defined for men and women in general.

A community governance assessment conducted by the Asian Development Bank in 20 communities of four Pacific island countries (Fiji, Vanuatu, Solomon Islands and Kiribati) in 2004 showed two key findings:[2]

a) A decline in knowledge of community values and respect for chiefly authority, particularly among the young and more highly educated members is seen as contributing to the proliferation of land disputes at grassroots level and crime among young people. The lack of paid employment and income-earning opportunities at village level has made young people drift to urban centres creating problems of urbanisation and associated crime and drug abuse.

b) At the grassroots level, while there is little understanding of the national governance systems and processes, communities have high expectations that national and lower levels of government will provide basic public services such as health, education and access to public utilities. In the traditional structures, the distribution of goods and services by the chief is no longer prevalent. Community members would contribute time and resources to their leaders and, in turn, the leaders provided services, assistance and protection. There is much expectation that national and other levels of government will continue to provide these social, educational and development services.

There are three different political systems existing in the Pacific:

a) A constitutional monarchy exists in Tonga but, in practice, the King wields considerable power in that he appoints the Cabinet, which makes up one-third of the Parliament.

b) In the north, the Federated States of Micronesia and Palau have adopted the US presidential system with a Congress and an elected President who has executive power and authority. In both countries' constitutions, the Council of Chiefs is recognised and its main role is to protect traditional customs and values.

c) The remaining Pacific countries adopted a version of the Westminster political system, with political parties, a Parliament and an executive and judiciary similar to the structure maintained in colonial governments.

In general, the close interaction and fit between the traditional culture of leadership and administration and the Western democratic paradigm is lacking in the Pacific. In Fiji, the colonial administration coopted the traditional leadership structure via the Fijian Affairs Act of 1874. Through this provision, the Bose Levu Vakaturaga/Great Council of Chiefs, lower level chiefs and a parallel administrative system were established to look after the welfare of indigenous Fijians. The

President and Vice-President are appointed to their positions on the recommendation and support of the Bose Levu Vakaturaga. In terms of political power, chiefs must compete with ordinary citizens for political power in elections. This is not the situation in Samoa where only the "matai" or members of the chiefly caste can become parliamentarians.

For most Pacific island countries, democratic principles are legislated and generally observed and there exists a clear separation of powers between the legislative, executive and judicial branches of government. However, the political instabilities witnessed in Fiji during the 2000 coups have highlighted the fact that delivery of good governance and respect for law and democratic principles is fraught with challenges when traditional leadership is directly involved.

Carbon trading and sinks

As signatories to the 1997 Kyoto Protocol, trying to grapple with ways to immediately address their commitments to reduce greenhouse gas emissions by an average 5.2% over the period 2008-2012, Pacific Island Forum governments have welcomed a proposal put forward by the government of Papua New Guinea to engage the Kyoto Protocol's *Clean Development Mechanisms* (CDM). The name for a system in which wealthy emission-producing countries help finance clean energy projects in developing countries (carbon trading initiatives).

Leaders attending the 36th Pacific Islands Forum Meeting in Papua New Guinea (PNG) noted the initiative and welcomed PNG's offer to draft a concept paper outlining the purpose, functions, regulations and benefit sharing framework of carbon trading for Forum members.

In doing so, leaders noted the many benefits that Forum members could derive from CDM projects. Leaders also expressed interest in advancing the idea of recognizing the ocean as a "carbon sink", as the Pacific Island Forum Leaders' communiqué went on to state.

Since oceans, lakes and forests are natural carbon sinks or storage areas, it is quite vague as to what Forum Leaders meant in their communiqué. Whilst acknowledging the fact that the Pacific region has a vast ocean base, it is hoped the leaders are not seriously looking at the Pacific Ocean, where carbon is sequestrated and stored in repositories in the Pacific's deepest seabed, because some uncertainties remain as to the amount of additional carbon storage space available and whether such measures may lead to unintended environmental consequences.

The first Kyoto refugees on the move

The scientific panel advising the UN Environmental Program believes sea levels could rise by up to a metre by 2100 because of melting polar icecaps and warmer temperatures linked to burning fossil fuels and industrial greenhouse gas emissions. The Executive Director, Klaus Toepfer, stated in a world conference in Montreal, Canada that, "the melting and receding of sea ice and the rising of sea levels, storm surges and the like are the first manifestations of big changes underway which eventually will touch everyone on the planet". As a scientific prediction this is all well and good but for the Pacific islanders it is already happening. According to Pacific islands delegate, Taito Nakalevu, attending the 189 nations conference, "king tides are flooding many places across the region". In French Polynesia, unusually high tidal waves forced the evacuation of tourists from Raiatea in the popular Bora Bora archipelago.

In Kiribati, two uninhabited islands have already disappeared. In some places in this very long chain of Kiribati islands, the land is retreating or becoming submerged as the sea battles the coastline. On Carteret islands off Bougainville in Papua New Guinea, 2,000 villagers are preparing to move to Bougainville. Their subsistence economy is devastated, there is no fresh water and gardens are being destroyed by advancing salt water. It is the same story on the island of Tegua in Vanuatu. Tegua Island is claimed to be the first in the world to have moved its community because of rising sea levels. The Canadian government, in partnership with the South Pacific Environmental Program and the UN, has provided funds for the relocation of Tegua islanders. Vanuatu's National Advisory Committee for Climate Change coordinated the international assistance. In another small island state, Tuvalu, the government has approached Australia and New Zealand to resettle its entire population as the islands are submerged over the next 30 years.

Waste management and renewable energy

The small island states of the Pacific are doing their bit in response to the Kyoto Protocol. These initiatives may look insignificant to the big nations but, for the small island communities, these are important solutions to address immediate environmental concerns and to reduce dependency on imported sources of energy. Waste management will continue to be a big challenge for the Pacific nations, considering the fragile nature of the islands' ecosystem. Governments and NGOs have stepped up awareness campaigns to match the ever-expanding consumerism. This year recycling activity in Guam reached the stage where it has become an industry. The government seized the momentum to legislate and provide policy directives to protect the industry. On energy, Vanuatu and Samoa have developed alternative biodiesel fuel from coconut oil. Increased production of this energy source could offset imports of diesel oil. In another development, the Kanaky (New Caledonia) based French company, Vergnet Pacific, has successfully developed wind-farming projects (wind energy facilities) and is now ready to export this clean technology to neighbouring islands. Fiji has conducted feasibility studies and has already placed an order for 37 units of this technology. With the same strategy of renewable energy, the University of French Polynesia (UPF) has successfully run half of its establishment on solar power, and this will gradually increase to cover the whole university.

Trade agreements

Negotiations with the European Union
In a European Commission Green Paper of 1996, it was announced that the trade preference for ACP (Africa, Caribbean, Pacific) countries would be replaced with reciprocal rights for Europe's goods to enter

ACP markets. It claimed that one of the ways to strengthen the participation of ACP countries in the global economy was for them to em-
brace two-way (reciprocal) free trade. ACP countries were urged to
open up their markets and allow for unrestricted foreign investment as
this would offer them greater opportunities for growth instead of their
continued reliance on non-reciprocal tariff preferences. Negotiations
are to be concluded by December 2007 and the European Union (EU)
has sought a waiver from the World Trade Organization (WTO) for the
continuation of existing Lomé arrangements only until that date.

The European Commission (EC) negotiating mandate is premised
on regional economic integration amongst different groups of ACP
countries. In Phase I of the EPA (European Partnership Agreement)
negotiations, ACP governments failed to secure agreement from the
EC on a set of principles and baselines that would protect their interests when negotiations moved to the regional level.

The 14 Pacific ACP countries[3] are currently negotiating with the
European Commission on the formulation of a Pacific Regional Economic Partnership Agreement as envisaged under the Cotonou Agreement between African, Caribbean, Pacific countries and the member
states of the European Union. The aim of the EPA agreement as contained in Cotonou is to foster "the gradual and smooth integration of
the ACP states into the world economy, with due regard to their political choices and development priorities, thereby promoting their sustainable development and contributing to poverty eradication in the
ACP States" (Article 34(1)).

The term Economic Partnership Agreement gives the illusion that
negotiations are premised on cooperation and partnership rather than
profits and power. It is outrageous to claim that reciprocal free trade
access into ACP markets for European goods will promote sustainable
development and poverty alleviation. Reciprocal trade in goods will
threaten the survival of small local business and wage-earning jobs.
Free access for European agricultural products will undermine the viability of local food producers and intensify pressure on subsistence
farmers to move to male-dominated cash crop production for export.
There is increased threat of food insecurity and famine.

The lifeline for Pacific islands' exports has rested on trade preferences and these are vital for sugar and canned tuna. The WTO had
earlier agreed to the EU's proposal for a temporary waiver on preferences up to 2007 on sugar products from ACP countries. The latest
decision ensures these arrangements for preferences can no longer be
made, renewed or extended. Despite this bleak picture, in response to
the WTO decision, Fiji's Ministry of Foreign Affairs and External Relations stated that, in the follow-up negotiations in Geneva in 2006, their
negotiators would be advocating for special treatment as a country reliant on long-standing preferences for its sugar produce.

Melanesian Spearhead Group
The Melanesian Spearhead Group was formed following an informal
meeting between the heads of government of Papua New Guinea
(PNG), the Solomon Islands and Vanuatu in 1986. It now includes New
Caledonia. The bloc is the only sub-regional grouping to have its own
trade agreement. In 2005, the Vanuatu government imposed two bans
on imports of Fijian products. The first one was bread and breakfast
cereals. FMF (Flour Mills of Fiji) had been exporting biscuits to Vanuatu since 2001, raking in a total of about US$2 million annually. In
March 2005, Vanuatu imposed a ban on biscuit imports, apparently in
a move to protect its own biscuit manufacturing industry. In retaliation, in June 2005 Fiji threatened to impose a total trade embargo on
Vanuatu. The Fijian government's proposed reprisals were targeted at
Vanuatu's main income earners: kava[4] and aviation. Following the 16th
Melanesian Spearhead Group Summit held in August 2005 in Goroka
on PNG's Eastern Highlands, Vanuatu finally lifted the ban on biscuits
on 25 October. The Fijian government responded on 7 December by
lifting its ban on kava.

Pacific Island Countries Trade Agreement
This trade instrument was signed by Forum Island Country Leaders in
2001 and entered into force on April 13, 2003 after being ratified by 6
Forum Island countries. By July 2005, ten Forum island countries had

ratified the Pacific Island Trade Agreement (PICTA), namely the Cook Islands, Fiji, Kiribati, Nauru, Niue, Papua New Guinea, Samoa, Solomon Islands, Tonga and Vanuatu. The agreement aims to provide progressive cuts to tariffs that will result in free trade of goods within 8 years (by 2011) for the developing states (Fiji, PNG and Tonga) and 10 years (by 2013) for eleven other Forum Island countries. Sensitive products can be protected until 2016. Each Forum Island country has a schedule of tariff cuts and sensitive products. Legally, countries can withdraw by giving 6 months' notice.

One of the concerns raised regarding this agreement is that there is not much trade amongst Forum Island countries and therefore the costs of implementing the agreement will be high. Fiji is considered to be one of the main beneficiaries because production may be centralised here, but there is also concern that most of Fiji's exports are re-exports and therefore may not satisfy the Rules of Origin (40% local content) to receive duty free treatment under PICTA. Although confined only to goods, there are strong moves to include services in the Agreement.

FIJI

Land leases

Fiji has a complex land tenure system which, in many instances, has been attributed to the discord between indigenous landowners (native Fijians constitute 51 % of the population) and settler groups, especially the Indo-Fijian community.[5]

Given the track record of difficulties faced by the indigenous landowners to competitively farm commercially, the fact that the Native lands cannot be sold but only leased has been viewed as a striking disadvantage for both the national economy and the Indian farmers in particular. In order to rectify this situation, which has long been a particular problem of Native Lands in the cane farming areas, the Agricultural Landlord and Tenants' Act (ALTA) was passed in 1967, enabling agricultural lessees to obtain a maximum of 30-year leases. Because the sugar that comes from these cane-farming areas is one of Fiji's main export earners, the expiry of the agricultural leases under ALTA from 1997 on constitutes the most critical issue facing Fiji at the moment. ALTA was devised to provide lessees with a secure tenure for the thirty-year term of their lease. It applies to all lands under agricultural use with the following exceptions: lands under 1 hectare, lands held cooperatively by a group or co-operative society, un-surveyed areas, such as land in Lau, the interior of Namosi, and Native Reserves.

The problem with ALTA is that it only applies to new leases and does not allow for extensions once these leases have expired. It is not entirely clear what will happen to all leases that are due to expire from 1997 on.

One option that the government has resorted to is to extend the leases under the Native Land Trust Act (NLTA). However, this does not provide lessees with the same security of tenure that ALTA provides because, under the NLTA lease, extensions can be refused if indigenous landowners are able to convince the Native Land Trust Board (NLTB) that the leased land is needed for their own use and long-term welfare. Consequently, questions facing the country now are whether to extend the ALTA leases or not.

Not extending the leases will give indigenous farmers the opportunity to reoccupy and control their own lands, providing that they are now capable of competing commercially with other groups in Fiji. However, past trends and studies have shown that indigenous landowners are not as productive as the more experienced and better-equipped Indian farmers and this, in the context of Fiji's national economy, is of great concern to the government. Furthermore, with the non-extension of leases, potential problems that may arise would be compensation and improvements and who would pay for these, as well as identifying sites for the mass relocation of farmers. In 2000, the Labour Government under Mahendra Chaudhry's leadership relocated a few hundred farmers from the Western Division to Navua after the indigenous landowners did not renew leases. To this day, the government and the Fiji Labour Party are still trying to find solutions to this long elusive problem of Fiji's land tenure.

Extending the leases, however, ensures that Fiji's economy will not be adversely affected. But this measure may antagonize the indigenous landowners who have increasingly gone into commercial farming, and have been crying out for the return of their lands on expiry of the present leases.

Monasavu Landowners Compensation
In a landmark ruling reaffirming the importance of traditional rites in contractual arrangements, indigenous landowners of Fiji's largest hydroelectric dam site received the biggest ever civil compensation claim of F$52.8 million (US$30.5 million).

A group of 12 mataqali (landowning units) from Monasavu in the central highlands of mainland Fiji (Viti Levu) sued the Fiji Electricity Authority (FEA) after it reneged on a deal negotiated in 2000 to pay that amount in goodwill for lands surrounding the dam catchment area.

In his 27-page judgment in October, Justice Gerard Winter also referred to the "significant cultural impact" of traditional ceremonies, such as the sharing of yaqona (kava). FEA lawyers had argued that the yaqona ceremony performed after the 2000 Deuba Accord was irrelevant as the case was to be "determined by conventional legal principles and not by reference to traditional ceremonies". "The fact is, however, that such ceremonies are an every day experience in the lives of our citizens and have real meaning," Justice Winter said in his ruling.

Government and Military Stand-off
An example of the stand-off between government and military was evident when the Auditor-General reported to Parliament that his office had been denied access to some trust funds controlled by the Commander of the Fiji Military Forces. Most people viewed this as unfortunate, because the executive power necessary for prosecution is rarely exercised.

In the course of the year, the Commander made various demands publicly on government to withdraw the controversial Reconciliation, Truth and Unity Bill (which critics fear will further divide the indigenous Fijians and the Indo-Fijians); called for the removal of the Chief Executive Officer of the Ministry of Home Affairs and its Minister and later, towards the end of 2005, released a public statement of intention to relocate his office to the Ministry of Home Affairs headquarters. This was followed closely by an ultimatum to the government that if it continued with alleged plans to release those charged under the law because of their involvement in the 2000 coup and those that may be implicated, the military would take control of the government.

The government, on the other hand, remained resolute that the Commander should adhere to the rule of law and uphold the constitutional provision by ensuring that the military conducted itself subject to the control of the Minister of Home Affairs.

The stand-off continued for the rest of the year with neither parties relenting, thus causing more public anxiety over long-term security in the country.

TONGA

Elections and Split

The ongoing debate on democracy versus the monarchy continues to be waged in the Pacific's lone Kingdom, Tonga. This year, the Friendly Isles experienced new precedents in the area of politics. In March, the kingdom went to the polls to elect 9 members for a three-year term to the 30-member Legislative Assembly or *Fale Alea*. Tonga is not a democracy whereby its government is formed through popular elections, rather through the appointments made by the king.

There are renewed hopes that, in the near future, the august assembly will all be appointed via popular elections and, given the conservatism of the establishment, things appear to be moving slowly in that direction. In 2005, much to the surprise of many people, the king decreed that two cabinet ministers should be chosen from the ranks of "commoner" members of parliament (which is made up of 9 people's representatives, 9 nobles' representatives and around 12 ministers). Prior to this, power rested solely in the hands of the nobles and others chosen by the king, while the people's representatives were called upon to act as the opposition.

A record number of 64 candidates stood at the elections, including 6 women. Apart from the pro-democracy Human Rights and Democracy Movement of Tonga (HRDMT), most contested seats as individuals. The elections did not spring any surprises in the Tongatapu group, where the people's veteran politician Akilisi Pohiva remained the number one representative with 11,225 votes. In all, the elections were a victory for the movement as they secured 7 of the 9 available seats, the same proportion as in the last parliament.

Contrary to media reports, the pro-democracy scene is thriving in Tonga. This is in the light of the fact that one of the movement's founders and mentors, Professor Futa Helu, felt the movement was not tough enough on the royal family and too close to leading businessmen. This brought about much media attention around the fact that the apparent split would reduce public support for the HRDMT's candidates in the lead-up to the polls. This did not happen, though what is clear is that aspirations for democracy are thriving and, after 18 years, another faction has emerged to take up the same struggle in anticipation of a systematic and gradual reform that conforms to democracy's "uncertain" nature.

On December 15, 2005, WTO ministers approved Tonga's membership at the WTO Sixth Ministerial Conference in Hong Kong. Tonga became the 150th member of the organisation. Tonga is also the fourth Pacific island state to join WTO after Fiji, Papua New Guinea and the Solomon Islands.

PAPUA NEW GUINEA

Enhanced Cooperation Program

In August 2004, Australia sent several hundred policemen to train the country's police force in an attempt to curtail the escalating crime rate in an operation entitled "Enhanced Cooperation Program" (ECP). In

May 2005, the Australians withdrew after Papua New Guinea's (PNG) supreme court ruled their claim to immunity from prosecution in PNG unconstitutional. A 2004 report in The Guardian newspaper stated that Australia had tied the approval of an Aus$800 million aid package to the granting of immunity from criminal prosecution to the Australian personnel. In the same report, PNG Prime Minister Michael Somare rejected the call, pointing to his obligation under the constitution not to permit such special privileges.

A report in the newspaper, *The National*, carried comments from unnamed PNG officials who provided a mouthpiece for the sense of outrage in PNG. "We have taken offense to the attitude of Australian officials. Australia insists on its jurisdiction over criminal immunity for its personnel while Waigani (PNG Government) maintains that PNG's jurisdiction should be applied because PNG is not in a crisis situation, or a failed or weak state."

The PNG government was "clearly worried" that its Australian counterpart viewed their country as another target for the sort of treatment handed out to the Solomon Islands in 2003 when 2,000 Australian troops and police were sent to the Solomon Islands to restore order in what the Howard Government had declared a "failed state". Australia displayed its first demonstration of its newly bestowed role as deputy sheriff of the US in the Pacific and, in doing so, assumed the right to impose its commercial and strategic interests in the region.

BOUGAINVILLE

On 10 June 2005, Joseph Kabui was sworn in as President of the Bougainville Autonomous Government (BAG) along with two other members of the caretaker Cabinet: the Central Bougainville Women's representative; Magdalene Toroansi and Vice-President, Joseph Watawi. The support for independence (from Papua New Guinea) had given Kabui (his party the People's Congress Party had earlier polled 14 seats) a majority of 34 out of the 40 seats in the Assembly. The elections that started in May 2005 were in line with Bougainville's landmark 2001 Peace Agreement adopted on August 30, 2001. By 23 June, a 10-member Cabinet was established to manage the affairs of the newly formed provincial government.

The Papua New Guinea government would, however, retain regal powers relating to military, police and defense and external affairs, currency and the judiciary until the planned referendum on independence in 10 – 15 years' time.

At the inauguration of the new government, Kabui announced that his government would give priority to finding funds and that he would launch talks around the future of the Panguna copper mine. The sixteen-year-old crisis in Bougainville had arisen out of differences over the operating of the mine and had resulted in the deaths of 20,000 civilians. In response, PNG Mining Minister Sam Akoita emphatically stated that the Panguna copper mine would remain closed for an indefinite period and called for an agreement to first be settled among the landowners, developers, BAG and the PNG Government.

TOKELAU

Tokelau is a non-self-governing territory currently in the final stages of the decolonization process. Formerly a British Protectorate, Tokelau was administered from 1889 as part of the Gilbert Islands, now the Republic of Kiribati. But because of its geographical proximity to Samoa it was transferred to New Zealand in 1925 to be administered from Samoa. In 1948 Tokelau was incorporated with New Zealand but administered separately under its own laws and political system. It consists of 3 islands and has a national representative body of 27 members, which has the power to make rules and impose taxes. As a rule New Zealand, as the administering power, makes annual reports to the United Nations on the progress of the socio-economic and political situation in the territory. This year, leaders of the territory finalized their constitutional arrangements with New Zealand. They want to have a free association status with New Zealand. But as part of the UN decolonization process, the 10,500 citizens of Tokelau have to cast their votes in a UN-organized referendum. The referendum is planned to take place in February 2006 and, when completed, may see the creation of another new nation state in the Pacific.

TE AO MAOHI
(French Polynesia)

In 1946, France withdrew its Pacific Territories including Te Ao Maohi from the United Nations List of Non Self-governing Territories. Since then it has administered them as Overseas Territories of the French Republic. But, after France began its nuclear testing on the islands of Moruroa and Fangataufa in 1966, some political groups emerged in the Territory openly calling for independence, partly as a measure to stop the testing. France officially ended its testing program in 1996 after it had conducted 46 atmospheric and 147 underground tests.

This year, the 230,000 people of French Polynesia democratically voted conservative anti independence politician Gaston Flosse out of office. He had dominated French Polynesian politics for almost two decades. On 4 March, one of Te Ao Maohi's foremost pro-independence campaigners, Mr. Oscar Temaru, was elected President of the French Polynesian government. He is leading a fragile coalition government with pro-autonomy parties. Mindful of this reality, he did not push his independence agenda. Instead he negotiated with Paris for more autonomous powers. He advanced this with his long-held platform of seeking closer cooperation with independent countries in the immediate Pacific region. These include fisheries, economic cooperation and trade agreements with the neighbouring Cook Islands, New

Zealand and Australia. He also moved swiftly to appoint a Permanent Representative to Brussels to access the European Union for economic cooperation, including the possibility of replacing the Pacific Franc with the Euro. He also built on his successful campaign the previous year when his country was granted observer status with the Pacific Islands Forum (PIF), an annual summit of Pacific leaders, by pushing for full membership. This year's PIF meeting in Papua New Guinea granted French Territories Associate membership. This will further facilitate the expansion of Temaru's Pacific cooperation policies. His rival politicians tend to favour close cooperation with parties and institutions in France. Locally, his coalition government did not waste time in responding to the call by Nuclear Test Veterans Association, the Moruroa e Tatou to set up a Committee with financial assistance to prepare documentation on the effects of radiation on humans and the environment. This will help in the applications for compensation.[6] Temaru's accomplishments after only a few months in office began to strengthen confidence within his coalition as well as the Metropolitan government in Paris. For the first time in the relationship between French Polynesia and Paris, the French High Commissioner paid a courtesy call on the Oscar Temaru-led coalition government. Normally it had always been the other way round.

Nuclear test legacy lives on

In June this year, in two separate military tribunals in France, two veteran nuclear test site workers were awarded compensation or a pension for life. The first court case in Tours involved 65-year-old André Mézières, a veteran of the French nuclear testing in Reggane, Algeria in the 1960s. He was suffering from polymyositis, a slow, degenerative illness affecting his nervous system, particularly his muscles. His case was supported by the French Nuclear Testing Veterans Association, AVEN. The second case was in the harbour town of Brest, involving Mr. Michel Cariou from the Moruroa and Fangataufa testing sites in French Polynesia where 46 atmospheric and 147 underground tests were conducted between 1966 and 1996. Mr. Cariou had to have his thyroid gland removed, for which he claimed damages. The court established that his urine samples taken during the testing period contained strontium 90 at a concentration 45 times higher than normal. These two cases gave the Nuclear Test Veterans Association, the Moruroa e Tatou (Moruroa and us) of French Polynesia hope that their members too may also claim compensation. Their hopes were strengthened by a decision taken by the newly-elected French Polynesian government led by Oscar Temaru to set up a special Committee to study and compile a report on the effects of nuclear testing in Moruroa and Fangataufa. The report would be available in 2006 and could be used by the members of Moruroa e Tatou to support their claims.[7] While the victims of radiation pinned their hopes on these new changes in France, they and the rest of the Nuclear Free and Independent Pacific Movement were saddened by the loss of anti-nuclear Leader and former Prime Minister of New Zealand, David Lange, who passed away in August. David Lange was well known for introducing a law to declare New Zealand a nuclear free country and for stopping port calls by US warships.

KANAKY
(New Caledonia)

Political developments

After Kanaky's re-registration with the UN Decolonization Committee at the end of 1986, the French government moved to sign an agreement called the Matignon Accord with the coalition of pro-independence parties, the FLNKS (Kanak National and Socialist Liberation Front) on 25 May 1988. The agreement approved a 10-year development program that would end with a referendum on independence in 1998. However, the FLNKS realized that they needed more time and a new agreement called the Noumea Accord was approved to last the next 15 to 20 years.

One area that is very sensitive yet crucial for the Kanak people is migration policy. The current population of Kanaky is 230,000, which is an increase of 15% on the 1996 census. It is the duty of FLNKS to make sure that electoral laws make strict reference to migration policies. Twenty years could qualify a new migrant to participate in the referendum. The Kanak are preoccupied with devising and running local governments, and also competing in economic activity, especially the mining sector, which provides a steady income for the country. There have been successes in promoting Melanesian Kanak culture, especially in returning the names of rivers, mountains and other prominent landmarks to indigenous or local names in provinces and municipalities controlled by FLNKS. The FLNKS has also been doing well politically by winning enough seats in the May elections to be able to share power with the parties supporting autonomy. Interestingly, the government is led by two women, the President, Marie-Noelle Themereau, of Avenir Ensemble (Future Together), which is anti-independence but pro power sharing. Her Deputy, Dewe Gorode, is from the Palika Party, a member of FNLKS. Another big change in New Caledonian (Kanaky) politics is the defeat of the conservative anti-independence leader Jacques Lafleur of RPCR (Rally for New Caledonia within the Republic) by the pro-autonomy party in this year's elections. He has dominated New Caledonian politics and government for over two decades.

Mining

Canadian mining giants faced unyielding opposition from all sides in New Caledonia, following the exploitative way in which they had been conducting nickel mining in the Goro region. In a show of general outrage at the development of the Goro Nickel Project, Kanaks and New Caledonians, including locally elected officials, called for a halt to mining activities until certain standards had been met.

Kanak organization Rhéébù Nùù, which was established as a local monitoring body for Inco's Goro Nickel Project in order to protect the fundamental freedoms and newly recognized rights of the indigenous Kanak people from violations as a result of this mining project, issued a communiqué calling on Inco to suspend its operations because the company had failed to respond properly to environmental, social and economic concerns. The local communities in opposition to the project asserted, "that the Goro Nickel project does not fulfil the conditions of respecting the environment and even less the conditions for sustainable development". They further called for a suspension in construction of the Goro Nickel project and a halt to the vast campaign of misinformation around the current project.

Where previously the local French administration had bowed to Inco's demands, it now asked for basic guarantees on standards from Goro Nickel. President Philippe Gomez of the Southern Province, in a media advisory, expressed concern at Goro Nickel's unwillingness to respect advice and recommendations made by the province in consultations with the company.

The frustration with Inco's conduct extends up the ranks of New Caledonia's authorities, with the French High commissioner Daniel Constantin having been recently quoted as saying "INCO is lying to everybody".

NIUE

Uranium Mining

There was excitement in the air when news first broke in August that the tiny island of Niue could be sitting on the world's biggest uranium deposit. The question on many people's minds was whether tiny Niue could survive uranium exploitation, or whether it would end up like Nauru after the guano mines, unfit for human habitation, its cash bonanza wasted and its people dispersed?

An Australian exploration company first discovered the prospects and was reported to be on the verge of drilling. Junior explorer, Yamarna Goldfields Ltd., says geological modelling confirmed the potential for a uranium deposit on Niue "equal or greater" to that of the world's biggest deposit at Olympic Dam in South Australia.

The company has signed an agreement with Canberra-based explorer Avian Mining Pty Ltd to take a stake of up to 80 per cent in the project and to spend over US$920,000 on exploration work. Yamarna will now work to prove the tonnage and grade of the potential resource, after which it will prepare a statement on the impact of mining on Niue and apply to convert the current prospecting license into a mining lease.

Dr Satish Chand of the Asia Pacific School of Economics and Government at the Australian National University says that if a large mine were to be set up it would have a big impact on Niue and, if there were a big find, it would raise the challenge of economic management. He said that if the resources were managed well then it could be a boom for Niuean development. However, a statement from the Pacific Concerns Resource Centre cautioned Niue's leaders to consider the impacts uranium mining would have on their land and marine environment.

GUAM

Foreign military access and the setting up of bases or their expansion are viewed by US strategic thinkers as critical to achieving "power projection", "forward deterrence" and the ability "to impose the will of the United States and its coalition partners on any adversaries" (Catherine Lutz, Brown University).

Asian hot spots such as the Taiwan Strait, North Korea and developments in China of a rapid military build-up of new warships, submarines and aircrafts are lending support for more US power and presence in Guam because of its close proximity to Asia. In early November 2005, Ms. Madeleine Bordallo, the Guam delegate to the US House of Representatives, announced that Japan and the United States would begin moving US marines from Okinawa to Guam in 2008 and finish by 2012. Out of the 18,000 marines stationed in Okinawa, 6,000 would be deployed to Guam and 1,000 elsewhere in Japan. The Japanese and US governments intend to begin building facilities in Guam in 2006 including housing and medical facilities, schools, utility infrastructure and bases as well as training facilities both in Guam and on the neighbouring Northern Mariana Islands. The cost is estimated at more than US$4 billion.

A group of indigenous Chamorros has, however, expressed concerns that the planned deployment will result in more problems for the US territory. The leader of Nasion Chamoru, Ms. Debbie Quinata, expressed concern that the "militarisation of Guam is detrimental to the well-being of their people and the community as a whole", "...the Chamorros have suffered the sociological, political and cultural impact of military personnel in the local communities, the lack of concerns for the environment and unjust taking of prime cultural lands, not to mention the strain on our fragile and limited resources".[9] ❑

Notes and sources

1 16 non-self governing territories – most of them small islands in the Caribbean and the Pacific – figure on the list of the UN Special Committee on Decolonization, a body of 24 members established in 1961 and charged with bringing to self-government or independence territories originally voluntarily submitted by United Nations member states as non-self governing. In doing so, the administrative powers agreed to bring these territories to self-government, with the United Nations overseeing the process. The list has been under attack, since many territories that consider themselves non-self-governing are not included. –Ed.

2 **Mellor, Thuy and Jak Jabes, 2004**: *Governance in the Pacific: Focus for action 2005-2009.* p. 41. Asian Development Bank, Pacific Studies Series, 2004.

3 These are Cook Islands, Federated States of Micronesia, Fiji, Kiribati, Marshall Islands, Niue, Palau, Papua New Guinea, Samoa, Solomon Islands, Tonga, Tuvalu and Vanuatu. Kiribati, Samoa, Solomon Islands, Tuvalu and Vanuatu are classified as Least Developed Countries (LDCs). Six island states are designated by the Pacific Islands Forum as "small island states" (SIS): Cook Islands, Kiribati, Nauru, Niue, Republic of Marshall Islands and Tuvalu.

4 Kava is a plant whose dried roots make a fine powder used in the production of kava, a social beverage widely consumed in the Pacific. Known for its calming and stress reducing effects, kava is today also turned into pills and used to relieve pain and stress. –Ed

5 The people of Fiji are made up of Fijians (51%), Indians (44%), Europeans, other Pacific Islanders, overseas Chinese and others (5%). Fijians are predominantly Melanesian with a Polynesian admixture. The ethnic Indians descended from contract workers brought over in the 1870s by the British to operate the sugar estates. –Ed

6   These reports appeared on the Dateline TV Program of SBS in Australia and also
     in reports by the Institute for Human Rights Study and Advocacy in Papua,
     Church and NGO groups.
7   Quoted in *Pacific News Bulletin* articles and *Pacnews.*
8   *Air Force Times,* January 20, 2006.

WEST PAPUA

West Papua covers the western part of the world's second largest island, New Guinea, bordering the independent nation of Papua Niugini (Papua New Guinea). Around 240 different indigenous peoples live in West Papua, each with its own language and culture closely related to those of the peoples in Papua Niugini.

In the late 19th century, West Papua became a Dutch colony while the British controlled the northern and the German the southern parts of the eastern half of the island. After World War II, the eastern half was administered by Australia, and gained independence in 1975. The Dutch government also recognized the Papuan peoples' right to self-determination according to article 73 of the Charter of the United Nations, and made preparations for West Papua's independence. Indonesia, however, laid claim to West Papua, arguing that it was part of the Dutch colonial territory. In an agreement between the Netherlands and Indonesia, ratified by the UN General Assembly on 21 September 1962, the Netherlands was to leave West New Guinea and transfer authority first to a United Nations Temporary Executive Authority (UNTEA) and then, on 1 May 1963, to Indonesia. The Papuans were never consulted. The Agreement stipulated that the Papuans had the right to self-determination and that they would, within six years, and in a free and fair manner, determine whether they wanted to remain under Indonesian control or not. Indonesia, however, immediately established tight military control of West Papua and, in 1969, in a staged "referendum", 1,022 hand-picked people out of a population of one million were made to publicly declare loyalty to Indonesia. The international community turned a blind eye on this fraudulent "referendum".

Ever since then, the Indonesian government has maintained a strong military presence and has suppressed with brutal force any attempts of the West Papuan people to assert their right to self-determination. Military operations have above all targeted the West Papuan resistance movement, the Organisasi Papua Merdeka (OPM - Free Papua Movement), founded in 1965. At least 100,000 Papuans have been killed and many more dispossessed and displaced by one of the most brutal colonial regimes the world has ever seen.

Resource extraction and resettlement

The Indonesian government is extracting West Papua's natural resources on a large scale. Its forests are plundered and mineral deposits exploited without any consultation of the indigenous communities, and without any benefits flowing back to them. By means of a state-sponsored transmigration program that started in the 1970s, the Indonesian government has resettled up to 10,000 families annually from Java and other parts of Indonesia. In addition to this, an unknown number of people have migrated on their own to West Papua. It has been estimated that over 750,000 Indonesians have settled in West Papua, now making up over 30% of the total population of 2.2 million. It is feared that the Papuans will eventually become a minority in their own land. Resource extraction and resettlement have resulted in dispossession and numerous large-scale conflicts between the Papuans and the Indonesian army.

Indigenous peoples' survival threatened

Massive violations of human rights have been reported ever since West Papua was occupied by Indonesia.[1] The most recent comprehensive report was launched on 18 August 2005 by the University of Sydney's Centre for Peace and Conflict Studies and Elsham, the Institute for Human Rights Study and Advocacy, based in Jayapura, West Papua.[2]

Entitled "Genocide in West Papua? The role of the Indonesian state apparatus and a current needs assessment of the Papuan people", the report documents the ongoing human rights abuses, systematic violence, including rape, torture and destruction of property in the West

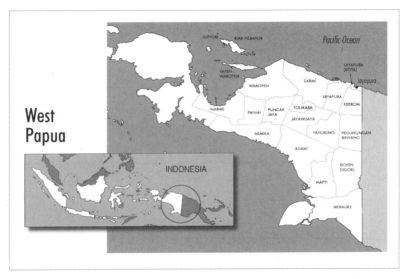

Papuan territory, occupied and claimed by Indonesia as one of its own provinces. In the authors' own words, it

> *details a series of concerns which, if not acted upon, may pose serious threats to the survival of the indigenous people of the Indonesian province of Papua. It covers the threats posed by the Indonesian military to the province's stability, the recent increase in large scale military campaigns which are decimating highland tribal communities, the HIV/AIDS explosion and persistent Papuan underdevelopment in the face of a rapid and threatening demographic transition in which the Papuans face becoming a minority in their own land.*[3]

Militarization

The report analyses in detail the role of the Indonesian security apparatus in West Papua and comes to the unambiguous conclusion that the Indonesian armed forces are the main source of suffering and instability in the province.[4]

A 'culture of impunity' exists in Indonesia which sees its highest manifestation currently in Papua and Aceh. Military operations have led to thousands of deaths in Papua and continue to cost lives, yet the Republic's armed forces act as a law unto themselves with no real accountability for crimes against the Papuan population. The report discusses a number of areas of Indonesian security forces' involvement, including: illegal logging and corrupt infrastructure and construction work; destabilization and manipulation of local politics, and orchestration of attacks blamed on pro-Papuan independence groups; the introduction of illegal arms and militia training and recruitment; and prostitution and the spread of HIV/AIDS.[5]

The deployment of 15,000 additional troops is planned for the period 2005 to 2009, which will bring troop presence up to between 45,000 and 50,000.[6] It is part of the armed forces' plan to set up a new division of elite troops in West Papua. Most of these will be stationed in the border area with Papua Niugini.

A new apartheid?

In their second chapter, the authors compare the restrictions on freedom of movement imposed by the Indonesian state to the system of apartheid in South Africa during the era before democratic elections and self-rule. Restrictions include the difficulty of free movement due to arbitrary acts on the part of the security apparatus, the requirement to have a travel permit when traveling to one's home village; arbitrary detention without charge for unspecified and often lengthy periods; Papuans who are members of the Indonesian army sometimes do not receive arms; Papuans often have to wait years to get a job while newcomers easily obtain one.

The demographic transition

As mentioned above, the Indonesian state has for decades been encouraging and sponsoring large-scale migration to West Papua. Officially, the migration program is a national government policy to develop West Papua and peripheral regions. The report however states that it leads to

> *a sharp inequity between migrants and locals. Papuans are becoming a minority in their homeland, unable to compete and being further stressed. Official transmigration programs and spontaneous migration alike have led to a rapid increase of the non-Papuan population in Papua, outstripping the Papuans, especially in district towns like Jayapura, which is immediately apparent in areas like shopping centres.*[7]

In transmigration areas, local communities lose their traditional land rights. One example given is Arso district in Keerom region. In 1970, the population numbered no more than 1,000. By 2000, it had reached around 20,000 and Papuans had become a marginalized minority.[8]

At the same time, low health standards and the bleak state of local clinics, which are ineffective, under-equipped and lack trained staff, result in high mortality rates among the Papuan population. Furthermore, HIV/AIDS cases in Papua are rapidly increasing. The report concludes that a "sustained, intensive, regular publicity program is needed on the dangers of HIV/AIDS and how to prevent it. HIV/AIDS will impact severely on the population growth and productive lives of Papuans."[9]

Failure of Special Autonomy

The report notes no noticeable progress with respect to the granting of Special Autonomy as set out in the Special Autonomy Law of 2001. Since the new government under President Yudhoyono came to power in 2004, however, even mere symbols of Papuan nationalism, such as the Morning Star flag and national anthem, have been denied once more. Furthermore, the government's proposal for an all-Papuan upper house of the local parliament has greatly diluted the powers envisaged for it in 2001, and provides for only 42 representatives. It is utterly cynical that the Special Autonomy funds of the central government should be used for military operations.[10]

At its Congress on 4 February 2005, the Papuan Customary Council *(Dewan Adat Papua,* sometimes also referred to as the Papuan Tribal Council) gave August 15 as the deadline for correcting the deficiencies in the Special Autonomy Law. Dissatisfaction with the law culminated in the council organizing demonstrations in many areas of West Papua, demanding that the West Papuan provincial government reject the unimplemented "special autonomy" offered by central government. Between 15,000 and 20,000 people demonstrated in the provincial capital, Jayapura, in support of the Papuan Customary Council.[11]

Human rights violations

According to the report, the human rights situation has deteriorated further over the last two years.

Particularly destructive have been the series of military operations which began in the Kiyawage area in 2003, then in the Puncak Jaya region in 2004/05 and since January 2005 in the Tolikara regency. According to the results of an investigation released by the Baptist Church of Papua in May 2005, military operations such as these have been cynically engineered by the TNI [the Indonesian armed forces, ed.].

Apart from the operations making large numbers of people homeless and leading to scores of deaths, the impacts have been exacerbated by poor delivery of aid to the refugee communities. Yet the siphoning off of Special Autonomy funds to the military to conduct these same operations, money that was targeted to help the communities through health and education projects, has made a tragic situation doubly evil.[12]

In September 2004, Law 27 was passed, providing for the establishment of a Truth and Reconciliation Commission by the Indonesian government. The authors of the report feel that President Yudohyono is trying to resolve the human rights violations of the past in a reconciliatory atmosphere but that "if no justice is served for the crimes in Papua there could be a feeling of betrayal and profound disappointment, compounding the lack of trust in Papua for Jakarta."[13]

Recommendations

The authors of the report conclude with the following recommendations:

- Indonesia to immediately commence demilitarization of the Papuan highlands, ending military campaigns and human rights abuses, which have included extrajudicial killings, rape, torture, arson, destruction and theft of property.
- Indonesia to cancel plans to deploy 15,000 additional troops to Papua. Existing troops should be transferred from military security operations against civilians to civil projects aimed at improving provincial infrastructure.
- An international agency (such as the International Commission of Jurists or Transparency International) to investigate the operation and funding of the Special Autonomy Law in Papua, including allegations by the Baptist Church of Papua concerning misappropriation of Special Autonomy funds by the Indonesian Army.
- An independent commission to inquire into the operation and funding of the Special Autonomy Law.
- The UN Refugee Agency to request immediate access to the Papuan highlands to assess the humanitarian needs of internally displaced persons who have been forced to flee their homes and villages as a result of army operations, especially in the Puncak Jaya region.
- Indonesia to grant access to UN mechanisms and international parliamentary and human rights delegations to report on the human rights situation in Papua.

- Indonesia to request international assistance in the investigation of crimes allegedly linked to pro-independence groups.[14]

Notes

1   Source for the paragraphs above: West Papua Action home page (http://westpapuaaction.buz.org/); West Papua Information Kit (http://www.cs.utexas.edu/users/cline/papua/); Mines & Communities website (http://www.minesandcommunities.org/Company/freeport6.htm); and J. Wing and P. King 2005 (see below).

2   **Wing, John, and Peter King, 2005:** *Genocide in West Papua? The role of the Indonesian state apparatus and a current needs assessment of the Papuan people.* The West Papua Project, Centre for Peace and Conflict Studies, University of Sydney, and ELSHAM Jayapura, Papua. The report is the result of research carried out by the authors during the years 2003 to 2005. It can be downloaded at http://www.arts.usyd.edu.au/centres/cpacs/wpp.htm

3   Ibid. p. v

4   Ibid. p. 2

5   Ibid. p. v

6   **Tani Amemori, 2005:** *West Papua military build-up threatens Land of Peace.* WestPan. Canada's West Papua Action Network.
      http://www.westpapua.ca/?q=en/node/399

7   Ibid. p. 16

8   Ibid.

9   Ibid.

10   Ibid. pp. 13 and 19

11   *Irian News* 10/19/05 (Part 1 of 2). http://www.kabar-irian.com/pipermail/kabar-irian/2005-October/000714.html

12   Ibid. p. 19

13   Ibid. p. 14

14   Ibid. p. 25

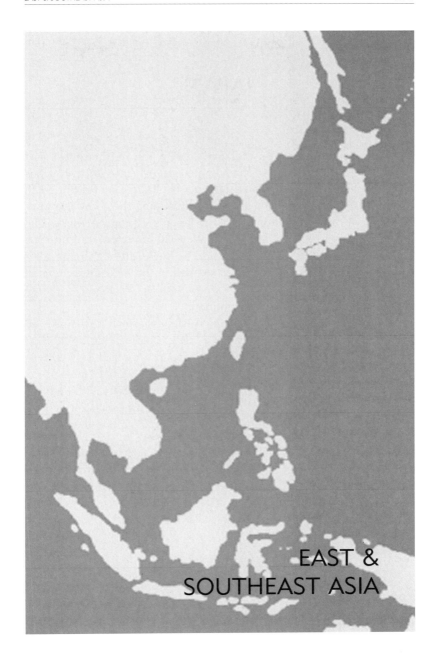

EAST &
SOUTHEAST ASIA

JAPAN

The indigenous peoples of Japan live in the northernmost and southernmost islands of the archipelago. Ainu territory stretches from Sakhalin and the Kurile Islands (now both Russian territories) to the northern part of present-day Japan, including the entire island of Hokkaido, which constitutes 20% of Japan's current territory. The greatest portion of Ainu land was unilaterally incorporated into the Japanese state and renamed Hokkaido in 1869. Although most Ainu still live in Hokkaido, over the second half of the 20th century tens of thousands migrated to Japan's urban centers for work and to escape Hokkaido's more prevalent discrimination.

The modern history of the Ryukyu Islands, which now make up present-day Okinawa prefecture, is a tale of colonization, militarization and struggle for self-determination. Japan colonized the Ryukyus in 1879 but later relinquished the islands to the United States in exchange for its own independence after World War Two. Although the United States' 27-year formal occupation of Okinawa ended in 1972 when the islands were reincorporated into the Japanese state, the US military presence increased. Today, the US still maintains 37 military installations occupying 20% of Okinawa's main island. It also controls 29 sea zones and 20 air spaces around the prefecture.

The Ainu

Today, the Ainu continue to face oppression at both institutional and individual levels. Despite the Japanese government's insistence that they enjoy rights as Japanese citizens, the government's persistent denial of their indigenous identity and right to self-determination prevents them from exercising their indigenous rights.

A new generation of Ainu in national politics

2005 saw a new generation of Ainu enter Japanese national politics, as well as national and international calls for recognition of Ainu rights. Ten years after Kayano Shigeru became the first Ainu member of Japan's parliament, a young Ainu woman named Tahara Kaori sought the position of Hokkaido representative to the *Diet* (the Japanese parliament). Tahara ran as a candidate for the Hokkaido-based, Hokkaido-focused New Party Daichi (NDP), which stands out as a counter to the ruling conservative party's efforts to push ahead with neoliberal reforms. Although the NDP is controlled by ethnic Japanese, its call for recognition of the indigenous rights of the Ainu is notable.

Although Tahara's candidacy was ultimately unsuccessful, it exemplifies a significant change in recent decades. Thanks in large part to Ainu rights activists and the many dedicated Ainu reviving and maintaining their cultural practices, more and more young Ainu are able to positively express their Ainu identity in public. However, it remains a central challenge for the Ainu to find the most effective means of collectively taking a lead in decisions about the future of their community, territory and resources.

Shiretoko declared a World Natural Heritage Site

A recent development that illustrates this challenge is UNESCO's designation of the Shiretoko Peninsula (located in eastern Hokkaido) as a World Natural Heritage Site. Although this promises a certain level of conservation of the biologically diverse region, ironically it also increases the potential for environmental damage as a result of the hordes of tourists that inevitably come with UNESCO recognition. Significantly, the World Conservation Union (IUCN), which serves as an advisory body to UNESCO's World Heritage Committee, called for the Ainu to play a central role in the protection of Shiretoko.

Although still largely pristine, the peninsula is threatened by the same state-led development practices that dramatically impacted on the rest of Ainu territory. In its examination of Shiretoko's qualification as a Heritage Site, the IUCN lists two issues of special concern: *protection of the sea* and *dams*. For example, the endangered Stellar sea lion inhabits the sea around the Peninsula, feeding on the schools of walleye pollack. Because the mammals often break fishing nets to reach the walleye, Japanese fisheries in the area view the sea lion merely as interference.

The more than 50 dams on the rivers around Shiretoko, ostensibly built to slow river bed erosion, were also criticized by the IUCN because they prevent the free movement required by salmon and other

fish to spawn. Salmon in particular were and still are considered a sta-
ple food of the Ainu, even though they are legally prevented from
catching them as they used to. At the request of the IUCN, the Hokkaido government will carry out a survey of salmon in 2006 to assess the
need for fish routes in Shiretoko rivers.

The IUCN pointed out that use of Ainu rituals and practices will
help promote ecologically sustainable tourism in Shiretoko. It still remains to be seen, however, if the national and local government will
indeed work together with the Ainu to consider appropriate ways of
employing Ainu practices in order to ensure sustainability.

The Ryukyus (Okinawa)

Massive presence of US military forces

The presence of US forces, and the resulting daily violations of the
Okinawans' indigenous rights as well as their rights as Japanese citizens, remains a key source of the Okinawans' most pressing problems.
Highlighting the United States' reliance on the colonial relationship
between Japan and Okinawa, 75% of US forces in Japan are located in
Okinawa, a mere 0.6% of Japan's territory. Moreover, all decisions regarding the US military presence in Okinawa are made between Washington and Tokyo, thus making Japan's denial of Okinawans' right to
self-determination the foundation of US military policy here.

In addition to increases in round-the-clock flight and ammunitions
training, US aggression in Afghanistan and Iraq has led to more crime
by US servicemen. The combination of being formally trained to resolve conflict through violence and the trauma of war itself has led to
a well-documented rise in the number of US soldiers suffering from
psychological stress disorders. A marked increase in violent criminal
behaviour among US servicemen stationed in Okinawa (and elsewhere) since 2002 reveals how the effects of this trauma are felt by
those who live alongside servicemen returning from war zones. 2005
saw both the Marine Corps and Air Force commands in Okinawa compelled to impose curfews on its personnel due to increased criminal

behaviour off-base, most notably the molestation of a 10-year old girl in July.

Okinawans are also affected by changes in US war targets and tactics. With the Japanese government's consent, the US built a live-fire urban warfare training facility just 250m from a residential neighborhood in the town of Kin. A year-long sit-in and formal opposition by the Okinawan authorities met with bittersweet success in September, when the US agreed to rebuild the facility away from town but insisted on using the current facility over the 2 ½ years it will take to rebuild.

Popular protests against military expansion

However, 2005 also saw achievements in the Okinawans' struggle to reverse the militarization of their lives and territory. Especially noteworthy was the continued success of a now decade-long popular campaign to halt the construction of a new US air base in the coastal waters of Henoko Bay. In March, a US federal judge denied the US government's motion to dismiss an Okinawan-led joint lawsuit to stop construction of the base. The ruling established the grounds for the case to move to trial.

In an unprecedented development, the widespread opposition to the new base – sit-ins, marches, hunger strikes, interventions at the United Nations, delegations to Washington DC, legal actions and daily non-violent direct action at the construction site for nearly 2 years – forced the US and Japan back to the negotiating table in October to revisit their agreement. Instead of abandoning the plan, however, the two governments announced what they called a "compromise": to merely shift the location of the new base closer to shore.

The 1.8km-long runway will now expand beyond Henoko Bay into neighboring Oura Bay. A large section of Oura Bay will be filled in to provide land for hangars, maintenance buildings and access to a deep-water pier. Building the base will thus involve massive landfill in an area known to be the habitat of the critically endangered Okinawa sea manatee and other endangered species. Environmental experts warn that construction and operation of the base will cause irreversible damage well beyond the area, dramatically transforming the culture and livelihoods of communities along the entire coastline.

Far from a compromise by the US, moreover, the October agreement fulfils plans created but not realized in the final years of the United States' formal occupation of Okinawa. The "new" plan is nearly identical to the military's 1966 plans to build an air base and a military port in the exact same location.

Although the October accord was a blow to those who hoped the project would at last be cancelled ‾ and could seem like the outright failure of the campaign ‾, to assume that the air base is now inevitable would be to miss the significance of what has transpired: the popular campaign prevented construction for a decade, ultimately derailing a major bilateral agreement. Moreover, the conviction and energy that made this possible remains strong

If anything, the revised plan merely demonstrates both governments' confidence in their ability to divide the Okinawan people over the base issue. However, by excluding Okinawans once again from major negotiations over US military presence in Okinawan territory, the US and Japan now face even greater local opposition. Five thousand Okinawans marched against the October agreement on the day it was announced. Recent polls show popular opposition to the new air base at over 95%. Not only has the previously submissive governor of Okinawa taken a strong stand against the revised plan, city councils around the island have passed formal resolutions opposing it.

Faced with such overwhelming opposition, the US government quickly resorted to tying its long-promised reduction of US forces to the new air base plan. In October, the US finally agreed to transfer 7,000 marines off of Okinawa. Confronted with even greater local resistance to the air base, however, the US announced in November that if the new plan failed "the marines would be obliged to stay". ❑

TIBET

A s in previous years, we include an article on Tibet in *The Indige-nous World* because Tibetans are confronted with similar prob-lems and the same lack of fundamental rights as indigenous peoples all over the world. The Tibetan Government in Exile in India does not regard Tibetans as an indigenous but as an occupied people.

Tibet was occupied by China in 1949/50. Around half of the 5.6 mil-lion Tibetan population lives in what China has named the Tibet Au-tonomous Region (TAR), while the other half lives in Tibetan areas now included in Chinese provinces. When Tibetans and Chinese speak about Tibet, they are not referring to the same thing. To the Chinese, Tibet is identical to the TAR.

As a result of having lost their independence, the Tibetan popula-tion is under pressure and marginalised by the large and growing number of Chinese settlers in Tibet. Their exact number is not known but they have economic and political power, and their position and impact on Tibet is therefore much greater than their actual number might indicate. Since the beginning of Chinese occupation, the Tibetan people have faced severe repression of basic human rights, most nota-bly the right to self-determination. They have also been excluded from active participation in the development of their country.

Political developments

In September 2005, the Chinese government marked the 40th anniver-sary of its establishment of the Tibet Autonomous Region (TAR). It was an important opportunity to reconfirm China's power over occupied Tibet. The event was officially celebrated by the Chinese authorities in the Tibetan capital Lhasa. In Europe, China chose two countries for its

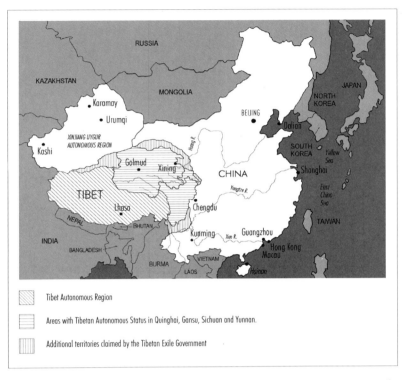

Tibet Autonomous Region

Areas with Tibetan Autonomous Status in Quinghai, Gansu, Sichuan and Yunnan.

Additional territories claimed by the Tibetan Exile Government

celebrations – Denmark and Italy. In Denmark, part government-financed institutions, including the Nordic Institute for Asian Studies (NIAS), were misused by the Chinese embassy to present its official view on Tibet at a seminar on China, despite protests from the Danish Tibet Support Committee.

Contacts between the Tibetan Government in Exile and the Chinese government continued during 2005. Two Tibetan delegations met with Chinese officials in Beijing in May and Switzerland in July. These continuing meetings are positive signs of a potential "opening up" of the Chinese government but they have not yet resulted in concrete moves towards negotiations. Some Tibetans fear that the Chinese government does not want to negotiate with the Dalai Lama and that it is awaiting the death of the now 70-year-old Tibetan leader in the hope that the issue of Tibet's status will disappear with him.

This fear was confirmed during the Fourth World Parliamentarian Convention on Tibet in Edinburgh in November, where 130 delegates representing 27 parliamentary groups supporting the cause met and agreed a resolution on Tibet. Along with a large number of Tibet Support Groups around the world, the parliamentary groups for Tibet have been instrumental in highlighting the issue of Tibet in the international community and bringing the concerns of the Tibetan people to the attention of the governments that have an influence over China. The resolution urges the Chinese leadership to commence negotiations and expresses its concern over development and human rights in Tibet.

Human rights

The human rights situation in Tibet remains grim. This was the conclusion of human rights reports during 2005. Despite China's pledge to improve its human rights record before the Olympic Games - to be held in Beijing in 2008 - little has been achieved.

In November, the United Nations Commission on Human Rights' Special Rapporteur on Torture visited China and the TAR. His conclusion was that although the situation has improved over the last years, torture and mistreatment of prisoners continues to be widespread. In his interviews with detainees, the Special Rapporteur observed fear and self-censorship. Although he could not make a detailed determination as to the current scale of abuses, he believes that the practice of torture remains widespread. Under international human rights law, governments are only permitted to interfere with the expression of political opinions and religious convictions when they constitute incitement to violence or a direct threat to national security or public safety. State surveillance of citizens with non-conformist views and severe punishments, such as re-education through labour - which is common throughout China and Tibet - leads to a culture of fear that is incompatible with the core values of a society based on the rule of law.

In Tibet, dissent of any form continues to be punishable by imprisonment and Tibetans are arrested for minor offences. The victims are often monks and nuns who uphold their allegiance to the Dalai Lama, for they are seen as endangering national security. The fate of some known Tibetan prisoners shows that prisoners still face unusual hardship. The number of political prisoners fell slightly in 2005, mainly as a result of the release of prisoners who had served their sentences. Fear of punishment keeps most Tibetans out of political activities.

Tenzin Deleg Rinpoche is still in prison (read more about his case in *The Indigenous World 2005, 2002-2003*). He was condemned to death in 2002 for his alleged participation in a bomb attack but the death sentence was commuted to life imprisonment in 2004 as a result of international pressure. According to some sources, he is in very poor health. The European Parliament appealed for his release in a statement on the situation in Tibet in March 2005. Bangri Rinpoche and his partner, Choedon Nyima, have been in prison since 1999. Bangri Rinpoche was head of an internationally-funded orphanage in Lhasa until it was closed down and he and several staff arrested on charges of "attempting to split the country". He has been hospitalized at least once during his sentence, and an eyewitness report cited by the International Campaign for Tibet in 2005 described him as being shackled to a bed by his wrists and ankles in a solitary ward, although he was too weak to move.

The 11th Panchen Lama, the now 16-year-old Gedhun Choekyi Nyima, has been held under house arrest in China for more than 10 years. Despite widespread international campaigns for his release and for independent visitors to be allowed to visit him, this was again denied in 2005 and his whereabouts remains unknown. During the 40th session of the UN Committee on the Rights of the Child, the committee expressed its concern over the boy's fate to the Chinese delegation and urged China to ensure full religious freedom.

A "work team" of officials at Drepung Monastery in Lhasa has been conducting patriotic education campaigns in the monastery since October. In November, the monks were ordered to sign a document denouncing the Dalai Lama as a "separatist" and to pledge their loyalty to the Chinese government by accepting "Tibet as a part of China". The monks refused and five of them were expelled from the monastery and handed over to the Public Security Bureau (PSB) Detention Centres in their respective places of origin. Following these arrests, more than four hundred monks sat in peaceful protest in the courtyard of the monastery. The protesters refused to follow the authorities' directives. They also called for the release of the five arrested monks. Fearing that the protest might escalate out of control, the government of the TAR imposed a crackdown and a curfew, which was later withdrawn.

The recent incident at Drepung indicates that although the authorities do permit the free practice of Buddhist rituals to some extent, there is strict control over religious life. In the eyes of Buddhist practitioners in exile, the control over monasteries and the ban on the transmission of wisdom from teacher to student undermines the ability of the Tibetan people to hold on to their spiritual and cultural heritage.

Development and economy

From a Chinese point of view, one of the major achievements in Tibet during 2005 was the near completion of the railway from Golmud to Lhasa. The railway is the most prestigious project within China's Western Development Programme (see *The Indigenous World 2005, 2004*), which has the objective of bridging the economic disparity between rich eastern China and the impoverished western regions. In Tibet, many of the development activities are concentrated around infrastructure. Tibetans suspect that the real reason for this is to enable China easier access to Tibet's rich mineral and other natural resources. The Tibetans say that this will make it easier for China to cart away resources to the mainland to fuel its development and to bring more Chinese settlers onto the Tibetan plateau.

They also assert that the vast majority of Tibetans do not benefit from the economic boom in Tibet. Chinese settlers are the main beneficiaries. The majority of Tibetans are increasingly marginalised and remain as poor as before, if not poorer. Recent reports show that Tibetans, apart from a small middle class, benefit little from the immense economic subsidies to Tibet. It is difficult for them to compete with the better-educated Chinese-speaking immigrants, who also have better access to those in power. A report from the Tibet Information Network in January 2005 showed that, according to official Chinese statistics from 2004, there have been drastic changes in the ethnic structure of the government sector in the TAR. The percentage of Tibetan government officials has fallen considerably. One reason may be the increased wages, which are now so high compared to wages in China that they attract many Chinese. Another possible reason is the fact that all applicants must now pass an examination in Chinese. Since more than 80% of the rural population does not speak Chinese, Tibetans are clearly discriminated against. If Tibetan language skills were a prerequisite for a government position in the TAR, Tibetans would be at an advantage. The new system is out of step with the Chinese law on minorities, in which the use of local languages is enshrined as a right.

In another report from September, the Tibetan Information Network showed that, according to Chinese government statistics, the level of education among Tibetans has fallen in recent years. The percentage of Tibetans with secondary education is around 15%, way below the average of 57% in China. One reason for the decline may be the low quality of schools, the high costs of schooling as compared to job opportunities, and the fear of many Tibetans that the schools are primarily a way of assimilating their children into Chinese culture.

China continues to promote Tibet as a major tourist destination, especially for the Chinese. In 2005, around 2 million Chinese visited Tibet.   ❑

TAIWAN

New act for indigenous peoples

The most important issue for Taiwan's approximately 460,000 indigenous peoples[1] in 2005 was the codification of the Indigenous Peoples Basic Act in January. This Act is the first legislative effort to address indigenous sovereignty and general indigenous rights issues. The Legislature gave the Basic Act a superior status to other legislation and made January 2008 the deadline by which all laws that are incompatible with the Act must be revised.

Many indigenous communities have continuously struggled for their livelihood, land and natural resources. Many of the current development projects and government regulations are designed to facilitate easy access to indigenous land and traditional resources on the part of corporations. Local communities have been fighting these development projects, including the Lao-nung River Water Diversion project, the Tai-an Hot Spring Resorts Project and the Sun-moon Lake Resorts Project, etc. In the newly codified Basic Act, article 20 clearly addresses the indigenous peoples' right to their traditional territory. It states: *"the Government recognizes indigenous peoples' rights to the land and natural resources"*. This article raises the importance of the many ongoing community-based participatory investigations of indigenous territories. It also provides an important legal foundation for the indigenous peoples' continuous struggle for their traditional territories and natural resources.

Since May 2004, there have been discussions proposing the inclusion of a special chapter on indigenous peoples in the Constitution. Although such an amendment has not yet been adopted, the Basic Act demonstrates that it is still possible to protect the rights of indigenous peoples by means of legislation.

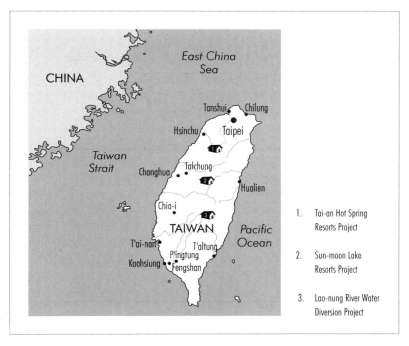

1. Tai-an Hot Spring
    Resorts Project

2. Sun-moon Lake
    Resorts Project

3. Lao-nung River Water
    Diversion Project

The Act has led to many disputes with other government bodies, whose authority has been challenged by it. Ironically, these disputes have highlighted the importance of a constitutional chapter that would provide the basic framework for indigenous sovereignty and the right to self-governance. In March, the National Assembly was convened to affirm a number of constitutional amendments. The proposal for the Special Chapter on Indigenous Peoples was not included this year but there is hope that indigenous sovereignty and the right to self-governance will obtain endorsement in constitutional revisions over the coming years.

Indigenous self-governance

The Saisiyat people[2] organized a preparatory committee for a Saisiyat Assembly in August 2005. The Truku people, after their successful campaign in 2004 that led to official recognition of their indigenous status as the 12th indigenous group in Taiwan, established a committee in October to advocate for self-government. In December, the Thao people also established a Thao Assembly, leading to the road to self-governance.

Reclaiming indigenous names

In 2005, the Taiwan government started a process of re-issuing national identification cards to all citizens. A campaign to reclaim indigenous names was mobilized by indigenous activists. More than a hundred indigenous persons were encouraged to register their birth names rather than the colonial ones that were imposed on them by the foreign ruling power. Although Taiwan's Ministry of Internal Affairs still declines to use the Roman spelling system without first rendering each person's name in Mandarin Chinese characters, the campaign has highlighted the more than two-decades-old demand of the indigenous movement to "reclaim indigenous names".

First iTV in Asia

Under the requirements of the Indigenous Education Act, the first Indigenous TV (iTV) was fully funded and established by the Taiwan Government on July 1, 2005. Although it is exciting for indigenous peoples to have a TV station devoted to them, the joy is tainted by the fact that this iTV has been awarded to a commercial television company through a bidding process. Commercial TV companies may not see indigenous issues as one of their major concerns, and commercial and political intrusion into iTV has raised concerns about the public service nature of the channel.

Unsatisfactory participation in international meetings

Although it is generally acknowledged that indigenous peoples are involuntarily governed by nation-states and their participation at international fora, such as those of the United Nations (UN), should not be denied them, the reality is quite the contrary. Indigenous peoples who are confined within Taiwan often find themselves falling through the cracks of member states at the UN and face constant constraints to their participation in international fora. Taiwan is not recognized as a member state of the UN. Its membership has been denied repeatedly, largely due to China's opposition.

The Ping Pu plains indigenous peoples

Indigenous Formosan Plains Peoples are collectively known as the "Ping Pu", a Mandarin Chinese term which means "plains". Like other indigenous groups in Taiwan, the Ping Pu are native Austronesian peoples. They do not identify themselves as Ping Pu but as 9 distinct peoples, each with its own language and cultural affinities.[3]

For the Ping Pu peoples, 2005 has been another year of frustration and further setbacks. Once again, their demand for official recognition as indigenous peoples was turned down by the Taiwan government. Despite claiming to uphold human rights for all citizens, the Democratic Progressive Party (DPP) government continued to ignore the real threat of cultural extinction faced by the plains indigenous peoples.

National and local associations of Ping Pu have organized a number of lobbying campaigns over the past years. These have included public hearings, press conferences, petition drives and even a lawsuit launched in 2005 to demand the restoration of their indigenous status and their historic indigenous rights. One of the main requests was for the establishment of a government council to look after the affairs of Ping Pu peoples and help to preserve their disappearing languages and cultures. However, these actions have been met with cold silence and continued stonewalling by the ruling DPP government.

The Taiwan government continues to deny the Ping Pu Peoples recognition of their indigenous status and continues to exclude the Ping Pu peoples from the indigenous political system and social welfare

scheme. Ultimately, the government's inaction denies them the possibility of obtaining indigenous status and self-governance.
❏

Notes

1   According to the Taiwan Government's Information Office, the number of indigenous people was 459,578 in June 2005 (http://www.gio.gov.tw/taiwan-website/5-gp/yearbook/p238.html (Jan 19, 2005)). –Ed.
2   See *The Indigenous World 2004, 2005* for a list of the major indigenous groups in Taiwan. –Ed.
3   Taiwan's Ping Pu Peoples are the Ketagalan, Taokas, Pazeh, Kahabu, Papora, Babuza, Hoanya, Siraya and Makatao (from north to south).

PHILIPPINES

The indigenous peoples in the Philippines are estimated at between 6 and 12% of the population. According to the standard 10% projection, they number around 8 million, comprising some 100 ethnolinguistic groups. The lack of basic aggregated data on indigenous peoples noted in the previous yearbooks still exists, such that one cannot give consolidated nationwide data regarding demography and human development indices. It is generally agreed that indigenous peoples are among the most marginalized groups, a situation that the promulgation of the Indigenous Peoples Rights Act (IPRA) of 1997 sought to address. After 8 years of existence, however, there is still much to be done.

Land rights

That indigenous peoples in the Philippines have managed to stay on in resource-rich areas after centuries of evading absorption into mainstream society means that they inevitably confront the difficulty of others being interested in those resources. Hence many of the problems indigenous peoples face are related to rights pertaining to access and control of the land and its resources. During 2005, the encroachment of mining companies, the intrusion of migrant landless farmers and the uncertain plight of indigenous peoples in Muslim areas continued. Issues regarding ancestral domains and protected areas, the imposition of infrastructure such as dams and plantation conversions also continued but did not receive as much attention in 2005 as in previous years.

Mining

Of the resources, minerals have taken a greater share of the limelight since 2004 when the government stepped up efforts to revitalize the mining industry (see *The Indigenous World 2004*). In most indigenous territories, big (thousands of hectares) or small (hundreds of hectares) mining possibilities have been identified or are already being pursued, many of them to the detriment of indigenous peoples. The hardships suffered range from being driven from their lands to being negatively affected by environmental and health hazards. In rare cases where there is a Memorandum of Agreement (MOA) between the mining company and the indigenous community, the latter is likely to experience non-compliance. Advocacy regarding mining, both pro and anti, stepped up in 2005. It remains to be seen how such advocacy is being undertaken at the community level, where it ultimately matters, because indigenous communities in the end are the deciding factors in allowing mining interests onto their lands or not.

Ancestral domain claim versus agrarian reform

Another land issue is the latent but emerging conflict between two distinct social-justice concerns pertaining to land – recognition of the ancestral lands of indigenous peoples and the awarding of lots to landless peasants. The conflict arises when the same tracts of land are claimed.

This is illustrated by a case in the central island of Mindoro. In 2005, the Buhid Mangyan found out that the Department of Agrarian Reform (DAR) had appropriated some 2,000 hectares within their ancestral domain claim. Peasant activists and their supporters could not understand why the Buhid Mangyan should deny landless farmers tracts within their ancestral domain claim when it was 93,000 hectares in size. This highlights two issues. One is that the majority of the populace sees land as property that can be owned and for which ownership can be transferred, as opposed to the view of indigenous peoples that land is a birth right that is taken care of rather than owned. The other is that the government has still not settled the matter of conflicting laws and policies on land ownership, use and management.

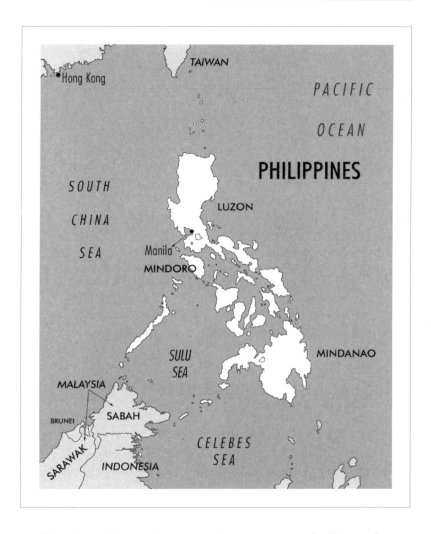

There is no data on how many hectares are involved in such conflicts nationwide. With the sheer number of landless peasants, however, it may be expected that the public and legislative sympathy will
not be in favor of indigenous peoples living on comparatively sparsely
inhabited tracts of land.

Indigenous peoples in the Autonomous Region of Muslim Mindanao

The Autonomous Region of Muslim Mindanao (ARMM) was created by an act of 1989 as one major step by the Philippine government to end the war with Muslims wishing to establish their own independent territory. In 2005, ongoing talks within a peace panel composed of government and Muslim representatives discussed the matter of indigenous peoples within the ARMM. The ARMM had declared that they would recognize indigenous peoples and their ancestral domains. However, indigenous peoples are apprehensive as the ARMM government has said that its definition of indigenous peoples and their land will depend on its interpretation of the Koran. Indigenous groups in the ARMM have been appealing for assistance in advocating for their genuine recognition within this region.

The National Commission on Indigenous Peoples

The National Commission on Indigenous Peoples (NCIP) is the government body mandated by the Indigenous Peoples Rights Act (IPRA) of 1997 to oversee the concerns of indigenous peoples.

Free, prior and informed consent

In 2005, the NCIP placed great focus on the matter of free, prior and informed consent, which means that any type of project or activity that entities outside of an indigenous territory wish to undertake within it has to be approved by the community in a manner that does not involve coercion or misleading information. This a particular right embodied in the IPRA, which the NCIP has given meat to with its Administrative Order No.3, series of 2002, and the guidelines on how the NCIP will issue certificates attesting that a particular indigenous community has given its free, prior and informed consent to a certain project.

The issue had come to the fore in the previous year when the NCIP commenced efforts to have the guidelines revised. The NCIP was bombarded from the two opposing sides. The mining industry had been complaining that the process was taking too long and thus limiting economic opportunities. On the other hand, indigenous peoples and support groups feared that any attempt to speed up the process would undermine traditional consensus-building practices and inhibit the full flow of information, particularly with regard to the negative long-term impacts of mining.

2005 saw a series of consultations organised by the NCIP with multiple stakeholders. It was becoming clear by mid-year, though, that any revisions would satisfy the mining industry rather than the indigenous peoples and their advocates. The finalization of the revision was expected within the third quarter but, as of year end, no final version had been approved by the NCIP's policy-making body.

Land titling
Land titling continued to be a major focus of the NCIP. Within the year, there were 8 new Certificates of Ancestral Domain Title (CADTs) awarded to indigenous communities, a 22% increase on the previous grand total of 29. The NCIP began awarding CADTs in 2002, and the present achievement is still a far cry from the original target of around 50 identified for processing in 2004 alone. In April 2005, the Ancestral Domains Office (ADO) of the NCIP issued a claim book outline. The claim book is the basic document which the NCIP studies and deliberates upon to decide whether or not a CADT is to be awarded. Feedback from assisting organizations is that, ironically, the NCIP's attempts to clarify procedures have resulted in further bureaucratization of the process, to the detriment of traditional concepts and practices. In other words: titling has not been made easier for indigenous communities.

The Ancestral Domain Sustainable Development and Protection Plan
Ancestral Domain Sustainable Development and Protection Plan
(ADSDPP) is the name given by the IPRA to the community development plan of an indigenous community. The NCIP has paid renewed
attention to this aspect, especially since it was placed under the Department of Agrarian Reform (DAR) in September 2004 (see *The Indigenous World 2005)*. Part of the reason given for the transfer of the NCIP
was that the DAR could help in facilitating financial support. One early DAR response was a block of grants to capacitate the NCIP in helping indigenous communities formulate their plans (ADSDPPs). It is
expected that, apart from processing ancestral domain titles and certificates on free, prior and informed consent, the NCIP will be placing
more focus on ADSDPP formulation in the future.

Change in Leadership
There was a change in NCIP leadership toward the end of the year
when the Philippine President Gloria Macapagal-Arroyo abruptly replaced Reuben Dasay Lingating with Jannette Cansing-Serrano as chairperson. This sudden turn of events must be understood within the wider context of what was happening in the country's political arena. In
mid-year, there was uproar when a tapped telephone conversation between Macapagal-Arroyo and a member of the Commission on Elections implied that there had been irregularities in the presidential elections of May 2004, which had been a close contest between the Presi-
dent-elect and a popular film star. Eventually, there were indignant res-
ignations within the Cabinet, including officials who were deemed close
to Lingating. This is believed to be the reason behind his replacement by
Cansing-Serrano. Lingating had enjoyed some measure of support from
indigenous peoples and support groups, and they are taking a "wait-
and-see" attitude with regard to the new NCIP chairperson.

The Consultative Body project
As a measure to help ensure that the government conducts genuine
consultation with indigenous communities, the IPRA has provided for

the creation of a Consultative Body comprising indigenous leaders. The NCIP fleshed out the creation by coming out with Administrative Order No. 1, Series of 2003, guidelines for the constitution and operationalization of the Consultative Body. There had been intensive negotiation between the NCIP and the indigenous peoples' movement and support groups as to how this was to be undertaken (see *The Indigenous World 2002-03* and *2004)*. The final agreement was to set up consultative bodies at three levels – provincial, regional and national. A joint project was undertaken to establish the consultative bodies at least up to provincial level, facilitated by the formation of coordinating committees at the said three levels.

The project was finally completed in early 2005. A total of 75 coordinating committees were formed, representing at least 350 national, regional and provincial indigenous peoples' organizations and support groups/NGOs, all NCIP offices from the national, regional and provincial levels and the Office of Southern Cultural Communities (or OSCC, which serves the four Muslim provinces in Mindanao with indigenous peoples). All told, about 60-70% of civil society organizations in the indigenous sector and 100% of the NCIP and OSCC were involved in the CB process. As of January 2005, a total of 63 provincial consultative bodies and three city-wide consultative bodies had been formed. The 63 provincial consultative bodies represent 65 provinces (82% of the country's 79 provinces, or 97% of the provinces with indigenous peoples) while the city-wide consultative bodies are found in three key cities which have ancestral domains and indigenous communities.

The formation of consultative bodies at the regional and national level is still outstanding. At this point, however, the indigenous peoples' movement and support groups are considering whether they intend to continue working with the NCIP on this project. There was some dismay caused, in part, by the NCIP's delay in processing proposals related to the establishment of the consultative bodies. But a greater uneasiness was triggered by the observation that, after a long period of inaction towards these bodies, the heads of the provincial consultative bodies were suddenly convened by the NCIP in the last quarter of 2005 for consultation on the charter change issue (see below). What is disturbing about this is the attempt to influence the Consultative Body heads to support the charter change without making provision for proper consultation with the indigenous groups on the ground, which was the spirit behind the Consultative Body formation.

Proposed changes to the Constitution

Within the broader political context, part of President Macapagal-Arroyo's attempts to allay the mid-2005 uproar regarding her involvement in election irregularities was to promise to call for an amendment to the Philippine Constitution. The amendment would make way for a parliamentary form of government and the establishment of a federal system of governance. In essence, it can be seen as supportive of local governance, including governance of and by indigenous peoples. The response from the indigenous peoples' movement and support groups has, on the whole though, been lukewarm. One concern is that the charter change opens the door to a dilution or even abrogation of the IPRA. Even groups previously opposed to the IPRA stated that whatever gains and opportunities were provided by the IPRA should be protected from further erosion.

Concluding Remarks

A chronicling of events and issues related to indigenous peoples in the Philippines shows that there has been little substantial change in terms of the types of events and issues ongoing, for example, development aggression, lack of government response to indigenous issues and the efforts at increased consolidation among the different ideologically-based networks of national and regional indigenous peoples' organisations.

The indigenous peoples' movement and support groups see that there has to be a greater focus placed on localized capacity building in the efforts to empower indigenous communities. For instance, the networking (including alliance building, information sharing, discussion and media profile) that has taken place around mining advocacy has not permeated down to community level, where such activity is most needed if a genuine community involvement in decision making is sought. It is hoped that 2006 will see improvements in this area. ❑

INDONESIA

Indonesia is one of the most diverse nations in the world. It is home to more than 220 million people from hundreds of ethnic groups speaking more than 800 languages spread across thousands of islands. Among these ethnic groups, the Javanese make up approximately 41 percent of the population. Other ethnic groups range from the second largest group, the Sundanese, who constitute 15 percent of the population, to much smaller groups in eastern Indonesia consisting of several hundred individuals. Despite this diversity, or rather because of it, Indonesia has no official government policy concerning the rights of indigenous ethnic minorities. The government works diligently to avoid issues of ethnicity and ethnic privilege that are characteristic of other nations in Southeast Asia. Government officials argue that the concept of "indigenous" is not applicable in Indonesia, as almost all Indonesians (with the exception of the Chinese) are indigenous and thus entitled to the same rights. Subsequently, the government rejects all calls for special treatment by groups claiming the label of "indigenous people". These objections to special privileges for indigenous minorities have hindered the ability of many communities to hold on to their land and provide no particular legal avenue to pursue compensation. In recent years, an indigenous rights movement led by the Alliance of Indigenous Peoples of the Archipelago (also called AMAN) has begun working on behalf of indigenous groups throughout the country and supporting the development of local organizations and networks aimed at promoting and defending indigenous rights. AMAN defines indigenous people as "communities which have ancestral lands in certain geographic locations and their own value systems, ideologies, economies, politics, cultures and societies in their respective homelands".

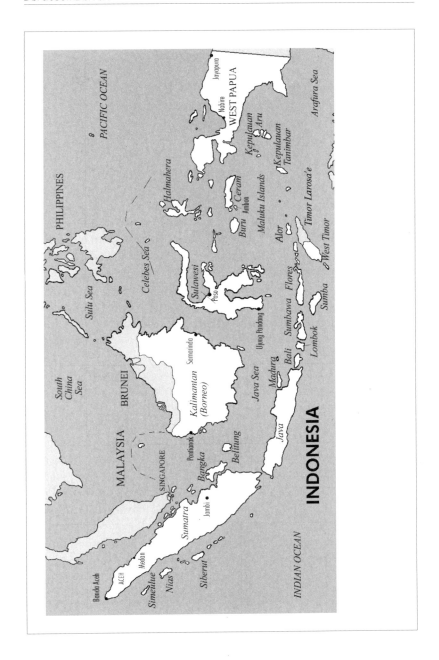

Decentralization and local governance

A continuing development in Indonesia in 2005 was the implementation of decentralization and regional autonomy throughout the country. This legislation is aimed at giving more power over natural resources and government to the more than 450 districts in Indonesia. One of the main selling points has been that it will provide more opportunities for local communities, including indigenous peoples, to participate in government. Many indigenous communities have seen these opportunities as a chance to return to local forms of governance and resource management (known as *adat*) that were ignored or discouraged under previous regimes. Older laws that dismantled local forms of leadership and required a standardised form of village administration throughout the archipelago have been repealed. Communities can now implement forms of government based on local customs (*adat*) and choose their own leaders. After decades of authoritarian rule that often disregarded local beliefs and customs as a hindrance to development, a return to *adat* promises more attention to local needs and local culture. The new autonomy also allows local communities more control over their educational systems. As a result, some groups are adding to the school curriculum to better reflect local history, culture and language.

Forest-dwelling indigenous communities in particular, such as the Punan in Kalimantan and the Orang Rimba in Sumatra, have seen the new legislation as a welcome change. Previous governments largely viewed these groups as "primitives" who needed to be brought into "mainstream" Indonesian society. The government set out to achieve this goal through social engineering programs that included resettlement and assimilation. However, these programs were often more about accessing natural resources than helping local communities. During the last decades of the twentieth century, many forest-dwelling communities were resettled into coastal communities, as their land was taken for large-scale development projects. It is hoped that local control over regional government will lead to a change in these policies and more respect for indigenous communities. For example, in

2005 three villages in the province of South Kalimantan passed laws on the use of natural resources that respect the needs of the forest-dwelling Meratus people. Their claims to the forest had previously been ignored by the government. The new legislation allows Meratus to exploit the forest for their own needs, but prevents large-scale commercial extraction.

The new decentralization legislation has its drawbacks, however, and these could negatively impact on indigenous communities. The new legislation has placed new financial burdens on local governments because they are now responsible for a larger portion of their operating budgets. There are thus pressures to raise new revenues that can often result in increased logging, mining and plantation expansion, which often disregard the land claims of indigenous communities. For example, on the eastern Indonesian island of Halmahera new logging, mining and plantation permits are under consideration as local governments try to increase their incomes. Most of the land targeted for these projects is claimed by indigenous communities, such as the Modole and Pagu people.

The results of this new regional autonomy are mixed. Some ethnic minorities in Indonesia are faring better. In Kalimantan, Indonesian Borneo, for example, politically powerful indigenous groups have been able to regain control of land and resources that they had lost under previous governments. Less powerful indigenous communities, however, have not been faring as well. Instead of providing more access to government and more control over their land, decentralisation has simply strengthened pre-existing power relations. Planned resettlements of some indigenous groups continue as local governments seize their land for new projects to generate revenue. In fact, forestry and mining projects appear to have accelerated since decentralisation, and now threaten some of the remaining forested areas in Indonesia.

An additional piece of legislation passed in 2005 is a new land law that allows the government to revoke people's property rights in the name of national development. This new regulation, Presidential Decision No. 36/2005 on Land Acquisition for Development of Public Facilities, has many indigenous rights groups worried that the government will use it to evict people, particularly forest-dwelling communities, from their land as large development projects are implemented. The law has already been used in several parts of the country to remove people from their land. For example, farmers in Southeast Sulawesi had their land taken for the establishment of a sugar cane plantation. The passage of the law was greeted with protests from both urban and rural populations throughout the country. Even the nation's parliament has criticized the law and has called for it to be reviewed.

Government programs aimed at indigenous minorities

As mentioned above, the Indonesian government has long had a development program aimed at particular indigenous communities. This program is focused on developing indigenous minorities deemed to be in special need of assistance, who are classified as "geographically isolated customary law communities". Run by the Department of Social Affairs, this program seeks to bring indigenous communities that the government considers "backward" and "primitive" into the mainstream of Indonesian society through a program of social engineering. The groups targeted by this program generally include forest-dwelling foragers and swidden agriculturalists. The program seeks to change virtually every aspect of the target population's lives, from settlement patterns and religious beliefs to eating habits and clothing. Groups that fall under this program are often resettled into more accessible areas near the coast or along roads. Despite several years of protest from the indigenous rights movement in the country, the program continues.

Another government program that impacts on indigenous communities is the transmigration program. Transmigration is a government policy that moves landless peasants and other impoverished rural and urban populations from the overcrowded islands of Java and Bali to the more sparsely populated parts of the country. Officials hope that indigenous communities in the receiving regions will learn from the example of the "hard-working" Javanese peasants and change accordingly. This generally means moving into a sedentary village and adopting wet-rice agriculture. The vast tracts of "empty" land needed for these projects are often claimed by indigenous communities, but these claims are usually disregarded. Occasionally indigenous groups are given the opportunity to take part in the program as compensation. Although the program has slowed in the last five years, it continues to resettle thousands of people annually. For example, the government signed plans in 2005 to create several more transmigration sites on the northern and central peninsulas of the island of Halmahera, on land claimed by indigenous communities. Although local communities can protest these moves, they often lack the legal and bureaucratic knowledge and connections needed to do so.

Indigenous minorities and natural resources

As in previous years, many of the threats currently facing indigenous communities in Indonesia are directly related to environmental issues, particularly the fate of Indonesia's shrinking tropical forests. These include illegal and legal logging and the expansion of oil palm plantations. The latter represents one of the greatest threats to indigenous minorities in the country. The government hopes to make Indonesia the world's largest producer of crude palm oil (an oil used in cooking and cosmetics) and has made the expansion of oil palm plantations a priority. These expansion plans include making more than 4.6 million hectares available for plantations throughout the archipelago. One of the worst examples of these expansion plans is a plan put forward in 2005 to create a proposed 1.8 million hectare oil palm plantation along the Indonesian-Malaysian border on the island of Borneo. This mega-project threatens the livelihoods and resources of hundreds of indigenous communities, such as the Iban, as well as the existence of three national parks.

Unfortunately, oil palm plantations often have devastating effects on indigenous communities. They are often planted on land claimed by them, leading to conflicts over land and the loss of livelihoods. Government officials and oil palm companies argue that the plantations will bring much needed development, employment and infrastructure to rural areas. However, the costs often outweigh the benefits. Many local people claim that in addition to land conflicts, the plantations lead to an increase in gambling and prostitution as plantation workers move into the area, and represent a threat to local cultural traditions as peoples' ties to their land are severed.

On a positive note, Indonesia's newly-elected president made stopping illegal logging one of his priorities for 2005 and numerous large operations were uncovered with several culprits arrested. However, illegal logging remains rampant, much of it done on land claimed by indigenous communities, often without their consent. Furthermore, large-scale legal logging continues to take place throughout the country, often on land claimed by indigenous groups. With the current rate of legal and illegal logging, Indonesia will lose its remaining rainforests. Some estimates claim that if current logging rates continue, much of the lowland rainforest in Indonesia will disappear over the next 15 years. This ecological destruction has a major impact on indigenous peoples who depend on these same forests for their livelihoods.

One positive development is an increasing recognition that the rights of indigenous peoples must be respected as part of biodiversity conservation projects. In the past, and often today, indigenous and other local communities were removed from areas designated as national parks or wildlife preserves. The government and conservation organizations claimed that these people represented a threat to biodiversity. This removal can have a disastrous effect on communities, particularly forest-dwelling peoples. The attitude of the Indonesian government and the international conservation organizations they work with appears to be changing. For example, in the province of Jambi on the island of Sumatra, the government signed an agreement in August 2005 with the Orang Rimba, a group of forest-dwellers that live inside the Bukit Duabelas National Park. This agreement respects their traditional rights and claims to the region and will allow them to remain in the park and continue to use the forest.

The indigenous movement

The indigenous rights movement in Indonesia continued to grow during 2005. The large umbrella organization, the Alliance of Indigenous Peoples of the Archipelago, also known as AMAN, continued to work with indigenous communities throughout the country. A number of newly-formed local organizations representing various indigenous peoples were formed and joined the alliance during 2005. For example, on the eastern Indonesian island of Halmahera, the Tobelo people have established a customary law council that they hope will represent the rights of indigenous minorities from the northern part of that island.

In Kalimantan, four major NGOs held a conference to examine the impact of the government's development plans for the island of Borneo. They demanded the government cancel the proposed 1.8 million hectare oil palm plantation mentioned above. This conference was attended by numerous communities affected by these developments as well as over 21 NGOs working in the region. Hopefully the indigenous rights movement will be able to influence policy decisions that affect indigenous minorities across the country in 2006 and beyond.

Religious Freedom

Religious freedom remains elusive in Indonesia, particularly for indigenous minorities who seek to follow their own belief systems. The government's policy on religion, which requires Indonesians to adhere to one of five official religions (Islam, Protestantism, Catholicism, Hinduism, and Buddhism), remains unchanged. As a result minority communities are subject to often unwanted proselytization from Christian and / or Muslim missionaries and their children cannot attend school without affiliating with one of the recognized faiths. It is also difficult for a person who maintains traditional beliefs to obtain a government identification card because a person's religion is noted on the card. Without a government identification card it is very difficult to vote in local and national elections or to register land.

Ethno-religious and separatist violence

One of the greatest threats to some of the smaller indigenous groups in Indonesia has been the ethno-religious and separatist violence that has plagued many parts of the archipelago since the mid-1990s. Much of the ethno-religious violence seems to have subsided, which bodes well for indigenous minorities and others living in areas previously engulfed in violence. The previous conflict zones of North Maluku, West and Central Kalimantan were largely peaceful in 2005. The province of Maluku saw sporadic small-scale violence throughout the year but was able to avoid a return to full-scale communal violence. 2005 also saw more violence in the central Sulawesi region of Poso. The violence in Poso, which began in 1998, has pitted Christians against Muslims and has led to the deaths of several thousand people, and forced more than 200,000 people to flee their homes over the last few years. Despite the signing of a peace agreement by both sides in 2000, 2005 saw a continuation of violence in the region, including the bombing of the Tentena market in May that killed 35 people.

Peace process in Aceh in wake of the tsunami

One of the longest running separatist disputes in the country was between the Indonesian government and the Free Aceh Movement in the province of Aceh on the northern tip of Sumatra. Aceh also suffered the brunt of the large tsunami in December 2004 that killed more than 100,000 people. This horrific natural disaster opened up the region and led to the signing of a peace deal between the national government and the Free Aceh Movement on 15 August 2005. The deal gives the people of Aceh certain rights, such as the right to implement Islamic law and the right to form provincial-based political parties in exchange for dropping calls for independence. The implementation of the peace process has been going well and an international monitoring force has been able to resolve the few small problems that have arisen.
❑

MALAYSIA

M alaysia's 26.13 million population in 2005 included the *Orang Asli* of Peninsular Malaysia and the natives of Sabah and Sarawak. Officially, there are 18 sub-ethnic groups in Peninsular Malaysia, 25 indigenous groups in Sarawak and 39 in Sabah. In Sarawak, the predominant ethnic group according to the 2000 census was the Ibans, accounting for 30.1% of the state's total population, while in Sabah the predominant ethnic group are the Kadazan Dusun (18.4%) followed by the Bajau (17.3%).

Land rights and court cases

Long-drawn out court battles over rights to land continued in 2005, with indigenous peoples celebrating the landmark decision from the *Sagong Tasi vs Selangor State Government* case. In June 2005, the appeal by the four defendants (the Selangor state government, United Engineers Malaysia, the Malaysian Highway Authority and the Federal Government) was heard before Judge Gopal Sri Ram and two others. The judges unanimously threw out the appeal and held that the High Court was not misguided when it decided, on the basis of substantial evidence and fact that was not challenged, to rule that the Temuans (an Orang Asli sub-group) did indeed have propriety rights over their customary lands. As such, these lands should be treated as titled lands and therefore subject to compensation under the Land Acquisition Act. But the 59-page judgment of Gopal Sri Ram in the Court of Appeal was more than just an affirmation of the rights of the Orang Asli to their traditional lands. It was a condemnation of the way the Orang Asli have been treated by the authorities and a wake-up call to the government to fulfill its legal responsibility to the com-

munity. In the judge's words, "*Here you have a case where the very authority – the State – that is enjoined by the law to protect the aborigines
turned upon them and permitted them to be treated in a most shoddy, cruel
and oppressive manner*".

Acknowledging that the purpose of the Aboriginal Peoples Act
1954 was to "*protect and uplift the First Peoples of this country*", Judge
Gopal asserted that, "*it was therefore fundamentally a human rights statute, acquiring a quasi-constitutional status giving it pre-eminence over ordinary legislation. It must therefore receive a broad and liberal interpretation*". The case showed the state and federal governments' neglect in
both under-gazetting and not gazetting areas they knew to be inhabited by the Temuans, thus placing their rights to land in serious jeop-
ardy. For the state and federal governments now to say that no compensation was payable to the Temuans because the disputed lands
were not gazetted was to add insult to injury – injury caused by their
own neglect and failure. This prompted Judge Gopal to comment
that, "*I am yet to see a clearer case of a party taking advantage of its own
wrong*".[1]

In Sarawak, however, the Court of Appeal sadly upheld the appeal by two companies - Borneo Pulp Plantation and Borneo Pulp
and Paper, along with the Superintendent of Lands and Surveys of
Sarawak, against the Iban of Rumah Nor, Bintulu on 8 July 2005 (see
The Indigenous World 2005). Even though the community of Rumah
Nor lost the case due to insufficient evidence, this judgment is seen
as a bitter sweet victory for indigenous peoples in Sarawak because
the appellate court re-affirmed the concept of native customary rights
on *temuda* (cultivated land), *pulau* (communal reserve) and *pemakai
menoa* (community's territorial domain).The community of Rumah
Nor currently has its appeal filed with the highest court in Malaysia,
the Federal Court, and this is still pending.[2]

In Sabah, no date for a further appeal by the company was set for
the Tongod case (see *The Indigenous World 2005*). The Sungai community in Tongod continued their efforts to unify and maintain their
spirit by hosting the revitalization of traditional land conflict resolution practices at a sacred site, "Tinompok", in June 2005. The community also managed to remain vigilant to any encroachment by the

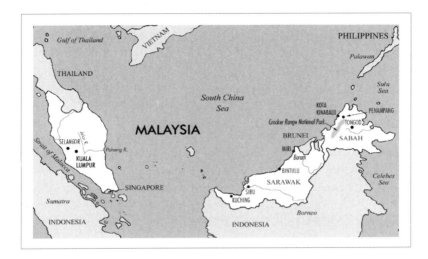

oil palm company, resulting in chainsaws being confiscated and workers being convinced to leave the area with their tractors.

In another incident, the hard work of community organizations finally paid off. Under Section 28 of the Sabah Land Ordinance, 4,940 ha of native customary rights land were acquired by the Sabah Forestry Development Authority (SAFODA) in Kanibongan for the planting of *Acacia Mangium* in 1983. The Rungus indigenous communities were given verbal assurances that the land would be returned to the people after the trees had been harvested. However the agreement was never fulfilled and the people were told that the government would be developing the land further. The communities had organised various protest actions since 2004 through a network of 21 villages under the leadership of KK Muringkat, the village headman and chairperson of the network. Their strategies included lobbying political leaders and organizing community land rights workshops with the PACOS Trust, an indigenous support organization. Finally, their struggle for the restitution of their land paid off and on 1 March 2005, the communities' traditional lands were degazetted from the land vested to SAFODA.

Communal Title

2005 also marked the success of the Terian community in Penampang district in getting their application for a communal land title approved by the government. The approval of the Terian Communal Title was attributed to the high-quality community maps presented in support of the application. Most indigenous peoples opted for individual native titles over their land, even though the process of applying for individual titles is much slower. The Sabah Land Ordinance 1930 actually has other options such as a communal title or native reserve or the possibility of registering their land as Native Customary Rights land.[3] Section 76 provides for Communal Titles *"in cases where a claim to customary tenure of land has been established or a claim to native customary rights has been dealt with by a grant of land and such land is held for the common use and benefit of natives and is not assigned to any individual as his private property"*. The Director of Lands and Survey will hold the title in trust for the community concerned, without power of sale. The success in Terian is expected to encourage other communities to apply for Communal Title.

The indigenous movement

As 2005 passed, indigenous issues gained increasing exposure, in the courts as well as in a number of dialogues and meetings. Indigenous representatives participated in numerous governmental and non-governmental meetings on environmental, human rights, women's and indigenous development issues. The Indigenous Peoples Network of Malaysia (JOAS-IPNM), comprising indigenous organizations in Sabah, Sarawak and Peninsular Malaysia, also held its General Assembly and elected new officers for the period 2006-2007. JOAS-IPNM gained more recognition and two national conferences were co-organised, one with the University Malaysia Sabah (UMS) on Indigeneity, Identity and Social Transformation, and one with the

Malaysian Environmental NGO (MENGO) on environmental sustainability.

With the realization that community mapping is important in proving land claims in court and in land applications, in 2005 the IPNM-JOAS established its community mapping programme with SPNS, an Orang Asli organization in Peninsular Malaysia. The Malaysian Human Rights Commission, SUHAKAM, also acknowledged the awareness-raising work of indigenous organizations, such as organizing a public function in conjunction with the launch of the new indigenous peoples' decade during the International Day of the World's Indigenous Peoples; national training for indigenous women in decision-making; and a youth dialogue. Support through the European Commission/UNDP's "Promoting Tropical Forest" programme and the inclusion of indigenous representatives on the programme's steering committee have also provided opportunities for several indigenous organizations in Malaysia to build their own capacity and improve networking efforts.

Government policies and programmes

Also being actively monitored are the developments of two mega-industries that have seriously affected the lives of indigenous peoples, i.e. the logging and oil palm industries. Indigenous organizations worked closely with other organizations in Europe to explain that certification by the Malaysian Timber Certification Council of a logging company in Sarawak did not meet international standards. Organisations also participated in the drafting of the Principles and Criteria for the sustainable production of oil palm by the Roundtable on Sustainable Oil Palm (RSPO), which comprises governments, companies, indigenous organizations, NGOs and trade unions involved in or affected by the oil palm industry, and monitored the implementation process.

In 2005 the government also showed some positive efforts towards recognising the indigenous system, such as the active promotion of the customary *tagal* concept of resource management, following its incorporation into the Sabah Inland Fisheries and Aquaculture Enactment 2003. The effort by the Sabah government resulted in an enhancement of the livelihood and dignity of communities in the Penampang district. However, such a strategy may not necessarily capture indigenous concepts adequately, as seen in the incorporation of indigenous land ownership into the definition of Native Customary Rights to land in the Sabah Land Ordinance 1930, as there is no recognition of customary law per se. Since customary law in general, and on natural resource management in particular, is either not well-understood or is undocumented, governments are often afraid of recognizing it. Unfortunately, past efforts by the government to recognize customary law often meant codification, which goes against the diverse customary laws of communities. The other weakness of the programme is the tendency to form committees to manage resources, taking away the control that was traditionally held by the community. Although such committees may in fact allow more participation, particularly from women and youths, it nevertheless means that the weakened traditional structure is sidelined altogether. In the long run, it may disempower indigenous communities from achieving aspirations for self-determination and a pluralistic society.   ❑

Notes

1   *Colin Nicholas* of the Center for Orang Asli Concerns (COAC) has contributed to this section.
2   *Mark Bujang* from Borneo Resources Institute (BRIMAS) has contributed to this section.
3   To register lands as having Native Customary Rights, the community needs to fill in a form (LSF1898) and submit it to the Lands and Survey Department with the accompanying proof. A ground survey will be made prior to approval by the Land and Survey Department based on the criteria set out in Section 15 of the Land Ordinance 1930.

THAILAND

The indigenous and tribal peoples of Thailand live in two geograph-ical regions of the country, indigenous fisher communities in the south of Thailand (the *chao-lae)* and the many different highland peoples living in the north and north-west of the country. With the drawing of national boundaries in South-east Asia during the colo-nial era, many peoples living in highland areas throughout the re-gion were divided. There is thus is not a single indigenous group that resides only in Thailand. Nine so-called "hill tribes" are offi-cially recognized: the Hmong, Karen, Lisu, Mien, Akha, Lahu, Lua,Thin and Khamu. According to the official survey of 2002, there are 923,257 "hill tribe people" living in 20 provinces in the north and west of the country.

The general political situation

2005 saw many events and changes in the political landscape in Thai-land at both a local and national level, and which impacted on the rights and freedoms of indigenous peoples in the country. On Febru-ary 6, national elections saw the Thai Rak Thai party (TRT) win a land-slide victory and form a majority parliament after completing a full term in office – an historical first for the nation. The overwhelming nature of the TRT victory led some commentators to voice concerns as to the dictatorial potential of the new government.

At the level of local elections there was some progress, with indig-enous peoples elected into both the sub-district *(Tambon)* and provin-cial administrative authorities. With the decentralization of some budget and regulatory controls the role of these authorities is growing, and indigenous representation is an important step in order to be able to reflect on the needs and perspectives of indigenous peoples in local government decisions on service delivery. In addition to elected bodies such as the local administrative authorities, the Constitution of Thailand also requires the establishment of a National Economic and Social Advisory Council as an advisory body to the government on implementation of the National Economic and Social Development Plan, a body that also serves as a channel for public communication. Not only does the new council include an indigenous representative, Mr Waiying Thongbue from the Karen Network for Culture and Environment, but the president of the Council, Mr Khothom Areeya, is also a well-respected figure from civil society. Both are important and positive steps towards increasing the role of civil society in national government decisions in Thailand.

The national political landscape altered in the aftermath of the national elections, with the Electoral Commission declaring the disbanding of some smaller political parties due to violations of the electoral rules. Some new parties have also emerged, established by veteran politicians unhappy with the positions of the major parties – although the platforms and positions of these new parties are still far from clear.

Violence in the south

Continuing unrest in the three southern border provinces could clearly be seen on the front pages of Thai-language newspapers, with almost daily reporting of new killings of state employees (such as teachers and police) and local residents (including monks). Some reporters and social commentators have linked the underlying causes of these continuing problems to the root causes of the problems facing indigenous peoples in northern Thailand: long-term local experience of unjust administration and conflicts of interest with local mafias. The tendency of local government to respond with violence, arrests and force only intensifies the conflicts – a point as true in northern border regions as it is in southern ones. The Thai government has established the National Reconciliation Commission as a mechanism

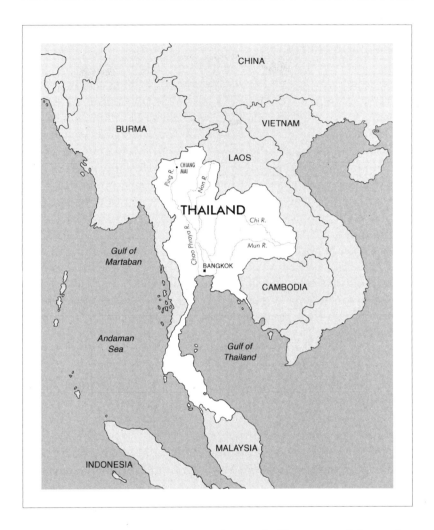

to address the unrest, with a mandate to facilitate non-violent solutions. Sustained progress continues to elude the Commission, however. An additional body, the National Justice Commission, was established at the end of 2005 but it is not yet clear how it will work to
change the situation.

Trade and privatization

In its second term, the TRT government continued to push for the privatization of some state enterprises, in line with the policies of its first term. Both the Petroleum Authority of Thailand (PT) and the Electricity Generating Authority of Thailand (EGAT) were partly or fully privatized as a result of government policy. Trade policy and trade agreements also blossomed, with Free Trade Agreements previously signed with China, New Zealand and Australia coming into effect at the beginning of 2005. The impact on the agricultural prices of key Thai products such as vegetables, fruits, dairy goods and soybeans was a sharp drop in average prices throughout the country in 2005. This has had a severe impact on indigenous farmers who, over the past decades, have been encouraged or forced by the government to adopt market-oriented cash-cropping of vegetables, fruit and flowers. Further talks on the part of the Thai government, which is considering additional free trade agreements, are being carefully monitored by civil society.

Local and national policies impacting on indigenous and tribal peoples

Personal legal status and citizenship

The government approach to finding durable solutions to stateless or under-registered peoples in the border areas of Thailand continued to be inconsistent, corruptible and haphazard throughout 2005 (See also *The Indigenous World 2004*). As close readers of this publication will know, an amnesty is declared on 24 August every year to extend the temporary residence permits of non- or under-registered people in Thailand. This amnesty was declared again in 2005 but only for 3 months, despite civil society and academics pressuring the government to extend it for a period long enough to effectively deal with the issues. Instead, insecurity and fear again characterized the situation of communities in the border lands and throughout the highlands, and a further extension of the amnesty was necessary in November 2005.

In allowing the extension of the amnesty in 2005, the Cabinet requested the creation of a strategy to deal with the issues of under- and non-registered people in a coherent and consistent manner – a call that was positive in its intentions. Earlier in 2005, on 18 January, a draft strategy of this type had been tabled to Cabinet, and indicated what form the final strategy may take. This strategy paper contains items of significant concern to indigenous peoples as it is intended to address the problems of indigenous peoples who have been excluded from previous surveys, migratory peoples who fall within the regulations for application of Thai citizenship and migrant workers who have only labour registration rights. The conflation of these groups, however, is dangerous as registration processes for migrant-labourer status are by far the quickest and easiest to access. This leads some to apply for this in order to gain at least some recognized status. It instantly cancels people's access to the right to citizenship or long-term residence, however, along with the right to land and the right to nationality. It forces indigenous peoples out from the forest lands and into the low-wage garment, agricultural or construction industries.

Natural resources and environment policies

Over the past few years, the Thai government has launched a pro-active policy to gain greater control over activities in forested areas, including forest management by local communities and peoples. Part of this policy approach was the initiation of a range of government-led projects such as the "Forest Village Reform", the "25 River Basins Management Initiative" and the "Joint Management of Protected Areas" (JoMPA) project launched in early 2005. Many of these projects claim to promote and ensure the involvement of local communities and peoples, and stress the importance of participation by communities and their leaders. However, in the execution of these projects, participation is practised merely in the form of consultations, with no access to decision-making power.

The reality of peoples and communities in areas under the remit of such projects is one in which they are expected to attend numerous meetings at which speaking is discouraged, with the site of real decision-making remaining far away. The projects are proving to be processes by which community rights to lands and forests are removed, and commercial management for business, tourism or other economic development is emerging.

Civil society and indigenous peoples have long protested these tendencies in Thai government policy on natural resource management. Public networks such as the Northern Network of Community Forests, the Thai Network of Community Forests, the Assembly of Indigenous and Tribal Peoples of Thailand and other allied organizations gathered 52,698 citizen signatures in support of the draft Community Forest Bill proposed to Parliament on 7 November 2001. The proposal was approved by Parliament and passed on to the Senate House as per the constitutional provision providing for public drafting and submission of legislation. The Senate's consideration was finalized on 15 March 2002 with some modifications in content, for example, "The declaration of community forest not to be allowed in forest conservation areas".

The parliament did not agree with the Senate's changes, however, and established a Joint House-Senate Committee comprising 24 members from the two houses in order to find a solution. The result is that the joint committee has added some phrases into the Bill banning the declaration of community forests in Special Forest Conservation Areas. The public disagreed with this distortion of content, which could be interpreted as banning the forest protectors from the forests by not letting them participate in the management of anything but degraded resources. In November and December 2005, forest dwellers from all parts of Thailand staged a rally by marching peacefully from Chiang Mai's Chiang Dao district in the very north of the country to Parliament House in Bangkok to insist on their right to protect natural resources, and the "people's version" of the Community Forest Bill. The "Long March" and subsequent gathering of 10,000 people in Bangkok, nearly half of whom were indigenous from highland areas, resulted in the Bill being removed from the agenda of the latest parliamentary session. Moreover, it generated a better understanding and attention on the part of the public and media with regard to the issue. By providing community rights to natural resource management, the Community Forest Bill is supposed to conform to articles 10c and 8j of the Convention on Biological Diversity, ratified by Thailand in 2004, and the 1997 Constitution of the Kingdom of Thailand.

Populism and free trade

Over the last year, the government has stepped up its populist policy and, at the same time, signed free trade agreements with several countries. This has negatively affected the poor, as prices for agricultural products have dropped, and debt and labour migration to the cities have increased. These are ultimately the results of the government's lack of commitment to solving the problems of the poor, and of its focus on building its image through propaganda and ill thought out populist policies. The government is trying to take over the management of natural resources, subsequently transferring plantation land to capital-rich entrepreneurs while leaving the poor and indigenous peoples facing even more problems.

Education policy

The government's educational reforms progressed very slowly over the year. By the end of the year, the government had initiated a decentralization policy by transferring the educational administration to Tambon (sub-district) Administration Organizations. This has triggered massive protests among teachers. The National Council of Teachers reasons that the local administrations are not ready to take on the effective management of the education system. They argue that the government has not really given them any power but only a burden; that there has been no decentralization of authority or financial administration. As a result, the idea of transferring the management of the education system to local communities, thereby making it more suitable to their specific needs, has had to be delayed.

The indigenous movement in Thailand

Significant developments took place within Thailand's indigenous movement during 2005. They consisted mainly of the formation of indigenous peoples' development organizations and networks, such as the Highland Peoples' Task Force and the Tribal Health Security Coordinating Centre, as well as an increase in the number of tribal peoples' networks. For seven of the indigenous peoples of northern Thailand, the Karen, Lahu, Lua, Iu Mien, Lisu, Hmong and Akha, support networks of communities and leaders have been in place for a number of years. In 2005 six further networks were established, facilitated by leaders of the existing networks and staff of indigenous peoples' organizations. The six new indigenous networks are the Kachin, Pa-long, Bee-Su, Lua, Shan and Tai-Ya, and they have joined with the pre-existing seven to form a national inter-tribal network of knowledgeable elders and leaders. This coalition aims to record and revive indigenous knowledge and culture including, among other things, the drafting and adoption of school curricula concerning indigenous knowledge and culture, and promoting a better understanding of health issues and the right to access public health care.

The Assembly of Indigenous and Tribal Peoples of Thailand (AITT) and the Highland Sustainable Agriculture Network, together with other allied networks and organizations, continued their work on land and forest, alternative agriculture and personal legal status. They also sought cooperation with regional and international networks such as the Montane Mainland South-east Asia Indigenous Knowledge and Peoples' Network (IKAP) and the International Alliance of Indigenous and Tribal Peoples of the Tropical Forests. ❏

CAMBODIA

Cambodia's indigenous peoples are facing a number of crises but there were nonetheless positive steps made by both government and the people in 2005. There is a growing awareness among indigenous peoples themselves that they are present in 14 different provinces and that they share many of the same issues.

Land Rights

The 2001 Cambodian Land Law contains provisions for indigenous communities to gain title to their land, either in the form of individual titles or as a communal title. This law defines indigenous community land as residential land, agricultural land or land kept in reserve as part of the traditional rotational cultivation system. Applying for a communal title requires that communities be able to register as legal entities. The legal instruments that will allow for this are currently being drafted.

In the meantime, apparently illegal land transactions have been plaguing many of the indigenous communities in the country, especially those in the north-east. This has been documented in a video produced by the NGO Forum on Cambodia in October 2005. The video presents community voices and opinions in this regard.[1] It documents how the land security of indigenous communities is being undermined prior to land titling by a system of illegal land transactions often involving officials and business people. This is theoretically illegal because the law includes articles that provide interim land security prior to titling. The trade in land has also involved many indigenous people, some of whom have not known about the laws, some of whom have been encouraged to sell and broker sales by outsiders, and some of whom have lost hope in the social and legal system and decided to follow the lead in thinking short term rather than following traditional indigenous social systems. In some villages, the problem has become so severe that a majority of the people have been involved in selling off their community land and, in some cases, the land of neighbouring communities too.

Groups of concerned community people have made a number of requests for a moratorium on the transfer of land away from indigenous communities but none of these requests have yet been acted upon. It is assumed that there are high-level and influential people involved in the illegal land acquisitions.

Also of concern is the proliferation of "land concessions" issued by the government over areas that include indigenous peoples' land in provinces such as Kompong Thom, Ratanakiri, Kompong Speu and Mondulkiri.

In Mondulkiri, a Chinese company, Wuzhishan, began to plant pine trees this year on land claimed by local Punong communities. Burial grounds were ploughed. Communities protested, and the government agreed to demarcate community lands before allowing the company to continue. However, the areas claimed by communities have not been recognized and this issue has not yet been resolved. In Kompong Speu, another Chinese company, New Cosmos, is preparing to develop a tourist resort on a site sacred to the Suoy community.

While this happens, work is continuing in 3 pilot areas (2 in Ratanakiri Province and 1 in Mondulkiri Province) to develop and trial procedures for communal land registration and to provide inputs for developing legal instruments for the land law. This work is being done by the Ministry of Land, with NGO collaboration. Consultations on land registration have been held with indigenous people from nine provinces, in the context of a national consultation forum of indigenous peoples. The Ministry of the Interior has developed draft by-laws for indigenous communities as part of the process of registering their lands.

Mines

Mining concessions are of great concern. Indigenous people have little or no control over the granting of mining concessions on their lands. It

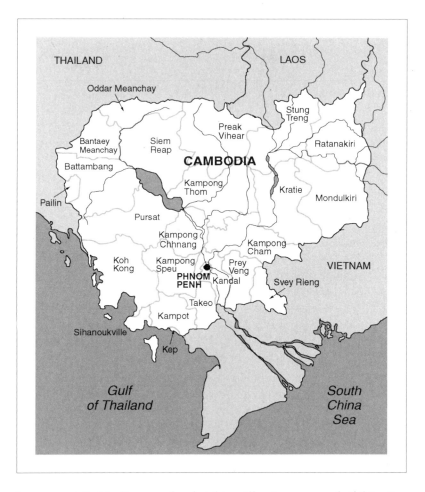

is apparent that indigenous land rights will not mean much if this situation is not corrected.

Mining concessions have been granted over areas that include indigenous peoples' land in Ratanakiri, Mondulkiri, Preak Vihear and Stung Treng provinces. In 2005, the Ministry of Environment received Environmental and Social Impact Assessments (ESIAs) for these ventures and opened the way for public comment. It appears, however, that these concessions have not been halted despite the obvious deficiencies of the ESIAs and the potential impact on indigenous communities.

Forestry issues

The Royal Government of Cambodia, donors and civil society have been looking at ways to reform forestry management in Cambodia. A number of disturbing practices have been seen to continue with the forest concession system. These have been universally condemned as an abuse of indigenous peoples' and non-indigenous people's livelihoods and rights. It is hoped that these concessions will be terminated definitively so that people are no longer under threat of the wholesale destruction of their forests.

Logging concessions remain in many areas where indigenous people live, though officially they are not currently operational. In Ratanakiri, a new concession was granted to produce timber for the construction of a new National Assembly building.

In the new era that is opening up, however, there is scope for community forestry to be officially recognised and it appears that the legal procedures and guidelines required for this are near to completion. This would offer indigenous and non-indigenous peoples an opportunity to obtain use and management rights over forest on a 15-year renewable basis.

Hydropower dams

Ever more hydropower dams are being planned on the Srepok River in Viet Nam. This is in addition to those currently being built on the Sesan River. They have the potential to affect indigenous communities throughout the Srepok river basin. This is continually being raised with various authorities but there appears to be very little effort to consider the impacts of these hydropower dams on the indigenous peoples of Cambodia.

Local government and decentralisation

The 2005 experiences of commune councils and local government have been mixed. In areas where there has been land alienation, it is often openly recognised that local authorities have been involved in the illegal sale of indigenous community land. In very few - if any – cases has there been any retribution dealt out to commune councils for supporting and benefiting from these illegal activities. In some cases there have been complaints about the role of commune councils but higher authorities have been involved with the deals too and so the complaints have not been acted upon. There is a very real danger that commune councils will remain uncorrected, and supported in their illegal activities.

On the other side of the coin, there has been significant progress in some areas, with community mobilisation and linking with commune councils and other local authorities. Where communities have become aware of their rights and the proper role of local government, they have been insisting that the commune and local governments fulfil their proper role. In some cases this has been a difficult and potentially dangerous situation. When powerful people are involved in supporting the local authorities, communities have had to be active in opposing their actions and there is still much potential for future conflict.

In still other areas, local government has responded with gratitude to community support in preventing abuse from outsiders, saying that they need the support of their communities in order to deal with the pressures put upon them.

Amidst this work with commune councils, there have been steps to produce the legal instruments needed for indigenous communities to be recognized as legal entities. This is a requirement for land ownership, as mentioned above. In other matters, too, it would empower the community to have this legally recognised status as a civil society entity. This would not only give communities the ability to apply for land title but would also give them legal recognition for other things such as receiving development projects, filing complaints and undertaking conflict resolution.

Organisation and advocacy

Following the first national indigenous peoples' forum in September 2004, there was a series of workshops throughout Cambodia. These workshops assisted indigenous people to come together and learn about indigenous peoples' rights and to discuss their future. At each workshop, provincial representatives were chosen by the participants. These representatives have since come together to form an interim national network of indigenous peoples and they are now trying to look at how they can work together to jointly support the rights and development of indigenous peoples. One of the first activities was to plan, obtain funding for and implement a national indigenous peoples' development forum, which was held in October 2005 in Stung Treng Province.

Concluding remarks

2006 will be an interesting year for the indigenous peoples of Cambodia. In many ways it will also be a pivotal one. Many communities and groups are at crisis point with regard to land and natural resource management issues. Many people are saying that, if there is no significant betterment of the situation in 2006, it may be too late and there will be considerable degradation and destruction of indigenous culture and communities.

2006 is an important year, too, for these issues to be discussed throughout the world. There is a unique opportunity and a legal framework in place to avoid many of these problems and it is imperative that the challenges are taken up if the worst possible consequences are to be avoided.

In this light, it is rewarding to see significant community networking activities developing ever more strongly and even some significant government and donor support for these initiatives.   ❏

Note

1   The video, entitled "CRISIS", is available on request by contacting the NGO Forum on Cambodia.

VIETNAM

Since 1979, 54 ethnic groups have been officially recognised in Vietnam. They make up about 14% of the current total population of 82 million. The Kinh or Viet are the majority, inhabiting the lowland deltas of the Red River in the north, the Mekong Delta in the south and the coastal land along the Truong Son mountain chain. The Hoa (1 million, making up ca. 1%) are the various Chinese groups, settled mainly in the large cities, while the Khmer (1 million), who are culturally linked to Cambodia, live generally in the Mekong Delta. There are also a number of quite large ethnic minority groups living in the Northern Mountains, such as the Thai, Tay, Nhung, Hmong or Dao, each with between 500,000 and 1.2 million people. But there are many with fewer than 300,000 people, sometimes only a few hundred. Around 650,000 people belonging to ethnic minorities live on the plateaux of the Central Highlands (*Tay Nguyen*) in the south. All ethnic minorities have Vietnamese citizenship.

In recent decades, the Kinh people have increasingly moved to the highlands and the ethnic minority communities have also left their original lands, resulting in an increasingly mixed population, particularly in the Central Highlands where land has been more accessible than in other areas of the country. Consequently, it is not known how many of the ethnic minority people are still indigenous in the sense that they live on their original land *(thô dan)*. The ethnic minorities are, on average, poorer than the Kinh and Hoa people, and with poverty reduction having a more rapid effect in the cities and the lowlands, the tendency is for the poverty gap between the ethnic minorities and the Kinh/Hoa people to increase. The latest data from the Living Standard Survey of 2004 indicates that 14 percent of Kinh/Chinese (Hoa) live in poverty whereas the rate for ethnic minorities is 61 percent.[1] In spite of this difference, the poverty level has declined considerably over the last 15 years, even for ethnic minorities.

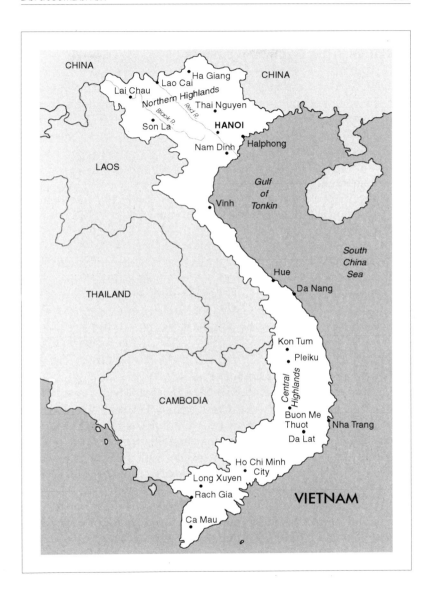

Conflicts in the Central Highlands

Religion and land can be said to be the core issues in the continuing problems of ethnic minorities in the Central Highlands, with demonstrations and clashes with police in 2001 and early 2004 (*The Indigenous World 2005*). Since Easter 2004, no new violent conflicts have been recorded but around 700 ethnic minority people who left the Central Highlands after 2001 and 2004 have asked for refugee status in Cambodia, where most of them were still living in early 2005.

The refugees were settled in UNHCR (United Nations Refugee Agency) refugee camps in Phnom Penh. Some families have returned voluntarily to Vietnam. Most wanted to go back or stay in Cambodia, and some opted to go to the United States (US), but not all were eligible. Tensions arose in early January 2005 between human rights organisations, particularly Human Rights Watch and the Montagnard Foundation, foreign-based organisations with an interest in the case such as UNHCR, the Cambodian, Vietnamese and US governments and, a little further out on the periphery, the European Parliament.

Indigenous refugees in Cambodia

On 11 January 2005, Human Rights Watch published a report with evidence of torture and mass arrest of *Montagnards* (an old French term for the various indigenous people in the Central Highlands) in Vietnam, and criticised Cambodia for slamming the door in the face of new asylum seekers from Vietnam. Human Rights Watch commented that people who had returned to Vietnam were being treated with suspicion and put under surveillance.

The accusations were denounced completely in an editorial in a Vietnamese newspaper a few days later. The article raised the issue of whether Human Rights Watch supported organisations hostile to Vietnam, such as FULRO,[2] an organisation active during the Vietnam War (called the American War in Vietnam). Its leader, Kok Ksor, originally from Ga Lai in Central Vietnam, is now the head of the Montagnard Foundation with his home based in South Carolina, USA. According to Vietnamese opinion, this organisation has the aim of establishing an autonomous Protestant state (referred to as a Dega state)[3] in the Central Highlands. The Montagnard Foundation is the most vocal organisation in denouncing the repression of indigenous people in the Central Highlands.

The Vietnamese government regards the refugees who fled to Cambodia after the conflicts in 2001 and 2004 as people "illegally departing the country"; and denies that they left the country because of repression. It maintains that the refugees were lured into Cambodia by hostile foreign forces. Some refugees said that broadcasts had promised them that the UN could help them get their ancestral lands back. Other refugees stated that they had been promised a house and money. The Vietnamese government was not willing to give foreigners access to the Central Highlands, which caused severe criticism from several sides.

A public trial of 7 people was held on 13 January 2005 in the Gia Lai provincial capital of Pleiku. Ksor Krok was one of those convicted, the younger brother of Kok Ksor, charged with causing social unrest. They received sentences ranging from 4 to 6 years.[4] A few days later, on 25 January, the Court in Dak Doa district, Gia Lai province, convicted 3 people to between 10 and 11 years in prison.[5] It was claimed that they had received instructions from foreign exiles to "foment the establishment of a Dega state, led by Kok Ksor, beat Kinh majority people, hold demonstrations and instigate people to flee to Cambodia".[6]

The Cambodian government perceived the refugees as being (illegal) economic migrants since they were not interested in conflict with Vietnam over this matter. However, being a country highly dependent upon aid, it also did not want to displease the international donor community. Cambodia was not willing to host the refugees from Vietnam for long if they were not willing to settle in a third country. The Cambodian government was asked by UNHCR to harbour the refugees until their cases had been processed. Some of the refugees were accepted for resettlement in the United States, some were interviewed for resettlement in Canada and Finland. Others did not accept such a solution but wanted the UN to get them their ancestral lands back in Vietnam, a demand that UNHCR declared it was unable to help with.

Memorandum of Understanding

In 2005, Vietnam, Cambodia and UNHCR met in Hanoi for the first time in three years for discussions to resolve the refugee issue. On 25 January 2005, they agreed a Memorandum of Understanding concerning 700 Vietnamese minority people under UN protection: they should either be repatriated to Vietnam or resettled in a third country. According to the Memorandum, those who had not made up their minds would be given one month to do so. After that date, the three parties would arrange to bring people back to Vietnam. The Vietnamese government affirmed its policy of ensuring no discrimination or legal action would be taken against the repatriates.

Repatriation of refugees

In March, 43 ethnic minority refugees in Cambodia returned voluntarily to Vietnam, while 297 opted for resettlement in the US, Canada or Finland. In April, 24 ethnic people, who had hidden in the Vietnamese jungle since 2001, turned themselves in and returned to their villages. In May, another group of people who were not found eligible as refugees were scheduled to return. After the trial and subsequent imprisonment of some of the alleged leaders of the 2001 unrest, and claims by Human Rights Watch and the Montagnard Foundation that many "Montagnards" continued to be mistreated and imprisoned, international pressure increased on Vietnam to allow foreign visitors to enter the Central Highlands. Vietnam accepted the first visit of the US Consul General in March, and in May and June two UNHCR delegations were allowed to meet with returnees. They reported that they were well-integrated and returning to normal life.

In July, the plans to repatriate 101 ethnic minority people from refugee camps in Phnom Penh who were not eligible for resettlement in a third country proceeded. Local and international human rights organisations protested at the repatriation. On 20 July, the Cambodian authorities took action and forcefully deported the refugees. Protests by other ethnic minority Vietnamese and human rights workers were met with force by the police. The repatriation was publicly criticised by Human Rights Watch, who denounced the violence used by the Cambodian police. The US State Department criticized both Vietnam and Cambodia for the forced repatriation before an international monitoring programme had been established for the refugees. Vietnam, which had not been particularly eager to receive the refugees back, confirmed the arrival of 94 people and declared that they would be treated well (7 were stopped at the border under suspicion that they were Cambodians who had tried to get to the US). The US authorities offered to accept a case-by-case resettlement of some of the repatriated ethnic minorities. In 2005, a total of around 600 refugees left for the US, Canada and Finland. A few hundred returned to Vietnam.

By September, UNHCR had established a programme of regular visits to the refugees. Another US delegation visited the Central Highlands to inspect the religious situation and the returnees, and reported that it appeared to be open for many Protestant groupings belonging to different chapters of Protestantism to practise their religion.

British, Austrian and European Commission ambassadors to Vietnam visited the Central Highland province of Dak Nong on November 21-22 to inquire into the local socio-economic situation. According to the Vietnamese press of November 27, the delegation approved the efforts of the government in integrating the "illegal" returnees.

Government relaxes conditions for churches

Alongside the conflicts over the refugees, the Vietnamese government relaxed the conditions imposed on the Protestant evangelical church. On 4 February, an instruction was issued by Prime Minister Phan Van Khai concerning Protestantism. It encouraged Protestants to follow their religious beliefs and offered public support for the creation of places of worship and training of clerics but stated that they should adhere to the eligible chapters of the Vietnam Protestant Church.[7,8] One of the messages underlying the new policy was that Protestants should follow their beliefs but not adhere to the Dega church. The new policy was moreover part of the policy of improving the conditions for religious communities generally in Vietnam during 2005. This may, at least partially, be a result of the campaign of the US Commission on International Religious Freedom, a US government agency monitoring the status of religious freedom abroad, which demanded sanctions against Vietnam. It was successful, in late 2004, in including Vietnam on the list of countries of particular concern for violating religious freedoms.[9]

Global response and local realities

Between September and December, Kok Ksor, the leader of the US-based Montagnard Foundation, appealed to the European Parliament and to individual country leaders to stop all support to Vietnam and to oppose Vietnam's membership of the World Trade Organisation. Some of the accusations were repeated in the resolution on human rights in Vietnam, Laos and Cambodia passed by the Parliament of the European Union on December 1. The religious repression and discrimination of indigenous minorities in the Central Highlands of Vietnam was noted in the strongly formulated resolution.

Tensions are continuing in the Central Highlands, evident in the arrival of new refugees in Cambodia in December 2005. They are now under the protection of UNHCR. It is not clear if the Memorandum of 25 January 2005 is still the basis for the present refugee policy or if the negotiations have to start all over again.

Considering the comparatively small number of refugees in question, international focus on the case has been disproportionately large. The tone of the discussions resembles the uncompromising statements of the Cold War era, and it is obvious that the issue has become politicized. There is no doubt that the Vietnamese state has shown insufficient consideration of the rights of ethnic minorities in the past. But evidence of the specific forms of repression of the ethnic minorities in Vietnam presented by organisations such as Human Rights Watch and the Montagnard Foundation could not be fully verified during inspection visits (such as that of UNHCR) to the Central Highlands. It is certainly difficult to properly assess local conditions by means of such inspection delegations. In the end, we are left with opposing and contradictory information ❑

Notes

1   **World Bank.** 2005. *Taking Stock. An update on Vietnam's economic development and reforms*, prepared for the Consultative Group Meeting for Vietnam, Hanoi 6-7 December 2005, pp. 14-16.

2   FULRO is an abbreviation of the French version of United Front for the Liberation of Oppressed Races. Its purpose was to gain autonomy for people in the mountains. http//:www.unpo.org/member.php?arg=40 (visited 14 Jan 2006)

3   Dega Protestantism is an evangelical form of Protestantism banned by the Vietnamese government. http//:www.vietnamvietcontacts.com/gpage.htlm (visited 10 Jan 2006)

4   According to the *Vietnam News Agency*, 13 January 2005.

5   Quoted from *Deutsche Presse-agentur* and *Vietnam News Link* by Stephen Denney 27 January 2005.

6   *Thanh Nien* newspaper, 27 January, 2005

7   The Confederation of Evangelical Alliances of Vietnam (CEAV) split into a "Northern" and a "Southern" branch after the 1954 partition of Vietnam, and most supporters went to the south. During the Vietnam War, about 20 Protestant denominations with mother organisations in the US entered the country. After the 1975 end of the Second Indochina War, the majority of the then 37 organisations and denominations retained member status in relation to mother societies abroad. Most were neither legal nor illegal. Some of them split from the CEAV as independent organisations. In 2001, CEAV was again officially recognised by the Vietnamese government, and is the largest evangelical organization. The Dega church, Vang Chu and Thin Hung, the last two practised among Hmong and Dao in the Northern Mountains, are not recognised by the government because they are considered political opposition movements in disguise (**Nguyen Minh Quang. 2005.** *Religious Issues and Government Policies in Viet Nam.* Hanoi, The Gioi Publishers, pp. 63-70).

8   *Vietnam News Agency /BBC,* 5 February 2005.

9   Ibid. 19 March, 2005.

LAOS

A round 5.5 million people inhabit Laos, one of the most ethnically diverse countries in mainland Southeast Asia. The ethnic Lao dominate both politically and economically but comprise only around 30% of the population. People who speak first languages in the Lao-Tai family make up about 66% of the population. The rest mostly have first languages in the Mon-Khmer, Sino-Tibetan and Hmong-Mien families. These latter groups are sometimes considered to be the "indigenous peoples" of Laos, although officially all ethnic groups have equal status, and therefore the concept of "indigenous peoples" is not generally applied in Laos. As was emphasised in *The Indigenous World 2004*, the ethnic makeup of the country remains quite confusing, even for Lao nationals.

Internal resettlement continues to attract attention

There is increasing concern amongst the donor community regarding the government promoted internal resettlement of ethnic minorities from remote mountainous areas to lowland areas and along major roads (see *The Indigenous World 2005, 2004, 2002-2003*).

In 2005, two major studies on internal resettlement in Laos were released. The first came out in August, and was entitled "Aiding or Abetting? Internal Resettlement and International Aid Agencies in the Lao PDR".[1] The report reviewed the growing literature on internal resettlement in Laos, which clearly shows many of its severe negative impacts on livelihood, health, culture and environment, etc. The report also examined how different international aid agencies, including multilaterals, bilaterals and NGOs, are addressing this important issue in Laos. Largely based on a series of interviews and some fieldwork,

the study shows that while some organisations are offering innovative alternatives to internal resettlement, most are either indirectly or directly supporting it. The report has generated considerable interest.

The second report, released in September, is entitled, "Lao PDR: Is Resettlement a Solution for Human Development?".[2] It has also generated considerable interest, and includes some important data on the government's internal resettlement plans for various parts of the country populated by ethnic minorities.

Despite the evidence against internal resettlement in Laos, it continued in various forms during 2005. Sometimes, resettlement has been associated with efforts to reduce swidden agriculture. For example,

the concentration of ethnic minorities in lowland areas as a way to reduce swidden agriculture is continuing in Houaphan province. It is
expected that 5,436 ha of swidden fields will exist there in 2006, as opposed to 9,333 ha in 2005.[3] In addition, in Kalum district, Xekong province, three villages of ethnic minorities from remote areas were "consolidated"[4] and moved to a new more accessible location in 2005.[5] In
Phongsaly province, in northern Laos, the government is also continuing to try to reduce the amount of area under swidden agriculture
(2,500 ha in 2005). However, it is recognised that it is unrealistic to expect people to give up shifting cultivation as there are no more appropriate areas for the people to conduct other forms of agriculture.[6] Although shifting cultivation in Laos continues to decline overall, in Vientiane province it actually increased in 2005, with ethnic minorities
moving in from places like Houa Phan, Phongsaly and Xaysomboun
Special Zone. Yet, the government hopes to reduce the area under
shifting cultivation there by 800 ha in 2006.[7]

Americans deported for interfering with resettlement process

On June 3, 2005 four American citizens, including two of ethnic Hmong
descent, were arrested in Phoukout district, Xieng Khouang province,
in northern Laos. According to the Vientiane Times, "They were
charged with having interfered in the internal affairs of Laos, causing
social disruption, and creating misunderstanding between authorities
and people. They were guilty of misleading and obstructing people in
the process of relocation to live together in order to implement the
government's poverty reduction plan." The article continued, "The
government has been bringing scattered villages together for the purpose of maximising the use of resources for development so as to raise
the people's living conditions."[8] The event apparently took place in
the Chomthua village focal development point, which the government
has been encouraging ethnic minorities in the area to move to.[9] Although the initial Vientiane Times article reported that the Americans
were being deported for interfering in the internal resettlement of eth-

nic minorities to a focal site, subsequent newspaper articles on the incident made no mention of internal resettlement, and instead stated that the Americans were, "causing social disruption, and creating misunderstanding between the authority and the people." The group was also accused of having "misled and obstructed local people's efforts to implement the government's poverty reduction plan."[10] The details of the events that transpired remain unclear, but it appears that they were advocating in some way against internal resettlement.

Opium cultivation officially eradicated

The Lao government set a goal to eradicate opium production in the country by March 2005 (see *Indigenous World 2005*), after the area under opium cultivation was reportedly reduced to 3,500 ha in 2004 (see *Indigenous World 2004*). By May 2005, the provinces of Houaphan, Luang Phrabang, Phongsaly and Xieng Khouang had all announced that they had eradicated opium production, as had Saysomboun Special Zone. Xayaboury was the last province to make this announcement. The Lao President signed an agreement with the United Nations to stop opium production by 2006. However, in a meeting in the province, the deputy Governor of Luang Namtha province, Mr. Singkham Phanthavong, questioned what crops could replace opium for the local people, given that one kilogram of opium was worth three tonnes of soybeans or ten tonnes of corn. There is a general recognition that stopping opium cultivation may be causing serious problems for ethnic minorities, and that they are likely to remain poor after they have stopped growing opium.[11]

The United Nations Office on Drugs and Crime (UNODC) has been more cautious in declaring Laos "opium free". According to a survey conducted for them in 2005, there has been a 73% decline in poppy cultivation since 2004, and a 67% drop in potential opium production. The UNODC Executive Director Antonia Maria Costa reported that, "For the first time in many years, we can safely assume that Laos is no longer a supplier of illicit opiates to the world market." However, he admitted that 1,800 ha of opium were grown in Laos in 2005, for local consumption. He also acknowledged, however, that more needed to be done to "help them [former opium growers] to escape the poverty associated with the shift from drug production."[12] Others have also raised serious concerns about the negative impacts on opium growers being caused by the drastic eradication of opium production, without providing the mainly ethnic minority producers with adequate alternative livelihoods (see *Indigenous World 2005, 2004*).

Lost group of ethnic minorities from Cambodia emerges in Attapeu

In November 2004, a group of 34 ethnic Kreung and Tampuen people originally from Ratanakiri province, northeast Cambodia, unexpectedly emerged in Attapeu province's Phouvong district in southern Laos. They had been accidentally discovered in deep and largely uninhabited forests along the eastern part of the Lao – Cambodia border. The group had been in the forests for over 15 years without any contact with the outside world. Being formerly allied with the Khmer Rouge, the people continued to hide in the forest from the Vietnamese army, unaware that the war had ended years ago and that the Vietnamese soldiers had long since left. They wanted to settle in Attapeu, but were resettled in their original villages in Ratanakiri province, Cambodia, instead.[13] Only one person died during the 15 years that the group stayed in the forest but, within a short period of coming into contact with other people, three had died of illnesses. This is not unusual when people who have not been exposed to outside diseases for many years are suddenly exposed to them.

Hmongs from Laos enter Thailand

In 2005, a group of about 6,500 newly-arrived ethnic Hmong people were residing in Phetchabun province in Central Thailand. Over two-thirds of them are believed to have entered Thailand from Laos. Many discarded all their Lao identity documents, and most are apparently hoping to be sent to the United States as happened to a number of Hmong originally from Laos in 2004. These Hmong were previously based at Thambrabok temple in Central Thailand. Many of the new group claim to have been associated with the secret army in Laos supported by the US Central Intelligence Agency in the early 1970s. A small number have been secretly deported to Laos from Thailand, but it remains unclear what will happen to the rest of the people.[14]

Large hydropower dams

There has also been a general surge in international investment interest in large hydropower dams in Laos over the last year,[15] and many prospective dams are presently being studied or have begun to be constructed.

A Vietnamese consortium is constructing the 250 MW Xekaman 3 dam in Dakchung district, Xekong province.[16] The 76 MW Xeset 2 dam in Lao Ngam district, Saravane province, is being constructed by Electricitie du Lao (EdL) with funding from the Export Import Bank of China and construction support from the Chinese weapons making company, Norinco Construction Company of China.[17]

There are other dams in advanced stages of planning, including the 640 MW Nam Ou 8 dam in Phongsaly province, which will be built by Sinohydro Corporation as a joint Lao-Chinese venture;[18] and the Nam Ngum 5 dam in Saysomboun Special Zone.[19] Another Chinese investor, the China Machine-Building International Corporation, is planning to build the 70MW Xepon 3 dam in order to supply electricity to the nearby Xepon gold and copper mine,[20] which is being run by the Australian company Oxiana and has been financed by the International Finance Corporation (IFC). Finally, the Garmuda Berhad Company of Malaysia and the Lao government are preparing to proceed with the 474 MW Nam Theun 1 dam in Bolikhamxay province. There are also many other large and small projects in the planning stages.[21]

After years of waiting, the World Bank approved the financial guarantees required to move the controversial Nam Theun 2 dam onto its construction stage, after years of uncertainty. The cost of the 1,070 MW capacity dam on the Nakai Plateau in Khammouane province, central Laos, has been estimated at US$1.2 billion. Apart from resulting in the resettlement of about 6,200 indigenous people from the reservoir area, the dam will also cause serious downstream impacts along the Xe Bang Fai River into which the water from the dam's reservoir on the Nam Theun River will be diverted via the project's powerhouse. The increased volume of water, along with the dam's erratic operating regime, will probably affect more than 100,000 people in Savannakhet and Khammouane provinces. The decision by the World Bank to proceed with the project was quickly followed by the agreement of the Asian Development Bank (ADB) to support the project as well. International NGOs who have heavily criticised and campaigned against the dam for many years were very disappointed with the decision, and continue to question the viability of the project.[22]

All of the above projects are or will negatively affect ethnic minorities situated in their project areas, and it is clear that ethnic minorities are paying the highest prices for hydropower development in Laos. For example, the Xeset 2 and 3 dams have been seriously criticised for the serious downstream negative impacts that these dams will cause, especially for people living along the Tapoung stream and other streams that will be diverted into the Xeset River to facilitate the project. At least 20,000 people will be negatively impacted by the projects, and the vast majority of them are from ethnic minority groups.[23]

Concerns about logging

In 2005, there were serious concerns raised by the Lao government regarding the extent of logging in the country. While the National Assembly only approved a quota of 150,000 m3 for 2004-2005, well over 500,000 m3 was actually cut down, according to official government statistics. The actual amount cut may be much more. For example, quotas for taking dead wood out of National Protected Areas have resulted in loggers taking advantage of the situation and cutting live trees as well.[24]

New list of ethnic groups approved for government use

In 2005, the National Assembly declined to approve the new list of ethnic group names proposed by the Central Lao Front for National Construction (see *Indigenous World 2005*). This was after the Central Party Politburo (leadership committee within the Central Party) had approved the list in principle in late 2001 (see *Indigenous World 2001-2002*). In 2005, the Lao Front decided to counter their setback at the National Assembly by successfully reaffirming the list's validity with the Politburo. The Lao government thus adopted the new list for classifying people by ethnicity during the 2005 National census. The list presently includes 49 ethnic groups and a large number of sub-groups, but the Lao Front is well aware that this figure is likely to change in the future. There is still not enough known about the diverse peoples of the country.

New book about ethnic groups in Laos

In 2005, the Lao Front for National Construction released its first official publication using the new ethnic group names adopted by them and the Lao government. Entitled "The Ethnic Groups in Lao P.D.R.,"[25] the book is being distributed throughout the country. It provides summaries of all the ethnic groups in Laos, in both the Lao and English languages. The Canada Fund in Laos provided funding to the Lao Front to produce the book. This book is significant as it is the first official publication that includes all the newly recognised ethnic group names included in the new list prepared by the Lao Front. ☐

Notes and references

1   **Baird, I.G. and B. Shoemaker, 2005:** *Aiding or Abetting? Internal Resettlement and International Aid Agencies in the Lao PDR.* Toronto: Probe International.
2   **Gonzales, G., E. Diaz-Boreal and P. Cottavoz, 2005:** *Lao PDR: Is Resettlement a Solution for Human Development?* Vientiane: Action Contre La Faim.

3   **Syvongxay, K.,** **2005:** Huaphan to reduce slash and burn. *Vientiane Times.* October 21.
4   Village consolidation involves taking two or more small villages and combining them together to make a large village, either by resettling people from all the communities into a new village location or by moving people from other villages into an already established village.
5   *Vientiane Times,* September 8, 2005. New village in Kaleum district.
6   **Latsaphao, K.,** **2005:** Slash and burn continues in Phongsaly. *Vientiane Times,* June 21.
7   **Syvongxay, K.** **2005:** Slash and burn cultivation in Vientiane province. *Vientiane Times,* September 26.
8   *Vientiane Times,* June 7, 2005. Three Americans deported.
9   *Vientiane Times,* June 7, 2005. Phoukout people support Govt. development policy.
10 *Vientiane Times,* June 8, 2005. Deported Americans admit their wrongdoings.
11 **Pansivongsay, M.** **2005:** Opium Cultivation to end forever. *Vientiane Times,* May 31.
12 *Vientiane Times,* June 23, 2005. Laos will be opium-free by year end.
13 **Phann, A. and C. Purtill, 2004:** Wanderers emerge from life of constant fear. *The Cambodian Daily,* 10 December.
14 **Ganjanakhundee, S.,** **2005:** 29 Hmong secretly deported to Laos. *The Nation,* December 14.
15 *Vientiane Times,* September 9, 2005. Mining, hydro-power boom.
16 *International Water Power and Dam Construction,* December 8, 2005. Vietnam to invest in Laos.
17 **Vongsay, P.,** **2005:** Xeset 2 to increase hydropower in the south. *Vientiane Times,* November 17.
18 **Phonpachit, S.,** **2005:** Nam Ou 8 hydroelectric power project underway. *Vientiane Times,* June 1, 2005.
19 *Vientiane Times,* September 9, 2005. Mining, hydro-power boom.
20 *Vientiane Times,* November 29, 2005. Xepon 3 hydropower plant agreed for Saravan.
21 **Pansivongsay, M.,** **2005:** Malaysians to build dam in Bolikhamxay. *Vientiane Times,* September 2.
22 **Imhof, A.,** **2005:** World Bank Approves Nam Theun 2 Dam. Project's Economic Viability Remains in Doubt. *World Rivers Review.*
23 **Sayboualaven, P.,** **2005:** The Xeset 2 and Xeset 3 Hydroelectric Projects: A Report on the Potential Social and Environmental Impacts. *Watershed* 10(3).
24 **Phouthonesy, E.,** **2005:** Govt moves to conserve forests. *VientianeTimes,* October 12, 2005.
25 **Department of Ethnics, 2005:** *The Ethnic Groups in Lao P.D.R.* Vientiane: Lao Front for National Construction.

BURMA

Burma is a diverse country, with ethnic groups speaking over 100 different languages. The majority — an estimated 68 percent of its 50-million large population — are Burman, and Burmese is the country's national language. Other major ethnic groups include the Shan, Karen, Rakhine (or Arakan), Karenni, Chin, Kachin and Mon. The country is divided geographically into seven divisions and seven ethnic states, the latter being located in the border regions. Buddhism is the dominant religion in Burma, although many Karen, Karenni, Chin and Kachin are Christian. Islam is practised widely in Arakan State, where it is the dominant religion of the Rohingya people.[1]

It is usually the non-Burman ethnic groups that are considered Burma's indigenous peoples. In accordance with more general usage in the country itself, this article will refer to them as "ethnic nationalities", in preference to "ethnic minorities", in order to avoid marginalizing the ethnic populations from Burma's broader political spectrum.

Burma continues to suffer from one of the longest-running civil wars in the world. In 1949, a year after independence from Britain, the Karen, unhappy at their political disenfranchisement, rose up against the Burman-dominated government. Numerous other ethnic-based resistance movements also took up arms. Conditions worsened after the 1962 military coup, which has seen Burmese of all ethnic backgrounds subjected to worsening violations of human rights. "Dying Alive", a detailed report by the British human rights researcher Guy Horton, published in April 2005, argues that the actions of the Burmese military against ethnic nationalities constitute genocide under international law.[2]

Despite multiparty elections in 1990 that saw the National League for Democracy (NLD) win a landslide victory, the junta refused to hand over power. NLD leader and Nobel Peace Prize laureate Daw Aung

San Suu Kyi, who was under house arrest from 1989 to 1995 and 2000 to 2002, was again imprisoned in May 2003 following an attempt on her life. At the end of 2005 she still remained under house arrest.

Continued oppression and militarization

Since 1989 the State Peace and Development Council (SPDC), Burma's military junta, has brokered ceasefire agreements with 14 - and thereby most - of the country's armed opposition groups.[3] Only the Karen National Union (KNU) and the Shan State Army South (SSA-S) have not entered into official ceasefires with the junta. However, the ceasefires have neither prevented widespread and systematic abuses against civilians nor have they led to any peace agreements. As a result, many of the ceasefire groups face mounting disaffection among their own people, who continue to suffer the consequences of the junta's exploitation of human and natural resources for their own benefit and that of neighboring countries.

SPDC leaders continue to press ceasefire groups to surrender without offering political rights. In 2005, the junta's War Office issued a directive to regional commanders to face any resistance by ceasefire groups with direct military action.[4] The junta also stepped up attacks on other armed ethnic nationality opposition groups. The ongoing armed conflict between the military regime's forces and opposition groups has resulted in hundreds of thousands of people becoming refugees or being internally displaced within the country. People flee to the forests, remote areas or across the border into Thailand or India, facing starvation, disease, landmines and other dangers.

In 2005, military operations and displacement continued unabated. Following the renunciation by the Shan State National Army (SSNA) of its ceasefire agreement in April 2005, there has been increased deployment of SPDC armed forces to cut off the SSNA from the Shan State Army South (SSA-S). As a result, between March and June 2005, over 10,000 civilians were reportedly displaced by the conflict in southern Shan State. During this period the SPDC armed forces relocated, burned or emptied several villages. Meanwhile, in Karen State, a large

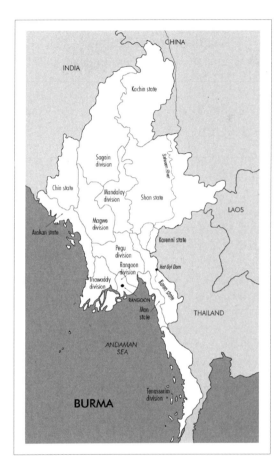

number of villages have also reportedly been burned down and the villagers forced to relocate as a result of continued military offensives against armed opposition groups.[5]

The National Convention

The National Convention, the junta-sponsored body first convened in 1993 with the objective of creating a new constitution and ultimately calling for new elections, was reconvened from 17 February to 31 March, and again on 5 December 2005. It took place without the involvement of a number of political parties, including the National League for Democracy (NLD) (read more about the National Convention process in *The Indigenous World 2005*).

Ethnic nationality leaders and ceasefire groups have been coerced into attending the National Convention in order to make the body appear nationally "representative". At the same time, the SPDC has tightened its grip on ethnic political leaders. Prior to the resumption of the National Convention, on 7 February, 2005, 31 political activists were arrested by SPDC authorities for participating in a meeting of senior Shan ethnic nationality representatives to discuss the formation of a "genuine federal union" of Burma. Those arrested on charges of conspiracy against the state included Khun Tun Oo and Sai Nyunt Lwin, chairman and secretary respectively of the Shan National League for Democracy (SNLD), the second largest vote winner in the 1990 elections. On 3 November, Khun Tun Oo was reportedly sentenced to 90 years in prison, while Sai Nyunt Lwin received an 85-year sentence.

In addition to the intimidation and detention of ethnic nationality political leaders, the National Convention has been characterized by restrictions on the participants' involvement, the lack of open debate and an intolerance of dissenting voices. On 13 February 2005, a group of six ceasefire groups tabled a proposal for changes to the National Convention's agenda comprising the following seven points:

1. To review the declared 6th political objective, which guarantees the military's leading role in national politics;
2. To review the 104 constitutional principles;
3. To allow free discussions with any individuals and groups;
4. To permit communications between National Convention participants and their organizations;
5. To allow the participation of those elected in the 1990 elections;
6. To conclude ceasefire agreements with the remaining armed opposition groups and enable their participation in the National Convention;
7. To repeal Law No. 5/96, which imposes lengthy jail terms on those who criticize the National Convention or propose alternative constitutions.

The junta however ignored the proposal. As a result, some ethnic nationality ceasefire groups reconsidered their policy of cooperation with the SPDC. Ceasefire groups such as the Shan State Army - North (SSA-N) and the New Mon State Party (NMSP) withdrew their official participation from the 2005 National Convention's first and second rounds respectively.

Human rights violations

The military regime continues to perpetrate serious human rights violations against Burma's ethnic nationalities as a strategy for maintaining
its control over their territories. Reports of forced labor, rape and other
sexual abuses, extortion and expropriation by the regime's authorities
continue to surface not only in areas where the regime is actively
engaged in military operations against armed opposition groups but
also in ceasefire areas, where the presence of large contingents of the
SPDC armed forces continues.[6]

Despite the atrocities suffered, civil society in ethnic nationality
areas has continued to play an active role, and ethnic community-
based organizations have produced a variety of reports documenting
and denouncing the abuses suffered at the hands of the regime.

Forced labor, Child soldiers, Human mine-sweepers

All over the country, men, women, and children continue to be forced
to perform duties such as road building and repair, portering for the
military, sentry duty, transport of military supplies, forced rice and
tea cultivation, rock-breaking, digging, construction, bush clearance,
fencing of military barracks and compounds and digging of military
bunkers and trenches. In August 2005, the Chin Human Rights Organization released the report "The Forced Labour Pandemic in Chinland",
documenting such patterns of abuse in Chin State.[7]

Civilians living in ethnic nationality areas are also forced to act as
human mine-sweepers by the military, resulting in loss of limbs and
sometimes death. In June 2005, the International Labor Organization
noted with concern the number of people under forced labor for the
military who had suffered "mutilations and violent deaths occurring
during mine-clearing operations."[8] Moreover, forced conscription and
training of children for the SPDC armed forces have also been reported
in 2005.[9]

Rape, sexual abuses and trafficking of women

Sexual violence such as rape, sexual slavery and forced marriage on the part of SPDC military personnel continued to be reported throughout the year but prosecution of the perpetrators rarely takes place. Civilians in Shan, Karen, Kachin and Mon states have been particularly vulnerable to such violations. In May 2005, the Kachin Women's Association Thailand released "Driven Away", a report analyzing the dynamics of the trafficking of Kachin women across the China-Burma border.[10] In July 2005, the release of "Catwalk to the Barracks" by the Woman and Child Rights Project and the Human Rights Foundation of Monland provided overwhelming evidence of the conscription of women into sexual slavery and other practices of sexual violence on the part of the military regime's troops in Mon areas.

Violations of economic rights

As in previous years, in 2005 the SPDC armed forces again confiscated land, livestock and fish catches, and harvested crops belonging to civilians. "Deserted Fields", a report released by the Shan Relief and Development Committee in January 2006, details how policies and initiatives of the Burmese military regime are impacting on farmers and agriculture in Southern Shan State.[11] In conflict areas, people suffered even more acute human rights violations, such as the requisitioning of possessions, forcible evictions and destruction of civilian dwellings.[12]

Religious freedom

Discrimination against non-Buddhist religions continued unabated during 2005. In January 2005, for example, SPDC armed forces vandalized and destroyed a Christian cross in Chin State's Matupi town. In May 2005, Chin Christians were forced to contribute money and labor to the construction of a Buddhist monastery in the same town. Discrimination also continued against the Muslim Rohingya in northern Arakan State, including the destruction of mosques by SPDC armed forces and the forced contribution of labor for the construction of "model villages" to resettle Buddhists onto Muslim land. Rohingya continued to be prevented from marrying or traveling outside their villages without official permission.

Development according to the junta

Natural resources extraction and infrastructure projects in areas inhabited by ethnic nationalities have often turned out to be a strategy used by the military regime to generate hard-currency income and a way of increasing and maintaining control over ethnic nationality regions.

Exploitation of natural resources

Of particular concern to ethnic nationalities living in Arakan and Chin states is the natural gas pipeline project presently unfolding in Western Burma. In cooperation with Burma's military junta, a consortium of Indian and Korean corporations are currently exploring gas fields off the coast of Arakan State. These fields – labeled A-1, or "Shwe", the Burmese word for gold – are expected to be one of the largest natural gas reserves in Southeast Asia and could well become the military regime's largest single source of foreign income. However, there is no evidence that ethnic nationality communities will derive any direct benefit from the project. On the contrary, it is feared that the ethnic nationalities will be negatively affected, as the "Shwe project" provides an excuse to further militarize and exploit the frontier areas of Arakan and Chin states. In order to transport the gas to India via Bangladesh, a pipeline corridor is already being cleared in those states. The area is already becoming increasingly militarized, and reports of forced labor in the context of infrastructure development have already emerged. Moreover, the military regime's poor environmental record and its failure to carry out any social and environmental impact assessments of the project precludes any determination of the extent of the impact on the local population and environment.

In 2005, two groundbreaking out-of-court settlements involving multinational oil companies Total and Unocal set significant precedents for corporate social responsibility. Unocal and Total agreed to compensate two groups of villagers from ethnic nationality areas in southern Burma for the serious human rights violations suffered in the mid-1990s at the hands of the SPDC military, who were providing security during the construction of the Yadana natural gas pipeline. Plaintiffs had alleged that Unocal and Total must have known that human rights violations, forced labor, rape and murder, were occurring.

Infrastructure projects

Another issue of serious concern is the construction of dams along the Salween River, which flows southward through Shan and Karenni states in the east of Burma and along the Thai-Burma border through Karen and Mon states. On 9 December 2005, Burma's military junta and the state-owned Electricity Generating Authority of Thailand (EGAT) signed a Memorandum of Understanding that paves the way for the construction of five dams inside Burma and along the Thai-Burma border on the Salween and Tenasserim rivers. The first structure on the Salween River will be the Hat Gyi dam at Haygui in Karen State. However, damming the river poses a threat to the livelihoods of local ethnic nationality communities and will inevitably lead to a massive population displacement in Karen State.   ❑

Notes

1   **Economist Intelligence Unit, August 2005:** *Country Report: Myanmar (Burma)*;
    Central Intelligence Agency (CIA), 2006: *CIA World Factbook: Burma.* Available
    online at:
    http://www.cia.gov/cia/publications/factbook/geos/bm.html#Intro
2   The 600-page report *"Dying Alive: A Legal Assessment of Human Rights in Burma"*
    was written by the British researcher Guy Horton, who traveled secretly in Bur-
    ma for four years documenting the 50-year war waged on the ethnic nationali-
    ties. It is only available in hard copy from the author at:
    hortonguy@hotmail.com
3   List of Cease-fire Agreements with the Junta, available at *Irrawaddy's* website:
    http://www.irrawaddy.org/aviewer.asp?a=444&z=14

4   The Politics of Peace, *Irrawaddy*, November 2005
5   United Nations General Assembly, 60th session, *Interim Report of the Special Rap-porteur of the Commission on Human Rights on the situation on human rights in My-anmar*; UN Doc. A/60/221 of 12 August 2005
6   Ibid.
7   Available at: http://www.chro.org/index.php/Home/193
8   **International Labour Organization (ILO), 2005:** *Report of the Committee of Ex-perts on the Application of Conventions and Recommendations, Report III (Part 1A), 93rd session, 2005.* pp. 175-176.
9   Covered by various reports, among them the *Interim Report of the Special Rap-porteur of the Commission on Human Rights on the situation on human rights in My-anmar*; op.cit.
10   Available at: http://www.womenofburma.org/Report/Driven_Away.pdf
11   Available at: http://shanland.org/articles/general/2006/Deserted_Fields.pdf
12   See also the report "They came and destroyed our village again", *Human Rights Watch*, June 2005, vol. 17 No. 4 (C). Available at: http://hrw.org/reports/2005/burma0605/burma0605.pdf; and Photo Set 2005-A, of the *Karen Human Rights Group*, May 2005, available at: http://www.ibiblio.org/freeburma/human-rights/khrg/archive/photoreports/2005photos/set2005a/index.html

NAGALIM

The Nagas number about 4 million people, inhabiting a mountainous landlocked territory of around 48,000 square miles that strad-
dles the present-day border between India and Myanmar (Burma).
When the Indian state gained independence from the British colonial
power in 1947, the Naga nation was denied sovereignty, and instead
arbitrarily divided and integrated into the new states of India and Burma (Myanmar). Subsequently, on 16 May 1951, the Nagas held a voluntary plebiscite in which 99.9% of the people voted for an independent Naga state. Even so, India and Burma defiantly ignored the legitimate rights of Nagas and unleashed a policy of genocide and militarization leading to thousands of deaths and wide-scale repression. The
Nagas are today further divided into different "administrative units"
such as Manipur, Assam, Arunachal Pradesh and the Nagaland state
within India, plus the Sagaing Division within Burma.

However, today, after many decades of armed political conflict, a
change in perception is being seen, with a formal cessation of military
conflict following the signing of a "ceasefire" agreement in 1997 between the Government of India and the National Socialist Council of
Nagalim (NSCN). The realization that the Indo-Naga conflict is of a
political nature, and that a political solution rather than a "military option" is necessary to solve it, has given rise to new hopes that the Nagas' right to exercise self-determination will be achieved.

Political negotiation

The fact that the ongoing peace talks are unconditional and at the highest level of the Prime Minister in a third neutral country indicates the
de facto recognition of the Naga people's sovereignty by the Govern-

ment of India. The 2002 recognition by the Indian government of the "uniqueness of Naga history and situation" has paved the way for serious negotiations between the NSCN leadership and India. After decades of living in exile, the NSCN leaders visited India in January 2003 and again in December 2004, both times invited by India's Prime Minister (read more about the visits in The Indigenous World 2004, 2005). The latest visit gave them the opportunity to visit Nagalim, where extensive consultations with the Naga public were held in order to prepare for future substantive talks. This also provided the space to intensively negotiate with the Indian government representative. From the Indian side, the talks have been upgraded from a bureaucratic level to a political level through the appointment of a Group of Ministers headed by Oscar Fernandes (Minister for Sports and Youth Affairs). This has created a more conducive atmosphere for the dialogue to continue.

Despite all this, after seeing no tangible progress in the talks with the Government of India, the NSCN insisted on extending the ceasefire for only six months when it was renegotiated in July 2005. This breaks the previous eight-and-a-half year practice of one-year extensions.

Civil society participation in the peace process

In recent years, Naga civil society has initiated a dialogue and sustained the peace process through various forms of democratic non-violent intervention, and has thus come to play a much more active role than during the first ceasefire in 1964.

The Naga people responded to the arrival of the NSCN leadership in Nagaland in December 2004 for consultation with the people, and the January 2005 Public Consultation on Peace at Hebron,1 with much appreciation. The Consultation endorsed and supported the confidence built thus far between the Government of India and the National Socialist Council of Nagalim (NSCN), and popular support was expressed for an honourable and acceptable settlement on the basis of the "uniqueness of the Naga history and situation" at the earliest possible moment. In addition, there was a call for unification/integration of the Naga homeland as a non-negotiable aspiration of the Nagas, and an appeal for sincerity from both political entities in the negotiation process.

Under the leadership of the Naga Hoho, the apex traditional tribal council, a number of Naga mass-based organisations have toured the different Naga areas, calling for active public participation in the ongoing peace-building process. A mammoth Public Rally was organized in Kohima on 31 August 2005 as "Naga Integration Day". More than 100,000 people participated, calling for unification of the Naga Homeland and demanding sincerity from the Government of India with regard the Indo-Naga political process.

The National Socialist Council of Nagalim (NSCN) also facilitated a series of Naga public consultations on the peace process. The latest of these was the 5th Naga People's Consultation on the Peace Process held in September 2005 in Bangkok, Thailand. The progress made and the challenges faced were extensively discussed, and an open statement was formulated at the conclusion of the two-day (6-7 September 2005) consultation. Its closing paragraphs read:

"... the Government of India also must accelerate its decisiveness to resolve the Indo-Naga Political conflict by exhibiting its 'Political will', lest the very purpose for which the ceasefire was signed is negated, which has become a serious concern for all. The Consultation also appreciated the continued efforts of all Nagas towards strengthening the peace process and further calls upon the civil society organizations, churches and individuals to re-enforce themselves with greater preparedness and responsi-

*bilities towards consolidating peoples collective potentials for nation
building and meaningful political settlement."*

Clashes in Manipur

On 16 June 2005, the United Naga Council organized a solidarity rally
across the Naga Hills, in present-day Manipur, calling for unification
of the Naga Homeland. In contrast, Manipur state declared 18 June as
Manipur State Integrity Day, thus provoking the Nagas to launch a
peaceful non-cooperation movement under the banner of the All Naga
Students' Association, Manipur (ANSAM), in the four Naga hill districts (Ukhrul, Tamenglong, Chandel & Senapati). Feeling that the government of Manipur did not represent the Nagas of Manipur, the
movement united around a resolve to uphold "Naga identity and dignity which cannot be safeguarded under the present Manipur state arrangement under any circumstances". The movement was answered
with a coercive hand, leading to indiscriminate firing upon innocent
Naga civilians on 8 and 9 July 2005. Many were injured in Senapati and
Ukhrul, and the Nagas were provoked to intensify their call for unification of the Naga homeland.

Nagas and neighbouring communities

The North East Peoples Initiative (NEPI) on demilitarization, peace
and progress organized a seminar on "Accords and Prospects of Peace
Initiatives in the North East Region" at Guwahati on September 9-10,
2005. This brought together nearly 100 peoples' organizations, among
these many indigenous peoples' struggle groups, women, students
and human rights movements. The observation was that the Government of India had entered into many peace processes after signing
"Suspension of Operations" agreements with many other armed
groups in the region, in addition to the "ceasefire" with the Nagas.
Moreover, the ongoing peace processes were indicative of the genuine
desire of the region's people for justice and peace.

Karbi Anglong in Assam, which is adjacent to Nagaland, has witnessed an upsurge in violence and ethnic tension between the Dimasas
and Karbis, leading to gruesome killings of innocent civilians. The immediate event that ignited the tension was the killing of 3 Dimasa
youths on 26 September 2005. The worst, however, was the 18 October
incident involving the hacking and burning of passengers on two bus-
es and the killing of some nearby villagers, causing the deaths of 38
persons. These events further snowballed into many criminal activities
causing torture, the destruction of more than 2,000 houses and the displacement of more than 40,000 villagers. Churches and human rights
organizations intervened with humanitarian assistance and much also
came across from Nagaland, while the Government in Assam and New
Delhi made only cursory interventions at a later stage. The systematic
provocation and tension in the initial phase of the violence later in-
flamed the communities' two armed groups to embark on a bloodbath,
shattering age-old neighbourly relations, while state agencies even
went to the extent of accusing the NSCN of involvement. This was rejected outright by the Naga group.

In a consultative meeting at Dimapur on 22 November 2005, the
Naga Peoples Movement for Human Rights (NPMHR) and the Assam-
based Manab Adhikar Sangram Samiti (MASS) expressed an immediate need to address human rights issues in a more comprehensive and
appreciative manner that would also reflect the solidarity of the peoples of the region. A team comprising eminent civil society activists
and organisations from the subcontinent, including the Naga Peoples
Movement for Human Rights, engaged in peace-building and reconciliation in the Karbi Anglong and North Cachar hill districts of Assam. A fact-finding team toured the affected area from 3-8 December
2005, and has published a report.

Obstacles to the peace process

The extension of the Disturbed Areas Act and the continuing use of
extraordinary powers under the Armed Forces Special Powers Act,
with incidents such as the killing of 3 NSCN cadres in Meghalaya and

the butchering of four civilians at Noney on 19 November 2005 by the 38thAssam Rifles battalion, the joint Indo-Myanmar military operation in the frontier areas, the use of other Naga splinter groups by the Indian agencies against the NSCN and the lack of a concrete response to the proposal made by the Naga negotiating team are all obstacles to a further extension of the ceasefire. Despite these difficulties, the Naga people's civil demonstration for an early solution to the Indo-Naga political process took place on 12 December 2005 at Dimapur. With more than 200,000 participants, the demonstration clearly showed the people's continued yearning for a just, honourable and lasting settlement to the conflict.   ❏

Note

1   The NSCN headquarters near Dimapur, Nagaland. –Ed.

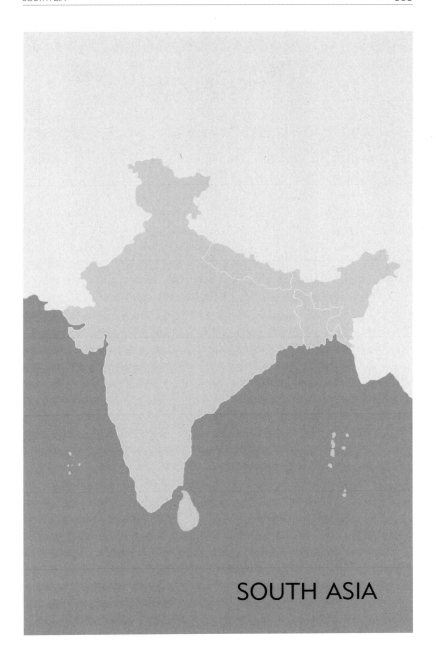

SOUTH ASIA

BANGLADESH

B angladesh lies in south Asia, bordering India and Burma (Myanmar) to the east, west and north, and bounded by the Bay of Bengal to the south. The majority of its 143.3 million population are Bengalis but there are also approximately 2.5 million indigenous peoples or *adivasi* (original inhabitants) belonging to 45 different ethnic groups. These groups are concentrated in the north and south-east of the country. There is no constitutional recognition of indigenous peoples in Bangladesh. The Constitution refers only to "backward segments of the population". Indigenous peoples remain among the most persecuted of all minorities in the country, facing discrimination on the basis of their religion and ethnicity.

Increased extremism

2005 was an eventful year in Bangladesh, with a significant rise in extremism, nationalism and intolerance towards minorities in general. On 17 August 2005, a series of over 400 coordinated bomb blasts in 63 out of the 64 districts of Bangladesh showed that Al-Qaeda-style terrorism was already well-established in the country. The assassination of former Awami League Finance Minister and Ambassador to the United Nations, Shah AMS Kibria, on 27 January 2005 also remains unsolved. This followed the assassination attempt on Anwar Choudhury, British High Commissioner to Bangladesh, in August 2004, when three others were killed by the bomb blast.

However, in spite of the deteriorating law and order situation and rising extremism, along with a drift towards calls for Sharia Law,[1] the international community remains unwilling to really tack-

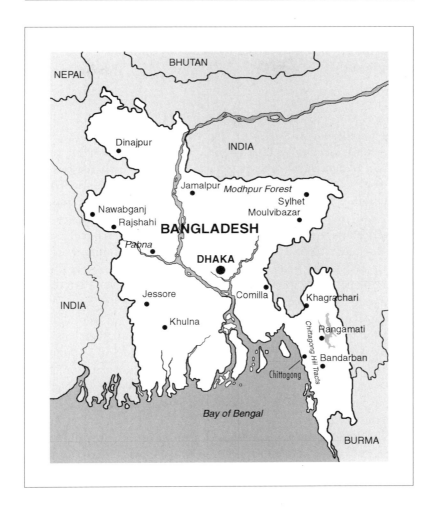

le the serious human rights abuses taking place in Bangladesh, one
of the oldest Muslim democracies and recipient of billions of dollars
of international development aid. Bangladesh continues to top the
list of most corrupt countries in the world,[2] and attacks on secular
figures and intelligentsia such as the judiciary, journalists and civil
liberty activists have reached alarming levels.

Government intolerance of freedom of speech
on indigenous issues

Indigenous representatives from Bangladesh were active at various international meetings last year, including the UN Permanent Forum on Indigenous Issues in New York, the Working Group on Indigenous Populations and the Working Group on the Draft Declaration on the Rights of Indigenous Peoples in Geneva. One of the main reasons why the indigenous peoples of Bangladesh are seeking redress within the UN system is because justice and equal rights are not guaranteed at home. This year, the statements made by indigenous delegates from Bangladesh were greeted with anger and intolerance inside the country. In August 2005, a Parliamentary Standing Committee on Chittagong Hill Tracts Affairs voted to summons four indigenous activists, Mrinal Kanti Tripura (PCJSS – the United Peoples Party of the Chittagong Hill Tracts), Mangal Kumar Chakma (PCJSS), Albert Mankin (Garo) and Ina Hume (Jumma Peoples Network International) for their alleged anti-state statements. Amnesty International and other international human rights organisations sent letters of protest to the Prime Minister and the Committee. A considerable amount of international pressure was placed on the Government of Bangladesh, and the summons was eventually withdrawn at the November meeting of the Committee.

In another show of increasing intolerance, the Government of Bangladesh sent police to break up a workshop to be held on Chittagong Hill Tracts (CHT) land rights issues from 23-24 November 2005. The event was funded by the Danish Embassy in Dhaka. Organisers of the event, including seven indigenous NGOs, held press conferences protesting at the prevention of the workshop, saying it was a violation of their fundamental right to expression of opinion and freedom of speech, as enshrined in the Bangladesh Constitution. An earlier workshop held in Dhaka on "Land Rights of Indigenous Peoples and Development Strategy" highlighted the need for politicians and policy makers to be progressive and liberal thinking, and find political solutions to the land rights problems. This meeting was not prevented by the government, perhaps due to the presence of international donors.

Struggle for constitutional recognition continues

Organised by the Bangladesh Indigenous Peoples Forum, more than 5,000 indigenous representatives gathered in Dhaka on the occasion of the UN International Day of the World's Indigenous People on 9 August 2005 and presented 10 demands to the government. These included constitutional recognition of indigenous peoples, the right to land, forest and natural resources, the right to mother tongue education at primary level, ensuring the security of indigenous women, special measures for economic and social development, reservation of membership in the parliament and local government councils etc. The national media, including television and newspapers, covered the event widely.

Inclusion of indigenous issues in Poverty Reduction Strategy

One step forward for indigenous peoples in Bangladesh is the inclusion of indigenous peoples' issues in the final version of the national Poverty Reduction Strategy Paper (PRSP).[3] The PRSP states that indigenous people have experienced social, political and economic exclusion, lack of recognition, fear and insecurity, loss of cultural identity and social oppression. It recognizes the fact that mainstream development efforts have either ignored their concerns or had a negative impact on them. However, the document lacks clear indications on how to address such issues, and nothing is mentioned about the participation of indigenous peoples in implementing and monitoring the PRSP.

Government project destroys Santal village

On 22 June 2005, the houses of 65 indigenous families in Parbatipur, Dinajpur district, were destroyed by order of the government. More than 400 people, including women and children, are now living under the open sky. The villagers, most of them Santals, lost their ancestral homes to the government's "model village project". Government officials, in the company of about 300 Bengalis, announced that the "old" village would be demolished to make way for an Adarsha Gram, a model village. The local administration did not deny the eviction although the Dinajpur deputy commissioner could not produce any written notice of eviction.

The General Secretary of the national Indigenous Peoples Forum, accompanied by journalists from national newspapers and members of civil society organisations, visited the village. As a result of the media reports, religious organisations, NGOs and civil society organisations organised protest rallies.

Continuing threat of eviction from forests

The Garo communities of Modhupur Forest are still under threat of eviction from the government's Eco-park project. More than 20 false cases were filed against Garos living in the forest after the killing of a Garo man in 2004 (see *The Indigenous World 2004, 2005*). Since 2003, the forest department has wanted to implement the project on Garo land without seeking their consent. In 2004, thousands of Garos were staging a peaceful protest rally against the project in the forest when the police opened fire on them. One Garo man was shot dead on the spot and 25 others were injured, including women and children. After the incident, the forest department could not continue to implement the project. However, to date the government has still not cancelled the project.

In Moulvibazar district, the Khasi indigenous peoples are also under threat of eviction from the forest department. An attempt to evict them in 2001 failed after large-scale protests were organised by indigenous peoples. On 3 August 2005, however, the forest department and more than 300 Bengali settlers attacked Notun Choilta village in Kulaura Thana. The outsiders, led by forest department officials, destroyed betel nut groves, fruit trees and other crops, and looted the properties of the Khasi villagers. The local union council chairman helped the forest department in the attack. The Khasis fled to save their lives. They had lived on the land for 20 years and demand recognition of their right to their ancestral land. The Khasi villagers reported the incident to the local police but nothing was done on their behalf. They obtained no compensation and no cases were filed against the forest department or the outsiders.

The eviction of 77 Santal families from their lands in northern Dinajpur led to protests in Dhaka in July 2005. The reason for the eviction was a "social forest" programme on their land. Calls were made by indigenous peoples and their leaders for the rehabilitation of the families.

Other Eco-Parks are planned in the Chittagong Hill Tracts, notably in Chimbuk in Bandarban district, where 5,600 acres have been acquired.

Chittagong Hill Tracts

The Chittagong Hill Tracts comprise 13,295 sq. km. of hilly land once densely forested. The area is home to 11 indigenous peoples, namely the Bawm, Chak, Chakma, Khyang, Khumi, Lushai, Marma, Mro, Pankho, Tanchangya and Tripura. They are commonly known as the Jummas due to their common practice of swidden cultivation (rotational agriculture), locally known as *jum*. The Jummas are, in ethnic, cultural and religious terms, very different from the majority Bengalis.

8th Anniversary of the Peace Accord

In December 1997, the 25-year-long civil war ended with a Peace Accord between the Government of Bangladesh and Parbattya Chattagram Jana Samhati Samiti (PCJSS, United Peoples Party of the Chittagong Hill Tracts), the organisation leading the indigenous peoples' resistance movement. The Accord recognises the CHT as an indigenous ("tribal inhabited") region and acknowledges the need to preserve its special characteristics. It also recognises the traditional governance system and the role of the chiefs, thus providing the building blocks for indigenous autonomy in the CHT. However, some of the major provisions of the Accord remain unimplemented, and the GoB and military have been in increasing breach of the Accord, through their further encroachments onto indigenous lands.

2 December 2005 was the 8th anniversary of the Peace Accord and the PCJSS organised protests all over the Hill Tracts against the Government of Bangladesh for its failure to implement key elements of the agreement. They called for implementation of the Peace Accord and the removal of military personnel and illegal settlers from the region.

Unfortunately, it is not only the indigenous people who have been victimised by the Government of Bangladesh and military personnel but also long-term Bengali residents of the CHT who have supported implementation of the CHT Accord. Many of them have resisted the fundamentalist state policies and supported progressive multi-ethnic politics under the banner of the Old and Permanent Bengalis Welfare Association. Many of the association's members were summoned to the local army headquarters, tortured and harassed, and forced to resign from the Association. It is clear that the army prefers the CHT people to organise along ethnic and religious lines, thus perpetuating ethnic tensions and helping to legitimise their presence and role in an otherwise post-conflict CHT.

Development programmes

2005 has seen an increase in development activities in the CHT. On 15 December 2005, the United Nations Development Programme (UNDP) approved a record amount of development funding for the CHT Programme. The joint programme of the Government of Bangladesh and the UNDP in Bangladesh entitled "Promotion of Development and Confidence Building in the Chittagong Hill Tracts" will invest US$50 million between now and 2009. With this development assistance to the CHT, the UNDP hopes to build confidence among its people and institutions and promote long-term peace. Funds have been made available to the UNDP primarily by the European Commission, along with Australia, Japan, Norway and USAID. Norway remains the only donor demanding the establishment of regional government bodies prior to large-scale investment, as set out in the Peace Accord.[4]

The UNDP's earlier attempt at implementing the programme met with protest from PCJSS and indigenous leaders, who complained that the UNDP was in breach of its own Indigenous Peoples' Policy by working with disputed settler communities and non-resident Bengalis (see *The Indigenous World 2004* and *2005*).

Continuing support to Bengali settlers

One worrying aspect of the amount of aid going into Bangladesh is the recognized corruption that exists. In addition, the fact that the Government of Bangladesh has been providing "free food rations" to 27,000 Bengali families within the CHT cannot be overlooked, even though equally impoverished indigenous families and widows rarely receive such rations. The GoB also recently passed a decision to increase the number of Bengali settler families receiving rations to 55,000. The provision of rations is an essential component in ensuring that Bengali settlers from the plains do not return to their original home regions. There have been reports that the Bangladesh Army is involved in settling a further 10,000 Bengali families in the Kassalong Reserve Forest in Sajek. A new road has been built from Baghaihut to Sajek, which borders the Mizoram hills of north-east India. This proposed settlement is in direct breach of the 1997 Peace Accord.

The legality of the Army's actions and the alarming and continuing policy of state-sponsored migration have been questioned by international human rights organisations. The source of funding of these discriminatory and militarily tactical policies was also highlighted in a recent report of the Asian Centre for Human Rights. In "Who funds the acts of Racism and Racial Discrimination in the Chittagong Hill Tracts?" donors, including the UK Department for International Development (DfID), the European Union and United Nations agencies are called upon to ensure that their funds are not used to sponsor the migration of Bengali settlers, the provision of their food rations or the settlement of Bengali families in Kassalong-Sajek, or any other programmes that continue to disregard the human rights and fundamental freedoms of the indigenous peoples. Sajek and the Kassalong Reserve Forest are already inhabited by indigenous groups who suffer from food insecurity on a yearly basis. There are still sizeable communities of internally displaced people in the area who have yet to be rehabilitated and who face an uncertain future and the likelihood of further displacement if this illegal resettlement programme takes place.

Militarisation and Human Rights Abuses
The continued presence and even expansion of military bases and the influx of settlers have contributed to ongoing human rights abuses and sexual violence in the CHT. The complete impunity that exists for such crimes has led to this culture of violence becoming acceptable within the military. The lack of access to justice for indigenous peoples has long been recognised as a serious issue by international human rights organisations.

Indigenous peoples are calling for an independent international body to investigate serious allegations of human rights abuses in the Chittagong Hill Tracts during and after the conflict. It is important to understand the causes of violence in the region if it is to be prevented in the future. However, the inextricable involvement of the military in abuses keeps the hands of the judiciary tied on Hill Tracts issues, no matter how serious.   ❑

Notes

1   Sharia is the traditional Islamic law based on the Koran.
2   Transparency International 2005 Corruption Perception Index 2005, at: http://
    www.transparency.org/policy_and_research/surveys_indices/cpi/2005
3   The process of formulating Poverty Reduction Strategy Papers in all low-in-
    come countries was initiated by the International Monetary Fund (IMF) and the
    World Bank (WB) in 1999. The formulation of the PRSPs is supposed to be coun-
    try driven, with the broad participation of civil society. Once formulated, a PRSP
    provides the basic framework of all policies and programmes aimed at promot-
    ing growth and reducing poverty. In many countries, indigenous organisations
    complain that they were not properly involved in PRSP formulation. –Ed.

4   See websites of UNDP Bangladesh (http://www.un-bd.org/undp/info/) and
    Underrepresented Nations and Peoples Organisation (UNPO) (http://www.
    unpo.org/news_detail.php?arg=16&par=3395)

Other sources

Amnesty International, 2005: Bangladesh, Harassment of leaders of the indigenous
people. *Amnesty International online documentation archive,* 13 October 2005.
Available at: http://web.amnesty.org/library/Index/ENGASA130102005
Asian Centre for Human Rights (ACHR), 2005: Bangladesh: Judges under the at-
tacks of the Jihadis. *ACHR Review,* 23 November 2005.
- Who funds the acts of racism and racial discrimination in the Chittagong Hill
Tracts? *ACHR Review,* 15 June 2005.
- Destruction of a people: Jummas of the CHTs, *ACHR Review,* 25 May 2005. All
available at: http://www.achrweb.org/countries/bangla.htm
United Nations Development Programme (UNDP), 2005: Largest ever develop-
ment project in the CHT approved. Press release 15 December 2005. Available at:
http://www.un-bd.org/undp/info/
Banglappedia (online source on Bangladesh): Parbatya Chattagram Jana-Samhati
Samiti. http://search.com.bd/banglapedia/Content/HT/P_0088.HTM
Bangladesh Human Rights Network, 2005: Constitutional recognition and self-de-
termination for Adivasis demanded. *Banglarights.net,* 10 August 2005.
- Adivasi leaders demand rehabilitation of 77 Santal families. *Banglarights.net,* 24
July 2005. Both available at: http://www.banglarights.net
Jumma Peoples Network-UK: http://www.jpnuk.org.uk/
- Statements of Bangladesh Indigenous peoples at UN Permanent Forum on
Indigenous Issues, UN HQ New York, May 2005
- Statements of Bangladesh Indigenous peoples at UN Working Group on Indig-
enous Populations, UN Geneva, July 2005
Underrepresented Nations and Peoples Organisation (UNPO), 2005: Chittagong
Hill Tracts: Largest Ever Development Project Approved. Press release 21 De-
cember 2005. Available at:
http://www.unpo.org/news_detail.php?arg=16&par=3395
Vanishing Rites
http://www.vanishingrites.com

NEPAL

Nepal is a country of great cultural diversity. The 1991 Constitution of Nepal also states that Nepal is a multi-ethnic, multi-cultural and multi-language country. Despite being a country of great cultural diversity, however, the constitution declares Nepal a Hindu kingdom and the *khasa Nepali* language as the only official language of the nation. The state policy of one language (*khasa Nepali*) and one religion (Hindu), and the state's institutional support to practising of the Hindu culture has eroded indigenous cultures, languages and religions and thereby contributed to a loss of ethnic identity among many indigenous communities. According to the latest national census, indigenous peoples constitute 37.2 % of Nepal's 23.4 million population. At present, 59 indigenous nationalities have been identified and listed in the official gazette but it is believed that many more are still outstanding.

The Nepal Federation of Indigenous Nationalities (NEFIN) is the umbrella organization for indigenous organizations in Nepal. It was established in 1991 with the aim of achieving social equality and justice for indigenous peoples by preserving their distinct identities and establishing ethnic autonomy, with the right to self-determination.

Armed conflict

After Sher Bahadur Deuba's government failed to respond to the 40-point demand of the United Peoples' Front, Nepal Communist Party (Maoist), they declared a people's war on February 13, 1996. Since then the armed conflict has been escalating in Nepal. Over the past 10 years, more than 40,000 people have been internally displaced and 14,000

have been killed. Indigenous peoples are the communities most affected by the armed conflict.[1]

Peace-building efforts have been made both at national and international levels. But the peace-building agencies have ignored the participation of indigenous peoples, ignoring the fact that they are the communities most affected by the armed conflict. NEFIN is therefore
strongly urging the government, political parties and international
communities first to recognize the identity and rights of indigenous
peoples and second to include their full and effective participation in
the peace-building processes. NEFIN also believes that the current
structure of the state is defective, discriminatory and non-inclusive.
The ongoing violent conflict is a result of structural problems in Nepali society. As long as the present structure of the state exists, conflict in
one form or another is unavoidable. One of NEFIN's clear demands is
therefore the restructuring of the state.

Royal coup: collapse of democracy

Since King Gyanendra dissolved parliament and dismissed the democratically elected government of Nepal on October 4, 2002, he has become more and more ambitious. With the royal coup of February 1,

2005, he has usurped all political and administrative power in the country, and democracy has collapsed. As a result, the political, civil and human rights of Nepali peoples have been denied. All sorts of democratic values and norms have been destroyed.

Indigenous peoples, who have been advocating for the protection and promotion of their rights and who have been raising issues of linguistic freedom, secularism, pluralism and national regional autonomy with the right to self-determination, have been badly affected by the collapse of democracy. The present regime is a replica of the pre-democracy panchayat regime, and the rulers are putting much of their efforts into reviving elements of the panchayat regime's autocratic state apparatus. They are trying to re-impose the monolithic policy of one nation, one culture, one language and one religion by any means. They have been advocating for homogeneity, despite the reality of a heterogeneous Nepali society.

Government ordinances and indigenous responses

At present there is no rule of law in Nepal, the government is ruling the country by ordinances. The king's government has abolished the reservation policy for indigenous peoples introduced by the previous government in the education and civil service sectors (see *The Indigenous World 2005*). The government's ordinances issued to regulate communication have violated the freedom of expression. The code of conduct introduced to regulate NGO activities has severely affected the freedom to open ethnic association as, according to the government, it supposedly disturbs communal harmony. In several districts of eastern and mid-western Nepal, government security forces, in the name of security, have restricted indigenous peoples from talking on the telephone with their distant relatives in their mother tongue. The security forces have also encroached historically and spiritually onto important lands and territories of indigenous peoples by putting up wire fences.

So far 33 ordinances have been issued, and the government is preparing to issue many more. Along this line, the Ministry of Forest and

Soil Conservation began preparing to issue an ordinance that was against the interests of indigenous peoples, as it could affect indigenous peoples' control, access and benefit sharing of the biological resources on their territories. NEFIN therefore led a delegation of indigenous peoples to the Ministry of Forest and Soil Conservation on June 5, 2005 and presented a memorandum to the Minister demanding that the government should not introduce any ordinances affecting the interests of indigenous peoples without the consultation and effective participation of those peoples.

On July 25, 2005, NEFIN delegates met the vice-chairs of the Council of Ministers and presented them with another memorandum demanding:

1) that the reservation policy introduced by the previous government be implemented;
2) that the founding General Secretary of NEFIN, Mr. Suresh Ale Magar, who has been kept in isolation since the Indian authorities handed him over to the government in 2004 be made public and be presented to the court for legal treatment;
3) that a special time schedule be allocated on Nepal TV and Radio Nepal for indigenous peoples' programs; and
4) that August 9 be declared as the national holiday to honor the international Day of the World's Indigenous Peoples and special programs be prepared for the social, economic, educational and environmental development of indigenous peoples.

Advocating for inclusive democracy

Indigenous peoples are experiencing a kind of political suffocation under the present regime. They find it very difficult to develop and preserve their cultures, languages, religions, norms, values and traditions. In the current situation, they cannot protect and promote their rights. Indigenous peoples have begun to realize that their rights cannot be guaranteed under the monarch's despotic regime. They are now aware of the importance of democracy. As a result, with their distinct identity and independent demands, and under the collective leadership of NE-FIN, indigenous peoples have been actively participating in the democratic movement of Nepal. But indigenous peoples are also aware of the fact that the type of democracy where "winner takes all" cannot serve the interests of indigenous peoples and does not address their multi-faceted issues. NEFIN is therefore advocating for inclusive democracy, whereby the participation and proportional representation of all communities is ensured. This has been a subject of national political debate among political leaders, academics, *janajati* intellectuals and activists in Nepal.[2]

Peace-building in a multicultural framework

In line with the above, a NEFIN seminar on ILO Convention 169 and Peace-Building in Nepal promoted a multicultural framework for a lasting solution to the armed conflict. The seminar took place on January 19-20, 2005. Its aim was to sensitize thinking at national level on the use of ILO Convention 169 as an international legal framework for peace-building in a multicultural country such as Nepal. Former ILO director and United Nations special representative to the Guatemala peace process, Mr. Ian Chambers, was among others to present a paper at the seminar. During his presentation, Mr. Chambers shared his experience of the Guatemala peace process. This was very relevant and useful to the case of Nepal. During the seminar, the then Prime Minister Sher Bahadur Deuba repeated his commitment to ratifying ILO Convention 169.

Other advocacy activities

Throughout the year, NEFIN has promoted indigenous peoples' rights and participation in the state mechanisms in Nepal through seminars, rallies, research, publications and a number of other activities. As in previous years, the International Day of Indigenous Peoples on August 9 was used as an occasion to attract the attention of the government bureaucracy, political leaders, society at large and public and private sector media.

Whereas the August 9 celebrations in previous years have been Kathmandu-based, this year NEFIN organized events to mark the day in many parts of the country. Activities to celebrate the day included seminars, talks, advocacy, a poem recital competition in mother tongue languages, folk songs, a folk dance competition, ethnic food festivals, an exhibition of indigenous art, dresses and ornaments, traditional games and cultural rallies. Thousands of indigenous people participated in the programs.

On December 21, 2005, NEFIN organized a huge protest rally against a massacre of indigenous Tamangs and Newars in Nagarkot. The massacre took place at 11 pm on December 14, 2005 when a bloodthirsty soldier indiscriminately opened fire on a crowd of local people who were gathering at the temple of Nagarkot (12 km north-east of Kathmandu) to celebrate a traditional festival. The massacre took the lives of 11 ordinary people, 10 of whom were indigenous Tamang and Newars. At least 16 indigenous people were seriously injured in the incident. In order to investigate the details of the incident, NEFIN visited the spot, met family members of the dead and wounded, questioned eye witnesses and collected first-hand information. Based on that information, NEFIN believes that the government is responsible for the mass killing.

It has demanded appropriate compensation for the families of the dead and wounded and that those involved in the crime be brought to justice. It has also formed a committee to conduct a detailed investigation into the massacre, and warned the government to put a stop to such killings immediately.

At international level, NEFIN representatives participated in the UN Permanent Forum on Indigenous Issues in New York in May 2005, in the Beijing Plus 10 meeting in February 2005,[3] also in New York, as well as in a number of international conferences. At the Permanent Forum, NEFIN's General Secretary Dr. Om Gurung and NEFIN's Public Relations Secretary Lucky Sherpa made oral interventions on poverty reduction and universal education under agenda item 3 on Goals 1 and 2 of the Millennium Development Goals (poverty reduction and

universal education). Participation in the Permanent Forum also provided an opportunity to meet with Mr. Rodolfo Stavenhagen, Special
Rapporteur on the Human Rights and Fundamental Freedoms of Indigenous Peoples within the Office of the High Commissioner for Human Rights. He was informed of the human rights violations committed both by the state and the Maoists against indigenous peoples, and
Mr. Stavenhagen was encouraged to visit Nepal.   ❑

Notes

1 According to a report published by the Informal Sector Service Centre (INSEC)
   in 2004, indigenous peoples constitute the largest group (21%) of victims of the
   conflict between the state and the Maoists.
2 On August 28-29, 2005 NEFIN hosted a seminar on *Re-structuring the state from
   an indigenous perspective.*
3 The 49th Session of the UN Commission on the Status of Women (New York 28
   February to 11 March 2005) is known as the "Beijing + 10 meeting", since review
   and appraisal of the Beijing Declaration and Platform for Action from the 1994
   United Nations Fourth World Conference of Women (held in Beijing in September 1995) was the main agenda item of the meeting. –Ed.

INDIA

In India, 461 ethnic groups are recognized as so-called Scheduled Tribes, and these "tribals" (also often referred to as *adivasis*) are usually considered India's indigenous peoples. With an estimated population of 84.3 million, they comprise 8.4% of the total population, making India the country with the largest indigenous population in the world. There are, however, many more ethnic groups that would qualify for Scheduled Tribes status but which are not officially recognized. Estimates of the total number of indigenous ethnic groups are as high as 635. The largest concentrations of indigenous peoples are found in the seven states of northeast India, and the so-called "central tribal belt" stretching from Rajasthan in the west to West Bengal in the east. India has several laws and constitutional provisions, such as the Fifth Schedule for mainland India and the Sixth Schedule for certain areas of northeast India, which recognize indigenous communities' rights to land and self-governance. These laws have numerous shortcomings, however, and their implementation is far from satisfactory. India therefore has a long history of indigenous peoples' movements aimed at asserting their rights, which have often provoked violent repression from the state. Sadly, this also continued in 2005.

Policy developments at national level

Draft Forest Rights Bill
On 13 December 2005, the Minister for Tribal Affairs, P.R Kyndiah, introduced the Scheduled Tribes (Recognition of Forest Rights) Bill 2005 into Parliament *"to recognize and vest the forest rights and occupation in forest land in forest dwelling Scheduled Tribes who have been residing in such forests for generations but whose rights could not be recorded and to provide*

for a framework for recording the forest rights so vested and the nature of evidence required for such recognition and vesting in respect of forest land." The Bill was then referred to the Joint Parliamentary Committee, a committee of parliamentarians set up specifically for this bill. The committee was to call for submissions from interested groups and persons, invite those who wanted to make depositions before the committee and place the final draft before Parliament in April 2006. The final draft of this bill is expected to be placed with Parliament for its passage in the first half of 2006.

The bill itself was introduced into Parliament amidst widespread nationwide protests demanding a pro-tribal and pro-forest dwellers' bill. A National Consultation on the Draft Forest Rights Bill organized, on August 7 and 8 in Delhi, ended with the passing of a declaration demanding the introduction of the bill during the then ongoing session of parliament. About 40-50,000 adivasis and forest dwellers across the country held protests on 15 August 2005, when India celebrates its Independence Day, demanding that the Bill be introduced into parliament. This was followed by people demanding "the bill or jail".

The act proposes 12 specific rights, heritable but not alienable or transferable, such as, among others, ownership of 2.5 hectares of land for each family from a forest-dwelling scheduled tribe, ownership of minor forest produce and the right to grazing. In turn, the communities are obliged to apply conservation and protection measures.

Rectifying historical injustice

On 21 July 2004, the Government of India - through the Ministry of Environment & Forests (MoEF) - finally confessed in an affidavit to the Supreme Court that *"the historical injustice done to the tribal forest dwellers through non-recognition of their traditional rights must be finally rectified"*. Earlier, the MoEF had issued a number of circulars on 18 September 1990 requiring the establishment of forest rights for all categories of forest dwellers as the forest laws in this regard were being violated by governments and forest departments. These were also being ignored by the states in question and the forest department. Matters reached a national crisis on 3 May 2002 when the MoEF issued an or-

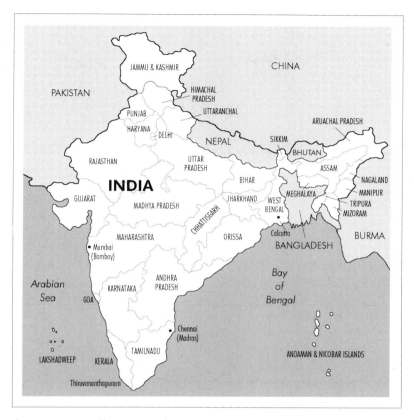

der requiring all states and Union Territories to evict all forest "en-croachers" within five months, based on a misinterpretation of a Su-preme Court order. This led to mass evictions of tens of thousands of forest dwellers. Between May 2002 and August 2004 alone, evictions were carried out over 152,000 hectares. Hundreds of villages were set on fire or demolished, leading to clashes and deaths from the police opening fire. About 300,000 people were evicted and another 3 to 4 million faced the threat of eviction. The MoEF was compelled to issue a clarification order in October 2002 stating that not all forest dwellers were encroachers. On 21 December 2004, the MoEF was forced to issue a letter to all states and Union Territories calling for a halt to evictions of forest dwellers until their rights had been settled. Even this had no effect.

Nationwide protests erupted. The Campaign for Survival and Dignity, a platform of mass organizations of adivasis and forest dwellers from 11 states, launched organized protests, publicising details of what was happening, the legal position, how their rights were being systematically violated and what should be done. The Campaign demanded a separate act to settle forest rights given that the present arrangement did not work either in law or in practice. At a high level meeting on 19 January 2005, the Prime Minister decided that the Scheduled Tribes and Forest Dwellers (Recognition of Forest Rights) Bill should be drafted and, by mid-2005, the draft was out.

Whereas environmentalists and the MoEF have objected to the bill, arguing that it would hinder efforts to prevent forest destruction and preserve endangered wildlife, most indigenous peoples' organisations and their supporters have welcomed it. They insist, however, that a number of crucial issues still need to be resolved, for instance, the non-inclusion of forest dwellers (the bill in the current form only provides for rights for Scheduled Tribes), and the fact that the bill only applies to people who were registered as forest dwellers before 1980. Another area of concern is the procedure, which leaves the authority to establish rights to the very same bureaucracy (the Forest Department) that precisely failed to implement the existing law and the repeated orders it received all these years.

Jharkhand

Arson and murder in Garhwa

The notorious Forest Department once again unleashed terror against indigenous communities in Jharkhand. The state's action against the so-called "encroachers" onto forest land turned violent when forest department henchmen, along with timber mafias from the district of Garhwa, attacked the villagers of Kumba Khurd, under the development Block of Nagar Untari in broad daylight. The villagers belong to the Uraos (Scheduled Tribe), Agarias (de-scheduled tribe now Back-

ward Caste) and Bhuinas (Scheduled Caste in Jharkhand but Scheduled Tribe in Orissa). On June 8, 140 houses were set on fire and people
were beaten mercilessly. The mother of a three-month-old girl child
cried and prayed to be allowed to save her baby, who was sleeping
inside one of the burning houses, but she was silenced by a forest department thug who hit her hard with a stick on her chest. The baby
was burnt alive. The carnage left many badly injured. All this happened after the circulation of an order by the central government's
Ministry of Environment and Forest, on 12 May 2005, asking all state
governments to avoid evicting any forest dwellers until the Forest
Rights Bill had been finalized and enacted.[1] The cause of this heinous
crime was the victims' opposition to timber contractors' felling of trees
in the forest. The victims are mostly landless and depend largely on
non-timber forest products for their livelihood.

The Forest Department of Jharkhand lodged a First Information
Report (complaint recorded at the nearest police station) on the case,
accusing the 50 people of Deonagri hamlet in Kumba Khurd village of
felling trees in the forest and constructing houses on forest land. They
were further accused of stealing timber. The Forest Department, in collaboration with the district administration, sent 17 of them to jail. The
people, however, decided not to be daunted by the state aggression
against them and to hold onto the land under their occupation at any
cost. Peoples' movements and human rights organizations are supporting them.

Hostile judiciary
In an ugly turn of events, in September 2005 the High Court of
Jharkhand ordered the state government of Jharkhand to halt implementation of the Panchayati Raj (Extension to the Scheduled Areas)
Act of 1996 (also known as PESA) in the state on the ill-founded ground
that the act was unconstitutional. The Chief Justice, along with another
judge from the court bench, said in the controversial ruling that the
act's provision to reserve posts at different levels of decision-making
for Scheduled Tribes was against the spirit of equality enshrined in the
Constitution of India. However, by doing so, the said judges them-

selves went against the Constitution. The PESA was passed by Parliament to ensure the functioning of self-rule of the Scheduled Tribes by empowering them in the areas where they are residing in large numbers, demarcated as the Scheduled Areas under the Constitution. In the judgment, the judges even resorted to falsehood by providing wrong data regarding the population of the Scheduled Tribes in the Scheduled Areas. The judges conveniently ignored the fact that nowhere in the Constitution was the demographic status taken into consideration when notifying these areas as Scheduled Areas. By trying to prove that the Scheduled Tribes were a minority in these areas and therefore not eligible to enjoy the status provided by the act, they were also refusing to recognize the inhuman aggression and ruthless exploitation these people have been subjected to by mainstream society. Factors that have resulted in their present pathetic condition, and in some areas have led to their becoming a minority in their own ancestral land. The act has already been implemented years ago in other states with the same demographic conditions as Jharkhand. In Jharkhand, the state government is using a delaying tactic in implementation of the act.

Threats of displacement
In an unprecedented move, the government of Jharkhand signed a Memorandum of Understanding (MoU) with 41 large and medium-sized transnational and Indian steel and mining companies to open up the ancestral land of the indigenous peoples for resource extraction on a large scale. Bearing in mind the demand for steel on the international market, the government is inviting foreign direct investment to the benefit of a few and at the cost of many, most of whom will be indigenous peoples. Of the estimated people who would be displaced, 80% would belong to Scheduled Tribes. The amount of land that is demanded is around 60,000 acres, a large part of which is forest land. However, the people have already started putting up strong opposition to this effort to sell off their ancestral land.

Chattisgarh

A "People's Movement" in Dantewada district?

The people of Dantewada district in Chattisgarh state in India, most of whom are indigenous, have had their lives completely transformed over the last year. Today they are living in the midst of an undeclared war between the government and the Maoist guerrilla. The administration, however, prefers to describe its war as a "people's movement" (locally known as the *Salwa Judum*), blaming any violence entirely on the Maoists. This, however, is far from the truth.

The Maoists, who were previously known as the People's War Group and have now expanded and renamed themselves the Communist Party of India (Maoist), have been active in Dantewada since the 1980s. In their writings, they claim that this is one of their "liberated zones" where they have their own parallel administrative structure through village level bodies called *sanghams*. The Maoists in this region have acted against extortion by police and forest officials, demanded higher wages for non-timber forest produce and also carried out some land redistribution. In their writings, they also maintain that they have undertaken some irrigation works, and launched seed banks and other developmental activities in their strongholds.

It is clear that the administration has hardly any presence here, especially in the interior villages. Development services such as schools and hospitals are minimal – the overall literacy rate is 21%, and only 26 villages out of 1,220 have primary healthcare centres. What is amply evidenced, however, is the presence of the paramilitary. As of now, there are five Central Reserve Police Force battalions, one Naga India Reserve battalion and at least one battalion of the Gujarat Armed Police, and the administration has requested more Naga battalions. In total, there are approximately 7,000 paramilitary forces deployed in the region. Although the region is located in the heart of India, roads are now being widened by the Border Roads Organisation, the road construction wing of the army, presumably to facilitate the movement of troops.

The region has very rich mineral resources and forests, and the government of Chattisgarh has major plans for industrialization here. As it is, the non-tribal population in the area expanded so dramatically between 1991 and 2001 that demands have been made to de-reserve two constituencies, i.e. lift the protection they enjoy under the Fifth Schedule of the Constitution (for example, the right to land and self-governance, as described above). There are three steel plants in the offing, owned by Tata, Essar and the National Mineral Development Corporation (a governmental enterprise), and two large dams, the Bodhghat Hydroelectric Project and the Polavaram dam, all of which will cause major displacements. Previous industrialization in the area, in the form of the iron ore mines at Kirandul, has not benefited the indigenous people at all. All it has brought them is pollution and sexual exploitation.

The immediate origins of the *Salwa Judum* in 2005 are unclear. According to a video made at the government's behest, "Operation Salwa Judum" was initiated in January 2005 when the police launched "overt and covert" operations to mobilise villagers against the Maoists. In an audio recording released by the Maoists to the press, a police official is heard promising 200,000 Rupees (around 4,500 US$) to every village that joins the Judum, and boasting of how the police had killed people and burnt villages that were supporting the Maoists. The official story being put out, however, is of a spontaneous people's reaction to years of left-wing militant oppression.

The administration glosses over Salwa Judum as meaning "peace campaign". Its literal meaning in the local Gondi language, "purification/pacification hunt", describes what it is far more accurately: a government-run "sanitization" campaign to exterminate Maoists and their supporters. Both the Bharatiya Janata Party, the ruling party in Chattisgarh, and the opposition Congress Party are supporting the Judum.

The leadership of the Salwa Judum consists mainly of urban non-tribal youth, sons and daughters of petty officials and traders, and some tribal politicians and their supporters. These people belong to the section that is directly threatened by the Maoists, and have the most to gain from unchecked industrialization. The Salwa Judum has taken the form of processions to villages, accompanied by politicians, members of the civil administration and paramilitary. Villages that support the Maoists are repeatedly attacked, their houses burnt, grain and cattle looted, and they are forced to surrender to the Judum and move to live in roadside camps. Some of these villagers have been forcibly brought to the camps by the paramilitary after combing operations in their villages, while others have come on their own to pre-empt attacks. There are also some people who are there because of their fear of Maoist retaliation for joining the Salwa Judum. People have little choice. Camp dwellers are made to participate in Judum meetings, and captured Maoists are forced to work as informers. Villages and even families have been divided, with people sometimes unaware of the whereabouts of others. According to the government's own estimates given in December 2005, some 15,000 to 30,000 people from approximately 400 villages in Bijapur tahsil[2] (West Bastar) have been affected. As of February 2006, the Judum has extended its operations to South Dantewada (Konta tahsil), and 40,000 people there have reportedly fled from their villages, either to the homes of relatives or across state borders.

The evacuation camps are in a terrible condition, and a report by Médecin Sans Frontiers (Doctors Without Borders) indicates that health problems are at crisis levels. Rations were stopped a long time ago and people are now engaged in food-for-work schemes. The government has plans to convert the camps into long-term strategic settlements, attached to police stations, with a permanent base of informers, chillingly reminiscent of Nagaland in the 1950s or the Vietnam War.

The Salwa Judum youth have also taken over the local administration. They man checkpoints along the road, stopping and searching vehicles, and preventing people they suspect of being associated with the Maoists from proceeding. Many of them have now been trained and armed and given the status of special police officers.

Since the emergence of the Salwa Judum, deaths have increased exponentially. According to the government, the Maoists have killed over a hundred people in the Bijapur region since the Judum began, on the grounds that they were informers or had joined the Judum. The Maoists have also killed the paramilitary and blasted government installations. The Maoist death toll of civilians rose dramatically on Feb-

ruary 28, when they blasted a truck carrying villagers back from a Judum meeting in Konta tahsil. Some 26 people were killed instantly,
and others seriously injured. Several people were reportedly kid-
napped in the same incident.

The government also has a mounting death toll to its credit but there
are no official figures. According to some estimates, it has surpassed a
hundred. An all-India team from different human rights organisations,
which visited Dantewada in December, found that in Mankeli village
five people had been killed and their bodies left around for the villagers
to dispose of. No police reports were registered. Mankeli, which had already been attacked three times by the Salwa Judum and forces, "surrendered" the next day. In other states, such incidents are at least recorded as "encounters" – here the bodies are just left to decompose, in
the confident knowledge that the state acts with complete impunity.

At the time of writing, it is not known how all this will end. What
is clear, however, is that Dantewada has become a military zone, and
its indigenous inhabitants have little chance of ever returning to normal lives in their villages.

Orissa

Police atrocities spread

The Orissa government, led by Biju Janata Dal's Naveen Patnaik, has
in the past year intensified the process of opening up its vast mineral
wealth for exploitation by various corporate interests, both Indian and
multinational. Corporate giants such as BHP Billiton (Australia and
UK), Rio Tinto (UK), Alcan (Canada), Posco (South Korea), Vedanta
(UK), Hindalco (Aditya Birla group, India) and L&T (India) have been
wooed to set up giant extraction projects in the state. It is proposed that
nearly 41 percent of Orissa's unexploited bauxite, 68 percent of its chr-
omite, 26 percent of iron ore reserves and 20 percent of manganese will
be consumed by these projects in the brief span of 25 years.

The ecological damage that this rampant exploitation would cause,
as well as the large-scale human displacement and deterioration in living conditions, are not matters of concern for this government. Its sole

obsession is to silence any opposition, as on the evening of 15 June 2005, when police battalions entered Guguput village near Kucheipadar in Kashipur, and indiscriminately charged the villagers with batons and tear gas to disrupt a peaceful meeting. Eleven villagers were picked up and sent to jail. This was merely one of a series of brutal police interventions recorded in the recent past.

What the outside investors and profiteers did not expect was that the dissent could not be stopped, that it would grow in the face of oppression and that the quiet, peaceful, indigenous inhabitants of the region, the adivasis, would give them such a dogged, imaginative fight: non-violent civil disobedience and mass resistance.

The *Prakritik Sambad Suraksha Parishad* (PSSP) has been spearheading the struggle against UAIL – a joint venture of Hindalco and Alcan in Kashipur district. In December 2000, three adivasis were killed in police fire, and many were injured. But resistance continued and the projects were stopped. Since December 2004, however, police repression has intensified. A heavy police force went, with the district collector, to Kucheipadar village, the tribal epicentre of the resistance, to set up a police barracks and outpost. People objected; they were subjected to a tear gas and baton charge. Many activists were sent to jail, some were locked up for four months. The Orissa government had made its intention clear: it was committed to "fast-track" industrialisation of the region, at any cost. The people did not matter, nor did the pristine environment of the area.

The police repression has since followed a pattern of rapidly increasing violence. On 15 May 2005, the PSSP called a rally against police atrocities. The local police chief, Kishore Mund, threatened dire consequences if anybody turned up. Despite the terror in the air, hundreds of people gathered and shouted slogans against the violence unleashed by the police and hired thugs.

The rally intensified the struggle. Villagers in the two blocks of Kashipur and Laxmipur sent a memorandum to the governor seeking his intervention to cancel the alumina projects. Many villagers refused the compensation offered by the UAIL, despite the police threat that if they did not take it they would be sent to jail. On June 8, villagers from Guguput blocked company vehicles and forced them to return. The

PSSP called a meeting on June 15 at Guguput to decide the future course of action. The police resorted to a baton charge. The link between the government and the companies is too apparent to be ignored.

Violence is not restricted to Kashipur. In Lower Sukhtel, villagers faced police violence on 11 May 2005 because they were demanding the cancellation of dam projects. One of the projects is supposed to supply water to the proposed aluminium plant in the Gandhamardan area of Bolangir district. In June, in Kalinga Nagar in Jajpur, adivasis were beaten up by the police because they refused to leave their land for a giant iron ore project. In Lanjigada, tribals who refused to leave their land were beaten up by thugs. Sukru Majhi, an activist at Nyamgiri, died in a mysterious accident on 27 March 2005. But no cases have been recorded by the police.

The presence of 10 platoons and five magistrates, along with senior officials of the police and administration in the region, points to the Patnaik government's determination to quell all peaceful struggles. The crackdown on democratic rights is evident in every realm of life. There have been five deaths in police custody in Chandanpur and Dhenkanal. The police resorted to firing in Champua when the people demanded that the rapist of a young girl be arrested. One villager died in the shooting. At Paradip, the police fired on slum dwellers who refused to shift during a demolition drive.

Various civil liberties groups undertook independent fact-finding investigations. All reports have held the government responsible for the violence unleashed by the mining companies and the police.

Kerala

Anti Coca-Cola struggle gains wide support

The struggle of adivasi communities against soft drinks giant Coca-Cola entered its 1,000th day on 15 January 2005 with a blockade of the factory at Plachimada in Perumatty Panchayat of Palakkad district, Kerala. The adivasis had established a picket in front of the Coca-Cola factory since 22 April 2002 (see *The Indigenous World 2004, 2005*). It was reiterated that the people would prevent the reopening of the factory at all cost after the Coca-Cola factory suspended production on 9 March 2004. The struggle is supported by a broad spectrum of organizations, ranging from adivasi peoples' organizations to youth federations, civil rights organizations and left-wing political parties. The struggle has forced the state and local government to raise the wider issue of the primacy of local people over ground water, of domestic use over commercial use, and the role of the state and local government in regulating use in the legal arena of the Supreme Court.

On 14 February 2005, the Investigation Team set up by the High Court, the apex court in Kerala, in 2003 submitted the Final Report on Investigations into the Extraction of Groundwater by Hindustan Coca-Cola Beverages Pvt. Ltd (HCCB) at Plachimada. On 23 April 2005 "Outlook", a popular news magazine, commissioned Sargam Metals Laboratories (Coca-Cola is one of their clients and they are recognized by the Indian government's Department of Science and Technology) to conduct an analysis of water from a well. The lab reported that the water did not meet the official requirements for potability in terms of chemical content and pH value.

Forced by a High Court order of 1 June 2005, the Perumatty Panchayat (local government), which had previously denied the HCCB renewal of their operating license, issued a three-month license, imposing conditions that were not acceptable to HCCB. But Coca-Cola resumed production on 8 August, fraudulently claiming that the High Court had permitted it to operate, although it had to shut down immediately thereafter.

On 19 August 2005 the Kerala State Pollution Control Board (KSPCB) rejected an application for renewal of the operating license on various grounds, but above all due to waste contamination, with the heavy metal cadmium at concentrations 400 to 600% above the permissible limit. Meanwhile, the Panchayat appealed to the Supreme Court to overturn the High Court ruling. Succumbing to the public and political pressure generated by the struggle, in a turnabout, the state government too appealed to the Supreme Court to overrule the High Court order.

On 19 November 2005, in another setback for Coca-Cola, the Kerala Water Resources Minister announced the government decision to declare 31 Panchayats, under clause 6 of the Kerala Ground Water (Control and Regulation), Act, 2002, as "notified areas", falling within the category of "over exploited". This further validated the charge of local communities that they had been facing acute survival problems on account of the debilitating quality and acute shortage of water. With this notification, the Ground Water Authority was empowered to further regulate or even ban the use of ground water for industrial purposes.

Meanwhile, the struggle has gained widespread worldwide support, including amongst students in Europe and the US, where Coca-Cola has been losing out on contracts in university campuses and colleges. HCCB has not only been violating the rights of the people and the laws of the land but it has even ignored the valid and lawful orders of government departments, institutions of self-governance, the state government and the courts.

Northeast India

Northeast India has seven states and is home to several indigenous groups, many of whom continue to be classified under the colonial category of "tribals" in the Indian Constitution. Since the inception of the Indian republic in the mid-twentieth century, the region has undergone massive militarization and, to this day, continues to remain on the political and economic margins of India. Today, counter-insurgency operations coexist alongside ambitious plans to open up the region to capital-intensive investment. Most indigenous groups that live along the eastern Himalayan rim that constitutes the region have enjoyed limited autonomy over their cultural and political institutions. This autonomy has been guaranteed under certain clauses within the Indian Constitution. With the focus now on altering land-use regimes, the government has been trying to further erode the limited autonomy prevalent in the region.

War and Peace

Assam and Manipur remained tense throughout 2005. Violence involving the Dimasa and Karbi indigenous communities in the autonomous district of Karbi Anglong (in Assam) claimed more than a hundred lives and displaced approximately 40,000 people from both communities. Despite efforts by civil society organisations in the district, armed militia have continued to target the lives and properties of innocent people, while the administration has done precious little to control the violence. It has to be mentioned here that, during the course of the violence, the government has been involved in ceasefire agreements with the two ethno-nationalist organisations active in the two autonomous districts, the Dima Halam Daogah, which ostensibly represents the Dimasas living in the state, and the United Peoples Democratic Solidarity, which is dominated by Karbis.

Civic protests against excesses of the armed forces continued in the state of Manipur. The state government compounded the problems by making partisan and politically motivated decisions which were opposed by Nagas who live in the hill districts of Manipur. This resulted in protests and boycotts, with a prominent Naga students' association in the state declaring and enforcing a 52-day long economic blockade of the valley, which they perceive as being the centre of local political power.

In Assam, the Indian army's counter-insurgency drive intensified during the year. The army entered the Dibru-Saikhowa reserve at the end of August and began an offensive against cadres of the United Liberation Front of Assam (ULFA) who were taking shelter there. The Dibru-Saikhowa area in upper Assam is one of the few bio-diversity hotspots in India. It is also home to many forest villages of indigenous peoples, whose livelihoods are based on subsistence cultivation and fishing. The army's operations in the area have resulted in large-scale destruction of the fragile eco-system and also led to the loss of livelihood and displacement of many of the indigenous communities from the area.

Despite ongoing efforts to arrive at a negotiated peace between ULFA and the government of India, via a group of prominent citizens who constitute the Peoples' Consultative Group (PCG), the army has continued its operations in upper Assam. Meanwhile, the ceasefire agreement between the National Democratic Front of Boroland (NDFB) and the government of India entered its first year. Meetings were organised by Boro organisations in western Assam to mark the event. The state of Meghalaya witnessed unprecedented protests against the move to shift the offices of the Meghalaya Board of Secondary Education from the Garo-dominated town of Tura to the state capital, Shillong. Following examination-related irregularities, civil society organisations, including the Khasi Students Union (KSU), demanded that the office be shifted to Shillong, a move that was opposed by Garo organisations. Civic protests led to police opening fire, with the deaths of nine people, including students, at Williamnagar and Tura in Garo Hills on 30 September 2005.

Exploitation of resources

State governments and international actors such as the World Bank and the Asian Development Bank held a series of closed-door consultations and meetings around issues related to the construction of big dams and the privatisation of the water and forests of the region's indigenous peoples in 2005. Such developments brought various rights-based organizations, including indigenous groups, to network and mobilize around broader issues of livelihood, development-induced displacements, the fallout of mass tourism and the involvement of security institutions in developmental works. Under pressure, the government of Arunachal Pradesh cancelled some proposed mega-dams that had been commissioned in the state. However, it is keen to proceed with the rest of the proposals. Though sporadic, the protests against the commissioning of dams have led state governments to rethink mega-projects in Tripura and Mizoram as well.

Three persons protesting against the Khuga Dam in Manipur were shot dead by security forces on 14 December 2005. At the same time, there has been strong resistance against the construction of the Tipaimukh Dam in the state. The proposed dam would submerge sizeable areas of land belonging to the Hmar and Naga people.

In Meghalaya, the campaign against uranium mining in Domiasiat drew wide support from several quarters in the region, as the

organisations in the state continuously opposed the project. Institutions such as the Uranium Corporation of India Limited (UCIL) and
the Bhaba Atomic Research Centre (BARC) have held a series of so-
called scientific awareness workshops around the state to dispel fears
and prove that uranium mining does not affect people's health.
Nonetheless, the reality is grim. Inhabitants of villages around the
mining area suffer from various health complications, for example
chest pains, dry cough and asthma. According to student activists,
livestock has also been diagnosed with mysterious diseases.[3]

Besides dams, the fossil-fuel based industry in Assam was also in
the news last year. On 7 August 2005, a crude-oil pipeline spilled over
and caught fire, destroying wide swathes of prime agricultural land
in eastern Assam. The area is inhabited by indigenous Assamese
tribes and is one of the major tea-growing areas of the region. The fire
raged for weeks and the nationalised oil agencies had to bring in
foreign experts to put it out after it had devastated the fertile coun-
tryside.

Even as Indian policy makers celebrated the country's vision of a
"Look East" policy that will link the resource-rich northeast region to
Southeast Asian nations, the indigenous peoples' voices have been
marginalised to an extent whereby identity-based protests have become accepted as an inevitable artefact of state policy. A disconcert-
ing reliance on archaic constitutional provisions that encourage ethnic competition and clamour for the fruits of unsustainable development has further exacerbated the social and political conflicts in
northeast India. In this process, many indigenous civil society organisations have come close to appropriating state symbols in their deal-
ings with other ethnic communities.   ❏

Notes

1   A tahsil (also spelled tehsil) is a local government unit. –Ed.
2   For details see "A nuclear divide" in *The Frontline*, 22 (27), December 31, 2005-
    January 13, 2006. pp. 72-4.

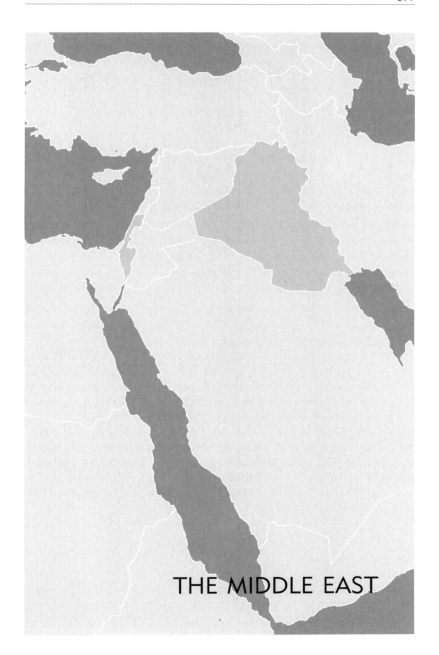

THE MIDDLE EAST

THE MARSH DWELLERS OF IRAQ

O f Iraq's more than 26 million people, approximately 75 to 80% are Arabs, 15 to 20% Kurds and roughly 5% Turkamans, Armenians and others. A distinct sub-group within the Arab community are known as Marsh Dwellers.[1] They have historically inhabited the Mesopotamian marshlands that once covered over 20,000 square kilometers of interconnected lakes, mudflats and wetlands within modern-day Iraq and Iran. Marsh Dwellers lived in harmony with the environment, constructing artificial islands made of layers of reed and mud on which they built their homes using woven reeds. They fed the sprouting reeds to their water buffalos and they used the dung of the water buffalo for fuel. They depended on fishing and hunting, and they planted rice and tended date palms along the margins of the marshes.

Following the end of the Gulf War in 1991, the Marsh Dwellers in Iraq took part in the rebellion against Saddam Hussein's regime and, as a consequence, were severely repressed. To control the region, the Iraqi regime implemented a program for the systematic desiccation of the marshes by diverting the water, burning the reeds and poisoning the waters. Many of the Marsh Dwellers died during that time and, by the beginning of 2003, only 85,000 out of an estimated population of 250,000 (1990)[2] remained in the marshlands, while 50,000 had been internally displaced in the Basrah Governate and 20,000 had fled to Iran. Less than 10% of the Mesopotamian Marshlands remained, the rest having been turned into wastelands.

Returning home

As soon as the regime of Saddam Hussein had been removed in 2003, the Marsh Dwellers immediately began to request the return of the water flow, and the local water authorities complied. To date, 41% of

the marshlands have been re-flooded. All of the re-flooding has oc-curred as a result of the direct actions of the Marsh Dwellers and via the Ministry of Water Resources at the request of the local populations. In some instances, the locals took things into their own hands and pooled their resources to hire backhoes to breach the embankments holding back the floodwaters; they opened sluice gates, stopped pumping operations, and re-directed water flow back to where it was wanted – in the marshlands. And the water complied, slowly yet faithfully flowing back along its ancient pathways.

Though some areas remain barren or have problems with high salinity, many of the re-flooded lands are now healthy marshlands. Fish have returned in abundance, fed from the rivers, and followed quickly by the fishermen. Birds, seeing the water from above, have reestablished their population in the marshlands. During a winter bird survey in 2005, 74 different species of birds were seen in the marshes and there are indications that the birds are utilizing extended or reestablished winter and summer breeding habitats. At least 10 species of rare birds have been recorded for the first time in 25 years and the Basrah Reed Warbler is now reconfirmed in low numbers in the marsh area.

With the return of water, the people continue to filter back to the marshlands. The returnees have rebuilt their villages with reed huts and exquisite *mudthifs* (guesthouses). And they are harvesting reeds, fishing, raising water buffalo and hunting again.

Future challenges

In 2005, Iraq saw two major elections[3] as well as a referendum on a new constitution, but the continued unrest in the country leaves many with an uncertain future. In the marshlands, the humanitarian situation continues to be difficult. With the help of international donors and NGOs, the Iraqi Ministry of Municipalities and Public Works conducted a survey of the three southernmost governates of Iraq (Missan, Thi Qar & Basrah), which encompass the three distinct wetland ecosystems that make up the Meso-potamian Marshland (The Hammar, Central & Huwaizah Marshes). They surveyed over 1330 settlements (including but not exclusively settlements of Marsh Dwellers) and found many disturbing trends.

Although power grids exist throughout the three governates (be-tween 80 to 87% of the settlements are served by power grids), the quality of service is poor. Water treatment plants exist but many are not functioning or are in poor condition. There are three waste water treatment plants in the entire area and none of them provide full coverage to the communities where they are located. Generally these services, if they exist, are only provided in the larger cities and thus the more rural areas, such as the Mesopotamian Marshlands where the Marsh Dwellers live, have no services at all. At a recent conference entitled "Health and the Environment in Iraq," [4] Laith Al Rudainy of the Department of Community Medicine at Basrah Medical College, stated,

The true incidence of waterborne disease in the marshes is not known because neither investigation nor reporting of waterborne disease is required. Nevertheless, many waterborne disease outbreaks per year have been documented in the south of Iraq.

This and other health hazards are a major problem in southern Iraq. Approximately 90% of all settlements, particularly in rural areas, are without any medical services.

The education sector also faces many challenges. Primary schools tend to predominate, both in terms of total numbers and distribution (primary schools exist in 60% of the settlements of Thi Qar Governate, 62 % in Basrah and 75% in Missan) but secondary and intermediate schools are lacking, showing that students are abandoning their education after only a few years.

Restoration of the Marshes

Land ownership remains a potential issue that will eventually have to be dealt with. The Marsh Dwellers traditionally held the land communally; later, sheikhs were given title over their territories. Many Marsh Dwellers were forcibly relocated to new areas when the drying occurred, and this has further complicated the ownership issue, impeding the process of marshland restoration.

There continues to be a debate as to the amount of water that is available to restore the former marshlands, and the procedure for addressing the equitable distribution of water resources amongst competing interests is still an important need. The Center for Restoration of the Iraqi Marshes, a part of the Iraqi Ministry of Water Resources, is creating a plan for the restoration of the marshes in cooperation with international conservation agencies, donor countries and other concerned Iraqi government institutes and non-governmental organizations. The plan will be finalized and presented to the Iraqi government by spring 2006.[5]

Reorganizing Marshlands and Marsh Dwellers

Tribal and family affiliations still dominate in the Marshland areas, but new indigenous organizations are forming.[6] To date, the Iraqi government has made no investments in the Marshland areas and the Marsh Dwellers have formed associations and village councils to promote their rights and organize their own projects to provide health care and other services to their members.

One example is the Chibayish Marsh Arab Council in Thi Qar Governate. This organization was formed to bring back and develop the marshes and help restore the rights of the people who live in the marshes by providing services in all aspects of life, including education and health. The Council has helped build a primary school and has conducted educational seminars for the people. In the future they hope to conduct an education and awareness raising program on fishing and hunting, particularly to discourage the practice of electro-shocking of fish, which has become a prevalent and unsustainable fishing practice in the marshes and rivers of southern Iraq.

There are at least two other groups in Thi Qar Governate, two to three in Missan, and up to eight groups in Basrah Governate. Each group tends to represent the members of specific villages but there is some movement towards working in larger associations in order to build a stronger voice for Marsh Dwellers in the country. ❑

Notes

1 The dwellers are also known as "Marsh Arabs" or "Ma'dan". The former specifically refers to Bedouin groups who moved into the marshes perhaps only 500 to a thousand years ago; the term Ma'dan is a pejorative term in Iraq but some believe that the Ma'dan are the truly indigenous people. The term Marsh Dweller is used here as it is more inclusive of the cultural values that are consistent between the two (or more) groups that live in the marshes.

2 According to some sources, the number may have been as high as 500,000. –Ed.

3 In January 2005 there was a legislative election for an assembly to draft a new constitution. In December 2005 the first assembly under the new constitution was elected. –Ed.

4 *Health and the Environment in Iraq: Status, Needs & Challenges,* 19-22, September, Amman, Jordan, Sponsored by Stony Brook University and the Agency for International Development, Higher Education and Development.

5   For more information on the Marshes: http://www.iraqfoundation.org and www.edenagain.org.

6   For a complete list of Marsh Dweller Organizations, see the Eden Again Website: www.edenagain.org. In addition the Amar Appeal: www.amarappeal. com/contact.php represents efforts to assist the Marsh Dwellers that started outside of the country.

THE BEDOUINS OF ISRAEL

A certain optimism was raised in early 2005 when Ofir Paz-Pines, newly appointed Minister of the Interior, promised that no houses would be demolished in the "unrecognized" Bedouin villages.[1] These 45 villages are home to approximately 86,000 Bedouins. Another 70,000 Bedouins live in government established townships. The Bedouins – or Negev Arabs – who are today Israeli citizens, are indigenous to the Negev Desert, and the "unrecognized" villages lie either on land that the Bedouins inhabited before the 1948 war or within the so-called Siyaj (Reservation) Zone[2] where many Bedouins were relocated to in the early 1950s. Although some of these villages have several thousand inhabitants, they do not exist officially - i.e. they do not appear on maps, are denied adequate access to a host of rudimentary services such as electricity, water and health care, and all buildings are considered illegal and therefore susceptible to demolition. However, their inhabitants stand firm on their wish to stay on their land where they are still – albeit in a very limited way - able to continue their traditional livelihood (herding and farming).

But the new minister reneged on his promise and, as in previous years, 2005 brought both house demolitions and crop destruction. Other events impacting on the situation of the Negev Bedouins were the adoption of an amendment to the Public Land Law that means a new threat of evacuation orders, the Government of Israel's Judaization policy for the Negev (making the Negev Jewish), and a number of cases that once more exposed the discrimination and hard-handed policy followed by the Israeli government in relation to the Muslim Negev Arabs.

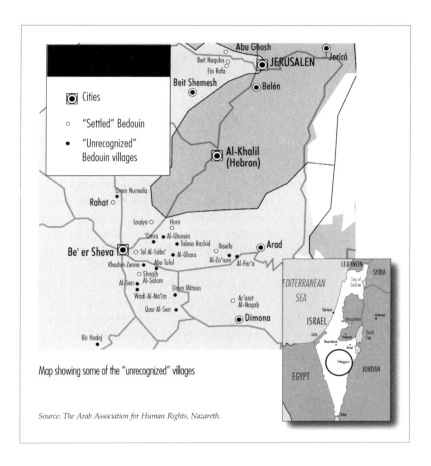

Map showing some of the "unrecognized" villages

Source: The Arab Association for Human Rights, Nazareth.

House demolitions

Some 1,000 house demolition orders were issued in 2005. Accompanied by police forces, the Israel Land Administration (ILA) comes to the villages and sticks the demolition order on the houses. Not all the homes that get demolition orders are demolished, only two or three homes every two or three weeks in different villages. This way the ILA keeps the people under permanent threat of seeing their home disappear. Once the ILA bulldozers have finished their work, the families, including many children, are left without shelter and most of their possessions are buried under the ruins.

Commercial buildings were also targeted: in June, inspectors from the Ministry of the Interior, accompanied by large police forces, destroyed two commercial buildings close to Hura, and new demolition orders were presented to tens of other commercial facilities.

Police violence in relation to house demolitions is on the increase, and several cases of injured people requiring medical treatment were reported in 2005. The worst case was in November, when inspectors from the Ministry of the Interior, accompanied by a large police force, arrived with demolition orders in the unrecognized village Bir Al-Mashash (located south-east of the Be'er Sheva – Dimona road). Trying to protect their homes, the residents blocked the road to their village, but in vain: with the help of a large number of special patrol officers, the police forced their way in by firing in the air and using clubs. Thirteen people were injured, including five pregnant women, all of whom were admitted to the Soroka Hospital in Be'er Sheva for medical treatment. A television cameraman from a local network who apparently refused to give the officers the footage he had shot at the location was beaten up and rushed to hospital. Forty-two villagers were arrested, including several women, the field coordinator and the chairperson of the Regional Council of Unrecognized Villages (RCUV). Most of the people were released after a few days. Eight were still under house arrest at the end of the year.

Even mosques do not escape

In March 2005, the District Court of Be'er Sheva issued a demolition order for a mosque in the unrecognized Arab village of Um-al-Hiran in the Negev. The claim was a familiar one – that the mosque had been built without the appropriate building permits. The court ruled that the mosque was to be demolished within 21 days of the verdict. Sheikh Mussa Abu El-Qian, who initiated construction of the mosque, will be subject either to a fine of NIS 30,000 (US$6,375) or 120 days in prison.

In June, the Omar Ibn-el-Hatab mosque was selected for demolition. In early 2005, the city of Be'er Sheva rejected a proposal put forward by the High Court of Justice to make the mosque available for
use as a community and cultural center for the Muslim population of
the region (the Negev Bedouins). The city justified its stance by claiming that allowing Muslims to pray in the mosque would increase tensions between the Jewish and Muslim populations and ultimately disrupt public order. The city instead wants to turn the mosque into a
museum.

Crop destruction

Crops, too, were destroyed in 2005. In April, a few weeks before harvest time, 1,500 dunams (375 acres) of crops were bulldozed in the unrecognized village of Sa'wa, east of Hura. More than 500 police officers
and Police Special Forces raided the area, setting up road blocks and
forbidding residents from leaving their houses.

The use of bulldozers and tractors for crop destruction was reintroduced after the Supreme Court in 2004 issued an interim order that
stopped the Israel Lands Authority using aerial spraying with chemical pesticides (Round Up among other chemicals). The interim order is
still in effect but the Supreme Court is expected to reach a final ruling
in 2006.

Olive trees were another target. In May, tens of olive trees were
uprooted from the graveyard of the Abu-Siam tribe. The ILA claimed
that the graveyard and the road leading to it were built on state lands.
A few days prior to the incident, ILA bulldozers damaged the road
leading from the Abu-Siam community to their graveyard.

In June, another 270 olive trees were uprooted in the village of
Hashem Zane, south of the Jewish community of Nevatim. These trees
were planted during the March 2005 Land Day. Land Day is celebrated
each year on March 30 as a protest against Israel's discriminatory policies toward its one million Palestinian citizens and to underline their
collective and individual rights.[3]

The Judaization of the Negev

The residents of the unrecognized villages regard crop destruction and tree uprooting as steps in the Government of Israel's attempt to expropriate their lands and relocate them to the townships. This was confirmed in July when the government authorized a comprehensive plan for the development of the Abu-Basma municipality (located east of the Be'er Sheva – Rahat road, north of Lagiya), home to 25,000 Negev Bedouin. This plan follows an earlier government decision concerning the establishment of eight new Bedouin townships in the Negev. The plan is expected to cost NIS 470 million (US$100 million), which will be invested in education, transportation, infrastructure, employment, housing, healthcare, welfare and agriculture. While government representatives claim that these newly planned villages will solve existing problems, critics insist that these villages, if approved and developed, will perpetuate the difficulties since no lessons have been learned from past mistakes in developing the seven existing Bedouin towns: the forced urbanization of the Bedouin population has been disastrous, with high rates of unemployment, and the townships rank among Israel's 10 poorest municipalities.

Further evidence of the government's Judaization policy for the Negev was the adoption in January 2005 by the Israeli Parliament (Knesset) of an amendment to the Public Land Law (expulsion of invaders) which extends the mandate of the ILA and local municipal authorities to evacuate "invaders" of public land without having first been granted an evacuation order from the Debt Enforcement Office or the courts. Furthermore, the amended law enables the ILA to issue evacuation orders up to three years after the date of the "invasion", and sets charges of up to one year's imprisonment for unauthorized trespassing or holding of public land. The majority of lands used by Bedouin in the Negev are under legal dispute with regard to ownership. The new amendment therefore poses the threat of the mass destruction of thousands of homes as well as the expulsion of Arab Bedouin civilians in the Negev from their lands.

According to the *Haaretz* newspaper[4] a private company named *Daroma Idan HaNegev Ltd.* (Southward: The Age of the Negev, Ltd.) will be in charge of one of the biggest plans ever to address the development of the Negev. Tal Dilian, one of the founders of the company, claims that, *"The project's goal is to develop the Negev, including all of the populations that are located in it, and in this context we have focused especially on the Bedouin population. The project stipulates that the Bedouins must be integrated in all of the development efforts"*. The plan was also presented to the US Government in order to recruit funds and includes a project for the creation of 100 more individual farms.

Another programme for individual farms – The Wine Road Programme – is already well underway. The National Council for Planning and Building plans to establish 30 individual wine producing farms in the Ramat HaNegev area (south of Be'er Sheva and near the main road). Despite the fact that the programme has not been finally approved, 20 farms have already been established and settled.

The case of Inas al-Atrash

Inas al-Atrash is a three-year-old cancer victim who lives with her parents in an unrecognized village. Doctors have recommended that Inas live in an air-conditioned home that can provide a healthy environment, particularly during the hot summer months, and thus prevent the possibility of contracting other illnesses that might prove lethal to her. She is also required to take medication that must be refrigerated. However, living in an unrecognized village, her family has no access to electricity, although the electricity lines run only a few hundred meters from the village. The NGO Physicians for Human Rights petitioned several ministries as well as several parliamentarians asking them to immediately bring electricity to the family's home, or at least provide a temporary solution to the problem. In November, the Supreme Court rejected an appeal that would have forced the Ministry of Health, Ministry of Infrastructure and the Ministry of the Interior to provide electricity to the home of Inas. The Supreme Court acknowledged that its ruling was insufficient to address the girl's cancer but that the parents had chosen to live in an unrecognized village which they knew lacked electricity. Instead, the court ruled that the ministries should assist the girl with 16,000 shekels (US$3,400), which could be used to buy gas for a neighbour's generator: Inas' family could then borrow from that source of electricity to prevent further deterioration in her condition.

Bedouins react

In reaction to their situation, in 1997 the unrecognized villages formed the Regional Council of Unrecognized Villages (RCUV). This community-based organization endeavours to respond to the daily challenges faced by the villages: home demolitions and demolition orders, crop destruction, lack of basic services, etc. At the forefront of their struggle, however, is the legitimization of the Negev Arabs' ownership of their ancestral land and opposition to the Israeli government's determination to uproot the residents of the unrecognized villages and concentrate them in townships. In 2005, the RCUV responded to house demolitions and crop destruction by setting up protest tents and organizing several mass demonstrations in Be'er Sheva and in Jerusalem.

The struggle of the RCUV is supported by and coordinated with national Arab and Arab Jewish organizations as well as local organizations such as the Negev Coexistence Forum for Civil Equality. The Forum was established in 1997 by Arab and Jewish residents of the Negev and its aim is to provide a framework for Jewish-Arab collaborative efforts in the struggle for equal rights and the advancement of mutual tolerance and co-existence.

The Negev Co-existence Forum recently published a new report entitled, "The Indigenous Bedouins of the Negev". The report was presented at the UN Working Group on Indigenous Populations in Geneva. This was the first time that an international forum had heard a first hand account of the situation of the Bedouins in Israel, and raising awareness of and putting the Bedouins (in Israel) on the international agenda signifies a step forward in their struggle.[5] ☐

Notes

1   *Haaretz*, 25 January 2005.
2   The Siyaj covers about 2% of the northern Negev and is located between Be'er Sheva, Arad and Dimona. Most recognized townships and unrecognized villages are located within this reservation.
3   Land Day also commemorates the killing of six Palestinians in Galilee on March 30, 1976 by Israeli troops during peaceful protests over the confiscation of Palestinian lands.
4   *Haaretz*, 22 September 2005.
5   The report can be downloaded from IWGIA's website at www.iwgia.org (noticeboard)

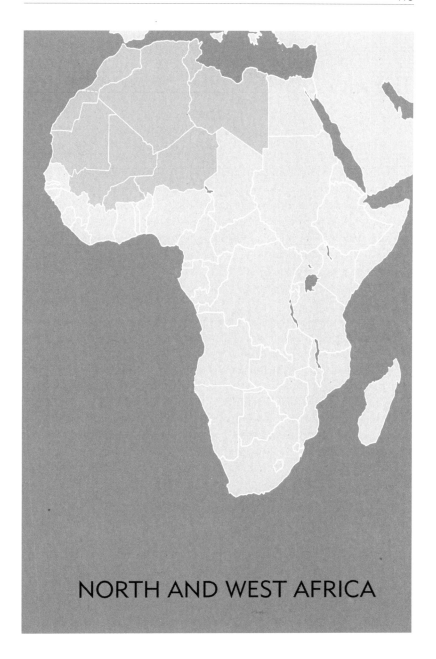

NORTH AND WEST AFRICA

THE AMAZIGH PEOPLE OF MOROCCO

North Africa, the land of the Amazigh people indigenous to this region, is witnessing a transitional period of reform paving the way for democracy. In Morocco, efforts are being made to rehabilitate the Amazigh language through its teaching in schools, and measures are being taken to integrate it into the media and all other sectors. The liberalization of the public sector is underway with the establishment of the Moroccan National Media Company. A new law on political parties was adopted by Parliament, while the 2007 legislative elections are being prepared. The Amazigh Movement is expected to participate massively.

In neighboring Algeria, in Libya and in Tunisia too, the Amazigh people witnessed positive developments in 2005. In Algeria, the Amazigh Movement took successful part in the municipal elections. In Libya, Colonel Kadafi declared that he would endeavour to recognize all Amazigh rights in his country, and promised to take all necessary measures in this regard. In Tunisia, the World Summit on the Information Society (Tunis, November 2005) saw the country's president talking about the importance of preserving cultural identity, with all its characteristics.

Report of the Equity and Reconciliation Commission

In November 2005, the Equity and Reconciliation Commission concluded its mandate, releasing its report to the King of Morocco. The commission was set up in 2004 and has since then organized several public and private sessions to hear the victims of human rights violations that took place during the period between independence in 1956 and 1999. The commission was tasked with establishing the truth of these violations, on the one hand, and compensating the victims, on the other. In its detailed report, the commission presents key recommendations, most importantly the need for the state to apologize to the victims and to amend the Constitution, and to provide more human rights guarantees in order to avoid the recurrence of such violations, to enact new laws, to guarantee the independence of the authorities, and provide supervisory mechanisms.

Continuing efforts to rehabilitate the Amazigh language

Rehabilitation of the Amazigh language has continued for a third year. In this connection, a school manual was published by the Royal Institute for Amazigh Culture, in the Amazigh language, for third-year primary school students. Moreover, it has been decided to broadcast many programs in the Amazigh language on the two national TV channels, which are now run by the National Media Company in the context of liberalizing and developing the media sector. In addition, the Royal Institute for Amazigh Culture has also published many books dealing with Amazigh culture, and for the first time organized a National Prize for Amazigh Creativity to honor many creative artists and writers.

Struggle for constitutional recognition of Amazigh identity, culture and civilization

The Amazigh Movement, represented by many local and national associations,[1] has continued its struggle for constitutional recognition of the Amazigh identity, culture, language and civilization. The movement believes that the lack of recognition in the current Constitution results in a number of violations of the rights of Amazigh organizations and institutions as they are denied the right to register or renew registration, their activities are sometimes hindered, and the use of Amazigh names is occasionally forbidden. All of this firmly establishes a policy of assimilation in all fields, hindering the development of Amazigh language teaching and its use in the media and other national level sectors.

The National initiative for Human Development

Prior to the UN World Summit in New York in September 2005, with its discussion on the Millennium Development Goals, King Mohamed VI announced the National Initiative for Human Development. This initiative will have a direct impact on many indigenous communities living in the plains and mountains, especially in some Amazigh regions where people have been excluded from the development process throughout the last fifty years of independence. Many board and lodging centres for girls have been established, with the aim of helping them carry on their studies. In addition, many schools have been opened in regions that were previously deprived of education. It is expected that this initiative will pave the way for a large number of indigenous people to take part in the country's development.

Creation of the Amazigh Democratic Party

Another important event in 2005 was the creation of a new party named the Amazigh Democratic Party on the part of a group of Amazigh activists. The party aims to build a democratic society in which people can live and enjoy freedom and equality, a society that recognizes Amazigh as an official language and gives the different regions of the country a right to enjoy their wealth, under state supervision, based on principles of tolerance, solidarity and redistribution of wealth.

Amazigh laws and the current legislation in the context of the partnership with the International Labor Organization

In the context of the partnership between the Tamaynut Association and the International Labor Organization (ILO), a study was carried out into Amazigh laws and current legislation. A historian, an anthropologist and a legal expert took part in the study. It is expected that this study will have a great impact on constitutional recognition of Amazigh identity, language, culture and civilization.

Translation of the provisions of Family Law into the Amazigh language

In the context of another partnership between the Tamaynut Association and the Women's Initiative Organization, the provisions of the new Family Law were translated into the Amazigh language, and an information campaign launched in the suburbs of Marrakesh, in Aït Ourir, and in the suburbs of Agadir, in Imintanoute, to make Amazigh men and women aware of the law. Volunteers from the Tamaynut Association introduced the law to men and women's groups in the Amazigh language. This translation is an important achievement because it is the first national law to be translated into the Amazigh language.

Publication of findings of the 2004 census

For the first time in Morocco, the findings of the census conducted in 2004 were published. The Amazigh Movement had protested against the omission of any reference to the Amazigh language in clear terms in the census forms, although the same census indicates that 28% of the population use the Amazigh language in their daily lives. That equates to around 10 million people. The report does not state, however, how many Amazigh people do not use the language daily, taking into consideration the fact that the majority of Moroccans are Amazigh people. The Amazigh Movement believes that the figures provided would double if clear questions were asked. In general, given the poor methodology behind the figures, the census is not considered reliable.

Creation of nature reserves without free, prior and informed consent of Amazigh landlords

The Moroccan government has continued the policy of creating nature reserves in the region of the Atlas Mountains on lands and forests historically owned by the Amazigh tribes by virtue of the customary laws that consider lands and forests to be collective property. The government has expropriated these areas to give large plots of land to local and foreign people, who are then entitled to manage large nature reserves without taking into consideration the wishes and interests of the local population. The result is conflict and instability in those regions.   ❑

Note

1   Among others, three national associations, namely the Tamaynut Association, Amrik Association and Ouasta Association, and three regional confederations (Tamunt Nifus, Ouamyafa and the Rif Confederacy).

THE TUAREG PEOPLE

The nomadic Tuareg people live in the south of Algeria, the north of Mali and Niger, with small pockets in Libya, Burkina Faso and Mauritania. Population estimates vary between 300,000 and 3 million. This article focuses mainly on the Tuareg of Niger.

Famine and starvation in the Sahel

The number of people across the Sahel region who died as a result of the 2005 famine is not known. Most attention was on Niger, the most seriously affected country, although Mali and neighbouring parts of Burkina Faso, Mauritania and northern Nigeria were all affected to a slightly lesser degree. At one point, it was estimated that as many as four million people in Niger, a country of only some 10 million people, were facing starvation and possible death. Most other estimates placed this figure a little lower, at around 3 million. UK charity Oxfam, for example, reported that 3.6 million people – one-third of Niger's population – were facing food shortages. By mid-year, the UN estimated that 150,000 children in Niger were suffering from severe malnutrition, with thousands of them dying.

Niger, classified as both a least developed and a low-income, food-deficient country, was ranked the second lowest country in the world (176 out of 177) on the UNDP (United Nations Development Programme) Human Development Index in 2000. With a population of approximately 10 million, including some 1 million Tuareg, the country's average annual earnings are under US$200 per capita. 63% of the country's population lives below the poverty line, with 34% of these living below the extreme poverty line. According to the World Food Programme, one child in every four dies before the age of five. An FAO

(UN Food and Agriculture Organization) report on the early stages of the famine in Niger, around June-July 2005, stated that severe child malnutrition was increasing rapidly and that the number of children being supported by feeding centres was rising. Out of 63 districts it surveyed, 11 had populations in an "extremely critical" situation, with the situation considered "critical" in a further 16 districts.

Pastoralists, in particular Peul populations, the Tuareg, Wodaabe and many others were having difficulty in accessing food staples and keeping their animals alive.

It is difficult and perhaps misleading to give figures for the precise loss of life as it varies considerably from region to region, with emergency relief reducing the worst outcomes in the most severely affected districts. A particularly reliable report from Agades in northern Niger estimated that one in every three families experienced loss of life. This figure is almost certainly higher in many of the more severely affected regions.

The tragedy of the famine, especially in Niger, is that it was entirely avoidable. A combination of climatic conditions in 2004 combined with a series of locust plagues across much of the Sahel made it obvious to everyone, including international aid agencies, the United Nations, the European Union and local populations, as long ago as October 2004 that famine was inevitable. A special report on the Niger food forecast prepared in December 2004 by the Global Information and Early Warning System of the FAO reported that the failure of the October 2004 harvest was two-thirds due to severe drought and one-third due to the locust infestation that swept through West Africa.

The Niger government, as well as many NGOs, blamed the outside world for being slow to respond. The UN World Food Programme (WFP) said that it needed at least US$ 16 million in aid. Nothing like this figure was forthcoming. In response to a US$ 4 million appeal for Niger in May, the FAO had only received $650,000, donated by Sweden. Apart from Canada's pledge of US$ 1million, other members of the G8 industrialised countries did virtually nothing to prevent the crisis. By July the WFP said that it had received the bulk of its US$ 4.2m appeal to feed 465,000 people. However, by that time the situation had turned into an emergency feeding programme, with the WFP needing

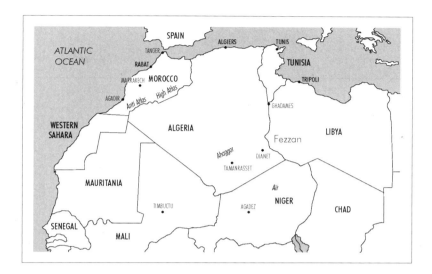

another US$ 12 million to cover the rapidly rising costs of expanding the emergency relief to 1.2 million people. Most immediately at risk, as always, were young children. *Médecins sans Frontières* (MSF) feeding centres reported admission rates nearly three times higher than during the same period the previous year.[1]

While it is true that WFP's initial response had been severely hampered by late funding and difficulties in buying food within the region, the Niger government itself, and notably its President, Mamadou Tanja, was also seen by many as an obstacle.

In spite of millet prices reportedly rising six fold in many regions, and notwithstanding widespread demonstrations, the Niger government insisted in January 2004 on raising taxes to 19% on staples such as milk, flour and sugar, worsening the situation of an already impoverished population.

As the impending crisis grew more serious, many representatives of "civil society", responding to rallies by several thousands of people protesting at the government's denial of their plight, demanded that the government make free food stocks available to the three million or so citizens teetering on the edge of a food crisis. Government spokesman Mohamed Ben Omar responded by saying, "What civil society is asking is poorly conceived and irrational. The state of Niger cannot engage in such a foolish adventure."

On top this, President Tanja's refusal to admit that his country faced a famine made it almost impossible for external agencies to respond to the disaster. Not only was it difficult for the UN World Food Programme and other relief agencies to raise extra funds to purchase additional food for Niger when the country's own President was denying such a crisis, but the difficulty was compounded by the fact that the same conditions that had devastated Niger's cereal production had also hit harvests in neighbouring Mali, Benin, Burkina Faso and northern Nigeria.

Amnesty for Tuareg rebels

In March 2005, the Tuareg leader, Rhissa ag Boula, was freed after thirteen months detention, without any charges being brought against him. One of his first moves after re-gaining his freedom was to try and negotiate an amnesty for 200-300 Tuareg in the Aïr region who had been provoked by his arrest into taking up arms. Anger at Rhissa's detention had led to increased political tension, especially in the northern mountainous region of Aïr, and an escalation in banditry, for which Rhissa's brother, Mohamed ag Boula, reportedly claimed responsibility. In September 2004, the Niger government sent some 150 troops into Aïr in a move which many thought likely to ignite a new Tuareg rebellion (see *The Indigenous World 2005*). However, the troops, recently trained by the US marines as part of the Pan Sahel Initiative, were ambushed by the Tuareg, with at least one soldier killed, four wounded and four more being taken hostage. RFI (*Radio France Internationale*) subsequently carried an interview in which Rhissa's brother said he was leading a 200-strong group that was fighting to defend the rights of the Tuareg, Tubu and Semori nomadic populations of northern Niger, and that he was personally responsible for the attack.

Northern Aïr remained tense and effectively cordoned off from the outside world throughout the winter months of 2004-05 but without any further serious incidents, due largely to Tuareg restraint and the good offices of Libya, which secured the release of the Niger soldiers on 8 February 2005.

In the wake of the return of the Niger soldiers and his own release, Rhissa assumed that the Niger government would be willing to grant an amnesty to the rebels. The Tuareg were surprised and angry, however, when the negotiations got bogged down.

Even more perplexing to the Tuareg leadership was the fact that France, which had hitherto always assisted them in such negotiations, played no part in the proceedings. They believed this was because France was becoming increasingly anxious regarding public exposure to the activities of two of its biggest companies in Niger and might be more than grateful for the protection afforded by America's military presence. COGEMA (*Compagnie générale des matières nucléaires*), a subsidiary of the AREVA Group, which is the major shareholder and operator of Niger's uranium mines, has been accused by its own workers of causing massive damage to both the environment and their health, and of blocking medical investigations.

Libya's Mouammar Qadhafi made a successful intervention in finally negotiating an amnesty with the Niger government on behalf of Tuareg rebels in northern Aïr. The amnesty was announced through the Libyan press on 17 July. The precise details of how the breakthrough in the negotiations was obtained are still not clear. Qadhafi's key role in securing the amnesty relates to a speech he made in Libya at Oubari in the Fezzan on April 20, 2005, in which he informed the assembled Libyan and Malian Tuareg that Libya regarded itself as the protector of the Tuareg people, whose ancestral home, prior to their expansion into those parts of the Sahara that now comprise Algeria, Mali, Niger, Mauritania and Burkina Faso, was Libya. These regions, so Qadhafi explained, could thus be regarded as constituting an extension of Libya. Moreover, Libya would always defend the Tuareg and not allow anyone to attack them as they were, as he put it, the "defenders of the Sahara, North Africa, Islam and this strategic zone".

"Social reintegration" programme for ex-rebels

Following the hand-over of arms at a ceremony in Libya on July 15, a delegation of dignitaries from the Tuareg tribes of northern Niger was received by Qadhafi at Sirte on July 31. The Tuareg delegation expressed its gratitude to Qadhafi for his expressions of solidarity and support. While thanking the Libyan leader for his country's help in alleviating the suffering inflicted on Niger's peoples by the recent famine, one prominent member of the delegation also asked the Libyan leader to assist them in overcoming the specific problems of northern Niger by breaking out of the circle of poverty and misery and creating a more permanent programme of economic, social and cultural development.

Part of Qadhafi's assistance is to "employ" some 3,000 Tuareg and Tubu (from Niger) and other Saharan peoples including, so it is reported, Algerian Chaamba in his army. The first legion to be recruited, reportedly numbering some 500-600, comprised the Tuareg rebels from Aïr, whose families will also be provided with financial support. It is not yet clear whether this initial recruitment consisted exclusively of Niger Tuareg or whether recruitment has yet begun from other areas. Nor is the precise number of Niger Tuareg recruited known: reports range from between 200-300 to 500-600. The end of Ramadan saw many young men from northern Niger packing their bags and heading for Libya.

The prospect of Niger's "ex-rebels" joining up in some sort of Qadhafi-inspired and financed Libyan foreign legion is not necessarily what either Niger, France, the USA or "big business" in the form of the uranium and oil industries (both established in northern Niger) might wish for. The Niger government and the UN have consequently moved quickly to try and counter such an eventuality. On 12 October in Agades, they jointly announced the launch of a "social reintegration" programme for 3,160 ex-rebel Tuareg in accordance with the Peace Accord of April 1995. The fact that this provision is being made little more than two months after the announcement in the Niger press that 500 former Tuareg rebels had enlisted in the Libyan army (denied by Libya), and more than ten years after such measures were stipulated as part of the Peace Accord, has not been lost on the Tuareg.

The programme, costing EUR 1.2 million, and funded by the UN-DP, France, USA and Libya, will give each of the 3,000 or so ex-combatants a US$300 payment with which to establish income-generating activities such as animal husbandry, handicrafts, market gardening, etc. Although this programme will stimulate some level of socio-economic development in the region, it is probably more a matter of "too little, too late". Nevertheless, the programme's mere initiation is a reflection of the complexity of Saharan-Sahelian politics and the issues that are at stake.

Rhissa ag Boula returns to mainstream politics

At the end of August 2005, the recently freed Tuareg leader Rhissa ag Boula accepted the leadership of the small political party, the UDPS *(Union pour la Démocratie et le Progress Sociale)*. Although focused predominantly around Agades and Aïr, it gives him a formal footing in Niger's official political system.

Algerian Tuareg feel increasingly marginalized

The Algerian Tuareg form two traditional groups, the Kel Ahaggar, centred around the administrative centre of Tamanrasset, and the Kel Ajjer, centred around Djanet. Their political repression by the Algerian government has intensified over the last three years, especially since Algeria became a close ally of the USA in the "war on terror" in the region. In July 2005, extensive riots broke out in Tamanrasset, with many government buildings being burnt down. At least 60 young Tuareg were arrested and jailed. However, when brought to court, they were all eventually freed. It was also revealed that the riots were largely instigated by *agents provocateurs* working for the secret police. According to some, one of the objectives of the secret security forces was to burn and destroy many of the files in the government offices. The reason for this was allegedly to destroy the evidence of widespread fraud by the *wali* (governor) and other members of the regional government, which was liable to be uncovered as a result of imminent investigations by the state procurator fiscal's department.

Subsequent grievances related mostly to the belief that the government was trying to further undermine tourism in the region, the main livelihood for many Tuareg. Tourism has already been decimated by the "war on terror". Local Tuareg now believe that any possible recovery in the tourist market is being deliberately blocked by the state airline, *Air Algérie*, making its schedules and connections inconvenient for foreign tourists. Local people also believe that the huge increases in internal airfares are partly designed to further their geographical marginalisation. While state officials have their airfares paid, most of the indigenous population can no longer afford to buy air tickets.

Death of Tuareg leader

On December 19, the 85-year-old Hadj Moussa, half-brother of Bey ag Akhemouk (d. 1973), the last traditional Amenukal (paramount chief) of the Kel Ahaggar, died. His death was seen by many Tuareg as "the end of an era". While Tuareg realise that the Algerians will never allow the appointment of another Amenukal, several Tuareg spoke at his funeral of the need for Tuareg across the different Saharan and Sahelian countries to unite together.   ☐

Note

1   Even in a good year, malnutrition rates amongst young children in Niger are extremely high. Some 82% of the population rely on subsistence farming and cattle rearing while only 15% of the land is suitable for arable farming. There is little irrigation, leaving most farmers at the mercy of the rains.

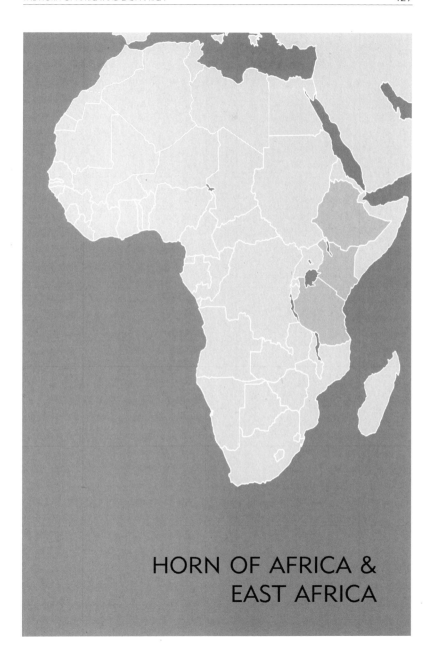

HORN OF AFRICA &
EAST AFRICA

ETHIOPIA

The year 2005 holds a special place in Ethiopia's contemporary history. Parliamentary elections were held in May 2005 and the hopes of various sectors of the population, including pastoral communities, were pinned on them to bring about social change. A number of factors contributed to the population's optimism. The most important, however, was the open public debate that took place between the ruling and opposition parties. Unlike previous elections, the debate began late in 2004 and was televised live as well as broadcast on the radio. The ruling party agreed to this arrangement following considerable internal and external pressure. It was through these debates that the ruling party was completely exposed, particularly its utter ineptness. The prevalence of the opposition during the debates prompted the population to vote. Yet there were still a great many people who did not register to vote because they had lost confidence in the process. By the time the debates had heated up, it was too late for such people to register. In the end, it was estimated that more than 90% of registered voters did cast their votes on May 15, election day. Compared to the previous two elections, voter registration in 2005 was at a record high. The results of the election were inconclusive as there were huge irregularities committed, as confirmed by international observers.

Pastoralists' hope for social change

Pastoral communities were among those who had been hoping for social change, after decades of neglect and repression from the three post-war governments. The opposition has quite similar views to the government on pastoralism, although the main opposition party, the Coalition for Democracy and Unity (CUD), offered a better position on

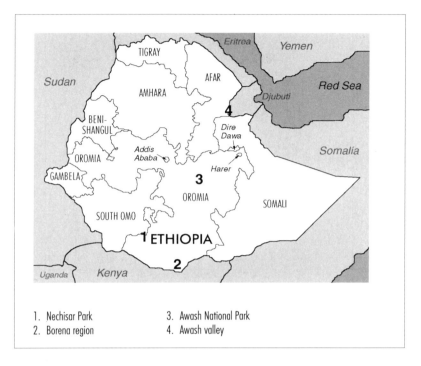

1. Nechisar Park   3. Awash National Park
2. Borena region   4. Awash valley

the question. Despite these weaknesses on pastoralism on the part of
the opposition, pastoral communities had high hopes that a new government could bring about much needed social change in areas such as
freedom, more space for participation and advocacy, an end to government pressure to settle them, provision of services such as water,
schools and clinics, an end to the various communal conflicts and so
on. As pre-election surveys indicated, most people in Afar and South
Omo, predominantly pastoral regions, would vote for the CUD.

The official results, which gave victory to the ruling party even before counting of the votes had been completed, were not popular in
pastoral areas. As the ruling party was to retain power in these regions,
pastoralists were in no doubt that there would be no change in pastoral
policy, meaning that poverty and under-development would continue.
On top of this, pastoral communities such as the Afar, Kereyu, Ittu and
the Ngangaton, Hamer and Dassenech in South Omo are beset by com-

munal conflicts and very much pressed by a recurrent drought. In the light of this, the plight of pastoral communities in Ethiopia has indeed become serious. Unfortunately, it has not attracted the attention of the policy-makers, who are bent on settling pastoral communities. With the results of the elections officially announced, the hopes of pastoral communities were buried.

Restrictions on freedom

Ethiopia saw more restrictions on freedom of expression and organization following the elections. The ruling party, which had played the stratagem of "maintaining law and order" from the start of the election debate, finally launched its onslaught on everyone that had opposed it. Those who challenged it openly and in the streets were thrown in prison, charged with treason and facing long-term sentences or death. Others had their freedom of expression and organization restricted. The same night the ballots were cast, i.e. May 15, the prime minister announced a state of emergency and all kinds of outdoor activities were banned for a month. This was renewed for another month. In the meantime, the clampdown against the opposition and social justice activists continued in a fashion paralleled only by the days of the red terror of the late 70s under the military regime. Hundreds of people were killed and assassinated, and more than 15,000 locked up in prison. This has created a situation of terror under which nobody dares challenge the government. To this day, outdoor activity is still banned, though not officially. NGOs and other civic groups do not dare to organize workshops.

In addition, most private newspapers are banned. Only a few were banned officially - most were banned unofficially with the use of threats and intimidation. Under such circumstances, it has become impossible to conduct advocacy work on pastoral rights and pastoral development. The regime has finally shown its true colors as a regime that does not offer space to civic sector and independent expression. Its long-time dream of quelling opposition and free expression has come true. In effect, the days of one-party totalitarian rule are back. Politically, Ethiopia is back in the dark ages.

The 7ᵗʰ Pastoralist Day

From the very start in 1998, the Pastoralist Day has been marked with the same spirit and the same purpose of policy advocacy. It started in the remotest areas of the country and, in 2005, it came to a large town called Dire Dawa. The government attempted to hijack the 7ᵗʰ Pastoralist Day in 2005 by dominating the event and sidelining NGOs, particularly the main organizer, the PFE. However, this did not stop the fury of the pastoralist representatives, who voiced their grievances with anger and disgust.

Pastoral representatives comprising elders, women and youth from throughout the pastoral regions of the country held their own workshop a day earlier. They first held their meetings according to language groups and met in the afternoon for a plenary. At the plenary, pastoralist representatives first considered what had happened to their 7-point demand passed at the 6ᵗʰ Pastoralist Day in 2004. As none of their demands had been met, pastoralist representatives angrily expressed their frustration at the government. After a thorough discussion, the pastoralists passed yet another13-point resolution. They reiterated their demands for a speedy response to their 6ᵗʰ Pastoralist Day resolution: 1) They called for the recent land-use policy draft to take pastoral livelihood concerns into consideration; 2) They urged water development; 3) They demanded a conducive environment for conflict resolution; 4) They called for the establishment of livestock marketing mechanisms; 5) They called for education and educational facilities; 6) They called for more cooperation between pastoral and government institutions; and 7) They demanded that the 8ᵗʰ Pastoralist day should be organized in the capital, Addis Ababa.

The 8ᵗʰ Pastoralist Day will be held on January 25, 2006. However, due to the political crisis and curtailment of freedoms, it cannot be celebrated as usual given that outdoor activities are effectively banned. Instead, it will be held in a hall in Addis Ababa. The Ministry of Federal Affairs, as one member of the organizing committee of the Pastoralist Day for 2006, recently came up with the imposition that it would be the sole organizer and host. This was rejected by the Pastoralist Forum and the previous arrangement was reinstated. It remains to be seen whether the government will respect this agreement or not.

Pastoral land-use rights

Like many indigenous peoples of the world, Ethiopian pastoralists suffer from a lack of land, it having been robbed from them for commercial farms, state farms, wildlife reserves and game parks. The eviction of pastoral communities from their ancestral land has not only caused poverty and destitution for the pastoralists but also contributed greatly to the degradation of natural resources and the environment. This has in turn contributed greatly to a decline in agricultural productivity. The natural resource base that pastoralists were evicted from had for centuries been maintained and protected through the indigenous knowledge systems of pastoralists. The main problem as far as pastoral land is concerned is the spread of commercial farms and expansion of state farms and game parks, which deprive the communities of their communally-owned land.

In 2005, the government came up with the long-awaited draft of the Proclamation on Rural Land Administration and Use. The need for this came about mainly because the government's policy of continuing with the nationalization of land was bearing no fruit. A much more detailed proclamation was necessary to clearly stipulate the rights of communities to use of their land. The government is basically concerned with peasants and the entire draft law is about land in peasant areas. Like other policy issues, such as the government's main strategy on agriculture-led industrialization, pastoralism is completely forgotten.

As usual, the government did not consult rural communities, the civic sector, academics or rural development experts before going ahead with this. At a public discussion to which the various sectors of society had been invited to reflect on the draft, several critical points and amendments were put forward. As far as pastoral land was concerned, the draft did not take into consideration the communal ownership of land in pastoral regions. At the end of the day, it was revealed that the draft did not even include the pastoral land rights that were granted in the country's Constitution. Although officials took note of the critique, it is unlikely to be considered in the final draft - just as has happened on many other occasions, such as in the PRSP (Poverty Reduction Strategy Paper) process.[1]

In the meantime, land in pastoral regions - supposedly owned communally - is being distributed to private "developers" engaged in commercial farming. This is quite common in Afar, where land grabbing along the Awash River has intensified. Private businessmen bribe local officials in the region and get land easily for cotton plantations. This is happening when demand for private plots by the Afars for farming is rising. Incessant drought over the past years has decimated pastoral animals and living off livestock rearing is becoming impossible for the Afar. As a result, pastoralists are increasingly shifting towards cultivation and the demand for farm plots has risen.

On top of all this, the government plans to expand the sugar plantation along the Awash River in Afar. Seven thousand hectares of land has been allotted for this enterprise. The problem is not the expansion of the sugar plantation per se. Government agro-industry (cane plantation and sugar production), from its inception, has never benefited the pastoral communities of Afar and Kereyu. Whether in terms of employment or in terms of compensatory schemes such as schools, clinics and other benefits, the government's schemes have not considered the interests of the indigenous owners of the rangeland. Pastoralists have been evicted without compensation. This is the problem.

In addition, the game park reservations such as in Awash have not benefited the communities either. The demands of pastoralists fell on deaf ears. As if adding insult to injury, the government recently evicted more than ten thousand Guji and Kore Oromo pastoralists from Southern Ethiopia for the purpose of a game park reservation at a place called Netchsar. This was done without any compensation. The park was leased out to a Dutch firm called the African Parks Foundation.

Indigenous rights and international instruments

The Ethiopian government, like many governments in Africa, is signatory to many international conventions agreeing to respect and protect the rights of its citizens, including women and indigenous peoples. The practice, however, is different.

Two important decisions that have been taken by the African Union include the recognition of the rights of indigenous peoples in Africa and the adoption of the protocol on African women. The Ethiopian parliament has not yet ratified the Protocol nor recognized the rights of indigenous peoples in Ethiopia. To conduct advocacy work on these issues can be considered tantamount to plotting to overthrow the government. After all, the Ethiopian contingent of the Global Call for Action Against Poverty, a global campaign targeting the G8 countries, was banned by the government as being part of the opposition's attempt to overthrow the government. Two leading figures in the movement are in prison accused of treason.

Communal conflicts

Recurrent drought and land grabbing by private "developers" as well as government has put pressure on pastoral communities and they are being squeezed out of their ancestral land. There is no visible development work involving those pastoralists that have been squeezed off their land. The government's so-called pastoral community development work has not yet benefited pastoral communities. It has not gone beyond constructing primary schools and a few clinics, and this mainly in Afar. It has not become involved in creating livelihood diversification schemes for pastoral communities, who have now become more desperate than ever. The pressure on the rangeland and the shrinkage of natural resources such as water points and grazing land has intensified communal conflicts among various pastoral communities. There is serious conflict between Afar, Kereyu and Ittu pastoralists along the

Awash River, while the various pastoral communities in South Omo (Hamer, Dasenech, Ngangaton, etc…) and Borana are at war.

The prevalence of conflict has had a huge impact on pastoral livelihoods over the past year. Small arms proliferation has aggravated the state of conflict. It has militarized society thereby highlighting the role of men and, because conflict has become the principal preoccupation, the role of men is taken as more important then that of women. In actual fact, however, it is the pastoral women who still play a crucial role in maintaining the pastoral household.

In a few cases, formal institutions are also party to the conflict. For instance, the Kenyan army post along the border with the Dasenech and Ngangaton in South Omo (Ethiopia) is involved in the conflict in support of the Turkana and other pastoral communities of Kenya. This is not government policy on the part of Kenya. According to the Dasenech and Gnangaton, the Kenyan army participates in cattle raids by Kenyan pastoralists and takes a share of the gains. On the other hand, the Gnangaton of Ethiopia, who are kith and kin to the Topaz of Southern Sudan, have access to arms and ammunition from the Sudan Peoples Liberation Army (SPLA). Ethiopian pastoralists strongly complain that their government is not doing enough to end the conflict or curb the involvement of the Kenyan army in cattle rustling along the border. Such conflicts require intervention involving communities and governments on both sides. Several NGOs are trying to implement development projects at micro-level, including conflict resolution. However, these projects will not get anywhere without macro-intervention. Macro-intervention in Ethiopia is the domain of government and, unless the government intervenes systematically, micro-projects will be only temporary solutions.

Conclusion

2005 gave the peoples of Ethiopia a hope that they had never before dreamed of, the hope of at last obtaining freedom. More than seven decades of rule by the so-called "modern state" had not brought that which is most precious for human beings: freedom. When an avalanche of humans, more than 3 million of them, descended on the Meskel Square of the capital on May 7 in a massive expression of the dream for social change and freedom, many concluded that there would be no return to totalitarian rule. The contemporary history of Ethiopia was about to change. The signs were all there. Unfortunately, all this changed in June when the government gunned down more than 40 people in the capital alone for protesting at a rigged election. Another round of massacres in November, again in the capital, shattered that dream for freedom and social change. Yet, the head of this same regime sat on Mr. Blair's Commission for Africa, was invited to attend the last G8 summit in Gleneagles, Scotland and was invited by the president of Germany to an Africa conference. Undoubtedly, this has encouraged him to pursue his repressive policies.

The plight of Ethiopian pastoralists must also be seen within the context of the debacle that the push for freedom has caused. It is only freedom and democracy that can facilitate changes for pastoralists. Without freedom, pastoralists - like others - have nothing, no base. Darkness looms over Ethiopia. Its people are muzzled and threatened at gunpoint. Under such circumstances, international solidarity is desperately needed.   ❏

Note of the editor

1   The process of formulating Poverty Reduction Strategy Papers in all low-income countries was initiated by the International Monetary Fund (IMF) and the World Bank (WB) in 1999. The formulation of the PRSPs is supposed to be country driven, with the broad participation of civil society. Once formulated, a PRSP provides the basic framework of all policies and programmes aimed at promoting growth and reducing poverty. In many countries, indigenous organizations complain that they were not properly involved in PRSP formulation.

KENYA

In Kenya, 2005 was an interesting year in many ways since it saw a number of developments affecting indigenous peoples. In this country, it is mainly pastoralists and hunter-gatherers who have identified themselves with the indigenous peoples' movement. According to the 1999 census, they comprise approximately 20% of the 28 million population of the country.

As in the previous two years since the new government took power, people still have high expectations of improved governance and more democratic space, reduced corruption and increased accountability. After all, the new government took office with clear pledges to improve the economy and people's livelihoods. In his inaugural speech of December 30, 2002, the President acknowledged the daunting task his government faced when he stated:

"Fellow Kenyans, I am inheriting a country which has been badly ravaged by years of misrule, disconnection between the people and government... I believe that governments exist to serve the people" ...."The government will no longer be run on the whims of individuals. ...My government's decisions will be guided by teamwork and consultations. The authority of Parliament and the independence of the Judiciary will be restored and enhanced as part of the democratic process .."

Three years down the line, the present government is being accused of repeating the same ills as its predecessor. It is said that the government has lost touch with the people and that some individuals are giving the President bad advice.

Constitutional review and referendum

The review of the constitution took centre stage, as popular demands continued to be made for a new Constitution. However, there were disagreements over some contentious issues in the original draft constitution (referred to as the "Bomas Draft" as it was finalized in a large conference in premises in Nairobi called "Bomas of Kenya"), and the manner in which those disagreements could be resolved could not be agreed upon. So the government, through the Attorney-General and some members of Parliament, decided to make some changes to the draft, resulting in a version that ended up being referred to as the "Kilifi" or "Wako" draft (Wako being the Attorney-General). This draft was put to a referendum whereby people were to vote "Yes", symbolized by a banana, or "No" symbolized by an orange. The government side, including the President, pushed for the "Yes" vote and campaigned hard for the draft to pass, with the Minister for Constitutional Affairs being quoted as saying they would use state resources to win the referendum. The majority of people, including some members of the cabinet and most indigenous peoples, voted "No" to the draft and urged their people to reject it.

The outcome of the referendum was a resounding "No" to the draft constitution, with just one out of the eight provinces backing the banana-led Wako draft. The province favoring the draft is situated around Mount Kenya, comprising the elite (Kikuyu, Meru and Embu people) closest to the President. This group of people is pejoratively referred to as the "Mount Kenya Mafia" on account of their being perceived as corrupt and conceited, since they see themselves as constituting "the government". Hence it is said that the referendum vote was as much against the draft as against this group, who were its proponents. The referendum defeat was said to constitute the "third liberation" (the first being from colonialism and the second being the overthrow of the ruling KANU party in 2002, after over 40 years in power).

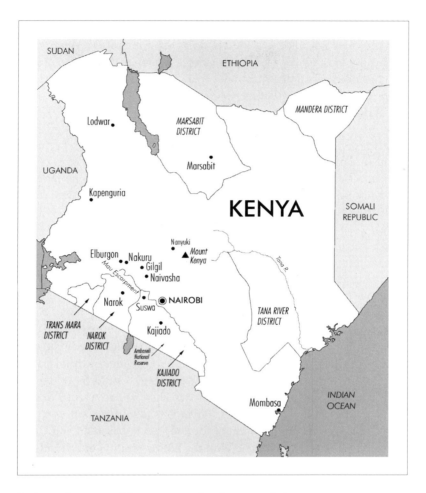

Referendum provides opportunity for organizing

The draft constitution was rejected mainly because it did not adequately address the issues of power sharing and devolution – this latter being a key issue of concern to indigenous peoples.

The referendum provided an opportunity for people, including indigenous people, to read the draft, understand it, share it, discuss it among themselves and organize around issues in order to make informed decisions. Through this process, some issues relating to land

and resources, and the possible negative impacts on indigenous peoples should the draft constitution be accepted, were raised. Views were shared (by sms, email, radio, workshops, meetings) and some apparent contradictions in the document were pointed out. It is perhaps appropriate to cite a few that made some indigenous communities wary of voting for the draft.

Article 80 (1) (b) defines Public Land as land lawfully held, used or occupied by a District Government or its agencies. Sub article 80 (1) (g) donates Game Reserves and Water Catchment Areas, National Parks, Wildlife Sanctuaries, especially Protected Areas to Central government. These areas are prohibited from being Community or District Government Land. Sub article 80 (2) states that Public Land under 80 (1) (b) shall belong to a District Government to be held in Trust for the people resident in the relevant District and administered by the National Land Commission. Sub Article 80 (4) gives parliament absolute power to legislate on the nature and terms of disposal of such protected areas. (Kilifi draft)

Indigenous peoples were against these articles because, once the new constitution became law, they would not be able to make further claims to productive resources in their areas since they would be under the jurisdiction of the central government. The proposed constitution could not be challenged in court. There was also suspicion as to the role, functions and composition of the proposed National Land Commission that was to be charged with the administration of all land.

Sub Article 78 (1) states that land is to be 'held, used and managed equitably, efficiently, productively and sustainably'. Sub Article 78 (2) defines a National Land Policy to ensure access to Land, and associated resources; security of land rights for all land holders, users and occupiers in good faith. (Kilifi draft)

The adjectives in these articles were read by most indigenous people as containing the possibility of alienation of land on a subtle pretext. In a similar vein, since indigenous peoples have no problem in accessing

their own land, the statement "ensuring access to land" was perceived
as being aimed at facilitating the settlement of farmers on indigenous
peoples' land. There was also the feeling that, even if there was good
faith, farmers would find it difficult to understand the land/resource
use systems of pastoralists and hunter-gatherers. In the thinking of
many farmers, and mainstream development discourse, pastoral land
set aside for seasonal grazing is dubbed "idle land", "inefficiently
used" or "poorly managed" and ownership is not clearly defined. The
criticism was thus that the aim would be to ensure access to pastoral
lands by outsiders.

All the discussions and analyses boiled down to the fact that indigenous peoples had no faith in the draft constitution since it was seen as
facilitating land and resource alienation. And in the process of reading,
analyzing and sharing the draft, they were able to organize and build
strategic alliances across political parties. In one such meeting, held in
the Rift Valley town of Suswa in southern Kenya - and also attended by
northern pastoralists - a declaration was made that all pastoralists
from Kenya should stick together.

Votes in exchange for own resources

The indigenous Ogiek hunter-gatherers have long fought for ancestral
rights to sections of the Mau Forest in the Rift Valley Province, gazetted as a National Forest. In order to woo their votes, the President suddenly declared that title deeds be issued to them. This was done despite protests from some sections of the government, who found that
the action was unprocedural. The ploy did not work, however, since
the Ogiek still voted against the draft constitution.

Similarly, the Maasai had long challenged the gazetting of the Amboseli National Reserve – the most lucrative wildlife park in the country - as a National Park in the mid 1970s. The park is situated in the
Kajiado District of southern Kenya. The Maasai claim that the alienation was carried out irregularly as a way of siphoning local resources
for the benefit of central government, at the expense of the Maasai. In
order to woo the Maasai to vote for the draft constitution, and perhaps

to split the votes of various regions, the President announced that the Amboseli National Park would be handed over to the local authority, the Olkejuado Country Council, to hold it in trust for the Maasai community of Kajiado District.

Again, as in the case of the Ogiek, the Maasai voted overwhelmingly against the draft constitution, stating that the government should correct the wrongs committed by returning the area to its rightful owners since it was fraudulently taken without the people's consent and without compensation. Local and international conservationists took the case to court, challenging the move of the President as unprocedural and against the principles of sustainable management of natural resources. They claimed that the President had no right to hand over any such resources and argued that local communities had no technical expertise to manage wildlife. The case is yet to be determined.

Land policy

Following delays in the constitution-making process and the many problems relating to the land question in Kenya, the Ministry of Lands was asked to work on a new land policy. The exercise started early in 2005 but it was delayed due to rejection of the draft constitution, whose central component was land. The new land policy document is expected to be shared with parliamentarians in an open forum before being sent to the cabinet. Once approved, it will be prepared as a Bill in order to pass through various reading stages in Parliament before it becomes law.

At this stage, where the document is still in draft form, a major concern for indigenous peoples is the lack of a legal framework in the present constitution to safeguard and protect collective rights to land and territories. It is apparent that unless an acceptable constitution is adopted, the land policy will not have the necessary legal framework for it to be operational.

Maasai human rights lawyer killed

In March 2005, a young Maasai lawyer, Marima Ole Sempeta, was gunned down outside his house in the outskirts of Nairobi. He had made a name for himself by representing the rights of the Maasai in a number of land cases. The motive for the killing has never been explained, neither has a suspect been arrested, but foul play is suspected. The director of Letangule and Company Advocates where Marima worked spoke of him as "a man who could mobilize people and gather evidence on the ground at the same time as he prepares evidence".

Delamere case and the killing of a ranger

In April 2005, Thomas Cholmondeley - the son of Lord Delamere, the famous settler who initially took 100,000 acres of Maasai land a century ago - shot and killed a Kenya Wildlife Service ranger named Samson Ole Sisina at the Delamere ranch at Gilgil. It was claimed that he was shot by accident while investigating the illegal trade in game meat.

The suspect was held and later freed by the Director of Public Prosecutions for lack of evidence. This release was received with shock from all corners of the country, particularly the Maasai community. So much noise was made in the media that the case was reinstated and Cholmondeley charged with murder, but later released. The Director of Public Prosecutions was sacked following the scandal and replaced with a Maasai.

Ethnic clashes continue

The beginning of 2005 was characterized by ethnic fighting in several parts of the country that left nearly 200 people dead. By July 2005, more than 60 people had been killed in inter-clan fighting in Mandera District and 92 in Marsabit. Scores more were also killed as violence erupted in Trans Mara, Kajiado and Narok districts. Following these clashes, there were accusations that the police had been unwilling to stop the spreading violence.

Massacre in Marsabit between Borana and Gabra

In Turbi, Marsabit District, an area occupied by Gabra pastoralists, at least 53 people - including 21 primary school pupils - were killed after a series of raids by Borana pastoralists. The fighting was partly a result of livestock theft but it was also reported that there were longstanding disputes between the two allied communities, who speak the same language, share the same names, live together and intermarry. The raiders were reportedly heavily armed with AK 47 rifles, sub-machine guns and hand grenades.

Although reports of the massacre reached the Marsabit police headquarters early in the morning and 20 officers were immediately sent to Turbi, it took them hours to reach the scene. The whole of Marsabit District is quite remote. Residents and leaders accused the police and army of taking too long to respond to the attack and treating the incident casually. This perception persists.

Clashes between Wardei famers and Auliyahan pastoralists

A clash in Tana River District began following the blockade of access routes to the River Tana for pastoralists and their livestock by the Wardei farmers. More than twenty herders drove their livestock to the river after cutting a fence, seriously injuring five protesting farmers. Two people were also killed and two others critically injured in clashes over grazing land in the same district.

Clashes over water and pasture in Mai Mahiu

In January, 20 people were killed and more than 40 homes burnt to the ground when Kikuyu and Maasai clashed over the fencing off of access to the water of the Kegong River in Mai Mahiu, Naivasha District. The volume of water had fallen drastically following a prolonged drought. Most of the people were killed by government security personnel using heavy weaponry. More than 30 leaders from nine districts met and criticized the action, dubbing it "government instigated terrorism". They castigated the use of excessive force by the police in quelling the violence, claiming that most of the victims of police shootings and arrests were Maasai. They cautioned that such violence by the government might result in civil war.

Peace agreement between pastoralists

In the midst of the many ethnic clashes, a peace agreement was reached between the Pokot and Turkana pastoralists of north-western Kenya who met and promised to put an end to cattle rustling between their two communities.

The government pays little attention to the area, so the two local communities voluntarily decided to end their long-drawn out hostilities through dialogue and peace building. Speaking at Tarkwel in Turkana District, elders from the two communities said that enough was enough and admitted that they had fought a meaningless war for many years that had not benefited them in any way.

Kenya-Tanzania border clashes

Many pastoralist communities reside in the cross-border areas of East Africa and, as such, any cross border skirmishes affect them. During this past year, two border areas were the scene of violent clashes. The first was the Kenya-Sudan border, which saw raids by 50 heavily armed attackers besieging Nimoit village, 40 kms from the Kenya/Sudan border and holding the herdsmen hostage. The Sudanese were said to be cattle rustlers.

A second cross-border clash took place on the Tanzania-Kenya border when raiders from Tanzania attacked Mausa village in the Narok District of Kenya leaving two people dead and three seriously injured. The raiders were thought to be from the Batemi (Sonjo) community of Mara province and the attack was the result of a longstanding land

TANZANIA

This article addresses issues related to indigenous peoples in Tanzania during 2005. The indigenous peoples of Tanzania discussed here are the hunter-gatherer communities of the Hadzabe and the Akiye, as well as the pastoral communities of the Barabaig and the Maasai.

Faced with a host of challenges, problems, negative bias and structural marginalization, pastoralist communities in Tanzania in 2005 continued to lose land, livestock, influence and workforce within pastoralism. Whereas agro-pastoral groups faired better, pastoral groups, especially those practising nomadic and transhumant modes of production, such as the Maasai and the Barabaig, lost out in the ongoing development processes.

Elections

At national level, the macro-economic position changed little in 2005. General elections were held and the fourth President of the United Republic of Tanzania came to power through the ruling party Chama Cha Mapinduzi (CCM) or the Revolutionary Party.

Elections were also held to elect councillors and village chairpersons. Despite the fact that elections were held during the dry season, when pastoralists are normally moving, the Maasai participated adequately and elected their preferred candidates.

Official political parties drew support from membership, businesses, professionals, research institutions, peasants and artisans. This support manifested itself in monetary contributions, campaigns and influence. The pre-election period in 2005 was dominated by *takrima* (translated as "African hospitality") in which various forms of gifts or dona-

tions were given in the name of "African hospitality" to help support political campaigns.

A new class of rich people and elites have emerged in Tanzania in recent years and, during the 2005 elections, they acted as power brokers. They have money, influence and power. Through interactions at various levels, these groups funded some of the political campaigns in different parts of the country, including in areas inhabited by indigenous peoples, and managed to influence the outcome of elections of village leaders and councillors in many parts of the country.

Whereas this was the reality in most parts of the country, the influence of the rich, the elites and other party activists was even more effective in rural areas - especially among the pastoral indigenous peoples - where the level of awareness of party politics and parliamentary democracy is still low.

Candidates who contested leadership positions in constituencies within the traditional territories of indigenous pastoral peoples were largely from the same ruling party (CCM), except in Kiteto district where one opposition party (CHADEMA) presented a candidate for the parliamentary seat. Access to land resources was an important parameter in the potential backing of candidates by power brokers. Candidates who supported investors from non- pastoralist areas received the backing of power brokers whereas candidates who were perceived to represent the interests of indigenous peoples found themselves opposed by them.

Land and livestock

Privatisation of public utilities continued throughout the year. This included some of the National Ranching Company (NARCO) ranches in pastoralist areas. This land, which once belonged to the Barabaig pastoralists in Hanang and was taken by a parastatal for wheat production, was up for privatisation in 2005 following the dissolution of the National Food Corporation (NAFCO).

A new livestock policy was formulated although it has yet to be approved by Parliament, probably in 2006. In an effort to influence the livestock policy in the pastoralists' favour, a joint committee was formed by the Pastoralist NGOs Forum (PINGOs) and the Tanzania Pastoralists & Hunter-Gatherers Organisation (TAPHGO). Through the committee, both organisations held consultative meetings that brought together various stakeholders in pastoral development to discuss, deliberate and communicate the new livestock policy to the relevant ministry.

Most of the comments presented to the ministry argued for a change in policy focus from pure productivity to supporting the livelihoods of

livestock keepers. Comments further tried to enrich the policy document by calling for an understanding and appreciation of flexibility,
movement and trekking as optimal forms of resource utilisation in an
unbalanced environment in which climate, rainfall and vegetation are
all variables.

Conflicts

The whole year was characterized by resource-based conflicts in all
areas inhabited by indigenous peoples. While such conflicts took different shapes and forms, the underlying causes remained the same
and the conflicts affected both pastoralists and hunter-gatherers.

The resource-related conflicts have had both internal and external
causes. Some of the internal causes include: poor governance of natural resources at the village level and weak village leadership. National,
regional and district level institutions[1] such as the ward land tribunals,
land councils, village governments and village adjudication committees, which are mandated by law to govern and administer land resources, have also impacted negatively on the indigenous local level
institutions (such as clans, territorial sections, traditional leadership
structures) that traditionally regulated access and management of the
same resources. Whereas in the past rights of access to resources were
negotiated at the local level through such social institutions, they are
now negotiated and secured at levels higher than that of the local communities, leading to different forms of resource-based conflicts. Allocation of hunting blocks and issuance of lands to foreign investors, conducted at a higher level of government without the involvement of
local level institutions, are cases in point.

Other causes include a lack of clear policies and procedures in relation to the acquisition and use of natural resources in Tanzania. Changes in property rights have in part been driven by development agents
and actors external to pastoral communities, and by creating market
conditions favourable to certain interest groups. This has aggravated
the competition between communal and private property resources
and, in this process, common property resources have been under-

mined. 2005 saw more pastoral households acquiring 3 to 4-acre plots of land for farming purposes. This move is in response to a need to diversify and to assert land rights, as privately-owned farming plots are seen as secure forms of landholding compared to communally held pasture lands. In 2005, households from the pastoralist communities put pressure on the different land authorities to give them private customary land titles as provided by the land law.

Population increase, climatic conditions, access to markets for specific products (especially maize) and the technologies that have become available in the last 20 years have become the engines of land-use conflicts in Kiteto district in northern Tanzania. Production and marketing of maize in Kiteto district has become one key engine of change in property rights, and local level institutions have become key players. As Kiteto district has proved to be the bread basket for various regions in Tanzania (Manyara, Dodoma, Arusha, Tanga, Morogoro, Coast and Dar es Salaam regions), more and more people from various regional capitals have gained influence over access, use and control of lands in pastoral areas, especially in Kiteto. High potential areas in Barabaig Hanang, Monduli and Simanjiro districts are experiencing similar scenarios.

Continued threats against pastoralism

Pastoralism in Tanzania as a unique way of production and life is experiencing serious threats because other forms of land use are competing with livestock production, and because political bias often favours forms of land use other than pastoralism. Various indigenous pastoralists have devised different coping mechanisms as a response to the threats to their livelihoods. Their experiences during 2005 are described below.

The Barabaig

The situation of the Barabaig pastoralists has changed little since 2004. The movement of farmers onto their indigenous territory (Hanang district) intensified unabated, forcing the Barabaig to migrate in even larger numbers to the south and west in search of pasture and water for their livestock.

Discrimination against the Barabaig by farmers also continued in the same way. Farmers still perceive them as aggressors who invade other people's areas and the farmers are urging the Barabaig to go back to their own areas. They do this without recognising the fact that the Barabaig's areas have been taken from them for other uses.

The exploitation of the Barabaig by different groups and local authorities has also continued. They are still used as a source of revenue for district councils since they are forced to pay both production and sales taxes in areas such as Kilombero and Kilosa. This is the case for most pastoralists in the country, especially those who live outside their traditional territories. As livestock is seen as destructive to the environment, there are different types of charges levied against pastoralists, ranging from fees for water use to various forms of council taxes before, during and after the sale of animals.

The Barabaig lands of Basuto in Hanang, which were once taken from them and used for a national wheat production scheme, are now to be privatized after repeated failures to reach production targets, along with environmental problems. While this land is being privatised, the situation of the Barabaig has moved from bad to worse in relation to landlessness. And while private investors are buying the Barabaig ancestral land, the Barabaig lack both capital and the political connections necessary for them to be considered its rightful owners and worthy of its return. Besides loss of pasture, which still forces the Barabaig to move far away to seek alternative grazing, the Barabaig are also still suffering the loss of spiritual sites, where the graves of their ancestors (which are of great cultural significance) are located and remain irreplaceable.

In 2005, more Barabaig moved further to the south as a result of land pressure. When moving south, the Barabaig had to travel through south Maasailand. In areas between Kiteto district and districts in Morongoro region (Kilosa, Kilombero and Ulanga), the Barabaig lost livestock to cattle rustlers, most of whom were fellow pastoralist Maasai. In some cases, the indigenous Barabaig were forced to hire young Maasai men, who escorted them beyond the Maasai borders to avoid losing more animals. The Barabaig who moved further to the south in 2005 thus experienced insecurity due to other indigenous groups i.e. the Maasai.

The Maasai

The indigenous pastoral Maasai people also continued to experience threats to their sources of livelihood in 2005. Key resources such as land and water have continued to shrink as farmers/miners/wildlife conservationists have continued to take more of their land from them. During 2005, Maasai in all five traditional districts (Ngorongoro, Monduli, Longido, Simanjiro and Kiteto) lost more land to farming and to various forms of wildlife protected/designated areas.

Towards the end of 2005, this resource loss, coupled with a serious drought, worsened the situation rendering indigenous coping mechanisms ineffective and leading to loss of livestock and great human suffering. By the end of 2005, there was still no official recognition of the seriousness of the drought and the acute food shortage.

Threats of evictions have continued to haunt the Maasai of the Ngorongoro Conservation Area (NCA). Over the past year, areas for resettlement have been identified outside the NCA, where people and their livestock are supposed to be moved to in order to reduce what conservationists perceive as environmental threats resulting from overstocking/overgrazing.

One positive development was celebrated in Monduli district in Central Maasailand: land which had previously been taken by the military for training purposes was returned to the inhabitants of the twelve villages to which the land belonged. This followed the land demarcation work carried out by the organization Community Research and Development Services (CORDS) by which the villages in question secured village land certificates. When the army tried to title this land, the Ministry of Lands and Human Settlement told them that they could not title any land that fell under villages that already had certificates to their land. The military was therefore forced to remove beacons[2] and had to place such beacons outside the village boundaries.

In Kiteto district, land-use conflicts have continued to intensify and more farmers are moving in, marginalizing indigenous peoples. Now the chairman of the district council is from a migrant farming community and two-thirds of the councillors are non-pastoralists. This is perceived by indigenous peoples as part of a systematic form of marginalization.

Increasingly, Maasailand is becoming home to non-pastoralists, most of whom are key actors in changing land-use patterns. Whereas some rich individuals, both Maasai and non-Maasai, have secured landholdings and are exploiting new opportunities for wealth accumulation in order to meet the increasing cash needs for education, health, food and other basic needs, there is an emerging trend of poor landless people among the Maasai. Egalitarianism, which was once a hallmark of the indigenous Maasai people, is now significantly reduced.

Hadzabe and Akiye (Ndorobo) hunter-gatherers

In 2005, the Akiye and Hadzabe hunter-gatherer communities experienced further loss of their land and other resources to both farmers and pastoralists. Shifting cultivation has destroyed their habitat, depleting berries, roots and the flowers necessary for the bees to make honey. All this places constraints on their coping strategies. Some foreign hunting companies have been allocated most of the Hadzabe territory as a hunting block by the Department of Wildlife. Hadzabe rights to subsistence hunting resources are thus eroded and their livelihoods have become increasingly insecure.

Both communities lived in near famine situations during the drought of 2005. Some groups of well-wishers provided food aid but this was inadequate and in most cases too little food aid arrived, and too late.

In 2005, the Hadzabe lost more land to hunting companies, and their subsistence hunting rights have now been seemingly lost indefinitely.

Development cooperation and indigenous peoples

Some bilateral donor organisations started working with indigenous communities in Tanzania in 2005. In Ngorongoro, the ERETO project, which is funded by Danish International Development Assistance (DANIDA) continued to work with the indigenous Maasai pastoralists, using restocking as a strategy for poverty reduction in a pastoralist setting. In 2005, the ERETO project further made serious attempts to address some policy issues in areas affecting pastoralism: conservation, poverty reduction and rangeland resources at district, regional and national levels.

A host of community-based organizations (CBOs) and NGOs, currently working with the pastoralists in Tanzania at local, district, provincial and national levels, continued to implement various projects involving different areas such as land rights, animal health, poverty reduction, HIV/AIDS and micro-finance.

The presence of international development organizations[3] continued to be felt in 2005. Support to their partners operating on the ground is noticeable. Most of them work mainly with the pastoralist Maasai, whose NGOs and CBOs are more organised and stronger than those of other communities.

Umbrella organizations

2005 saw close collaboration between the two pastoralist/hunter-gatherer umbrella organisations in Tanzania: the Tanzania Pastoralist & Hunter-gatherers Organisation (TAPHGO) and the Pastoralist Indigenous NGOs Forum (PINGOs) in certain areas of research, lobbying, advocacy and policy work. Most of their work has been with the pastoralist Maasai people. Work involving the pastoralist Barabaig and other agro-pastoral groups has been limited, less focused and irregular.

Both organizations have worked most in the northern part of the country, in Arusha and Manyara regions, with isolated activities with pastoral groups living in other regions such as Kilimanjaro, Tanga, Morogoro, Dodoma, Iringa and Mbeya. Thematically, TAPHGO and

PINGOs have worked in similar areas, such as livestock policy, wildlife management issues, land tenure and policy, HIV/AIDS and paralegal training.

While hunter-gatherer communities of the Ndorobo and Hadzabe have formed part of the constituency of the umbrella organisations, they have received little attention from either and remain the least visible group in the activity profiles of both organisations.

PINGOs has built its core competencies around legal issues. TAPHGO has yet to refocus its work in areas where it has a comparative advantage. Already, it has shown potential for networking within policy circles and state organs, hoping to change things from within instead of adopting a confrontational approach.

More indigenous peoples and their organisations participated in the sessions of the African Commission on Human and Peoples' Rights in 2005. These processes have proven instrumental in informing indigenous activists and their supporters about indigenous peoples' issues in Africa and the world. ❑

Notes

1   Ministry of Lands and other land boards that previous played a role in land allocations and transfers.
2   "Boundary beacon" means a survey mark constructed by cement and placed for the purpose of indicating boundary points.
3   These include Development Corporation Ireland (DCI), Oxfam UK and Oxfam Ireland, the Swedish International Development Agency (SIDA), CORDAID, NOVIB (Oxfam Netherlands), Danish Association for International Cooperation-Tanzania (MS-Tanzania), IWGIA, Trocaire (Development Agency of the Catholic Church in Ireland), TRIAS, VETAID, WaterAid and FarmAfrica.

References

African Commission on Human & Peoples' Rights, 2003: *Report of the Working Group on Indigenous Populations/Communities in Africa.* Adopted during the 34th Ordinary Session of the Commission in Banjul, Gambia, 2003. Co-published by IWGIA and the African Commission.
The International Work Group for Indigenous Affairs (IWGIA), 2002-2003, 2004, 2005: *The Indigenous* World 2002-2003, 2004, 2005. IWGIA, Copenhagen.

Organization of African Unity (OAU), 1983: *African Charter on Human and Peoples' Rights.*

United Republic of Tanzania (URT), 1977: *Constitution of the United Republic of Tanzania.*

United Republic of Tanzania (URT), 2001: *Agricultural Sector Development Strategy*

United Republic of Tanzania (URT), 2002: *Agricultural Sector Programme Support, Phase II.*

United Republic of Tanzania (URT), 2003: *ERETO 2 Ngorongoro Pastoralists Project 2nd Phase. Final project document.*

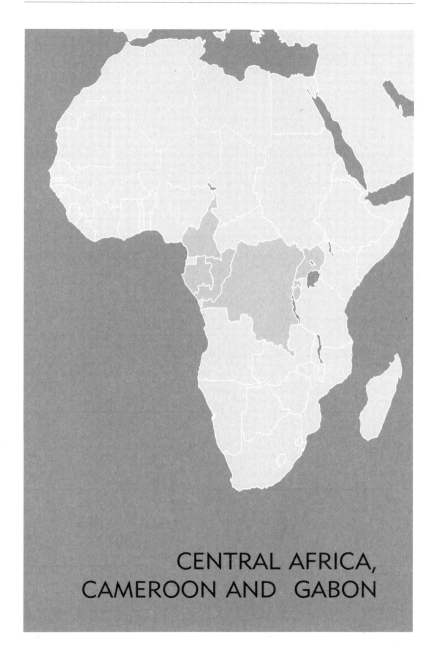

CENTRAL AFRICA, CAMEROON AND GABON

UGANDA

During the 2005 election campaign – the first Ugandan multiparty elections in 25 years will take place in February 2006 - the main opposition candidate Besigye was accused, acquitted and re-accused of various crimes, including treason plus links to insurgents in the Democratic Republic of Congo (DRC) and to the Ugandan rebel group the Lord's Resistance Army (LRA). The end result of this acrimonious affair was the re-election of President Museveni for an unprecedented third term in office.

Continued instability

A peace agreement and ceasefire in southern Sudan, established in January 2005 with Ugandan participation, ended in July with the unfortunate death of Sudan's vice-president John Garang, a former southern Sudanese rebel leader, in a helicopter crash. This means there is no end in sight to the conflict for an estimated 1.7 million internally displaced people, mainly in the north, and the hundreds of thousands of children who commute by foot to nearby towns every night to avoid abduction or worse at the hands of the LRA.

In south-west Uganda, continued instability in eastern DRC is being complicated by the alleged involvement of both Rwandan and Ugandan forces. At the end of 2005, the International Criminal Court found Uganda guilty of violating human rights laws with its 1997 invasion of the DRC, and the government is therefore liable for compensation. This will put even more pressure on Ugandan government budgets, already insufficient to implement the country's indeed progressive social and human rights programme. The continuing insecu-

rity in eastern DRC continues to impede tourism in south-west Uganda, which is also the home to around 3,500 indigenous Batwa.

Batwa land loss and current responses

Due to increasing competition from immigrants over land, and the impact of some conservation projects that have taken over their remaining traditional lands since the early 1990s, indigenous Batwa people in south-west Uganda have become landless and lost access to their traditional semi-nomadic hunting and gathering lifestyle. Most Batwa livelihoods have always been linked to forests and, as forests have disappeared or been taken away for conservation, their livelihoods have become extremely insecure, with many now facing extreme poverty. Their continuing social marginalisation, lack of access to adequate compensation for their lost forest access, low literacy rates, lack of access to social services and chronic poverty has led to a serious threat to Batwa's livelihoods, and to the survival of their culture. Up until now government, donors and NGOs have failed to address Batwa needs or deliver fully their promises to address their poverty. Batwa have therefore decided to work towards promoting the acquisition of land for themselves, while also securing education, training and income generation opportunities for Batwa communities.

During 2005, Batwa continued to build up their own representative organisation - the United Organisation for Batwa Development in Uganda (UOBDU) - which continued to seek funds to pay for a long-term programme of work that started in 2004. Since then, UOBDU has been working to establish its activities with local partners around the Echuya Forest, Bwindi Reserve and Mgahinga Park, to widen support for its programme, and to strengthen its own capacity to deliver on UOBDU community development plans. During 2005, UOBDU began to secure funding and has now established offices in Kisoro, Kabale and Kanungu districts, staffed by 9 Batwa fieldworkers and managed by an unpaid management committee drawn from communities from all three districts. Pilot funding allocated in 2005 for its capacity development programme addressing land and housing, education and adult literacy, income generation (including agriculture) and forest access and conservation benefit-sharing, will lead to implementation of activities during 2006.

Securing land continues to be the top priority for Batwa from southwest Uganda, and UOBDU is continuing to seek additional lands for the up to 50% of Batwa who are still landless, along with the establishment of Batwa land titles. During 2005, UOBDU completed community consultations on the land issue as part of its long-term legal strategy, spurred on by the successful outcome of the indigenous Benet community's land rights struggle. During 2005, the Benet community won a landmark battle over rights to lands lost when they were forcibly removed to make way for the Mount Elgon National Park. After

many years of work on the part of the Benet community and its supporters, the Ugandan High Court finally recognised the community as
the rightful owners of their land.   ❏

RWANDA

The system of traditional village courts, known as *gacaca*, was expected to start in earnest throughout Rwanda in 2005, having previously begun as a pilot scheme in 2002. *Gacaca* was established to process thousands of defendants accused of genocide-related crimes – which would have overwhelmed the official court system and taken decades – and blends a customary system of community hearings with a more formal court structure.

Despite the authorities' announcement that over 700,000 people would be tried in 2005, fewer than 3,000 cases were heard and trials have yet to start in every province. It is considered unlikely that the courts will have completed their work by 2007, as previously estimated. Despite President Kagame's announcement in April that government members must testify before courts if summoned, many Rwandans are suspicious of the *gacaca* system and have stayed away from sessions. As courts began their pre-trial inquiries in April 2005, thousands of Rwandans fled to neighbouring Burundi and Uganda, claiming to be escaping from arbitrary arrests and "persecution". Despite initially welcoming the refugees, the Burundian authorities cooperated with Rwanda in forced repatriation, flouting international conventions to which both countries are State parties.

In July, approximately 20,000 detainees, who had either confessed to genocide-related crimes or who were elderly, unwell or were children in 1994, were provisionally released from jail to stand trial at a later date. An official complaint by genocide survivors was lodged with the government in August following the release. In May a senior army official, Major-General Laurent Munyakazi, stood trial before a *gacaca* court, accused of helping militiamen kill thousands of Tutsis during the genocide. In September, the authorities arrested a Belgian priest, Guy Theunis, who was expected to stand trial for

inciting genocide; however, in November he was transferred to Belgium for possible trial there. Pasteur Bizimungu, Rwanda's post-genocide President, began his appeal at the Supreme Court. He was detained in the run-up to the 2003 presidential elections - in which he intended to stand as a candidate - and subsequently sentenced to 15 years in a trial widely regarded as politically motivated.

Relations continued to improve between Rwanda and the UN's International Criminal Tribunal for Rwanda (ICTR), which handed over files for 15 genocide suspects still at large to the national prosecutor. Relations with France remained delicate; however, in November a French judge began investigating claims that France helped the pro-Hutu administration during the genocide.

Land law

A national land law finally came into force in 2005, after years of deliberation. The law is based on the assumption that small parcels of land are not viable, and promotes land consolidation. A new land registration system is being established with major support from the UK's Department for International Development (DFID). The authorities will decide how land will be grouped and to what use it will be put. The law also contains provisions for the state to compulsorily requisition land that it deems is being inadequately used without compensation, and denies the customary use of marshland by the poor, which will have adverse consequences for the Twa potters who source their clay there.

The Twa are an indigenous "Pygmy" people living in Rwanda, Burundi, eastern Democratic Republic of Congo and south-west Uganda, estimated to number 86,000-112,000 people (33,000 in Rwanda). The Twa were originally semi-nomadic hunter-gatherers living in the high altitude forests of the Great Lakes region. Forest clearance and settlement and takeover of forest lands for agri-business and conservation eroded the Twa's forest-based subsistence economies. Some Twa found alternative livelihoods as potters, dancers and entertainers but most survived from labouring for others and begging. Their customary rights to land were not recognised, and they had no recourse to compensation, resulting in widespread landlessness. As itinerant squatters living on the edges of society, the Twa encountered prejudice and discrimination from the dominant culture, which persists to this day. During 2005 the human rights situation in Rwanda continued to cause concern. There were reported cases of arbitrary arrest and detention; trials and convictions based on inadequate evidence; cases of forced repatriation of Rwandan refugees from Burundi; and clampdowns on freedom of speech and the media. Despite hosting a regional seminar on human rights (during which the Minister for Justice, Edda Mukabagwiza, called for measures to promote the protection of human rights) an independent review of the implementation of the UK and Government of Rwanda (GOR) Memorandum of Understanding found that there continue to be violations of civil and political rights which also threaten the achievement of social and economic rights.[1] Rwanda's international donors, particularly the UK and USA, made no public comments about the human rights situation, although some (like the EU) did fund civil society projects, including those targeting indigenous peoples and organisations. Rwanda reached World Bank and IMF HIPC (Highly Indebted Poor Country) completion point during the year, receiving US$ 1.4 billion in debt relief, and has been approved for a second Poverty Reduction Support Grant (PRSGII) worth US$ 55 million. The HIPC Initiative is a debt-reduction tool which enables countries to benefit from debt relief if they initiate macroeconomic and structural adjustment policies specifically agreed with the World Bank and IMF.

Ethnicity banned in public discourse

Further to the parliamentary commission report of 2004, which accused several NGOs of "divisionism" and promoting a "genocidal ideology", the Senate has commissioned another report into international NGOs, which has yet to be published.

The authorities continued to deny legal registration to CAURWA (*Communauté des Autochtones Rwandais*), the main national Twa organisation, and others whose statutes and names refer to the words "indigenous" ("*autochtone*" in French) and "Twa".

As noted in *The Indigenous World 2005*, since the 1994 genocide, the Rwandan authorities have sought to remove all reference to ethnicity and, under Rwandan law, advocating ethnic differences is a crime. However, critics continue to believe that the government has used the excuse of ethnicity to suppress freedom of expression and political opposition. Organisations and individuals who refer to ethnicity are likely to be labelled "divisionist" by the authorities, who assert that all Rwandans share a common language, religion and culture and that any differences are not "ethnic" but the result of the colonial "divide and rule" policy which was perpetuated by subsequent post-independence administrations.

The Rwandan authorities believe that all Rwandans are "indigenous" and that CAURWA's affirmative actions in support of one ethnic group are unconstitutional and "divisionist", undermining the unity and reconciliation process.

Rwanda was one of the first countries to submit itself to NEPAD's (New Partnership for African Development) Peer Review mechanism. The NEPAD report notes that with regard to the Twa the authorities appeared to be adopting a policy of assimilation, and recommended the government begin intensive dialogue with the Twa. The government's official response states that it has never had a policy of assimilation but admitted that the *"Batwa community continues to have a disproportionate number of vulnerable members, and seem not to benefit sufficiently from the national policy that supports socio-economic integration of all Rwandans."* The authorities also noted that *"it is clear that a targeted response to [the Twa's] specific problems is recommended and shall be reflected in the plan of action."* [2]

Work on Twa issues

CAURWA implemented a wide-ranging consultation on the legal registration issue with its members, beneficiaries and the wider Twa community, which culminated in a summary report unanimously adopted by the membership at an extraordinary Annual General Meeting convened in August 2005. The report calls on the government to understand that the terms "Twa" and "indigenous" are not "divisionist", to put in place special measures to improve the socio-economic conditions of the Twa, and to continue a dialogue with CAURWA to allow the latter to continue its work.

Despite the ongoing negotiations on legal registration, CAURWA has continued its activities with beneficiaries in 9 provinces. CAURWA is supporting 148 Twa cooperative associations (3,043 people) and providing them with training and inputs to increase food security and revenues. The increased incomes have enabled association members to invest in their children's school costs, join health insurance schemes, obtain credit, buy additional livestock and improve their housing. Twa access to land, and know-how to use land productively, has increased. Twa communities' self-confidence has increased as has the recognition by local authorities of Twa needs.

Sensitisation by CAURWA staff and volunteers has led increasing numbers of Twa families to send their children to primary school. During 2005 CAURWA supported 80 Twa secondary school students throughout the country. CAURWA supported 529 adult learners in 19 literacy circles (189 men, 340 women) and, by the end of the year, 51.8% could read and write (88 men, 186 women).

Throughout 2005, CAURWA's human rights department was dominated by the issue of legal registration and the question of revising the organisations' name and statutes. Despite this preoccupation, CAURWA's work on human rights and advocacy continued to make progress during the year, including continued lobbying on the land law; attendance at several regional and international human rights seminars; training 200 Twa beneficiaries and community volunteers on human rights. CAURWA also provided legal support to 10 Twa communities whose land had been expropriated by neighbours or the local authorities, and intervened on behalf of 3 Twa victims of crime. ☐

Notes

1 **Killick, T. et al., 2005:** *Implementation of the Memorandum of Understanding between the Governments of Rwanda and the United Kingdom: Report of Independent Monitors* , p.24. Department for International Development (DFID), May 2005.
2 **Government of Rwanda, 2005:** *Response to Issues Raised and Best Practices Suggested in the Country Review Team (CRT)'s Report.* Section on "Democracy and Good Political Governance", p.4, June 2005.

BURUNDI

2005 began with continued violence in the western provinces, result-ing in hundreds of internally displaced people. Army and rebel sol-diers carried out massive violations throughout the year, including murder, rape, abduction and theft, although not on the same scale as seen in previous years.

Following the transitional period, Burundians had their first elections in 12 years and chose Pierre Nkurunziza of the CNDD-FDD (National Council for the Defense of Democracy-Forest for the Defense of Democ-racy) as their President. A new constitution was adopted by an estimated 90% of voters in a February 2005 referendum. The constitution calls for power sharing amongst the Hutu, Tutsi and Twa ethnic groups, and re-quires 30% of parliamentary seats to be reserved for women.

Despite presidential guarantees to protect human rights, violations continued, with opposition supporters detained, beaten and killed. Soldiers from the CNDD-FDD and the former Burundian Armed Forc-es were integrated into a new National Defence Force (FND) in early 2005, however many suspected of violations were given new positions of responsibility. Militia groups were disbanded and their members demobilized during the year. However due to delays in receiving the US$100 each had been promised, they have demonstrated several times, and only a few have handed in weapons to the authorities.

Many injustices remain uninvestigated – the reformed judicial sys-tem is weak through lack of resources, incapacity and corruption. Dis-illusioned with the system, several cases of "public" justice and lynch-ings were reported.

In December 2005 the UN extended the mandate of its mission in Burundi (UNOB) to July 2006, when it said it would end. UNOB has

about 5,000 peacekeepers in Burundi, which is expected to be gradually reduced throughout 2006.

The situation of the Twa

The situation of indigenous Twa in Burundi continued to be precarious in light of ongoing violence and conflict.

The Twa are an indigenous "Pygmy" people living in Rwanda, Burundi, eastern Democratic Republic of Congo and south-west Uganda, estimated to number 86,000-112,000 people (approximately 60,000 in Burundi). The Twa were originally semi-nomadic hunter-gatherers living in the high altitude forests of the Great Lakes region. Forest clearance and settlement and takeover of forest lands for agri-business and conservation eroded the Twa's forest-based subsistence economies. Some Twa found alternative livelihoods as potters, dancers and entertainers but most survived from labouring for others and begging. Their customary rights to land were not recognised, and they had no recourse to compensation, resulting in widespread landlessness. As itinerant squatters living on the edges of society, the Twa encountered prejudice and discrimination from the dominant culture, which persists to this day.

Following the constitutional referendum in February, approximately 200 Twa fled Kirundo province for Rwanda. According to the Twa Senator Liberate Nikayanze, the Twa had run away following intimidation from Hutu neighbours, who had accused the Twa of overwhelmingly voting "no" in the referendum. The post-transition Constitution accords 3 Senate and 3 National Assembly seats to the Twa community (out of a total of 49 Senate and 118 National Assembly seats), the rest being divided ethnically amongst the Hutu and Tutsi communities. Many Twa believe they should be accorded more seats in the National Assembly and Senate.

The Twa organisation UNIPROBA (*Unissons-Nous pour la Promotion des Batwa* – Let Us Unite for the Promotion of the Batwa) carried out several activities at the national and international level during the year. At the national level it performed advocacy on behalf of Twa communities in cases of land expropriation, supported Twa community food security and income-generating projects (e.g. agriculture; brick making), distributed school materials to Twa children, and conducted community sensitization workshops on HIV/AIDS and human rights training. UNIPROBA representatives participated in the UN Working Group on Indigenous Populations, and made an oral intervention condemning the lack of consultation with Twa communities over the power-sharing provisions in the Constitution, calling for more seats.

Representative of UNIPROBA participated in the 38th Ordinary Session of the African Commission on Human and Peoples' Rights in the Gambia in November 2005 and highlighted the situation of the Twa people.

In March 2005 the Working Group on Indigenous Populations under the African Commission on Human and Peoples' Rights conducted

ous ministries, international agencies and NGOs and carried out field trips to Twa communities. The Burundi mission report and its recommendations were adopted by the African Commission at its last session in November 2005 and will be published in 2006. The report concludes that the Batwa are one of the most vulnerable sections of the Burundian population. The report stresses the high level of poverty in Batwa communities, the inaccessibility of their children to education, their inaccessibility to land and health care, their quasi-institutional exclusion from employment, the threat of extinction of their culture and their subjection to the inhuman practice of bondage.

Youth network

The newly-established Twa youth forum, *Réseau des Jeunes Batwa/Bambuti de la Région des Grands Lacs* (RJB) held meetings in Bujumbura, Burundi in May 2005 and Bukavu, DRC in July 2005. The role of the RJB is to coordinate the activities of young Batwa and Bambuti, to strengthen capacity, and promote indigenous rights and education amongst young indigenous peoples in the region. It has formed an executive committee comprising representatives of indigenous organisations, and produced a three-year work plan.   ❏

DEMOCRATIC REPUBLIC OF CONGO
(DRC)

Conflict and violence continued throughout 2005, particularly in the eastern region of DRC. Both army and militia forces have been accused of multiple human rights violations including murder, rape, abduction, torture, arbitrary detention and theft against civilians, thousands of whom were forced to flee their homes.

Despite having planned elections for 2005, the transitional government's mandate has been extended into 2006. Civilians protesting against the delay in elections were killed and detained for long periods without trial. Approximately 2.5 million voters took part in a constitutional referendum in December. Although there was some voluntary disarmament by militia forces, it was on a much smaller scale than had been hoped. The UN peacekeeping force in DRC (MONUC - *Mission de la Organisation des Nations Unies en la République Démocratique du Congo*) had its mandate extended to October 2006. The UN mobilised a further 800 peacekeepers, and there were further accusations of peacekeepers sexually abusing civilians.

The ongoing presence of Ugandan and Rwandan rebels in DRC exacerbated violence within the country and continued instability within the region. In September, the Congolese government set a deadline for all foreign, armed groups to leave the country, and with support from the United Nations peacekeeping forces in DRC (MONUC) launched operations in October and December to oust rebels from the Ugandan Lord's Resistance Army. It has not yet taken similar action against the Rwandan *Forces Démocratiques de Liberation de Rwanda* (FDLR) – the Hutu-dominated militia force comprising ex-*Interahamwe* and Rwandan army forces responsible for the genocide and opposed to the Rwandan government, and Rwanda has threatened to invade DRC if it does not disband these rebels.

The DRC transitional government brought cases against Uganda and Rwanda for invading its territory and committing human rights violations to the International Court of Justice. Aldo Ajello, the EU special representative to the Great Lakes Region, said that the EU might support military action against the Rwandan Hutu rebels in DRC if they continued to refuse to disarm and return home.

The murder of prominent human rights activist, Pascal Kabungulu, Director of the NGO *Héritiers de la Justice,* which had prominently supported indigenous rights, highlighted the impunity that rights violators enjoy after the soldiers accused of the killing were released.

Advocacy for indigenous peoples' rights

There are a large number of indigenous "Pygmy" peoples scattered throughout DRC, although there is little information for some of these groups. The four main groups are the Bambuti, the Bacwa, the western Twa and the eastern Twa. This report focuses on the Bambuti and the eastern Twa for whom we have more information. The eastern Twa live in the far east of DRC, predominantly in Kivu province. Some may refer to themselves interchangeably as Batwa or Bambuti. The total number of Batwa in this area is estimated at around 16,000. The Bambuti are divided into several groups all living in the area of the Ituri forest in the north-east. Estimates for the total Bambuti population vary between 35,000 and 150,000.

Twa and Bambuti communities in the east continued to suffer grave rights violations, including abduction, rape, murder and torture. In April some 2,300 indigenous people demonstrated against rights violations in the eastern town of Isiro. For many it was the first time they had left the forest, their traditional home. Representatives of MONUC, who had supported the gathering and the transitional government, participated in a meeting with the Twa following the march. On Idjwi Island several cases were reported of Batwa homes being destroyed and land expropriation by the *Mwami* (king) who wished to give the land to his own relatives / friends.

Indigenous, national and international non-governmental organisations continued their activities on the forestry and mining codes, including a formal complaint to the World Bank Inspection Panel because the Bank has failed to take into account the impact that its plans would have on the people depending on the forest for their survival. The World Bank has taken a lead on forestry "zoning", which divides the forest into areas for timber felling and other uses, and encourages foreign investment in the timber industry. An estimated 150,000 km2 of forest concessions have been given to companies by the government since 2002, despite a moratorium banning the process.

The Twa network, RAPY (*Réseau des associations autochtones Pygmées*, or Network of Indigenous Pygmy Peoples' Organisations), produced sensitization guides on the country's new forestry and mining codes, and carried out community consultations to inform Twa communities about the proposed new laws and gauge Twa reactions. RAPY also lobbied for recognition of indigenous "Pygmy" peoples as the first peoples of DRC in the new constitution, as well as supporting Twa voter sensitization and registration prior to the national elections.

Representatives of Twa indigenous organisations, including APD-MAC (*Action d'Appui pour la Protection des Droits des Minorités en Afrique Centrale*), CAMV (*Centre d'Accompagnement des Autochtones Pygmées et Minoritaires Vulnérables*), and UEFA (*Union pour l'Emancipation de la Femme Batwa*) participated at the UN Permanent Forum on Indigenous Issues and in the UN Working Group on Indigenous Populations, and made oral interventions about violations of indigenous rights and the concerns surrounding the forestry and mining codes.

Representative of UEFA and PIDP-KIVU (*Programme d'Intégration et du Développement du Peuple Pygmée au Kivu*) participated in the 38th Ordinary Session of the African Commission on Human and Peoples' Rights in the Gambia in November 2005 and spoke about the human rights violations suffered by the "Pygmy" people in the DRC. ❑

REPUBLIC OF CONGO
(Congo Brazaville)

The Republic of Congo, commonly known as Congo Brazzaville, forms part of Central Africa and has borders with Cameroon, Gabon, the Central African Republic and the Democratic Republic of Congo. Independent since 1960, this country of 342,000 km² and around 3.8 million inhabitants is sub-divided into nine departments, namely: Cuvette, Cuvette Ouest, Kouilou, Lékoumou, Likouala, Niari, Plateaux, Pool, Sangha and the town of Brazzaville.

The socio-economic and political context

Like many of the continent's countries, the Republic of Congo is a mosaic of multiple ethnic groups, the most dominant of which are the Bakongo (48%), the Sangha (20%), the M'Bochi (12%) and the Teke (17%). The remaining 3% is composed not only of foreigners but also of a number of other small ethnic groups, such as the "Pygmies".[1]

The economy of the Republic of Congo relies primarily on oil, with production of around 267,100 barrels per day[2] making this the third largest producer of "black gold" in Africa, after Nigeria and Angola. Alongside oil, the Republic of Congo's economy has an emerging forestry sector. By 1999, the Congolese forestry sector was employing more people than the oil industry (9,000 employees as opposed to 1,300).[3] In fact, this country has around 20 million hectares of tropical forests, being the 4th largest forest mass in the Congo Basin after the Democratic Republic of Congo, Cameroon and Gabon. With annual timber production approaching 1 million m³, the Congolese forests are primarily seen as a source of income.

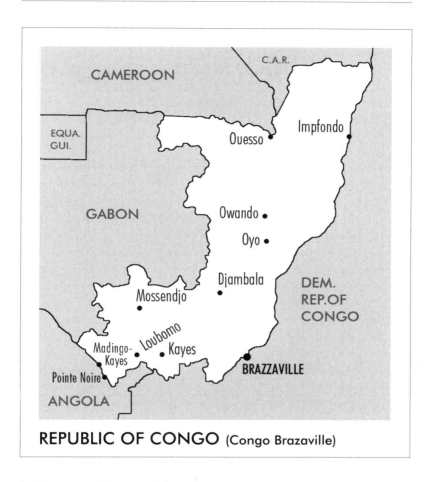

REPUBLIC OF CONGO (Congo Brazaville)

Indigenous Pygmy rights

And yet the African tropical forests are not only a source of income for governments. They are also the ancestral lands of one of the continent's indigenous peoples, known as "Pygmies" for want of an overarching term. These people, recognised also in the recent report of the African Commission's Working Group on Indigenous Populations/Communities[4] as the most longstanding occupants of the African tropical rainforests that stretch from Cameroon to Uganda, are estimated to number

more than 300 million. Their members are known by different names
in different countries, particularly Bagyeli, Baka, or Medzan in Cameroon and Batwa in a part of the Democratic Republic of Congo, Rwanda, Burundi and Uganda. In the Republic of Congo, they are also
known by different names, including Babenga, Babongo, Bambendzele,
Baka, Baluma and Bangombe. There is as yet no exact figure as to their
number, but there are large populations in Sangha, Likouala, Cuvette,
Lékoumou and Niari departments.

The situation of indigenous Pygmy peoples' rights in the Republic
of Congo is a worrying one. A recent information mission conducted
by the African Commission's Working Group on Indigenous Commu-
nities/Populations revealed a high level of discrimination, lack of access to health care, education, justice and employment as major features of these people's daily lives. In education, for example, although
the Republic of Congo was at one time reputed to have a school attendance rate of more than 70%, in some departments such as Lékoumu,
this rate among Pygmy children is only 2.9%. The reason for this is not
only poverty; there is also the prejudice, abuse and contempt these
children generally suffer at the hands of their fellow pupils and, sometimes, even their teachers.

Practices similar or comparable to slavery also persist in relation to
the Pygmies of the Republic of Congo. There are individuals who have
Pygmy individuals or entire Pygmy families in their pay, over whom
these "masters" hold a virtual right of life or death. In some corners of
the country it is common to hear people talk of "my Pygmies", as if
they were chattels to be bought and sold. Forced labour, unpaid services and sexual privileges over the women and girls of Pygmy subjects
are all forms of abuse generally committed by these "masters". This
phenomenon, certainly widespread but the extent of which has not
thus far been accurately estimated, was also highlighted by the African
Commission Working Group's mission.

Another major problem facing the Pygmies of the Republic of Congo is the failure of the state and other communities to recognise the
indigenous their land rights. Customary law and written law do not
recognise non-visible use of the land as a source of land rights. In legislative terms, however, this country has just adopted a land law abol-

ishing the principle of the state as one and only owner of land. In fact, Law no. 9-2004 of 26 March 2004, containing provisions governing state ownership, was complemented by Law no. 10-2004 of 26 March 2004, which established the general principles applicable to the Congo's land and state ownership systems. Among their innovations, these two new legal instruments restore and recognise customary land rights, previously abolished by Law no. 52/83 of 21 April 1983, containing provisions governing state ownership and the land code. It remains to be seen whether the context of application of these new legal provisions will also enable the indigenous rights of the Pygmies to be recognised. How this principle of customary land rights recognition will be reconciled with the provisions of law no. 16/2000 of 20 November 2000 on the forestry code is another question, given that several thousand hectares of logging concessions have already been allocated in the ancestral lands of the Pygmies.

Reasons for hope

But there is hope for the cause of the indigenous Pygmies of the Republic of Congo, and not only because of these new land law provisions. There is also the draft bill on special protection of this people, which is in the process of being formulated, in consultation with civil society. If this were to be adopted, it would be the first law of its kind in Africa. It would thus form a positive precedent for Pygmy rights in the region. The logging companies' efforts to obtain certification also represents an opportunity for the protection and promotion of indigenous Pygmy rights in the Republic of Congo, provided the negotiations are not conducted "on the cheap" but out of a respect for international standards. It is a question of recognition, respect, promotion and protection of indigenous land rights based on their occupation since time immemorial and a strong cultural link with the lands at issue. It is also a question of applying the consequences of recognising indigenous land rights, in this case the principle of the free, prior and informed consent of indigenous peoples with regard to managing the natural resources that abound on their lands.[5]

The regional forest forum of the Congo Basin, namely the *Conférence sur les Ecosystèmes de Forêts Denses et Humides d'Afrique Centrale* (Conference on Central African Moist Forest Ecosystems - CEFDHAC) should also be mentioned, in which a key role has been given to the indigenous "Pygmies" of the region. This forum is unique in the sense that if offers a totally new opportunity for direct dialogue between the different stakeholders in the management of the Congo Basin's tropical forests.

To these positive signs must be added ratification by the Republic of Congo of nearly all international conventions relevant to the indigenous cause, notably the International Covenant on Civil and Political Rights, the International Covenant on Economic, Social and Cultural Rights, the Convention on the Elimination of all Forms of Racial Discrimination, the Convention on the Rights of the Child, the Convention on Biological Diversity and the African Charter on Human and Peoples' Rights. Plus there is also an emerging indigenous civil society in the country due, among other things, to exchange visits by indigenous "Pygmies" from other countries in Central Africa, particularly Rwanda and Cameroon, where indigenous NGOs are more vibrant.
❏

Notes and sources

1 Whilst aware of the pejorative and derogatory nature of the word, this article uses the term "Pygmy" for lack of an alternative that can encompass the different groups that make up this community in the Republic of Congo.

2 CIA- The World Factbook: http://www.cia.gov/cia/publications/factbook/geos/cf.html

3 FAO, Forests department: http://www.fao.org/documents/show_cdr.asp?url_file=/DOCREP/003/X6778F/X6778F06.htm

4 African Commission on Human and Peoples' Rights, Report of the Working Group on Indigenous Communities/Populations. The report was adopted by the African Commission in November 2005. It can be downloaded from IWGIA's web site at: http://www.iwgia.org/graphics/Synkron-Library/Documents/InternationalProcesses/ACHR/Factfindingmissions/CongoReport-ENG.pdf

5 See an analysis made of this principle by the Forest Peoples Programme: http://www.forestpeoples.org/documents/prv_sector/eir/eir_ips_fpic_jun04_fr.pdf

GABON

In June 2005, the *Association pour le Développement de la Culture des Peuples Pygmées du Gabon* (Association for the Cultural Development of Pygmies in Gabon - ADCPPG) produced the latest population figures for forest peoples in Gabon (often referred to as Pygmies). Based on existing research and the current national census, ADCPPG produced the document *Organisation Territoriale du Gabon Demographie Chiffree Des Peuples Autochtones Pygmées du Gabon* (Demographic and Statistical Census of the Indigenous Pygmy Populations in Gabon)[1] and estimated the total Pygmy population (consisting of groups such as the Baka, Babongo, Bakoya, Baghame, Barimba, Akoula, Akwoa, etc.) at 20,005 out of a national population of approximately 1,400,000. These figures are the highest ever produced (most estimate 7,000-10,000). The greatest concentrations recorded were in the provinces of Ngounié and Haut Ogooué.

Gabon officially recognises three indigenous organisations: *Minorités Autochtones Pygmées au Gabon* (The Indigenous Pygmy Minorities of Gabon - MINAPYGA - representing Bakoya and established in 1997), *Edzendgui*[2] (representing Baka and established in 2002) and the *Association pour le Développement de la Culture des Peuples Pygmées du Gabon* (ADCPPG - representing Babongo and established in 2003).

Current threats and challenges to Gabonese Pygmy communities include resettlement and sedentarisation plans, logging, infrastructural transformations (roads and railways) and conservation initiatives.

Political and legislative developments

The key event of 2005 for the Forest Peoples in Gabon was the Gabonese government's commissioning of an Indigenous Peoples' Devel-

opment Plan (IPDP).[3] This was later adopted as the guideline for its interaction with indigenous people in the World Bank-supported Forest
and Environment Sector Programme (the programme is also supported
by the Global Environment Facility (GEF)). Through the signing of the
World Bank Operational Policy on Indigenous Peoples (OP 4.10), the
Government of Gabon officially recognised the existence of, and responsibility for, its indigenous populations in all forest-related issues. As part
of the loan agreement between Gabon and the World Bank, this has the
status of a treaty. Previously, the government had not endorsed legislation or international conventions that specifically protect the interest of
indigenous and tribal peoples or minority groups. According to the IP-
DP, it is now the responsibility of the Gabonese government to:

- Establish community forests for indigenous people of at least 1
  km² per capita. Compensate land loss.
- Protect traditional land-use areas and patterns e.g. guarantee
  free movement in all protected areas, including the right to live
  and hunt (except commercial hunting); recognise settlements as
  villages equal to other settlements, establish community forests.
- Ensure equal opportunities e.g. legal, financial, organisational
  and cultural.
- Provide Pygmy organisations with full information and support to:
  - Effectively represent their communities in all forest-related is-
    sues.
  - Ensure communication between stakeholders and indigenous
    peoples.
  - Safeguard traditional knowledge.
- Ensure indigenous participation in all relevant structures of the
  forest sector programme (decision making, implementation,
  management and benefit sharing); sensitise indigenous people
  to development risks. Monitor and evaluate IPDP.

The National Council of National Parks, ministries, park managers,
legal experts and indigenous leaders are now faced with the daunting

task of bringing existing law into line with these standards and producing a law on national parks and park-specific regulations and management guidelines for inhabited buffer zones. According to the existing law, traditional activities of local peoples are prohibited within
parks, with the exception of eco-tourist activities and certain fishing
zones.[4] During 2005, the council worked closely with the various
stakeholders, including indigenous organisations, on a park-by-park
basis towards this goal.

The second half of the year was dominated by preparations and
campaigns surrounding the presidential elections. On 27 November,
Omar Bongo Ondimba (in power since 1967) was voted in for another
seven-year term with a 79.2 % victory, making him Africa's longest
serving leader. Many Pygmy leaders took an active part in campaign-
ing for the President and participated in outreach poll programmes to

encourage rural poor to take part in the election process. Mr Massandé (leader of the ADCPPG) reported prior to the elections that his organisation was focusing on supporting the re-election of the President as the latter had said he would address the special needs of Pygmy communities, in particular, poverty and assimilation issues in the new year (personal communication 11/05). In December, several Pygmy leaders had audiences with the President of the Republic. They discussed the challenges faced by Pygmy communities in the country, and shared information about the activities of Pygmy organizations.

Indigenous representation

In March 2005, the Indigenous Peoples of Africa Co-ordinating Committee (IPACC) visited Gabon. Dr Nigel Crawhall (Director), together with Judith Knight (Consultant), carried out the mission, facilitated by the Wildlife Conservation Society (WCS) and the World Wide Fund for Nature (WWF). IPACC travelled with the leaders of MI-NAPYGA and Edzengui to their home communities near national parks. The team also visited Babongo communities near Waka National Park. IPACC consulted government officials, park managers and local communities regarding socio-economic change, knowledge loss, access to basic resources e.g. information, education, health care, and the development of national parks. In Libreville, IPACC worked closely with Pygmy leaders, major stakeholders and government officials.

Cultural promotion and development programmes

Since 2003, Gabon has become a party to the UNESCO instruments for Safeguarding and Promoting Tangible and Intangible Cultural Heritage. In February, UNESCO continued its ICT for Intercultural Dialogue Programme through support of the second phase of the "*Projet de Formation Audio-visuelle du Peuple de la Forêt du Gabon*" jointly organised by MINAPYGA and film producer Jean-Claude Cheyssial and his company Latitude Film. Six representatives of three separate Pygmy ethnic groups have now been trained in all aspects of film-making. Their first film "*Chasse aux Escargots*" is complete and their second "*La Sentier de l'intégration*" is in production.

The Ministry of Culture is presently involved in assessing potential Heritage Sites in Gabon. During this process, Minkebe National Park was identified as a possible World Heritage Site, primarily as a Baka "sacred landscape". Mining industry in the area, and land rights complications arising from Baka's ancient versus current land usage, have made this prospect problematic.

In May, in collaboration with UNESCO, MINAPYGA hosted a conference on literacy in Pygmy communities.[5] MINAPYGA held two meetings with the International Labour Organization (ILO) to discuss health issues, in particular hygiene and AIDS. UNICEF visited Pygmy communities as part of its outreach immunisation programme 2005 and is planning a Pygmy Birth Certification Programme in collaboration with the local NGO PRECED (*Promotion et Revalorisation des Cultures en Voie de Disparition*). During 2005, Edzengui obtained funding for a number of projects with the Baka on forestry, agriculture, culture and health, and MINAPYGA received a small grant from the US government to support agricultural development in Mekambo. The Forest Peoples Programme (FPP) visited Minvoul province and Minkébé (late 2004 and early 2005) and have carried out preliminary studies on the Baka in Gabon with the Centre for Environment and Development (CED, Cameroon). ❏

Notes

1   Association pour le Développement de la Culture des Peuples Pygmées du Gabon (ADCPPG), June 30, 2005.
2   The name is derived from "Ed! Zengui", the name of a Baka protective forest spirit.
3   Schmidt-Soltau, K., 2005: *Indigenous Peoples' Development Plan (IDPD)*. Report published by the World Bank, July 2005.
4   Code Forestier HEBDO 452.
5   Entitled *Defining a strategy for achieving literacy in Pygmy communities in Gabon*, the conference was opened by the Minister of Culture.

CAMEROON

In recent years, and especially since President Biya's 2004 election, Cameroon political discourse has been dominated by calls from civil society and international donors to reduce corruption in the forestry and natural resources sectors, central pillars of the Cameroon economy. In 2005, new corruption allegations against senior civil servants were made by the Cameroon government, but so far no significant prosecutions have been secured. Continuing delays in addressing this issue cause doubts among the international community as to the government's ability to target the rural poor.

Pygmy communities' livelihood threatened

The failure to invest in rural public services, coupled with support for logging and an addiction to donor funds for biodiversity conservation, helps to maintain structural discrimination against forest communities in Cameroon. The effects of this discrimination are particularly serious for indigenous Pygmy communities from across the southern forest zone, whose livelihoods rely on forests and who continue to remain socially and economically marginalised, receiving few benefits from the small amounts of funds which do eventually trickle down to the regions. The distribution of forestry revenues between central and local authorities and communities is the source of furious local and national debate. During 2005, indigenous hunter-gatherers saw almost no benefits from the tax revenues generated from the forests upon which they have always relied, and most do not know what is planned for the forests that provide their livelihoods.

Communities continue to be marginalised in discussions over forest planning, despite the establishment in 1994 of community partici-

pation as a central plank of the government's forest law and more recent moves towards decentralisation, now framed through the World
Bank-funded National Participatory Development Programme
(PNDP). Despite these potentially positive developments favouring
participation in planning, logging companies and conservation organisations continue to dominate negotiations with governments over
plans for the exploitation and conservation of forests. The allocation of
forestry concessions is still an opaque process which regularly conflicts with the rights of forest communities, especially since sanctions
against rule breakers are rarely applied.

The extreme poverty of the rural poor across the southern Cameroon forest zone and the lack of investment in basic social services,
coupled with growing rural populations and the continuous growth of
a national bush-meat trading network is leading to growing pressure
on the rights of Cameroon's indigenous forest communities such as the
Bakola, Bagyeli and Baka. The Cameroon government aims to protect
30% of the national area and, over the past decade, international conservation organisations have been very active in building up an extensive network of national parks and reserves. Unfortunately, local communities were rarely consulted about these plans and, when they were,
indigenous hunting and gathering communities were almost never involved. This situation continues today. The result is that Baka and
Bagyeli have little say in the management of their lands and, in many
cases, they are losing access to forests they have inhabited for centuries. Their continuing dependence upon these forests to secure their
livelihoods, combined with their lack of access to lands to cultivate (or
a decent wage to do so for others) causes severe social marginalisation.
Most still have little access to formal schooling or basic health services,
and virtually no influence with government agencies or other civil society institutions.

During 2005, the World Bank formally ended the Chad-Cameroon
Oil Pipeline project, rating it a success despite continuing complaints
from communities about environmental damage, compensation and
the failure of the Foundation for Environment and Development in
Cameroon (FEDEC) to work with indigenous communities, both in the
pipeline zone and around Campo Ma'an National Park, which it is also

supposed to fund. Changes to FEDEC's management and the suggested changes to consultation approaches by field staff have been crip-
pled by a weak and divided board and, for many, FEDEC's credibility
continues to fall.

Towards recognition of forest rights

During 2005, Bagyeli from around Campo Ma'an National Park used
their land-use maps to secure an agreement with government agencies, the Worldwide Fund for Nature (WWF) and FEDEC to reconsider
the park's draft management plan. Campo Ma'an National Park is
one of the environmental offset projects of the Chad-Cameroon Oil
Pipeline Project. In response to international pressure, the World
Bank International Advisory Group called for the establishment of a
multiparty commission to examine the specific issues faced by the
Bagyeli around establishment of the park, and this led in 2005 to a
revision of the park management plan in their favour. During 2005,
Bagyeli communities from Campo Ma'an were told that they could
continue to access and use forests inside the park. Other similar discussions are ongoing around the Dja Reserve and Boumba Bek, which
finally became a national park in 2005.

Bagyeli and Baka continue to build their capacities in negotiation
skills, to secure identity cards, to gain access to legal advice, to create
their own land-use maps and to develop alternative sources of income. However, their incomes, institutional capacities and confidence still remain very low and long-term support from government
and donors to promote their rights is still difficult to obtain. In spite
of these constraints, Bagyeli and Bakola from Ocean Department
have continued to engage directly with donors such as the World
Bank over the oil pipeline project's impact on their rights and, through
their own efforts, 14 Bagyeli communities from the pipeline zone
have secured formal recognition of their land rights. Baka from the
south and south-east are also active, some with their own, young
NGOs, and both communities are establishing their own community
associations. Baka and Bagyeli are building up their links with inter-

national and national conservation authorities, who are beginning to openly accept that their rights have been neglected in previous conservation plans.

New forestry projects

New funding to the Cameroon forest sector on the part of the World Bank in 2004 resulted in very limited development of a national Indigenous Peoples Development Plan (IPDP) by the Cameroon government in 2005. There is still no established process by which indigenous communities' participation in the development of the IPDP will be assured, and much of the programme remains a theoretical prospect due to slow implementation. The *Réseau Recherche Actions Concertées Pygmée* (RACOPY), a network of organisations supporting indigenous hunter-gatherer communities in Cameroon, continues to raise this issue as yet more conservation and logging initiatives are formulated for community forests in the national capital Yaoundé.

Likewise the Congo Basin Forest Partnership, a transboundary conservation initiative between the governments of Cameroon, the Republic of Congo, Gabon and the Central Africa Republic.[1] All the parks and associated forests that will form part of the new transboundary conservancy overlap lands that Cameroon's Baka communities rely on. The so-called TRIDOM and Sangha projects will lead to the development of regional land management plans that will govern access to and use of forests used by up to 70,000 indigenous forest peoples, mostly Baka, Baaka, Ba'aka and Babongo Pygmies, but also including many other farming groups. No mechanism has been introduced in any of the countries that will enable these forest users to participate in developing the forest plans, and a series of negative impacts on local and indigenous community rights and welfare is predicted.   ❑

Note

1   The project will join together a four-country conservation space bordered by the existing Minkébé, Boumba-Bek, Nki and Odzala, Ndoki, Dzanga-Sangha and Lobéké National Parks, and the Dja Wildlife Reserve.

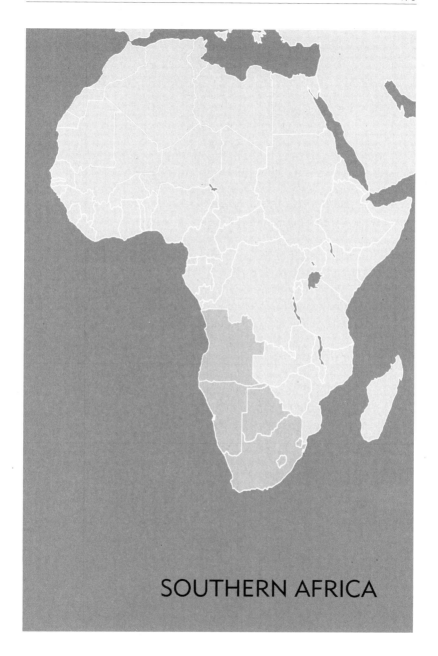

SOUTHERN AFRICA

ANGOLA

Although many San groups living in southern Africa are oppressed and impoverished, the situation of the Angolan San has given the most cause for concern over time, and the scale of the problem has required immediate emergency interventions. For 27 years, civil war raged throughout Angola and the severe damage to infrastructure and subsequent presence of landmines meant that it was very difficult to obtain information about the condition of these San. In 2003, following concerns raised by other San groups throughout southern Africa, an assessment of the situation of the Angolan San took place and emergency measures were implemented.[1] During 2005, the food security and livelihoods of the Angolan San have been greatly improved as a direct result of the work and commitment of OCADEC (*Organização Cristã de Apoio ao Desenvolvimento Comunitário* - Christian Organisation Supporting Community Development), and its partners – WIMSA (Working Group of Indigenous Minorities in Southern Africa), UN agencies, the Angolan Government, various donors and Trócaire Angola (Irish Catholic Agency for World Development – Angola).

Emergency interventions

The 2003 assessment established that, in Cuando Cubango, Cunene and Huíla provinces, there were at least 3,400 (predominantly !Xun) San facing very harsh and even life-threatening conditions. The assessment (reported in detail in previous editions of *The Indigenous World*) found that these San were suffering greatly from food insecurity, malnutrition, poor health, lack of education, discrimination and virtual dependence on their Bantu neighbours. Due to the presence of landmines, it was impossible for the assessment team to reach the Khwe

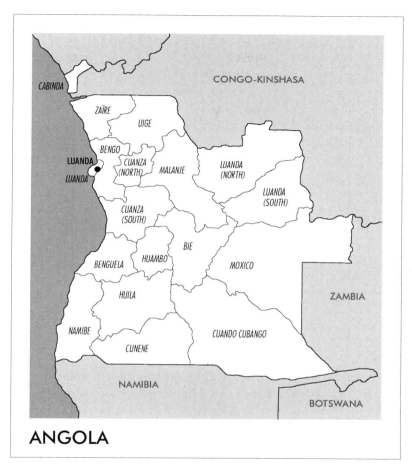

ANGOLA

San, mainly living in Cuando Cubango, and until landmine clearance is carried out this situation will unfortunately continue.

Practical interventions formed the basis of the assessment's recommendations. An Emergency Project was implemented by OCADEC in 2003/4, with the support of WIMSA. Its aim was to distribute food, seeds, agricultural equipment, clothing and blankets and these items were received by 3,500 San. An evaluation of this first stage of the intervention took place in May/June 2004. It found that this was the first time that 94% of San families registered with OCADEC had ever received any form of assistance and that 80% had now been able to take up agricultural cultivation. In February 2004, the first ever workshop held with the Angolan San took place in Luanda and project progress was reported back to Angolan society. This event, combined with the efforts of OCADEC and its partners, has contributed significantly to building trust at the grassroots level between the San and OCADEC. The second stage of the Emergency Project was subsequently implemented in 2004 and, in February 2005, representatives from WIMSA and OCADEC visited Huíla and witnessed the determination and hard work with which the San were carrying out the project. The team found that the crop yield for 2004/05 was more substantial than the previous years and had benefited 3,964 San. Information received from the Cuando Cubango and Cunene provinces provided similarly positive news and it was estimated by those visiting that some communities had reached up to 80% food security.

Achieving a sound level of food security has had an enormous influence upon both the physical and mental well-being of the Angolan San. As a direct result, many of the San are now more confident and able to concentrate on planning longer-term development interventions. In 2005, funding was secured for a three-year pilot project to be carried out by OCADEC, to support San communities in Quipungo (Huíla Province) in their efforts to become fully independent from neighbouring Bantu groups. This programme focuses on: achieving land rights, undertaking agriculture and maintaining food security, the management of livestock, the provision of reliable water supplies, the cultivation of various plants containing medicinal properties, access to formal education, health care and transport, income-generating opportunities and establishing San-led community structures.

Government interest in San issues

During 2005, OCADEC and its partners continued the important work of seeking to establish positive relationships with government representatives. The initial assessment of the Angolan San had created interest and influenced various Angolan government departments. Meetings that took place with the Huíla Provincial Government in 2005 proved to be very encouraging - with the government indicating its willingness to grant land ownership to some of the San who are already living on their ancestral lands or to move San not living on such land to areas where they could apply for collective land titles. A significant achievement for the San was gained in 2005 when the Huíla Provincial Government - in co-operation with the FAO (Food and Agriculture Organization of the United Nations) and OCADEC - carried out a survey of the land of two San communities. As a direct result of this survey, plans are now underway for the provincial government to issue the first collective land titles to Quipungo San communities in 2006.

During 2006, OCADEC will continue to be the lead organisation within Angola working with the San, and will further its groundbreaking work in assisting with development and in creating firm relationships with the Huíla Provincial Government. In addition to carrying out the three-year assistance programme, one of the important tasks to be undertaken by OCADEC during 2006 will be that of obtaining identification documents (ID) for the San. These documents are essential for Angolan citizens to be able to apply for state assistance, access public services or claim land rights etc. During 2005, all partners involved with the Angolan San were pleased to hear that this important aspect of work will be funded by the Angolan Department of Justice of Huíla Province.

At the time of writing, OCADEC is currently in discussions with San communities in relation to developing a model of San leadership within each village. The communities are looking at whether its leaders should assume responsibility for sharing the management of its various assets, including: land, water pumps, drinking water, draught power for tilling the land and livestock breeding. Because it will take some time before the government is able to provide formal education and healthcare, the communities will also undertake in-depth discussions on whether they can provide their own traditional schools and clinics.

During 2006, it is envisaged that the first "San Conference for southern Angola" will take place and will be hosted by the Angolan Government. This has emphasised the recent government commitment to assist the San. It is hoped that this event will further the development dialogue between the San themselves and the various organisations working to assist them. Another positive development occurred in 2005 when both Namibia and Angola relaxed conditions for travel between the two countries. Although the majority of Angolan San still do not possess the necessary documentation required to travel outside of the country, this measure meant that a small number were able to attend San regional networking events in Namibia.

The commitment of OCADEC and its partners, and the hard work of the San communities themselves, mean that the hopes of the San of Angola are now being realised. Securing funding for future projects and building upon promising relationships with Angola's Huíla Provincial Government will be imperative over the next twelve months in order to improve the situation of the Angolan San. ❑

Note

1   **Pakleppa, Richard and Kwononoka, Americo. 2003.** *Where the First are Last – San Communities Fighting for Survival in Southern Angola.* The three partners initiating and supporting this assessment were WIMSA, Tròcaire Angola and OCADEC.

NAMIBIA

Namibia gained independence from South Africa in 1990 and abolished the brutal and oppressive apartheid system that had been used to govern the country. Since then, many ethnic groups in Namibia have experienced significant improvements in their quality of life, yet this has not been the case for the estimated 33,000 San. The day-to-day reality of life for many Namibian San continues to be one of poverty, dispossession, disempowerment, abuse of human rights and virtual enslavement. The Himba of Namibia are also considered by many to be a group indigenous to Namibia and, like the San, they suffer from extreme poverty and social exclusion.

Advocacy developments

In 2005, Namibian San experienced a dramatic increase in interest and publicity regarding their plight. Under the previous President, Dr Sam Nujoma, the government's attitude towards the San had proved to be one of indifference - and even hostility - as President Nujoma himself had said on several occasions that the San were traitors to Namibia.[1] Namibia's second President, Hifikepunye Pohamba, took office in March 2005 and his Deputy Prime Minister, Dr Libertine Amathila, led the impetus for a change in sentiment towards the San. During 2005, Dr Amathila visited several San communities and publicised her concern at the terrible living conditions and oppression that they were suffering at the hands of other ethnic groups.

The government's "revelation" of the plight of the San was, however, quite a calculated move. The new rhetoric, which began in July 2005, was clearly influenced by the visit of the Working Group on Indigenous Populations/Communities of the African Commission on

Human and Peoples' Rights during the same month. The mission was headed by Commissioner Andrew Chigovera and the objective of the visit to Namibia was to investigate the living conditions and human rights situation of the San and the Himba. The delegation announced its intention to scrutinise the Namibian Government's policies and practices in relation to its indigenous peoples and to publish its findings in 2006.

The publicity surrounding high-ranking government officials' visits to the San provoked a considerable reaction from civil society, which took the opportunity to outline the scale of development work that had been undertaken with the San since independence but which certain sections of government had previously shown little interest in. It was disappointing to note that rather than accepting such criticism in a constructive manner, the Office of the Deputy Prime Minister responded by attacking San development organisations and projects and by questioning the work of the development community – particularly those the government felt to be "foreigners".

Despite the government's new interest in the San, a valuable opportunity to assist with their human rights was lost in 2005 when San groups, NGOs and Namibia's Legal Assistance Centre (LAC) led a campaign to get new identity cards issued for the San using their true San names.[2] However, despite popular support for this campaign, including from the Afrikaans-speaking community via the national "Die Republikien" newspaper, the government failed to negotiate this issue.

Organisational development and land

2005 proved to be a challenging period for many of the San organisations in Namibia. Traditional leadership struggles and internal organisational difficulties meant that many working with the San spent a great deal of time undertaking conflict resolution and working to secure organisational capacity, sustainability and security.

WIMSA (the Working Group of Indigenous Minorities in Southern Africa) undertook a preliminary investigation into the situation of the

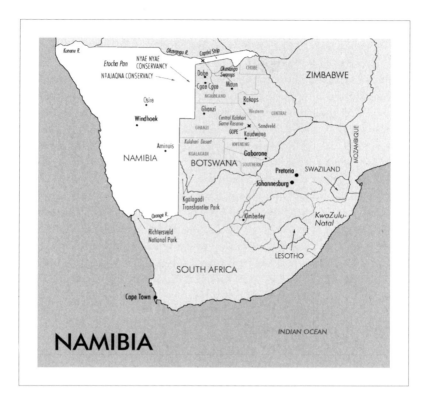

NAMIBIA

San living in the far north of the country (in the Regions of Oshana, Ohangwena, Omusati and Ohshikoto) in October 2005 and the study's findings underscored the need for intervention and assistance in these regions.[3] For the large number of Khwe San living in the West Caprivi area who suffer almost yearly from devastating floods, the invitation extended to WIMSA to advise the government's Emergency Management Unit, in conjunction with the UN, on its Disaster Response Planning initiative was a welcome development.

A number of achievements were made in relation to land and natural resources during the year. The San governing the N‡a Jaqna Conservancy successfully introduced a new income-generating measure via the adoption of a government-regulated hunting quota and also applied for Community Forest status.[4] At the Nyae Nyae Conservancy, garden development pilots were started for the San with funding from the World Bank and the support of the Ministry of Agriculture, Water and Forestry. The World Bank ICEMA (Integrated Community-Based Eco-System Management) programme also entered into negotiations to establish a 5-year partnership with WIMSA. The Khwe San of West Caprivi had their new organisation, the Kyaramacan Trust, officially recognised by the Ministry of Environment and Tourism and a Memorandum of Understanding was signed so that the Khwe could develop land-use rights within the area.[5]

Those Himba in the far north-west of the country who have recently had their own conservancies gazetted by the Namibian Government began to witness real gains.[6] The organisation IRDNC (Integrated Rural Development and Nature Conservation) reported to "National Geographic" in 2005 that a survey of the Himba had found that, by managing their own natural resources, direct income had been generated via tourism activities undertaken within the conservancies.

Education and culture

The Namibian Government's Ministry of Basic Education, Sports and Culture has demonstrated a firm working interest in assisting San and Himba learners in recent years.[7] The "drop out" rate of these children from school continues to be exceptionally high in comparison to other ethnic groups, largely due to registration difficulties, bullying, stigmatisation, a misunderstanding of indigenous culture, the long-distances required to travel to school and the lack of support available to those children living within the hostel system.

Perhaps the greatest problem facing the San in relation to formal education is the language barrier. The San in Namibia speak a variety of San languages including: Ju' l hoansi, !Kung, Khwe, Naro, Hai l l om and !Xõõ. Very few San can speak fluent English (adopted as the national language of Namibia in 1990) although the majority are able to speak Afrikaans. It is estimated that at least 60% of San are illiterate and the main obstacle to mother tongue education is the fact that hardly any schools in the country are able, or encouraged, to teach San languages.

Despite this, the work of WIMSA, SASEF (the Southern African Education Forum), NIED (the National Institute for Educational Development) and San community-based organisations such as the OST (Omaheke San Trust) has led to significant improvements. The NIED recently included San representatives on its Khoekhoegowab Language Committee and Namibia was the first country in the southern African region to formally introduce a San language – Ju' I hoansi - into its curriculum.

San language activists witnessed important gains in 2005 for the Khwedam-speaking San of West Caprivi. The Namibian Government's Directorate of Adult Basic Education lent its support to a Literacy Programme for the Khwe in order to develop non-formal teaching materials for Grades 1 to 3, along with a Khwedam dictionary.[8] Khwe-speaking volunteers are now trained to help carry out the initiative. Following the speeches made by two young Khwe men at the International Symposium on the World's Indigenous Languages in Aichi, Japan in July 2005, strong international interest has been generated in relation to the issues facing Khwedam speakers.

A Regional "Mother Tongue Conference" was held in June 2005. This was organised by SASEF, the University of Botswana and WIMSA. Both the teachers and the government representatives attending took the issue of San mother tongue education seriously. The conference report, designed also to be used as a "good practice manual", will be published by WIMSA in early 2006. It includes relevant research and findings from previous events organised by WIMSA and SASEF.[9] In 2005, WIMSA continued to provide support to San communities by assisting individual San to undertake Early Childhood Development (ECD) teaching courses, along with the provision of San pre-schools, in co-operation with UNESCO and the Ministry of Gender Equality and Child Welfare. IRDNC reported that one of the greatest achievements for the Himba in 2005 was the adoption of mobile "field schools" aimed at Himba children in the north-west remote areas of Namibia. During 2005, the San youth of Namibia continued to prove their ability in generating a cultural revival. The Hai I I om Youth Groups received a great deal of moral and financial support from WIMSA and developed traditional dance groups, encouraging San elders to teach them previ-

ously unknown dance steps and songs. This inter-generational bridge-
building exercise has done much to raise the collective self-esteem of
this group of mainly urbanised San. With the support of WIMSA, the
dance group travelled to the Botswana Kuru Dance Festival in D'Kar
in August 2005 and received much acclaim following their performance. In April 2005, the University of Cologne, Germany, returned Ha-
rold Pager's original San rock art research on the Brandberg to Namibia. A conference was held in order to celebrate this event and WIM-
SA was invited to write a paper on behalf of the San.[10] In 2005, the
Khwe San also celebrated positive achievements. In December 2005,
the Khwe launched their own Youth League and the Governor of
Caprivi Region attended in order to sign the Constitution. The new
Youth League asserted its intention to strengthen Khwe culture, language and literacy, and to build organisational capacity.

Health

Despite these encouraging initiatives, perhaps the most persistent and
disturbing issues affecting the day-to-day lives of both San and Himba
in Namibia continued to be the HIV/ AIDS pandemic. Namibia's HIV/
AIDS infection rate is 19% (and much higher in some areas) and, due
to their poverty and lack of access to education, the virus disproportionately affects its indigenous people.[11] In November 2005, a group of
San from both the Hai I I om and Khwe Youth Leagues undertook
WIMSA training in order to learn how to carry out HIV Community
Assessments.[12] During the training, it was found that knowledge in
relation to basic HIV and sexual reproduction / health information
was very low amongst the trainees. However, one important initiative
at the Nyae Nyae Conservancy involved the distribution of solar-pow-
ered radios in order to enable the villagers to receive the newly-established NBC (Namibian Broadcasting Corporation) local language radio station and to ensure that HIV/AIDS information is frequently received. This measure was backed up by the training of 16 local people as HIV/AIDS "peer educators". However, greater efforts now need
to be made in order to ensure that Namibia's indigenous people re-

ceive accurate information and that the infection rate of the virus is minimised in Namibia. ❑

Notes

1 These accusations originated because some San communities were exploited and used as trackers for the South African Defence Force during the War of Independence between Namibia and South Africa.
2 Under apartheid, many San were given Afrikaans or German names (due to the fact that the ruling ethnic groups found San names, with their series of "clicks", to be unpronounceable). However, in recent years, the collective confidence and identity of the San has increased greatly, and many San now wish to possess official ID containing their own, real names. Unfortunately government policy demands that if an individual wishes to change the name on their ID, they must pay an administration fee. This is impossible for most San as they cannot access the money needed to do this.
3 See www.wimsanet.org for more details.
4 Following Namibia's independence in 1990, the government introduced communally-owned "conservancies" where communities can achieve some control over some of the natural resources. This includes the possibility of generating income from game management and tourism, etc.
5 The Khwe San of West Caprivi cannot apply to establish a Conservancy because the area is a National Park. However, the Memorandum of Understanding has granted them similar land-use rights – such as trophy hunting.
6 The Himba Conservancies in Namibia are Marienfluss, Orumpembe and Sanitatas. Puros is a mixed Himba-Herero Conservancy.
7 In 2005 the new government re-arranged its ministries – with a new Ministry of Education, along with a Ministry of Higher Education, Training and Employment Creation.
8 This initiative is being undertaken in partnership with the University of Cologne, Germany.
9 **Hey, Jennifer, 2006:** *For the benefit of All: Mother Tongue Education for Southern African Minorities.* Report published by WIMSA. The report – and two other new publications published by WIMSA in 2005, include: **Longden, Christina and Pickering, Yvonne, 2005:** (comp and ed) *The Way it Used to Be – Lives of Our Elders* and *Voice of the Child,* 2005 and can be obtained by writing to wimsareg@africaonline.com.na
10 "A Homecoming of Rock Art" Conference, Windhoek, April 2005.
11 At the present time there are no official statistics available detailing the rate of infection amongst San communities.
12 This training took place with groups of youth from Otavi, Outjo, Otjiwarongo, Oshivelo and Omega communities 1,2 and 3.

BOTSWANA

The Republic of Botswana in southern Africa is committed, at least on paper, to social justice, equity and broad public participation in the political system. In spite of this, the majority of the approximately 50,000 San (or, as they are termed in Botswana, Basarwa/Remote Area Dwellers) continue to face a number of serious problems, including widespread poverty, lack of secure land and resource access, and human rights abuses.

In many ways the San are on the lowest rung of a multi-tiered socio-economic system. A substantial proportion of the San population live below the poverty line, and they face problems ranging from lack of access to land and social services to high rates of unemployment. In a number of cases, San were moved from their ancestral territories into large-scale settlements where water, schools and health posts are provided, but little else. Many of these settlements are characterized by poverty, disease, nutritional stress, internal conflict and social dissatisfaction.

The following is a short résumé of some of the main issues that are relevant to understanding the situation of the San.

Constitutional rights

The Government of Botswana (GOB) recently presented a Constitutional Amendment Bill 34 (2004-5), aimed at making the Constitution "tribally neutral". Sections 77, 78 and 79 of the Constitution in particular were criticized for being discriminatory since they guarantee automatic membership of the House of Chiefs to the eight Setswana-speaking paramount chiefs while minority groups, including the San, are

represented by only three members, regarded as sub-chiefs, elected to the assembly on a rotating basis for four-year terms.

The bill was met with heavy criticism from the minor tribes and civil society organizations. The argument is that the new constitutional amendment does not do away with the privilege of the eight major tribes, whose chiefs will continue to be members of the House. The minor tribes will have their representatives increased to 20 but these individuals will have to be selected by district electoral colleges chaired by a civil servant appointed by the Minister of Local Government. There is concern that San traditional leaders may not make it to the House of Chiefs via an electoral process, as the San do not have the same kinds of institutionalized chief or "headman" (traditional authority) roles in their societies as do other groups in Botswana. The

Constitutional Amendment Bill also deletes subsection 3c of Section
14, which guarantees "Bushmen" freedom of movement, allegedly in
an effort to make the Constitution more tribally neutral. This amendment will limit the special provisions for the San just at a time when
they and the Bakgalagadi are seeking to re-establish their land rights in
the Central Kalahari Game Reserve.

Land rights

According to the Constitution of Botswana, all citizens of the country
have land rights. In addition to the constitutional guarantees, Botswana Government white papers, such as the Tribal Grazing Land Policy
(TGLP) of 1975 (Government Paper No. 2 of 1975), state specifically
that all Batswana (people of Botswana) have the right to sufficient land
to meet their needs. The Sans' land rights, however, have never been
recognized fully. When they lived traditionally as hunters and gather-
ers, they were seen as having no land of their own and as having no
need of any. Since the latter part of the 19th century, they have gradually lost their customary land areas to settlers, cattle farmers, mines,
natural parks and game reserves, and to government programs such as
quarantine camps for livestock and agricultural experiment stations.

  For the San, the land reform process, starting with the Tribal Grazing Land Policy of 1975, has entailed the loss of land tracts that had
economic as well as cultural significance. They have experienced a
long series of relocations into government-established settlements.
And the process continues - the Central Kalahari Game Reserve and
the Western Sandveld region of Central District are cases in point. In
the case of the Western Sandveld, San were being displaced from
ranches in 2005 and their attempts to obtain compensation for loss of
their assets was making little headway. Even more problematic is the
fact that even those San who were resettled years ago are sometimes
faced with the threat of a potential relocation, as is the case, for example, with the community of Ngwatle in Kgalagadi District, which is in
an area that the Botswana Government would like to turn into a wildlife zone, connecting the Kgalagadi Transfrontier Park in south-west-

ern Botswana to the Central Kalahari Game Reserve. Many San today continue to face the prospect of losing their homes and lands because of government decisions or the actions of non-governmental organizations or the private sector in Botswana.

Although the Government of Botswana maintains that land boards provide the resettled San with land, relatively few have legal title over their arable plots and practically no San have business plots. The adjudication process is long, complicated and expensive. In some cases, the land boards have not issued certificates because there was a possibility of resettlement. Few, if any, San have been granted rights over grazing or water, which means that they have little control over blocks of land sufficient for them to earn a livelihood, and they lack control over the water points that are crucial for the care of livestock as well as for meeting domestic water needs.

The Central Kalahari Game Reserve issue

The situation facing the G/ui, G//ana, Tsilla, and Kua San and Bakgalagadi of the Central Kalahari Game Reserve worsened considerably in the last half of 2005, and the court case on their land rights is still pending (for an introduction to the court case see *The Indigenous World 2005, 2004, 2002-2003*). In June 2005, a group of San men hunting in the reserve were arrested and allegedly tortured. One member of this group, Selelo Tshiamo, died from his injuries in early September.

The Government of Botswana announced in early September 2005 that people would be required to leave the Central Kalahari Game Reserve and that the reserve was off limits to them. The Department of Wildlife and National Parks refused entry on the part of lawyers supporting the San and Bakgalagadi who were seeking the right to return and live and use the resources in the reserve. This was in contradiction to the orders of the High Court, which said that they should have the right to enter the reserve to confer with their clients.

On 12 September 2005, the Central Kalahari Game Reserve court case was adjourned until 6 February 2006. This case is already the longest and most expensive of its kind in Botswana history. The same day, armed police and wildlife officers entered the reserve and told people living there to leave. This began a process whereby (1) people were allegedly prevented at gunpoint from hunting and gathering, (2) dozens of people were loaded onto trucks and removed from the reserve against their will, and (3) goats were removed from the reserve or, in some cases, allegedly killed, ostensibly due to their suffering from a disease, sarcoptic mange.

On 28 October 2005, the High Court ruled that one San man, Amogolang Segotsane, and his family, had the right to go back into the reserve and to take water with them. The court also ordered that his goats, which had been confiscated, be returned to him.

It has been recommended that the Government of Botswana should enter into negotiations with all of the stakeholders involved in the Central Kalahari court case and come to an equitable, fair and just solution which guarantees the former and current residents of the reserve basic human rights and the right to return to their ancestral areas.

San standard of living and poverty

Despite Botswana's economic performance over the past few decades, one of the major problems still to be overcome is poverty.[1] This is particularly true in the case of the San in remote rural areas where their loss of land and traditional livelihoods has left them severely deprived and marginalized.

Whether cattle post labourers, settlement or slum dwellers, most San live at or below the Poverty Datum Line (PDL). They also exhibit some of the highest rates of illiteracy, morbidity and mortality in the country. Although HIV/AIDS prevalence rates are not as high for San as for some other groups in Botswana, these rates are increasing rapidly. One particular concern of HIV positive San in Botswana today is access to anti-retroviral drugs and care, which in many cases are both hard to come by in remote areas with relatively small medical facilities and a limited number of doctors, pharmacists, nurses and other medical practitioners.

For over two decades, San were able to supplement their subsistence and income with wild meat that they obtained legally with the

use of Special Game Licenses (SGLs). By the beginning of the new millennium, the Government of Botswana had ceased issuing Special
Game Licenses to individuals. The only way that the San can hunt legally now is if they apply for a citizen's license through government
channels or if they are living in a Community-Controlled Hunting
Area within a Wildlife Management Area which has a community trust
recognized by the government and whose members have opted to allocate some of the wildlife quota for subsistence hunting. Even with
these limited guarantees, the numbers of arrests and detentions of people for violating wildlife conservation laws is high.

Being deprived of their land and their traditional livelihood and
moving to new environments has also created social disruption and
distress among the San. Resettlement has sometimes (e.g. in Kaudwane and New !Xade) resulted in family members being relocated to
different places, and in different San groups having to live side by side.
It has also meant that San people have to live with other ethnic groups
who sometimes discriminate against them and, on occasion, abuse
their human rights. In the case of the former Central Kalahari Game
Reserve residents, their relocation outside the reserve means that they
no longer have access to their ancestors' graves and other culturally
significant places.

Language rights and education

Botswana has one of the most successful formal education systems in
Africa, claiming universal basic education of up to ten years. It has also
invested a great deal of resources in providing remote area children
with the opportunity to attend government schools, at least up until
Standard (grade) 4.

However, indications are that San children do not reap the same
benefits as children of more dominant groups in the country. San students have a lower rate of attendance and drop out much more often
than students from other ethnic groups. Even when students stay in
school, they may face greater disciplinary treatment, including corpo-
ral punishment, than members of other groups. There are particular

problems in schools with boarding facilities, the so-called Remote Area Dweller hostels, where San children are sometimes exploited both physically and sexually. The idea of separating parents and children is foreign to San culture; the pain and alienation that San students feel at boarding schools can be acute, and many of those who drop out cite missing home and family as their reason for leaving. An additional problem is that many of the remote area schools lack sufficient numbers of fully qualified teachers, and some of the teachers do not speak languages with which at least some of the children are familiar.

A serious educational obstacle for San students (and other linguistic minorities) is the GOB language policy. An important part of Botswana's state-building strategy since independence has rested upon the identification of all of its citizens with the *Batswana* ethnic identity. The building of this national identity has relied heavily upon the promotion of *Setswana* as the primary language of its citizens. Accordingly, the first years of schooling are taught in Setswana before switching to English as the medium of instruction by Grade 4. There is no provision for mother tongue primary education for minority-language children, who must begin primary school in a foreign language (Setswana) then switch to another (English) before they have even mastered the first. In 2005, there were discussions within the Ministry of Education and civil society groups in Botswana concerning the importance of learning mother tongue languages and developing curricula that are culturally relevant.

Cultural rights

A major concern of the San and other minority groups in Botswana is cultural rights – the right to protect their intellectual property and sacred sites. The protection of sacred places has received some attention from the San who helped push, for example, for the declaration of the Tsodilo Hills - an important place in north-western Botswana containing thousands of rock paintings and engravings and dozens of important archaeological and cultural sites - as a World Heritage Site in 2001. This declaration has helped fuel a tourist boom in the Hills which has meant greater access to income for Tsodilo residents, on the one hand, but competition for resources such as firewood on the other. In 2005, San and Mbukushu in Tsodilo sought to establish a set of guidelines and a land use and development plan that will allow for sustainable utilisation of the Tsodilo Hills and other places of natural or cultural importance.

In many parts of Botswana, however, there are no mechanisms for protecting sacred sites, and the situation in the Central Kalahari Game Reserve reveals that people can be removed from their ancestral territories without any provision for allowing them to return to visit their ancestors' graves or places of historical and social significance. Without some changes in Botswana government policies that recognize the cultural rights of all peoples in the country, San and other minority groups will continue to face challenges and will be unable to exercise their rights as full citizens of the state.

Visit by the African Commission

In June 2005, the Working Group on Indigenous Populations of the African Commission on Human and Peoples' Rights made a country visit to Botswana. The mission team was headed by Commissioner Andrew Chigovera from Zimbabwe. The mission met with various government ministries and institutions and with NGOs and visited San communities in Kugama in the Central Kalahari Game Reserve as well as the settlements of Kaudwane, New !Xade and West and East Hanahai. The mission report was adopted by the African Commission at its session in November 2005 and will be released in 2006 upon adoption by the African Union. ❏

Note

1 **Ministry of Finance and Development Planning, 1997**: *National Development Plan 1991-1997*. Gaborone, Botswana: Government Printer. **Nteta, Doreen and Janet Hermans, eds. with Pavla Jeskova. 1996**. *Poverty and Plenty: The Botswana Experience. Proceedings of a Symposium Organized by the Botswana Society, October 15-18, 1996*. Gaborone: Botswana Society.

SOUTH AFRICA

The most important event in 2005 was the visit to South Africa by the Special Rapporteur on the situation of human rights and fundamental freedoms of indigenous peoples, Professor Rodolfo Stavenhagen, from 28 July to 8 August 2005. Those groups claiming an indigenous status in South Africa are the descendants of aboriginal (i.e. pre-Bantu) peoples, which today include three ethnically distinct San communities, the Nama herders, Griqua communities and a revivalist movement of "Khoisan" peoples.

The invitation was extended by the Minister of Foreign Affairs, Dr Nkosozana Dlamini Zuma. This is the first time an African country has officially invited the Special Rapporteur to visit and report on the situation of indigenous peoples. The visit involved co-operation between government departments, United Nations agencies, universities, indigenous peoples' organisations, IWGIA and indigenous communities. The Special Rapporteur visited four of South Africa's provinces, including a visit to the remote Kalahari settlement of Andriesvale where he heard presentations by San and Nama leaders and community people. At the Krags near Plettenberg Bay, hundreds of Griqua people gathered to welcome the historic visit of the Special Rapporteur. The National Khoe-San Consultative Conference hosted a public consultation and speech at the University of the Free State.

The results of the visit will be released in 2006 and are expected to praise the policy progress of the South African government while encouraging it to improve the implementation of these policies. It will likely call for disaggregated data and statistics that are relevant to monitoring the situation of indigenous peoples. South Africa still excludes indigenous Khoe and San languages and identities from its census taking. As most San and Khoe people in the Northern Cape Prov-

ince are classified Coloured (mixed race), their intense poverty is not revealed in the census data.

An official response to the Special Rapporteur's report will follow the release of the final document, which is expected in April. Thus far, community responses to the visit have been positive. There are expectations that the recommendations will lead to greater focus by government on indigenous peoples' situation and survival. Early reactions from government include the fact that lower levels of government are only now understanding the international significance of South Africa's domestic treatment and policy development on the issue of indigenous peoples and their survival. The Special Rapporteur's visit was one of the first times that national, provincial and local government officials had spoken to each other about indigenous peoples.

Inter-Departmental Working Group on Khoe and San Issues

2005 was the first operational year for the Inter-Departmental Working Group on Khoe and San Issues. This Pretoria-based forum brings together various line-function civil servants from different ministries to review policy and implementation issues relevant to indigenous Khoe and San peoples in South Africa. The Working Group reports directly to Cabinet and the President's office, which also indicates a greater chance of coherence in government actions. The focus for 2005 was on the operational procedures and mandate of the Working Group. The Department of Constitutional Affairs is meant to play a greater role in the process. Indigenous leaders have been keen to have the backing of the dynamic Minister from that Department, Dr. Brigitte Mabandla. Weaknesses in the Working Group include the absence of key departments such as Environmental Affairs and Tourism and the Department of National Education. There is also no mechanism at present for the national departments to be able to dialogue directly with provincial and municipal counterparts, who are usually the ones having the direct interface with the communities.

Policy issues

Indigenous South African activists, in co-operation with the Indigenous Peoples of Africa Co-ordinating Committee (IPACC)'s Executive Committee, committed themselves to lobbying the South African government to put its full support behind the United Nations (UN) Draft Declaration on the Rights of Indigenous Peoples. South Africa has been supportive of indigenous peoples at the UN but could not formulate an official policy position until the Cabinet mandated an equivalent domestic policy based on existing constitutional values. After eight years of negotiations, the Cabinet adopted a memorandum in 2004 setting out a policy process to recognise Khoe and San as "vulnerable indigenous communities". It was hoped that the memorandum would

be a sufficient mandate for the Department of Foreign Affairs to articu-
late a foreign policy position in favour of the Draft Declaration. In December 2005, activists were disappointed to hear that Pretoria had sent
no instructions to its mission in Geneva. It is unclear whether the Cabinet has concerns about upsetting its neighbours or whether it is an
indication of how slowly foreign policy develops during the cooling
off period after the first ten years of democracy.

The Department for Environmental Affairs and Tourism (DEAT)
met with an IPACC delegation in November 2005. DEAT has not engaged indigenous peoples in the processes related to the Convention
on Biological Diversity but has expressed an interest in learning more
about how indigenous knowledge systems can play a role in the protection of biological diversity. South Africa is the only country in the
region that can nationally certify game trackers based on their actual
skills, and without reference to schooling or literacy levels. The evaluation system, designed by Dr. Louis Liebenberg, is based on San expert
tracking knowledge. This approach valorises indigenous peoples' specialist skills. IPACC is assisting both civil society and government to
strengthen their co-operation and capacity with regard to biodiversity
management.

The Griqua National Conference is working with government and
the World Wide Fund for Nature (WWF) to create a biosphere reserve
on their semi-arid territory of the Knersvlakte where the Western and
Northern Cape Provinces meet. The reserve will involve different levels of biodiversity protection and traditional sheep herding, as well as
cultural heritage interpretation sites.

UNESCO (United Nations Educational, Scientific and Cultural Organization) has supported one indigenous project in the Kalahari. In
2005, DEAT proposed that the ‡Khomani and rock art of the extinct
|Xam people be added to the tentative list of World Heritage Sites.
Other UN agencies have not engaged with indigenous peoples, reflecting in part the marginalisation of indigenous peoples in South Africa.
UNDP (United Nations Development Programme) is considering supporting Nama initiatives in the Richtersveld. Richtersveld Nama people feel excluded from the management of land claims, even though
they play a key legal role as aboriginal owners of the territory. Nama

518IWGIA - THE INDIGENOUS WORLD - 2006

villagers have created a representative structure with an elected traditional authority.

One of South Africa's influential Cabinet members, Lindiwe Sisulu, has joined the Nordic-sponsored High Level Commission for the Legal Empowerment of the Poor. Her inclusion indicates President Mbeki's support for multilateral approaches to fighting poverty, as well as his preference for neo-liberal capitalist solutions. Mbeki has sometimes antagonised trade union leaders in South Africa with his strong endorsement of investment-driven capitalism and privatisation. The High Level Commission emphasises formalising and legalising of private property for the poor. This approach poses a direct threat to indigenous peoples, who are calling for better African-centred land ownership mechanisms that recognise existing (precolonial) collective management of natural resources and territories.

In October 2005, ‡Khomani San activist, Annette Bok, travelled to the University of Tromsø for the Forum for Development Co-operation with Indigenous Peoples' annual conference. This year's theme focussed on indigenous peoples mapping their territories and cultural systems. Bok travelled through Norway and spoke on television about the ‡Khomani efforts to regain their territories and maintain their endangered culture and language. ❑

PART II

INTERNATIONAL
PROCESSES

UN WORLD SUMMIT
REFORM OF THE HUMAN RIGHTS BODIES

2005 World Summit

More than 170 Heads of State gathered at the United Nations (UN) headquarters in New York for the 2005 World Summit to mark the 60th anniversary of the UN. At this international event, world leaders addressed the main challenges facing the global community - including development, security and human rights - as well as reform of the United Nations so that it can more effectively address global challenges. This reform has been a priority for Mr Kofi Annan since his appointment as UN Secretary General in 1997.

Establishment of the UN Human Rights Council

In March 2005, Kofi Annan proposed the establishment of a UN Human Rights Council. This body would replace the existing UN Commission on Human Rights, the legitimacy of which has been increasingly undermined by the politically selective character of its work. International human rights NGOs welcomed the proposal and shared the concern that the Commission on Human Rights lacked credibility. During the negotiation process throughout 2005 the same organizations have, however, raised many concerns as to the possible results of the states' negotiation process regarding the mandate and functions of the new Human Rights Council. One concern is whether the new Council will maintain independent special rapporteurs and retain active NGO participation.

Together with other UN reform proposals, the proposal to create the Human Rights Council was considered at a UN World Summit in New York on 14-16 September 2005. Following weeks of intense negotiations and numerous draft texts, world leaders approved a final outcome document of the Summit. Delegations expressed mixed feelings about the document – very few were pleased with the text, while many others felt that priority issues had become diluted to the point of meaninglessness. The final UN Summit document included the creation of a Human Rights Council but passed on the responsibility for turning this into a reality to the 2005 session of the General Assembly. The president of the General Assembly, Jan Eliasson of Sweden, was charged with conducting negotiations to establish the "mandate, modalities, functions, size, composition, membership, working methods and procedures for the Council".

Since the World Summit, negotiations on the new Human Rights Council have been moving forward at a fast pace. But despite intensive governmental negotiations carried out throughout the whole of the 61st session of the General Assembly (October-December 2005), states have not been able to reach final consensus on some major issues regarding the mandate and procedures of the new Human Rights Council. At the end of the General Assembly session, the issue remained unresolved. The General Assembly President's Office therefore decided to continue further negotiations in January 2006.

The World Summit outcome document and indigenous peoples

The outcome document[1] agreed on at the 2005 World Summit represents an extremely important step forward for indigenous peoples as it consolidates recognition of the term "indigenous peoples" and reaffirms UN member states' commitment to uphold the human rights of indigenous peoples. Paragraph 27 of the outcome document reaffirms the commitment to continue to make progress in advancing the human rights of the world's indigenous peoples at local, national, regional and international levels, including through consultation and collaboration with them, and to present for adoption a final draft United Nations Declaration on the Rights of Indigenous Peoples as soon as possible. ❑

Note

1   The Outcome document can be downloaded from: http://www.un.org/summit2005/presskit/fact_sheet.pdf

THE UN COMMISSION ON HUMAN RIGHTS
61ˢᵗ session

The United Nations Commission on Human Rights, composed of 53 states, meets every year in a regular session in March/April for six weeks in Geneva. Over 3,000 delegates from member and observer states and non-governmental organizations participate.

Item 15 "Indigenous Issues": Since 1995 the Commission on Human Rights has had "Indigenous Issues" as a specific agenda item at all sessions. Under this item, reports from the Commission's subsidiary organs dealing with indigenous peoples' rights, such as the Working Group on Indigenous Populations, the Working Group on the Draft Declaration, and the reports from the Special Rapporteur on the Situation of Human Rights and Fundamental Freedoms of Indigenous Peoples, are presented and discussed.

The 61st session of the UN Commission on Human Rights took place in Geneva from March 15 to April 23, 2005. On April 11, the Commission considered agenda item 15 "Indigenous Issues".

Reports of the Special Rapporteur

The first presentation was from Rodolfo Stavenhagen, the Special Rapporteur on the Human Rights and Fundamental Freedoms of Indigenous Peoples. He discussed his main report focusing on indigenous peoples and the right to education, as well as his country visits to Canada and Colombia. In terms of his study on indigenous peoples and education, Stavenhagen mentioned how indigenous children tended to have less access to proper education than their non-indigenous counterparts, and noted that education was not just the right to go to school, but also to receive a proper and non-discriminatory education. Many indigenous children have no choice but to attend schools where assimilatory education is taught, encouraging the loss of their indigenous languages, erasing the indigenous history of genocide common to all parts of the world, as well as devaluing their traditional educational systems and culture in general. Stavenhagen pointed out that his next main report would focus on national legislation and indigenous peoples.

Colombia

In his presentation of the report on his official mission to Colombia, Stavenhagen stated that although there had been legislative advances in the country, there were huge problems with violence against indigenous communities in the light of government policies, and also the armed conflict that had been going on for many years. He discussed assassinations of indigenous human rights defenders and spiritual leaders, displacement of indigenous communities, forced recruitment into the armed forces, widespread rape of indigenous women and children and organized crime, among other human rights violations. Stavenhagen affirmed the near extinction of several Amazonian tribes due to these violations, and encouraged the Colombian government to protect non-combatants. He remarked that much of the rape and violence against indigenous populations was in fact carried out by the Colombian armed forces.

After the presentation, Colombia's governmental delegation was given the floor to comment on the report. The government refuted Stavenhagen's claims that human rights violations were taking place against indigenous populations. Colombia claimed that all of the violence against indigenous peoples was caused by the persistent terrorist actions of the guerrilla and armed groups operating in the territory. The government would continue, in a transparent manner, to guarantee the security of its people, particularly the indigenous citizens.

Canada

In terms of his visit to Canada, he stated that even though Canada ranks very high in the Human Development Index, aboriginal populations live far below acceptable standards in terms of health, education and non-discrimination. Although there are a great number of treaties between Canada, the Queen of England and indigenous populations, historical reclamation of indigenous rights continues to be a contested issue. Stavenhagen encouraged Canada to lessen the gap in human rights protection between indigenous and non-indigenous sectors of Canadian society, especially with regard to the penal system.

In its comments on the presentation, Canada said that all of the issues mentioned as problem areas in Canada had already been identified by the government and measures had been taken to improve the "unacceptable" situation of aboriginal Canadians. They noted the various pieces of legislation they had enacted to protect and promote the human rights of indigenous peoples and to redress the injustices of the past, especially in the area of health.

Report of the Working Group on a Draft Declaration on the Rights of Indigenous Peoples

Luis Enrique Chavez, the Chairperson-Rapporteur of the Working Group on a Draft United Nations Declaration on the Rights of Indigenous Peoples, presented the work of the 10th session of the Working Group (WGDD). Chavez said that, although the WGDD was not able to adopt the Declaration as mandated by the Commission by the end of the 1st Decade of the World's Indigenous Peoples (1995-2004), he wanted to point out a few things for the Commission to keep in mind as to why this had not been possible. Firstly, consensus was simply not possible in the short amount of time for the Draft elaborations. Secondly, there was a huge group of contentious articles that still needed far more discussion in the WGDD, articles dealing with self-determination and lands, territories and resources. But, there was another large group of articles that had indeed obtained consensus, and this group would be the starting point for the next meeting.

Chavez pointed out to the Commission that he had created a Chairman's Text that consolidated proposals from indigenous and government representatives, that attempted to bridge the gaps between the disparate positions held within the WGDD, and that he hoped this text could help build further consensus and lead to adoption in future sessions. He requested the extension of the WGDD mandate so that by the end of this year the WGDD would be able to complete its task and adopt a strong text.

In their interventions before the Commission, indigenous representatives also regretted the fact that the WGDD had been unable to complete its work within the International Decade but indicated that this was largely due to a lack of political will on the part of many governments to adopt a text in line with the demands and needs of indigenous peoples. However, they considered that progress had been made during the last session in terms of building a consensus, and the vast majority of indigenous organisations present called on the Commission to extend the Working Group's mandate. A very small number of indigenous organisations requested that the Commission adjourn the process.

The Saami Council read out a petition, signed by more than 200 indigenous organisations from around the world, supporting an extension of the WGDD's mandate and asking the Commission not to suspend the process, as this would be highly damaged to adoption of the Declaration.

Sovereignty over natural resources

Ms Erica-Irene Daes, the Special Rapporteur of the Sub-Commission on indigenous peoples' sovereignty over natural resources, presented her final report. The report traced the history and highlighted the importance of the concept of "permanent sovereignty over natural resources within the United Nations system" and the nature and scope of the right of indigenous peoples to own, use, control and manage their lands, territories and resources and further noted its importance to the cultural survival of indigenous populations. It also contained principal conclusions and basic recommendations, including a recommendation for an expert UN Seminar on indigenous peoples and permanent sovereignty over natural resources. She urged the UN to include this report as part of the UN Studies series.

Resolutions

The following resolutions were adopted by the 61st session of the Commission on Human Rights:[1]

Resolution on the Working group of the Commission on Human Rights to elaborate a draft declaration on indigenous peoples' rights, sponsored by Canada

This resolution extends the mandate of the Working Group on the Draft Declaration for one more year. Following this resolution, the Working Group will have a two-week session in September and an additional week before the end of the year (December) in order to obtain concrete results in the drafting process before the next Commission session.

Resolution on Human Rights and Indigenous Issues, sponsored by Mexico and Guatemala

This resolution focuses on the work of the Special Rapporteur and welcomes the intention of the Special Rapporteur to devote his next report to topics of constitutional reform, legislation and implementation of laws regarding protection of the rights of indigenous people and the effectiveness of their application.

This resolution also included a workshop to be organized within the year, which would be sponsored by the Government of Mexico. The workshop in Mexico was intended to foster a dialogue between governments and indigenous peoples on issues of self-determination, land and territory and collective rights. The Special Rapporteur, the Permanent Forum and other experts would also be invited.

Resolution on the Working Group on Indigenous Populations, sponsored by Cuba

This resolution highlights the continuing need for the Working Group on Indigenous Peoples, on account of its mandate, which is distinct from that of either the Permanent Forum or the Special Rapporteur.

Resolution on the protection of indigenous peoples in time of conflict, sponsored by Cuba

This resolution aimed at ensuring that the Special Adviser for the Prevention of Genocide appointed under the Action Plan to Prevent Genocide should take into consideration the need to protect indigenous peoples and their territories. ❑

Note

1   The resolutions can be found at:
    http://ap.ohchr.org/documents/sdpage_e.aspx?b=1&se=59&t=11

THE SPECIAL RAPPORTEUR

Overview 2005

Since his appointment as Special Rapporteur in 2001, Rodolfo Stavenhagen has been closely following the human rights situation of indigenous peoples around the world. During this time, he has been able to gain an in-depth knowledge of the regulatory developments and efforts underway in some countries to recognise indigenous rights. Despite legislative advances, the scenario facing millions of indigenous people around the world is one of serious violations of their human rights, both as individuals and as peoples. The Special Rapporteur has been able to find out about these situations in detail through his *in situ* visits to communities and dialogue with community members, through information brought to his attention via a large number of sources and through his participation in a large number of seminars and thematic meetings. An analysis of these situations led the Special Rapporteur to focus his main report to the 62nd session of the Commission on Human Rights on the gap between the progress that has been made in many countries in terms of national legislation recognising indigenous peoples and their rights, and the reality on the ground.

Legislative progress and day-to-day reality

During the First International Decade of the World's Indigenous Peoples (1994-2004), many countries introduced legislative processes and constitutional reforms in recognition of indigenous peoples and their rights, including recognition of their languages, cultures and traditions, the need for prior and informed consultation, regulation of access to natural resources and land or, in some cases, recognition of autonomy and self-government.

Despite these advances, the Special Rapporteur warned in his report that there was still an "implementation gap" between legislation and day-to-day reality and that enforcement and observance of the law was beset with myriad obstacles and problems. The Special Rapporteur drew attention in his report to two types of problem: firstly, there are many cases in which legislation on indigenous issues is inconsistent with other laws. Secondly, in most of the documented constitutional reforms there is a delay in adopting statutory and secondary laws. The main problem is the "implementation gap", the vacuum between existing legislation and administrative, legal and political practice. This divide between form and substance constitutes a violation of the human rights of indigenous people. To close the gap and narrow the divide is - in the Special Rapporteur's words - a challenge that must be addressed through a programme of action for the human rights of indigenous people in the future.

Part of the problem is to be found in the legislative formalities themselves, in the membership of legislatures, in the scant representation and participation of indigenous people in legislative work, in the lack of consultation of the indigenous peoples, in the biases and prejudices against indigenous rights observed among many actors on the political scene, among legislators and political parties of different persuasions. The problem is not only one of legislating on indigenous issues but also of doing so with the indigenous peoples themselves. Generally speaking, there are no proper mechanisms for monitoring the effectiveness of indigenous legislation and evaluating its application in the day-to-day practice of the public administration and society. The Special Rapporteur also highlighted the difficulties facing those who publicly defend the indigenous when carrying out their work, as well as the pressures to which civil society organisations who take up the defence of indigenous rights are often subjected.

One aspect of the same problem is the lack of a coordinated or systematic policy – with the participation of the indigenous peoples – that cuts across the various ministries and state bodies with regard to indigenous issues, such as ministries of agriculture, energy, mines and natural resources, education and health, to name but a few, in order to guarantee the rights of indigenous peoples.

One of the clearest illustrations of the "implementation gap" is to be found, according to the Special Rapporteur, in the public administration. With a few exceptions, the state bureaucracy reacts slowly to new legislation in favour of indigenous rights; it is not functionally prepared to address the new challenges. Another problem lies in a lack of consultation and participation mechanisms, established jointly with indigenous peoples so as to envisage the needs and views of both parties, with which to measure the impact of the visions expressed by indigenous peoples. Unilaterally developed mechanisms impose subordination regarding methodology and therefore make for such frustration that the consultation process is doomed to failure from the outset.

The judicial sector has been increasingly called upon to become involved in this area, along with the international and regional human rights defence mechanisms. The courts are instrumental in resolving conflicts between laws, non-enforcement of those laws, and measures taken by the authorities that are at variance with the reforms and jeopardize the rights of indigenous peoples.

Based on these conclusions, the Special Rapporteur recommended, among other things, that governments assign high priority to the quest for concrete measures and actions that will help close the existing gap between laws for protecting the human rights of indigenous peoples and their practical implementation, and that they should develop a coordinated and systematic policy with the participation of indigenous peoples. The Special Rapporteur recommended establishing consultation and participation bodies on all particular and general measures that affect them, with special attention to legislation, natural resources and development projects. The Special Rapporteur considered the need to establish, in parallel with the new laws, monitoring and evaluation mechanisms and mechanisms for implementing the standards established, with the participation of indigenous peoples.

Through different human rights and indigenous affairs commissions, parliaments play a very important role in monitoring the use of budgets allocated to the areas of protection and promotion of indigenous rights and it is thus recommended that the work of these bodies be strengthened.

The Special Rapporteur called for the adoption of the necessary statutory and organic laws as soon as possible, and in consultation with the representative institutions of the indigenous peoples, for the effective implementation of the standards established in legislation on the human rights of indigenous peoples. In cases of inconsistency between laws, priority and precedence should be given to those that protect the human rights of the indigenous peoples, and conflicts that may result from such inconsistencies should be resolved in good faith and by common agreement. In addition, in his report Rodolfo Stavenhagen recommended that independent mechanisms be established, such as, for example, citizen observatories, in order to determine the appropriate criteria and indicators for systematic monitoring of the enforcement of laws governing the rights of indigenous peoples as well as others that affect these peoples' fundamental rights and freedoms. The Special Rapporteur also called for respect for and enforcement of international human rights standards relevant to indigenous peoples, ensuring that they are applied correctly at national level, producing the system of guarantees for which they were created. Finally, the Special Rapporteur proposed a series of recommendations for the international system and civil society.

Country visits

The Special Rapporteur undertook two official visits during 2005 with the aim of observing *in situ* the situation of the human rights of indigenous peoples.

South Africa

Rodolfo Stavenhagen visited South Africa from 28 July to 8 August and, in his report, he noted the tragic consequences of apartheid and its legacy in the country. In this context, the Special Rapporteur noted his awareness of the tremendous efforts made by the democratic governments of South Africa to redress the many injustices inherited from the previous regime. Since 1994, the date of the first democratic elections, the South African government has been committed to the promotion and protection of human rights.

Indigenous peoples tend to be more marginalized than other sectors, being at the lower end of the socio-economic scale. In his report, the Special Rapporteur expressed his encouragement at the commitment made by the government to respond to the demands of indigenous groups in the country and at the efforts underway to formulate and implement the necessary legislation and policies to respond to issues such as land restitution, multicultural and multilingual education, the representation of traditional authorities in public life and the delivery of health and other social services.

The Special Rapporteur recommended, among other things, that the existence of indigenous communities be constitutionally recognised and that the legal institutions from the apartheid era that maintain the stigma of their classification as "Coloureds" be dismantled. He recommended that the government maintain an official national register of recognised indigenous communities and that their associations and chieftaincies be granted the necessary statutory recognition. He recommended ratifying ILO Convention 169. The Special Rapporteur also advised that the restitution of land claims should not be limited to the cut-off date of 1913 and that a study into land needs be conducted along with an acceleration in the land restitution process. He also recommended the use of economic, social and human development indicators for indigenous peoples as well as improving access of indigenous peoples and communities to the justice system by establishing visiting circuit courts in outlying areas.

New Zealand

The Special Rapporteur's second annual visit was to New Zealand. from 16 to 26 November 2005. Relations between the Maori people and the government are based on the well-known Treaty of Waitangi signed in 1840. As a result of land sales and breaches of the Treaty by the Crown, Maori lost most of their land, resources, self-governance and cultural identity. A new approach since 1975 has led to numerous settlements of Maori land claims and the enactment of new legislation.

In his report, the Special Rapporteur took note of the government's commitment to reduce the inequalities between Maori and non-Maori and to ensure that the country's development is shared by all sectors of society. Despite the progress made, Maori are impatient with the pace of redress for breaches of the Treaty of Waitangi. Of particular concern to them is the Foreshore and Seabed Act, which extinguishes customary Maori property rights to the coastal areas, and provides a statutory process for the recognition of customary or aboriginal title. In the light of these conclusions, the Special Rapporteur recommended in his report, among other things, that a convention should be convened on constitutional reform aimed at clearly regulating the relationship between the government and the Maori people, on the basis of the Treaty of Waitangi. He also recommended considering the Iwi and Hapu (tribes and sub-tribes) as valid units for strengthening the Maori system of self-governance and that their access to legal services be ensured in terms of legal aid. He recommended that parliament repeal or amend the Foreshore and Seabed Act. In addition, the Special Rapporteur recommended that Maori rights to participate in managing their cultural sites according to customary precepts should be recognised in all treaty negotiations; that the Iwi and Hapu should be enabled to self-determine an appropriate corporate structure for receipt and management of assets; that more resources should be made available for Maori education, including teacher training programmes and the development of culturally appropriate teaching materials; and that the provision of social services, particularly health and housing, should continue to target the needs of the Maori. Finally, he recommended that the New Zealand government should continue to support the efforts underway to achieve a UN Declaration on the Rights of Indigenous Peoples by consensus, including the right to self-determination and that it should ratify ILO Convention 169.

Monitoring activities

Following his oral presentation to the Commission's session in April 2005, the Special Rapporteur provided information on his activities underway to monitor the recommendations included both in his thematic reports and his country visits. In 2005, the Commission on Human Rights asked him to commence preparing a study into best practices for implementing the recommendations in his general and country reports and told him that he should present a progress report on his work to the Commission at its 62nd period of sessions, with the completed study ready for its 63rd period of sessions. In preparing the report, the Special Rapporteur had received a great deal of information from governments, UN agencies and many indigenous communities and civil society organisations on the different activities underway to monitor the recommendations.

The Special Rapporteur's visits, and particularly the publication of his visit reports, has created great activity among indigenous organisations, and civil society organisations in general, in all countries. The organisations have welcomed the Special Rapporteur's recommendations warmly and, in all countries, mechanisms and projects for monitoring government fulfilment of the recommendations have been established. In some countries civic observatories have been established to gauge the level of implementation of the recommendations.

The Special Rapporteur hoped that he would be able to present his completed study to the future Human Rights Council, which will substitute the current Commission on Human Rights, during 2007. For this report to be of value, the continuing collaboration both of governments and indigenous organisations, of non-governmental organisations, agencies and programmes of the UN system and academic institutions working on the subject would be necessary. For example, in his progress report, the Special Rapporteur found the joint action between the governments of Guatemala and Mexico and the Office of the UN High Commissioner for Human Rights to implement the Special Rapporteur's recommendations from his visit reports to both countries particularly important. This action is receiving significant financial support from the European Commission and is in full implementation. In addition, the government of Canada, for example, announced the monitoring of the Special Rapporteur's recommendations during the Permanent Forum in May 2005, plus the granting of 5 million Canadian dollars for the period 2005 to 2010 as funding for the work of the Association of Native Women of Canada (*Asociación de Mujeres Nativas del Canadá* - NWAC). These funds will be aimed at supporting the work of the NWAC with other organisations involved in activities aimed at bringing racial and sexual violence against indigenous women to an end. The Special Rapporteur, who has twice been invited by the Sami Parliament in Norway to find out more about their situation, stated that he was particularly pleased at the adoption of the new "Finnmark Act" in that country, the result of negotiations between the Sami Council and the Norwegian Parliament. In addition, a number of governments such as, for example, the Spanish government, have also produced strategies and guidelines on indigenous issues in relation to their bilateral cooperation and have requested the Special Rapporteur's opinion or have included elements relevant to some of the issues referred to in the Special Rapporteur's report. Some UN agencies, such as the United Nations Development Programme and the UN High Commissioner for Refugees, have used the Special Rapporteur's reports, both general and country, as a basis in the design of new activities and strategies for indigenous people.

In the Special Rapporteur's opinion, this was the type of information that should be gathered and analysed for his final study. For this reason, he intends to encourage all the above mentioned players to analyse in detail the reports presented to the Commission, along with the actions underway or in the planning stages, in order to respond to the needs of indigenous peoples in relation to the protection and promotion of their human rights. ❑

THE PERMANENT FORUM
ON INDIGENOUS ISSUES
4th session

The UN Permanent Forum on Indigenous Issues is a subsidiary body of the United Nations Economic and Social Council (ECOSOC). It is mandated to discuss indigenous issues related to economic and social development, culture, the environment, education, health and human rights.

The Permanent Forum is made up of 16 independent experts. Governments nominate eight of the members, and the other eight members are indigenous experts to be appointed by the President of ECOSOC. The Permanent Forum on Indigenous issues meets every year in a regular session in May for two weeks in New York. Over 1,000 delegates from states, UN agencies, indigenous organisations, NGOs and academic institutions participate.

The fourth session of the Permanent Forum on Indigenous Issues met from 16 to 27 May 2005 at the United Nations headquarters in New York. Around 1,200 participants from indigenous organisations, non-governmental organisations, intergovernmental organisations, states and UN specialised agencies attended.

The special theme of this session was the Millennium Development Goals (MDGs) and indigenous peoples, with special emphasis on goal 1 (Eradicate extreme poverty and hunger) and goal 2 (Achieve universal primary education). The Permanent Forum also engaged in a discussion of the ongoing priorities and themes of human rights, data collection and the disaggregation of data on indigenous peoples (making sure that statistical information includes separate data on indigenous groups so that their particular situation is reflected in the statistical materials), particularly indigenous children, youth and women.

As in previous years, the session also scheduled numerous side events in the form of films, panel discussions and exhibitions. Furthermore, various groups of indigenous peoples organised caucuses throughout the session to discuss developments, prepare joint interventions and co-ordinate strategies. Caucuses were either regionally focused (Latin America, North America, Africa and Asia), or topic based. In addition, an indigenous preparatory meeting was held for two days preceding the fourth session. During this meeting, representatives from indigenous peoples' organisations shared experiences from previous sessions, reviewed major issues to be discussed at the Permanent Forum and developed a common strategy plan for the fourth session of the Permanent Forum.

Opening session

Following the formal inauguration, the Permanent Forum proceeded to elect the Bureau. Ms Victoria Tauli Corpuz was elected Chairperson and Mr Hassan Id Balkassm, Ms Otilia Lux de Coti, Ms Ida Nicolaisen and Mr Pavel Sulyandziga were elected Vice–Chairpersons; Mr Michael Dodson was elected as *Rapporteur.* The high-level panel that opened the session emphasised the accomplishments of the Permanent Forum and important issues for indigenous peoples and the MDGs. Permanent Forum Chairperson Ms Victoria Tauli-Corpuz presented the Permanent Forum's recent reports on Free Prior and Informed Consent (FPIC) and data disaggregation and suggested that the 4th session should result in implementation proposals rather than more recommendations.

Poverty eradication and indigenous peoples

The topic was addressed under the thematic approach of Millennium Development Goal 1: Eradicate extreme poverty and hunger - good practices and barriers to implementation. As the Permanent Forum devoted nearly three days to this topic, participants were able to address a wide range of issues concerning the origins of extreme poverty and hunger within many indigenous communities.

The discussion began with an intervention from the United Nations High Commissioner for Human Rights Ms Louise Arbour. Ms Arbour stressed that programs implemented to achieve the MDGs must be rooted in a human rights framework and noted the importance of including indigenous peoples in the process of defining "poverty" so that it does not exclude the cultural dimension.

Following the opening speeches, a number of UN agencies reported on their work in relation to Goal 1 and indigenous peoples. Many agencies acknowledged the importance of a rights-based approach to achieving the MDGs and the inclusion of indigenous peoples.

Throughout the debate, indigenous representatives expressed concern about the definition of "poverty" in the MDGs. Many statements from indigenous organisations stressed that it was restricted to the idea of economic deprivation and did not account for the denial of social and cultural rights, which are a definitive component of poverty for indigenous peoples.

Several interventions expressed concern over the exclusion of indigenous peoples from the Poverty Reduction Strategy Papers (PRSPs) that governments are required to prepare in order to receive development aid from the World Bank. Several speakers also cited the lack of disaggregated data on indigenous peoples as a limitation of the PRSPs and directly contributing to a lack of understanding of the extent of indigenous peoples' poverty and the deficiency of culturally sensitive poverty alleviation programs.

Most of the Forum's recommendations on Goal 1 referred to the importance of assessing the impact of the MDGs on indigenous peoples and including such assessments in country reports. The Permanent Forum also acknowledged the importance of developing disaggregated data on indigenous peoples within the MDG context and beyond.

Indigenous representatives representing nearly all regions raised territory and land issues during the debate on the MDGs. Many were concerned that the loss of traditional lands due to development projects, displacement and armed conflict was not being acknowledged as a root cause of poverty and hunger for indigenous peoples.

The principle of Free Prior and Informed Consent (FPIC) and the lack of meaningful participatory mechanisms available to indigenous peoples regarding development projects were also issues raised by indigenous peoples' representatives. In their interventions they stated that the FPIC was integral to the exercise of self-determination and rights to lands and territories, and that they were thus very troubled by the new World Bank Operational Policy, which applies the concept of consultation rather than consent.

The issue of the environment arose during discussions on Goal 1. Many indigenous delegates drew attention to the relationship between the destruction of indigenous peoples' ecosystems, poverty, hunger and human rights. The Chairperson of the UN Forum on Forests (UNFF) acknowledged the relationship between poverty and deforestation, and that global agreements and initiatives aimed at combating deforestation had been largely ineffective.

A number of indigenous interventions maintained that a critical component of impoverishment for indigenous peoples was their continued loss of intellectual property rights. Members of the Permanent Forum and indigenous groups both expressed concerns at the World Intellectual Property Organization's (WIPO) approach to the preservation and protection of indigenous intellectual property. Several members of the Permanent Forum were concerned about the conflict between WIPO's state-driven mandate and its responsibility to protect indigenous knowledge systems. In particular, members were troubled with WIPO's inability to recognise indigenous peoples' collective rights to their traditional knowledge. In response to some concerns raised during the discussions, in its recommendations on Goal 1 the Permanent Forum urged UN agencies and other international organisations to implement existing policies on indigenous peoples or develop such policies if they did not yet exist.

Universal primary education

In the discussion on Goal 2 (Achieve universal primary education), indigenous representatives again expressed concern at the absence of an indigenous perspective. Many indigenous representatives said that without respecting the importance of indigenous languages, culture and traditional knowledge, programs designed to achieve Goal 2 would be carried out at the expense of the basic human rights of indigenous peoples.

Throughout the discussion on education, indigenous representatives stressed the need for native-language education programmes. Many interventions expressed concern over the lack of resources devoted to developing and sustaining education programmes for indigenous peoples. Interventions also focused on other impediments to education for indigenous peoples, such as remoteness, financial burden and discrimination.

In its recommendations, the Permanent Forum called on states to elevate intercultural education to a matter of national priority. In addition, it recommended that states review current educational materials to identify and remove culturally discriminatory references as well as enhance knowledge of indigenous cultures.

Discussion on priorities and themes

Human rights

The Permanent Forum session on human rights included a new interactive dialogue with the Special Rapporteur on the Situation of Human Rights and Fundamental Freedoms of Indigenous People for one day. Following an overview of his work, the Special Rapporteur, Mr. Rodolfo Stavenhagen, reported that he had received an increased number of individual communications alleging violations of human rights of indigenous peoples. He informed the Forum that in many countries indigenous peoples suffer from extra-judicial executions; arbitrary detention; torture; forced evictions; and lack of access to health services, food, appropriate education and adequate housing. He reported that the condition of indigenous women and indigenous human rights defenders had worsened. Concerning the MDGs, Mr. Stavenhagen said that persistent poverty among indigenous peoples was the result of a continued denial of human rights.

With regard to the progress of the Working Group on the Draft UN Declaration on the Rights of Indigenous Peoples, in their statements indigenous representatives strongly recommended that it should continue its work. Many states encouraged the Working Group to complete the Draft Declaration as soon as possible.

Human rights were discussed under almost all agenda items of the Permanent Forum. Many participants echoed Ms. Arbour's call for MDG strategies to be rooted in human rights and that it was crucial to understand the Millennium Goal commitments as commitments to implementing human rights.

Many indigenous representatives said that the indigenous peoples' right of self-determination should be expressly recognised, along with the collective nature of indigenous peoples' rights generally.

The Permanent Forum's recommendations under this item recommended that the adoption of the UN Declaration on the Rights of Indigenous Peoples be a top priority of UN agencies, states and indigenous peoples. It recommended strengthening the means for addressing "urgent, gross and ongoing human rights violations, militarisation of indigenous lands and systemic violence committed by Member States against indigenous peoples". It also asked states to ratify ILO Convention No. 169.

Data collection

As in previous sessions, indigenous representatives gave data collection as a principal area of concern. Almost all interventions affirmed the importance of disaggregated data for indigenous peoples. Ms Tauli-Corpuz (Chairperson) said that data disaggregation of the MDGs based on ethnicity was crucial because country reports did not usually reflect the realities of indigenous peoples. If the process did not take into account indigenous people, she noted, they would continue to be marginalised.

The Permanent Forum's recommendations included many suggestions made by participants, including the development of data collection standards and regional workshops on data collection. The Permanent Forum called on the UNDP, the World Bank and other relevant agencies to ensure that disaggregated data on indigenous peoples was included in all UN agencies' human development and poverty reports.

Free, prior and informed consent

After last year's session identified this issue as a priority, the Secretariat of the Permanent Forum convened an international workshop from 17 to 19 January 2005. The Conclusions and Recommendations from the workshop appear in the Report of the International Workshop on Methodologies regarding Free, Prior and Informed Consent and Indigenous Peoples. The workshop presented a series of recommendations to the Permanent Forum, including: promoting better methodologies on free, prior and informed consent; making governments, the private sector and indigenous peoples aware of the principle when planning development projects; and developing the capacity of indigenous peoples to participate in the process.

Indigenous youth, women and children

Following previous discussions on the particular needs of indigenous youth, the Permanent Forum called again on UN agencies to provide funding and incentives for indigenous youth organisations to create informal educational activities targeting girls and women. Furthermore, it called on states to develop poverty reduction strategies focussing on indigenous youth.

With regard to indigenous women and children, the Permanent Forum recommended that UN agencies and states continue to implement the recommendations from the third session of the Permanent Forum.

It called on states to improve the condition of indigenous women by expanding employment opportunities.

Future work

The Permanent Forum's discussion of future work focused on plans for the Second International Decade on the World's Indigenous Peoples and the agenda for next year's session. The Permanent Forum decided to organize a special day of discussion on a Programme of Action at its next session. Consistent with indigenous peoples' interventions, it recommended that the priorities of the Second Decade include: the adoption of the UN Declaration on the Rights of Indigenous Peoples; the establishment of regional councils to monitor the progress of the Second Decade; and linking the Second Decade to achievement of the MDGs. Furthermore, the Forum decided to devote a half-day session to Africa at its next session under the agenda item "on going priorities and themes". The Permanent Forum decided to focus on the remaining MDGs in its 2006 session.

The Permanent Forum closed its session with the adoption of seven sets of draft Recommendations, on Millennium Development Goals 1 and 2, human rights, indigenous children and youth, indigenous women, data collection and on its future work. The Permanent Forum also approved the following three decisions: to organise an international expert group meeting on the Millennium Development Goals, indigenous participation and good governance; the venue and dates for the fifth session of the Permanent Forum and the provisional agenda and documentation for the fifth session. All of the draft Recommendations and decisions were later submitted to ECOSOC for adoption.[1] ❑

Note

1 To download the report: http://daccessdds.un.org/doc/UNDOC/GEN/N05/377/61/PDF/N0537761.pdf?OpenElement

THE UN WORKING GROUP
ON INDIGENOUS POPULATIONS

The UN Working Group on Indigenous Populations (WGIP) is a subsidiary body of the UN Sub-Commission on the Protection and Promotion of Human Rights, and meets annually in Geneva, usually during the last week of July.

The WGIP comprises five UN experts who prepare the documents to be discussed at the session. The session itself is open to anyone wishing to attend. For the last two years, the experts have prepared some of the documents jointly with indigenous organisations.

The WGIP has a dual mandate. First, to consider developments that have taken place over the year in relation to indigenous issues and human rights. Second, so-called standard-setting activities, that is, the establishment of standards for indigenous rights. The WGIP has a number of permanent items on its agenda and chooses a main theme each year.

The 23rd Session of the Working Group on Indigenous Populations (WGIP) was held in the United Nations Office at Geneva (Switzerland) from 18 to 22 July 2005. The main theme of the 23rd session was "Indigenous Peoples and the International and Domestic Protection of Traditional Knowledge".

As is now customary, indigenous representatives met in caucus for two days prior to the meeting to prepare their involvement in the session. The caucus examined proposals on the WGIP's main theme and decided to present joint statements on several issues such as, for example, traditional knowledge; free, prior and informed consent; the future work of the WGIP. The indigenous caucus decided to present a statement on possible activities during the Second Decade of Indigenous Peoples (2005-2015) within the context of the Commission on Human Rights. A number of drafting groups were established to prepare the statement.

Among other issues considered by the indigenous caucus were the process of the Working Group on the Draft Declaration on the Rights of Indigenous Peoples and the possible impact of the UN reforms, particularly that of the Commission on Human Rights, on indigenous issues within the UN system.

The WGIP session commenced on Monday 18 July and Miguel Alfonso Martínez was elected Chairperson-Rapporteur for the session. Of the 5 WGIP members , Mr. Yokota did not attend, and Ms. Motoc participated only for the two last days. The new WGIP member, Mr. Gaspard Biró, was present. Under general issues and recent events, a number of indigenous organisations presented statements on the current situation of indigenous rights. Under the consideration of this year's main theme, and in the absence of Mr. Yokota, WGIP member who had been involved in its drafting, Mattias Åhrén of the Saami Council presented the report *Principles and guidelines for the protection of the heritage of indigenous peoples*. Statements from indigenous organisations were then heard in this regard. These were generally supportive of continuing future work on this issue within the WGIP

The second report to be presented as a result of joint work between the WGIP and indigenous organisations was the legal commentary produced by Ms. Motoc and the Tebtebba Foundation. There were few indigenous interventions in this regard but those present reiterated the lack of respect on the part of governments, multinationals, development agencies and international financial institutions in relation to the free, prior and informed consent of indigenous peoples. It was agreed to work with the Permanent Forum on Indigenous Issues (which held an expert seminar on free, prior and informed consent in January 2005) in order to make further progress on standard setting in this regard. One of the conclusions reached after listening to the participants' comments on this issue was the need to ask for more contributions from the states, indigenous organisations etc., on the application of free, prior and informed consent.

A further two points on the agenda (the impact of globalisation and the threat of extinction due to environmental degradation) were debated, and statements were heard from the organisations present. The indigenous organisations also contributed possible activities for the Second Decade and future standard-setting activities for the WGIP. Among these was a suggestion to consider the issue of colonialism, a situation still experienced by many indigenous people today Another proposal suggested that the WGIP examine the impact of the international financial institutions on indigenous peoples.

Two special sessions were also held, the first being to celebrate International Day of the World's Indigenous People. The High Commissioner for Human Rights was unfortunately unable to attend. The second was an interactive session on the Friday morning between the current Chairperson of the Permanent Forum on Indigenous Issues (Victoria Tauli Corpuz), the Special Rapporteur on the situation of human rights and fundamental freedoms of indigenous peoples (Rodolfo Stavenhagen) and WGIP members. Everyone emphasised the need for greater collaboration in order to guarantee complementarity between their different mandates and to ensure more useful mechanisms with which to respond to the needs of indigenous peoples. The Special Rapporteur suggested that complaints of indigenous rights violations submitted to the Permanent Forum and WGIP could be passed on to the Rapporteur for his consideration as part of his mandate but the Chairperson-Rapporteur of the WGIP indicated that this decision would need to be taken at the highest level within the system. Ms. Hampson, WGIP member, suggested that coordination between bodies dealing with indigenous affairs should become a permanent agenda item.

The session ended after the interventions on the last agenda item had been heard but without draft recommendations and conclusions to the Sub-commission having been presented.

The report was later posted on the Office of the High Commissioner for Human Rights' web page and presented for further adoption to the Sub-commission session in August 2005.[1]   ❏

Note

1 The report can be downloaded from: http://daccessdds.un.org/doc/UNDOC/
   GEN/G05/156/40/PDF/G0515640.pdf?OpenElement

THE UN DRAFT DECLARATION ON
THE RIGHTS OF INDIGENOUS PEOPLES

In 1995, the Commission on Human Rights decided to establish an Inter-sessional Working Group with a mandate to draw up a draft Declaration for consideration and adoption by the UN General Assembly within the framework of the International Decade of the World's Indigenous Peoples (1995-2004). The Working Group's mandate expired in January 2004, without consensus having been reached on a final text. In April 2005, the 61st session of the Commission on Human Rights considered the final report of the Working Group on the Draft Declaration on the Rights of Indigenous Peoples (WGDD). It was decided to extend its mandate for a further year so that it could convene an 11th session in order to complete its work before the 2006 session of the Commission.

The Declaration is a human rights instrument that will set the standard for the relationship that should exist between indigenous peoples and states. Its 59 paragraphs address the historical injustice and continuing discrimination of indigenous peoples' rights to language, education, self-government, cultural expression, the collective right to use of lands, territories and resources, restitution of lands and territories, and treaty rights.

As reported in our article on the 61st session of the UN Commission on Human Rights, the vast majority of indigenous representatives have fought fiercely for a renewal of the Working Group's mandate. However, both the indigenous participants and the governments who expressed their commitment to the process and to the adoption of a strong Universal Declaration on the Rights of Indigenous Peoples were aware that it was going to be difficult for the Working Group to be able to complete its work in only one year. Both were also fully aware of the fact that if no progress was made, the Working Group would not be able to demonstrate to the Commission that it was truly in the final stages of its work, and it would then be most likely that this body would decide not to renew its mandate in April 2006, thus bringing the process to an end. In this context, the need to carry out inter-sessional meetings aimed at moving the process forward was discussed both by indigenous peoples and governments. Among the initiatives considered were:

1. Organising of an indigenous expert meeting with the aim of developing strategies, discussing issues and producing documentation and arguments that could help promote and strengthen consensus among the indigenous delegations.
2. Organising of an informal meeting with government delegations and indigenous representatives, plus experts and NGOs involved in the Draft Declaration process, with the aim of promoting frank and open discussions between all parties.

In this context, two indigenous organisations (the Grand Council of the Crees and the Inuit Circumpolar Conference) decided to organise the first initiative while the Mexican government offered to sponsor the informal meeting with government delegations and indigenous representatives, plus experts and NGOs. The Mexican initiative was welcomed by the Commission on Human Rights in one of its resolutions.

Indigenous experts' strategy meeting

The indigenous experts' strategy meeting on the UN Draft Declaration on the Rights of Indigenous Peoples took place in Montreal from 10-13 August 2005. It was aimed at preparing discussions for the Patzcuaro workshop in Mexico as well as for the 11th session of the Working Group on the Draft Declaration, to take place in December 2005. It brought together about 30 indigenous experts from all regions. The participants addressed the crucial issues of the indigenous right to self-determination; lands, territories and resources; and the general provisions. In relation to self-determination, representatives affirmed their support for the indigenous proposal presented at the 10th session of the WGDD. With regard to lands, territories and resources, they reaffirmed the importance of the articles on lands, territories and resources, especially indigenous peoples' right to restitution under international law. Finally, their discussion on general provisions stressed the importance of indigenous peoples' collective human rights being affirmed in the declaration and of safeguarding against such distinct rights being undermined by state proposals. They agreed to take coordinated measures to secure provisional adoption of those articles that were agreed by indigenous peoples and states at the Working Group session in December 2005.

At the Montreal meeting, a number of documents were discussed and approved for submission to the Mexican government in order to be included in the documentation materials for the informal meeting in Mexico.

International workshop with government and indigenous representatives

The workshop, which took place in Patzcuaro, Mexico, from 26-30 September 2005, was organized by the Mexican Government and the Office of the High Commissioner on Human Rights. Its aim was to provide an opportunity for informal discussions among the participants with the purpose of reducing some of the obstacles to adoption of the draft Declaration and thus contributing to progress at the next session of the Working Group in December 2005 and January-February 2006.

About 90 representatives of governments, specialists from the main indigenous regions of the world, non-governmental organizations, as well as scholars and the Special Rapporteur on the situation of the human rights and fundamental freedoms of indigenous peoples, participated. The workshop was extremely important in the consensus-building process developed during 2005 to prepare for the discussions to take place at the 11th session of the WGDD.

It was organized around three themes: self-determination; land, territories and natural resources; and general provisions. In short, the workshop in Patzcuaro provided an outstanding opportunity for a frank and sincere exchange of different views and thereby contributed positively to a better understanding of the issues and provided ideas on how to narrow the gaps between positions in order to achieve a strong declaration. The Mexican initiative was highly appreciated by all participants and without doubt helped to improve the level of dialogue between governments and indigenous peoples and create a new momentum in the Draft Declaration process.

The 11th session of the Working Group on the Draft Declaration

Indigenous peoples and governments of nations met at the United Nations in Geneva from December 5 -16, 2005 to discuss the Declaration on the Rights of Indigenous Peoples. Although the Declaration has been approved at lower levels of the United Nations (the Working Group on Indigenous Populations and the Sub-commission on the Prevention of Discrimination and Protection of Minorities),[1] it is now being debated by the Commission on Human Rights. This approval process is comparable to any type of legislation or international treaty, which must be accepted by several levels of governance before it becomes a legal instrument. Eventually, if successful, it will be passed by the United Nations General Assembly as a standard to be followed by all countries in the United Nations when dealing with indigenous nations and communities. In this way, it has the potential to hold countries accountable for numerous historical and ongoing violations of indigenous peoples' human rights. For example, the violation of treaties, the abuse of sacred sites, military occupation and the unjust disposal of hazardous materials on indigenous peoples' territories are all addressed by the Declaration. When passed, it will provide indigenous peoples with a new and powerful weapon in combating oppression and colonization, namely redress through the United Nations.

By the end of the two-week December 2005 session, signs could be seen of some forward movement in the process of finding consensus on a useful and meaningful Declaration. In spite of efforts by some states to hinder the effective content of the document, the last day of the session saw increased understanding between the indigenous caucus and a number of states, including Mexico, Norway, Canada and Denmark, among others. The December 2005 session is to be followed by a second meeting from January 30 - February 3, 2006. The goal of this two-part meeting is to adopt the language of a substantial portion of the Declaration, including the critical language in the paragraphs on self-determination.

Negotiations

The 11th session of the Working Group on the Draft Declaration was devoted to negotiations on the exact text of the Declaration for approval. Because it is such a wide-ranging document, covering all kinds of human rights of indigenous peoples, these negotiations with governments are slow and hard. Many governments (especially the United States, Australia and New Zealand) want to dramatically limit indigenous peoples' rights so that the Declaration will help give the countries control over indigenous peoples. They seek international support for colonial policies such as plenary power (giving governments the ultimate right to decide the destiny of indigenous peoples) and the right to resources on indigenous peoples' lands. However, many others (including Norway, Sweden, Denmark, South Africa, Mexico, Guatemala, Venezuela, Cuba, Switzerland and even Canada) are siding with indigenous peoples and acknowledging the right to self-determination, the international status of treaties, and the critical right to indigenous control over their own lands and territories.

Support from these countries was demonstrated during the two-week 11th Session held in Geneva in December 2005. Although the United States, along with New Zealand and Australia, introduced language that basically maintains indigenous peoples as wards of the governments and colonized peoples, other countries have supported indigenous peoples' unwavering position on the right to self-determination, the international status of treaties, and the right to collective protection of lands and territories.

The Chairman of this meeting, Señor Luis Chavez from Peru, has often sided with countries like the United States, making the process more difficult for indigenous peoples. However, years of dealing with indigenous peoples' issues at the United Nations seems to be having its effect. When the United States, Australia and New Zealand introduced their very discriminatory language on self-determination early in the 2005 11th session, he questioned their motives. Many other countries (especially Guatemala and Mexico) went as far as to challenge the US/New Zealand/Australian position on the floor of the United Nations, calling it "inappropriate" and damaging to the efforts to build consensus[2] around indigenous peoples' rights. Even more encouraging, of the dozen or so countries who took the floor on this issue, not one of them supported the changes proposed. Every indigenous representative that spoke also made it clear how the US/New Zealand/Australian position would have a devastating effect on the international human rights of indigenous peoples.

The indigenous caucus

To more effectively present the indigenous world view in the plenary sessions and negotiations, indigenous peoples always gather in caucus meetings at the United Nations. Although we cannot expect diverse indigenous nations to always have the same perspective (no more than we would expect South Africa and France to have the same perspective), it is always the goal to build consensus whenever possible. Although members of the indigenous caucus have differing positions on specific language, there has been general agreement on the principles. When some indigenous groups are unable to consent to specific language, they have, by and large, not been willing to block consensus. This is organizing on an international level and 100% agreement cannot be expected. However, a united front of indigenous peoples is a powerful weapon against the countries most anxious to limit their human rights and there is a strong commitment to continuing the work to build agreement amongst indigenous peoples.

Provisional Adoption

In addressing the indigenous caucus close to the end of the session, Canadian and Danish representatives went as far as to say that they looked forward to the passing of a strong and effective Declaration by the General Assembly in 2006.[3] This, they noted, was consistent with the 2nd Decade of the World's Indigenous People and with the General Assembly's affirmation earlier this year in which it undertook *"to continue making progress in the advancement of the human rights of the world's indigenous peoples at the local, national, regional and international levels including adoption of a final draft United Nations declaration on the rights of indigenous peoples..."* (General Assembly Resolution A/RES/60/1 24 October 2005, p. 127).

During the Working Group, Norway chaired numerous meetings with indigenous peoples' representatives and states in order to find common ground and effective final language for the text of the Declaration. These meetings occurred both in and out of the formal plenary sessions with all delegations present.

On the final morning of the Working Group in December, Ms. Guri Hestflatt of the Norwegian delegation presented the outcomes to the chairperson of the Working Group. In her statement she said that progress was *"encouraging in both form and substance"* and that all delegations had *"demonstrated considerable effort to reach consensus"*. As a result, ten preambular and thirteen operative paragraphs were presented as ready for provisional adoption. (Provisional adoption simply refers to agreement on the text while noting that none of the articles of the Declaration are considered adopted until the entire Declaration is accepted.) In addition to the 23 paragraphs now considered ready for provisional adoption, an additional 15 are "very close". This would represent acceptance of more than half of the total 59 paragraphs that constitute the text of the Declaration.

Remaining hurdles

However, major obstacles still remain. The difficult issue of the total package of paragraphs on self-determination has not been resolved. The United States, New Zealand and Australia continue to put forth substantial objections. In a complicated twist of legalese, the United States has actually used circumstances surrounding national disasters as a reason to limit this critical right of indigenous peoples.[4] These states (US, New Zealand and Australia) are still insisting on language that would protect their "territorial integrity" and plenary power over indigenous peoples.[5]

Compelling arguments against the position of these few states have been presented and supported by indigenous peoples and other states. A group of non-indigenous human rights organizations made an intervention in an attempt to hold states accountable for their positions:

"With the obvious imbalance of power between states and Indigenous peoples, it is not clear to us why this discussion is preoccupied with perceived threats to states, rather than the very grave and pervasive threats to Indigenous peoples."

"Indigenous representatives have expressed concern that the concepts of political unity and territorial integrity are already being used by some states to justify denial of Indigenous peoples' rights and repression of the defenders of those rights."

"As human rights organizations, we are concerned that the inclusion of a specific reference to the principles of political unity and territorial integrity in a Declaration on the Rights of Indigenous Peoples would at best, reinforce an unacceptable status quo and at worst may encourage even greater human rights violations against Indigenous peoples."

"Furthermore, the proposal of New Zealand, Australia and the United States for article 45bis is particularly concerning as it would allow states to invoke the concepts of political unity and territorial integrity to justify the denial of any and all rights in the Declaration, no matter how fundamental to the welfare and survival of Indigenous peoples." [Intervention of IWGIA, Amnesty International, International Federation of Human Rights Leagues, KAIROS: Canadian Ecumenical Justice Initiatives, Rights and Democracy, NCIV, Friends World Committee for Consultation (Quakers)]

The text of this intervention reflects the principles supported by a majority of states and indigenous representatives. Together we are working to agree on langauge that would preserve the original text on the right of self-determination. States that cannot support the total expression of human rights will hopefully find themselves increasingly isolated.

Treaty provisions
Additionally, Willie Little Child presented revised articles on treaties (preambular paragraphs 6, 13, and Article 36), which had also been the subject of intensive negotiations. However, when presented to the Working Group, the United States again took the floor to state that they did not concur and would be introducing their own language on these paragraphs.

Coming in January 2006
Although many of the essential elements have yet to be tackled in the January-February 2006 session of the Working Group, there is clear indication that progress is being made. The more text that is agreed between states and indigenous peoples' representatives, the less room there is for the Chairperson to introduce his own interpretation of a compromise. Returning to the February session with 23 paragraphs ready for provisional adoption and a positive starting point for the discussion on self-determination, indigenous peoples believe that we will be in an excellent position to begin fine-tuning the actual language. In this way, the strongest possible Declaration, representing the minimum standard for indigenous peoples, will be presented to the Commission on Human Rights and, hopefully, adopted by the General Assembly. It will then be up to local indigenous communities, tribal governments, traditional leadership and international coalitions of indigenous communities to breathe life into the Declaration and use it in the daily struggles for everything from adequate shelter to adherence to treaty rights. With passage of the Declaration, the United Nations becomes a more powerful partner in this process.   ❑

Notes

1   Indigenous peoples do not of course consider themselves minorities and many United Nations studies have supported this opinion. However the original Working Group on Indigenous Populations was responsible to the Sub-commission on Prevention of Discrimination and Protection of Minorities and it was therefore required to approve the Declaration. This occurred in 1994.

2   Within the context of passage of the Declaration, the term consensus has been explained by the Chairman, Señor Chavez, as meaning that none of the parties to the discussion openly <u>oppose</u> the text. They do not have to necessarily support it; they just have to be willing to accept it. This apparently applies to both indigenous and state delegations.

3   This would mean that the January-February 2006 session would see provisional adoption of the entire text, with submission of the Declaration to the Commission in the spring and on to the General Assembly in its 2006 session. A rumor is circulating that because provisional adoption is so close, several days or a second week may be added to the January-February 2006 session to ensure adequate time to reach consensus.

4   One might ask if the Declaration's passage would have further reduced the inadequate response to Hurricane Katrina – it seems like a hollow argument at best.

5   As a result of several press releases sent out by Indigenous peoples from the floor of the United Nations relating to the position of Australia, the United States and New Zealand, many Maori people reacted and several articles appeared in New Zealand on the government's position. A petition was also started to urge the New Zealand government to review their position. This can be accessed at: http://www.thepetitionsite.com/takeaction/489895927

THE AFRICAN COMMISSION ON HUMAN AND PEOPLES' RIGHTS

During 2005, the African Commission on Human and Peoples' Rights (ACHPR or African Commission) continued to focus on protecting and promoting the human rights of indigenous peoples in Africa. IWGIA continues to be actively involved in this process, particularly via the Working Group of Experts on Indigenous Populations/Communities (referred to below as the Working Group). The Working Group has received an extensive mandate from the African Commission which includes gathering information on the human rights situation of indigenous populations, undertaking country visits, as well as raising the awareness of African governments and other key stakeholders on indigenous issues. During 2005, the Working Group began implementing this mandate in earnest.

The Working Group's activities during 2005

The Working Group met twice during 2005: once in May 2005 prior to the 37th Ordinary Session of the ACHPR and again in November 2005 prior to its 38th Ordinary Session. At these two meetings in Banjul, The Gambia, the Working Group planned its many activities and evaluated those already undertaken. The main activities undertaken during 2005 were:

Publication and distribution of the report

The expert report of the African Commission's Working Group on Indigenous Populations/Communities was published in English and French. The report debates the criteria for identifying indigenous peoples in Africa, documents violations of indigenous peoples' human rights, analyses the African Charter on Human and Peoples' Rights with respect to indigenous peoples' rights, and makes recommendations to the African Commission on how to improve the protection of indigenous peoples' human rights.

Subsequent to the report's publication, an extensive distribution strategy was initiated. Reports were sent to African governments, African and international NGOs, African human rights institutions, international institutions and academics in Africa, Europe and America. Demand for the report has been, and still is, high and very positive feedback has been received in this regard. The report has been widely used for advocacy and lobbying purposes, and has been cited in order to show that involvement with indigenous peoples' rights in Africa is legitimate, and in accordance with the African Union's own stance.

Country visits

During 2005, the Working Group undertook country visits to Botswana and Namibia. During these visits, the Working Group held meetings with the respective governments, NGOs, academic institutions and indigenous communities in order to gather information about the human rights situation of indigenous communities, and to engage the government and other stakeholders on how the situation could be improved. Both visits confirmed the marginalized position of indigenous peoples (for instance in terms of political representation and access to social services) and made a number of recommendations for improving the situation. The resulting reports were adopted by the African Commission at its 38th Ordinary Session in November 2005.

Research and information visits

During 2005, the Working Group carried out research and information visits to Burundi, Libya and the Republic of Congo. During these visits, meetings were held with a wide range of stakeholders with a view to disseminating information about the expert report and the ACHPR's position with regard to the rights of indigenous peoples. The visits also sought to gather information about the human rights situation

of indigenous populations, and produced a number of recommendations directed at both governments and the African Commission. The
reports from the visits to Burundi and the Republic of Congo were
adopted at the 38th Ordinary Session of the African Commission in November 2005, whilst the report from the visit to Libya is pending approval.

Establishment of an advisory network

An advisory network of experts was established during 2005. There
are currently 25 members of the network, all of whom have expertise on indigenous issues in Africa. The Working Group can consult
members of the network on different issues and can request members to carry out specific tasks. Thus far, the network has proven
especially important in terms of rendering assistance to the Working Group when carrying out research and information visits.

Compilation of database

A database of indigenous organizations in Africa currently exists in
a draft format. New entries may be added as information and contact details are obtained. It is hoped that this database will initiate
and ease communication between the many stakeholders across Africa.

Research on constitutions and legislation

The Working Group has, in cooperation with the ILO, undertaken
the preparatory work for carrying out research on the constitutions
and legislation of all African countries with indigenous populations. The research will document the extent to which the constitutions and legislation protect the rights of indigenous populations,
and will produce a comprehensive reference document for the
forthcoming work on protection and promotion of the human rights
of indigenous peoples.

The African Commission's 2005 sessions

Representatives of indigenous organizations continued to participate in the sessions of the ACHPR during 2005, with a total of 24 indigenous representatives participating in the two sessions. Seven indigenous organizations have been granted observer status, and others are in the process of applying. Indigenous representatives raised many important human rights issues in their statements during the ACHPR sessions and the commissioners are giving these issues increased attention. During the examination of state reports, commissioners are increasingly asking the governments questions about the situation and protection of the human rights of indigenous populations in their countries. This was the case in 2005 during examination of the state reports from Mauritania and South Africa.

Other mechanisms in the ACHPR are also expressing an interest in this area, for example the Special Rapporteur on the Rights of Women has expressed interest in including indigenous women as a specific target group in her work and contacts and initial discussions were established during 2005.

UN agencies, such as the International Labour Organization (ILO) and the UN Office of the High Commissioner for Human Rights (OHCHR), have taken an interest in the ongoing process in the ACHPR, and the OHCHR as well as the UN Special Rapporteur on the Situation of Human Rights and Fundamental Freedoms of Indigenous Peoples participated in the 37th session, expressing their interest in collaborating with the ACHPR and the Working Group.

In conclusion, the ACHPR has taken a very important step in recognizing the existence of indigenous populations in Africa and in prioritising the promotion and protection of their basic human rights. The ACHPR report on the rights of indigenous populations has proven to be a key instrument for advocating the rights of indigenous peoples on the African continent, and the country specific reports from the different visits will hopefully also serve as effective instruments in raising awareness and strengthening constructive dialogue between all relevant stakeholders.

Forthcoming activities

The Working Group plans to undertake the following activities during 2006:

- Publish and distribute the Working Group's report in Arabic,
- Continue distributing the English/French version of the report,
- Undertake country visits to Niger and Tanzania,
- Carry out research and information visits to Uganda, Ethiopia and Algeria,
- Improve the database on African organisations working on indigenous issues,
- Organise a regional sensitisation seminar,
- Continue strengthening cooperation with the UN human rights mechanisms,
- Produce an information folder on the activities of the Working Group,
- In cooperation with the ILO, continue the research project on African constitutions and legislation. ❏

INDIGENOUS PEOPLES AND THE CONVENTION ON BIOLOGICAL DIVERSITY IN 2005

The UN Convention on Biological Diversity (CBD) was finally negotiated at the Earth Summit in Rio de Janeiro in 1992. To date, well over a hundred countries have ratified it. The CBD sets out the states' obligations to protect and sustainably use their biological diversity. Some of its articles deal with issues of particular relevance to indigenous peoples' rights, so the processes surrounding it are becoming an increasingly important arena for indigenous peoples' struggle for the promotion and protection of their rights at the international level. The CBD's decision-making body, the Conference of Parties (COP) meets every other year and, between the sessions, working groups and other subsidiary bodies dealing with its different articles and programmes of work meet to prepare input for the coming COPs. The Convention deals with the conservation and sustainable use of biodiversity, and with access to biological diversity and sharing of the benefits arising from this access. Among others, areas of the Convention that are of particular importance to indigenous peoples include article 8(j) on traditional knowledge of indigenous and local communities, article 10(c) on customary sustainable use, and article 15 on access and sharing of the benefits arising out of the utilization of genetic resources. The Convention has developed programmes of work on such important issues as protected areas or the protection of traditional knowledge. Indigenous peoples coordinate their work on the Convention through the International Indigenous Forum on Biodiversity (IIFB).

2005 was an intersessional year in the negotiations on the Convention on Biological Diversity (CBD), between the Seventh Conference of the Parties (COP7, Kuala Lumpur, February 2004)[1] and the future COP8, which is to be held in March 2006 in Curitiba (Brazil). Intense activity has nonetheless continued within the different subsidiary bodies to the Convention, in order to implement the decisions taken at COP7.

Although in the past indigenous participation - primarily channelled through the International Indigenous Forum on Biodiversity (IIFB) - has focused on the Working Group on article 8 (j) and related provisions (WG8J) and on the COPs themselves, indigenous representatives are now taking advantage of the new opportunities for impacting on the negotiations by participating in the Subsidiary Body on Scientific, Technical and Technological Advice (SBSTTA), in the advisory group on article 8 (j), and in the new working groups created by COP7: one on protected areas (WGPA) and the other on reviewing implementation of the Convention (WGRIC).

The main intersessional meetings of the CBD in which indigenous people participated were the following:

- Tenth (7 to 11 February, Bangkok) and Eleventh meetings of SB-STTA (28 November to 2 December, Montreal).
- Third meeting of the working group on access to genetic resources and benefit sharing - WGABS (14 to 18 February, Bangkok).
- First meeting of the working group on protected areas – WGPA (13 to 17 June, Montecatini, Italia).
- Regional workshops on integrated reporting of the situation of, and trends in, traditional knowledge.

In addition, the advisory group on article 8 (j) was convened. Indigenous representatives from all regions form part of this group, whose job it is to prepare the WG8J meeting. The first WGRIC meeting also took place in September, with scant indigenous participation.[2]

What follows is a brief summary of the results of, and indigenous positions in, these meetings.

The SBSTTA meetings

As the CBD's negotiation process has progressed, the meetings of the SBSTTA - a theoretically technical body to prepare documents on CBD issues for discussion in the COP - have also come to form part of the political decision-making process.

It was because of this new dimension to the SBSTTA's meetings and the greater government involvement in its reports that the indigenous representatives realised that it was also essential for them to play a full and proactive role in these meetings, if they wanted their positions to be taken into account in the different issues from the start.

A small group of indigenous representatives participated in the two intersessional meetings of the SBSTTA (10 and 11)[3] in 2005,and so they had to prioritize a number of issues from the wider agenda. In SBSTTA 10, the priority issues for the indigenous organisations were: discussions on the work programme related to the biodiversity of islands and the discussions on genetic use restriction technologies (GURTs), popularly known as sterile seeds or "terminator" technology.

On the first issue, the CBD had already organised a number of preparatory meetings to formulate a possible work programme, with no indigenous participation. The discussions in the SBSTTA ignored indigenous proposals to a worrying extent. As is often the case in deliberations on the Convention, some countries were opposed to the introduction of texts relating to indigenous rights, despite the fact that these were the result of decisions already adopted by the COP. This lack of consistency in the negotiations on different issues, which generally tends to occur in all areas of the CBD's work, is exhausting for the IIFB and the indigenous organisations, who have to be present at ever increasing numbers of meetings in order to emphasise what has already been adopted. The SBSTTA's meetings do not enable active participation on the part of indigenous organisations to the same extent as other CBD bodies, in particular the WG8J, and so not even the reading out of indigenous opening and closing statements is permitted. In relation to the GURTs, the precedent lies in a decision taken at COP5 in which clear opposition was demonstrated to the use of these technologies, given the serious risk they could imply for biodiversity. In order to analysis this issue further, an ad hoc group of technical experts met to examine the possible impacts of GURTs from an environmental, social, cultural and economic point of view. This group's report reiterated the opinion that the possible negative impacts greatly outweighed the possible advantages of these technologies. Some Parties were opposed to this report at the SBSTTA meeting, describing it as "unscientific", and so the final SBSTTA recommendation for COP consideration is more flexible in terms of the possibility of conducting practical field tests on modified sterile seeds. The WG8J has already considered the economic, social and cultural impact of GURTs on indigenous peoples and local communities[4] and has accumulated a large amount of documentation presented by, amongst others, many indigenous organisations. This all offers a clearly negative assessment of these technologies. The issue will be considered again from this perspective by the WG8J's meeting prior to COP8, to be held in Granada in January 2006. The results of this meeting, along with the SBSTTA recommendation, will form the context of the discussions within COP8. It has been made clear in the meetings held that, despite the great opposition to GURTs within indigenous, NGO and environmental sectors, and among many Parties, the industry group and a number of countries will attempt to block any prohibition or moratorium until there is more certainty on the safety or not of these technologies, ignoring the principle of precaution.

Working Group on access and benefit sharing

The Working Group Acces and Benefit Sharing (WGABS)[5] met in Bangkok following the SBSTTA 10 meeting, and preceded by the usual preparatory meeting of indigenous representatives of the IIFB. The WGABS has a mandate from COP7 to produce and negotiate an international regime for access to genetic resources and benefit sharing in application of articles 8 (j) and 15 of the Convention. The impact this regime will have on indigenous peoples' rights to resources and knowledge is clear and explains the presence of indigenous representatives in the WGABS meetings since its creation in 2000.

Basically, the position maintained by the indigenous representatives in relation to the international regime has been to ask that recognition and respect for indigenous rights be guaranteed within the future regime. It is still difficult to forecast how these negotiations will pan out, with some Parties very interested in a strong and legally binding regime to regulate access and distribution of benefits (basically the "supplier countries" as they are known, such as the African Group, GRULAC (Latin American and Caribbean Group) and megadiverse countries), and others determined to adopt flexible and, it would seem, voluntary mechanisms (in general, the "user countries", or rich countries). In this context, the IIFB has tried to do two things within this WG: to increase its participation and to propose the inclusion of text recognising indigenous rights, including free, prior and informed consent, along with the adoption of international human rights instruments as the international legal framework that the regime must comply with, offering legal precedents with regard to indigenous peoples' sovereignty over their natural resources, for example.

The Bangkok discussions focused on the nature and scope of this future regime, along with the elements it will need to contain, the use of terms and a discussion of options, such as international certificates of origin. The IIFB presented additional elements for the consideration of the Parties, such as measures that would guarantee respect for and protection of indigenous peoples' rights not only over traditional knowledge associated with resources but also over the genetic resources coming from their territories. It should be noted that the Parties recognise indigenous rights to traditional knowledge to a certain extent but there has been no progress in recognising indigenous ownership of the biological and genetic resources coming from their territories, as the principle of national sovereignty is imposed without restriction.[6] With the support of some Parties, such as Ethiopia and the EU, who presented the texts, a number of elements proposed by the IIFB were included in the final WGABS document for future discussion.

Given the difficulties encountered by the IIFB in intervening or being able to participate in the negotiations, the organisation presented a proposal on participation that is included in the WGABS' final report as follows:

> *"Reaffirming the importance of the full and effective participation of indigenous and local communities in the work of the Ad Hoc Open-Ended Working Group on Access and Benefit-sharing and recognizing the progressive nature of the working practices of the Ad Hoc Open-Ended Working Group on Article 8(j) and related provisions,*
>
> *"Decides to continue to support the participation of the International Indigenous Forum on Biodiversity through the adoption of measures such as: (a) providing timely and appropriate indigenous participation in debates; (b) enhanced participation in Friends of the Chair and contact groups; (c) advising the Bureau; and (d) to provide the administrative support necessary to facilitate the participation of the International Indigenous Forum on Biodiversity in its advisory roles to Parties in meetings of the Ad Hoc Open-Ended Working Group on Access and Benefit-sharing."*

The discussion on whether to present the IIFB's proposal as a draft decision to the Parties or not has been postponed until the next meeting of the WGABS (Granada, January 2006). In terms of the international regime and related measures, the next meeting will need to consider all proposals presented in Bangkok and move towards producing a clearer negotiation document. This is something the supplier countries will push for with a view to obtaining clear results at COP8. Negotiations on the international regime will undoubtedly be one of the most important processes within the CBD over the coming years.

Working Group on protected areas

The programme and working group on protected areas (WGPA) were adopted at COP7[7] (see *The Indigenous World 2005*). The work programme includes very interesting aspects from an indigenous point of view as it not only generally accepts the need to recognise and respect indigenous rights when establishing and managing protected areas but also includes a whole area of work related to governance and participation in which concrete objectives and activities are defined in support of full participation and in support of a model of community conservation of protected areas that has been proposed as an alternative to the old model of exclusion and expulsion, still in place in many parts of the world and which has given rise to flagrant violations of indigenous peoples' human rights.

The IIFB's hard work during long negotiation sessions in the COP7 contact groups appeared to have done little good when the documents to be debated during the first meeting of the WGPA were examined. There were proposals for developing most of the work programme's goals and objectives but almost nothing about aspects of governance, participation, respect for the rights of indigenous peoples and local communities or community conservation. The Indigenous Peoples' Committee on Conservation, a working group of IIFB organisations formed to coordinate the specific monitoring of this issue, realised with disappointment that they would again have to defend positions already adopted by the COP in order to transfer them to the practical tools to be developed by this working group, if what had been achieved was not to remain dead letter. After a week of intense activity, preceded by the IIFB preparatory meeting, they managed to obtain recognition of the need to move towards formulating tools with the full participation of indigenous peoples. But it was also clear that the work of the CBD on this crucial issue was not in line with the "new paradigm" of protected areas established at the IUCN World Parks Congress, held in Durban in 2003.

COP7 had adopted the decision to hold two WGPA meetings prior to COP8 and the second meeting was planned for December in Montreal. But the meeting was cancelled in November and so progress in this area remains in the balance, pending decisions to be taken at the future COP8.

Conclusion

2005 came to an end with the usual highs and lows that are always present in negotiations within the context of this Convention. Full participation, and recognition of and respect for indigenous rights, are becoming central and recurrent themes in the discussions on every aspect and work programme, and this arouses suspicion and even hostility among some of the Parties. There are serious attempts to reduce indigenous participation through the IIFB, which has achieved the adoption of some really progressive procedures in the WG8J and the introduction of many positive elements in COP decisions. Some Parties do not wish to see these procedures extended to deliberations on issues such as protected areas or the international regime governing access. The IIFB and the indigenous organisations monitoring the CBD are thus facing a double challenge: to consolidate their full and effective participation and to produce clearly defined proposals in defence of their rights for adoption by the Parties. This is a complex task, all the more so given the uncertain funding available for this task and the complexity of constructing systems of work and consensus among different peoples. Despite this, the obvious importance of indigenous peoples, both in terms of the conservation and sustainable use of biological diversity and in relation to their valuable heritage of traditional knowledge, makes it impossible for the Parties to ignore them in discussions on CBD issues. The IIFB has been maturing and growing within this process as an indigenous participatory organisation that is flexible and effective, with specific internal work groups on areas such as conservation or the crucial work on indicators. It is hoped that it will be able to face up to both the challenges of internal functioning and the pressures from the Parties in order to be an effective instrument in the defence of indigenous rights within the CBD process. ❑

Notes

1 See *The Indigenous World 2005*.
2 The first meeting of this WG established by COP7 was held in Montreal from 5 to 9 September 2005. In principle, the work of this group is of great importance in terms of increasing the effectiveness of the CBD in general. Over the years, the Convention has been carrying out work programmes both in its thematic areas and in relation to what are known as cross-cutting issues, and the coherence between these programmes has not been the best. The CBD also adopted a Multi-annual Work Programme and a Strategic Plan that needed coordinating. In addition, the World Summit on Sustainable Development gave work related

to biological diversity a clear objective (the 2010 goal to reduce the rate of loss of biodiversity) and various mandates such as to formulate a benefit-sharing mechanism. Harmonizing all these goals, objectives and work programmes and providing them with a timeframe and indicators of achievement was to be the task of the new work programme. For reasons of funding, indigenous participation in this meeting was extremely limited (Joji Cariño attended for the IIFB/Fundación Tebtebba), and so it is not included in this report. But it is very important to bear in mind the new "rationalized" work contexts that are being proposed, in particular those referring to indicators related to indigenous participation (strategic plan objective) and indigenous rights to traditional knowledge (2010 goal).

3   This summary draws on the reports of Debra Harry and Lourdes Amos for the AIPP/IIFB on the IIFB's positions. For further information on the issues and positions of the Parties, see the corresponding issues of the **IISD's** *Earth Negotiations Bulletin* (www.iisd.ca).

4   Although in this article we refer to "indigenous peoples" or "indigenous peoples and local communities", the expression used within a CBD context is always "indigenous and local communities".

5   This summary draws on the report written for AIIP/IIFB by Le'a Kanehe on the IIFB's positions. Report on this meeting to COP8 at UNEP/CBD/COP/8/5.

6   On this issue, see *Indigenous Peoples' Rights, State Sovereignty and the CBD* by the FPP at www.forestpeoples.org.

7   Decision VII/28 on protected areas.

PART III

GENERAL INFORMATION

BECOMING A MEMBER

IWGIA welcomes new members. If you wish to apply for membership and become part of our dedicated network of concerned individuals, please consult our homepage at **www.iwgia.org** for details and to download a membership form.

Membership fees for 2006 are:

US$60 / EUR 50 (US$35 / EUR 30 for students and senior citizens) for Europe, North America, Australia, New Zealand and Japan. US$25 / EUR 20 for the rest of the world.

For IWGIA, membership provides an essential element of support to our work, both politically and economically.

All members receive IWGIA's journal *Indigenous Affairs* four times a year, IWGIA's Annual Report, and the yearbook *The Indigenous World*. In addition, members benefit from a 33% reduction on other IWGIA publications. If you want a support membership only and not receive our publications, the annual fee is US$10 / EUR 8.

SUBSCRIPTION RATES 2006

INDIGENOUS AFFAIRS / ASUNTOS INDÍGENAS

Individuals: US$ 35 / EUR 27 / DKK 200
Institutions: US$ 45 / EUR 36 / DKK 265

THE INDIGENOUS WORLD / EL MUNDO INDIGENA

Individuals: US$ 30 / EUR 24 / DKK 175
Institutions: US$ 40 / EUR 32 / DKK 235

BOOKS / LIBROS

Individuals: US$ 60 / EUR 47 / DKK 330
Institutions: US$ 80 / EUR 63 / DKK 445

INDIGENOUS AFFAIRS & THE INDIGENOUS WORLD / ASUNTOS INDÍGENAS & EL MUNDO INDÍGENA

Individuals: US$ 65 / EUR 51 / DKK 375
Institutions: US$ 85 / EUR 68 / DKK 500

INDIGENOUS AFFAIRS, THE INDIGENOUS WORLD & BOOKS / ASUNTOS INDÍGENAS, EL MUNDO INDÍGENA & LIBROS

Individuals: US$ 125 / EUR 98 / DKK 705
Institutions: US$ 165 / EUR 130 / DKK 940

Subscribe through: iwgia@iwgia.org